Individual Therapy in Britain

INDIVIDUAL THERAPY IN BRITAIN

Windy Dryden
(Editor)

Open University Press
Milton Keynes · Philadelphia

Open University Press
12 Cofferidge Close
Stony Stratford
Milton Keynes
MK11 1BY

and
242 Cherry Street, Philadelphia, PA19106, USA

British Library Cataloguing in Publication Data
Individual therapy in Britain.
1. Psychotherapy
I. Dryden, Windy
616.89'14   RC480

ISBN 0 335 09810 X

Typeset by Book Ens, Saffron Walden, Essex
Printed and bound by Butler & Tanner Ltd,
Frome and London

Contents

To my wife, Louise – a very therapeutic individual

Preface

During the last ten years I have searched in vain for a comprehensive British edited text on different approaches to individual psychotherapy, where each approach is outlined by a leading British exponent. My purpose was to use such a text on my training courses, but in the absence of such a book I had to rely on American works. My students over the years have joined with me in bemoaning an important gap in the British therapeutic literature. Remembering the cliché 'If you want something done, do it yourself', I decided to edit such a text. This is the result. It is really a joint effort, and I wish to thank my fellow contributors for participating in the project, for tolerating my infuriating habit of attending to detail and for their hospitality when I visited them to gather material.

The scheme of the book is as follows. In Chapter 1, I attempt to put individual therapy in context, showing that psychotherapists have to make decisions concerning which therapeutic arena to work in with clients and indicating where the arena of individual therapy may be placed in such a context. In Chapters 2–11 ten different, well-defined approaches to individual therapy are presented. Each chapter follows a common format: historical context and developments in Britain; theoretical assumptions; practice; and case example. This is to allow the reader to make comparisons among the different approaches. Two frameworks are presented in Chapter 12 to facilitate such comparative analyses. In Chapter 13, the limitations of these approaches are outlined, each contributor being given 1,000 words for this purpose. In Chapters 14–16 the topic of eclecticism in individual therapy is covered from three different perspectives. Finally, an appendix of addresses is provided for readers who wish to pursue their interest in any of the therapies covered.

I wish to thank the following people who have helped me to bring this project to fruition: Mark Aveline, John Davis, Albert Ellis and Ian Gilmore for their valuable comments on my own chapters; Michele Markham for typing portions of the book; Trevor Hartley for his graphic work and Naomi Roth, my editor, for her encouragement, conscientiousness and lunches at Tuttons.

WINDY DRYDEN
Birmingham, March 1984

Acknowledgements

The author and publishers would like to thank the following for permission to reproduce copyright material:

The Dorsey Press for Table 14.2 from Prochaska, J. O., 1979: *Systems of Psychotherapy*

Clare Hill for Table 14.3

F. E. Peacock Publishers, Inc, Itasca, Illinois, for Table 12.1. from Corsini, R.J., *Current Personality Theories.* © 1977, P.12–13, Table 1.4.

Pergamon Press for figures in Chapter 12 adapted from Beutler, L. E., 1983; *Eclectic Psychotherapy: A Systematic Approach*, Figure 8.6.

Psychotherapy: Theory, Research and Practice for Table 1.1, adapted from Prochaska and Norcross, 1983, in Volume 20, P. 165 and for Table 14.1, adapted from Prochaska and DiClemente, 1982, in Volume 19, P. 284.

John Wiley and Sons Inc., for material in Chapter 13 from Ellis, A., 1983 'Failures in Rational-Emotive Therapy' in Foa E. B., and Emmelkamp P. M. G., (eds.): *Failures in Behavior Therapy*.

Chapter 1   Therapeutic Arenas

Windy Dryden

Introduction

The main purpose of this book is to present the major approaches to individual therapy as practised in Britain today, each chapter being written by a leading British advocate of a particular approach. Most texts (almost exclusively American) which adopt a similar format fail to place a discussion of the different individual therapies in context. The aim of this chapter, then, is to present the issues facing psychotherapists who have the task of selecting the most appropriate arena for helping their clients. A *therapeutic arena* refers to the interpersonal context in which therapy takes place.

When clients seek psychotherapeutic help they may well find themselves being invited to work on their problems in a variety of different therapeutic arenas, individual, marital/couple, family or group therapy being the most common. It would be comforting for clients and therapists alike to know that such treatment decisions could be based on commonly agreed criteria which were in turn founded upon extensive research investigation; a perusal of the research literature, however, leads to the conclusion that the current state of affairs is more haphazard. Thus novice therapists are faced with a situation where decisions concerning how best to help their clients – in terms of selecting the most appropriate therapeutic arena(s) – may not be well informed. Much advice to novice therapists seeking such guide-lines is of course given in the literature, but in the main such advice is based upon the advisors' predilections and values as well as upon their way of construing the nature, acquisition and perpetuation of psychological disturbance. My purpose here is not to add to this body of advice, but to sensitize psychotherapists to the issues involved in the choice of relevant therapeutic arenas. In doing so I shall include material gained from in-depth interviews carried out with the other contributors to this book. In keeping with the book's theme, the later emphasis of the chapter will be on individual therapy.[1, 2] First, then, how widely is individual therapy practised, and who practises it?

Individual Therapy: Its Prevalence and Practitioners

One of the major developments in psychotherapy in the late 1970s and early 1980s has been the emergence and growth of the family therapies. This trend has been accompanied by a growing awareness on the part of psychotherapists of the important role that clients' relationships and environment play in the development and maintenance of their problems. To some degree, the sacred cow of individual therapy has been under attack. What effect has this trend had on the practice of individual therapy?

There has, unfortunately, been a dearth of research into how British psychotherapists spend their working time; a consideration of American research on this issue is thus in order. Prochaska and Norcross (1983) recently conducted a survey of 410 psychologists belonging to Division 29 (psychotherapy) of the American Psychological Association, and also reported on a similar survey (Norcross and Prochaska 1982) of a representative sample of psychologists who were members of APA Division 12 (clinical psychology). Table 1.1 shows the involvement (Division 29) and the percentage of time devoted by both groups to work in the respective therapeutic arenas.

It can be seen that individual therapy is still practised widely; and on

Therapeutic Arena	Division 29 (Psychotherapy)		Division 12 (Clinical Psychology)
	% Involved in	Mean % of Therapy Time	Mean % of Therapy Time
Individual Therapy	99.0	65.3	63.5
Group Therapy	45.8	7.5	7.3
Marital/Couple Therapy	73.7	12.9	11.5
Family Therapy	53.6	8.1	9.0

Table 1.1 Involvement and percentage of time deovted to work in various therapeutic arenas. APA members divisions 29 and 12 (Prochaska and Norcross, 1983)

comparing this data with that gathered by Garfield and Kurtz (1974) from 865 members of Division 12 it will be seen that the practice of individual therapy is not on the wane, at least not among members of the American Psychological Association.

Other pertinent, significant findings which emerged from Prochaska and Norcross' (1983) research on Division 29 members include the following:

(a) Male therapists were more involved in the arenas of marital, family and group therapy than were female therapists.
(b) Female therapists spent a larger percentage of their therapy time doing individual therapy than male therapists.
(c) Less experienced therapists were more involved in family therapy than were therapists with greater experience – a fact that is probably attributable to the recent emergence of this field.

While such information is interesting, and comparative British research is needed, this type of inquiry does not reveal what factors influence therapists in making 'therapeutic arena' decisions. Possible sources of influence will now be discussed.

Sources of Influence on 'Therapeutic Arena' Selection

The wider context

The wider contexts in which therapists work often exert an influence on arena choice. This may happen in a number of ways. First, therapists may work in different settings in which different norms of practice have developed. Thus therapist A may work in a setting in which group therapy is commonly practised, while therapist B may work in one which favours marital/couple therapy. It is likely, then, that the same client may be offered group therapy by A and marital/couple therapy by B for the same problem. There is, unfortunately, little research into the impact of institutional norms on therapeutic decision-making; yet such norms are likely to affect both how therapists think about the determinants of their clients' problems and how such problems may best be tackled.

Second, therapists often work in a wider context in which referring agents play an important role – for better or worse. When therapists develop good referral networks, they succeed in communicating how they work and what clients they believe they can best help; consequently, they are likely to receive appropriate referrals. However, the danger may exist that they come to believe their preferred therapeutic arena to be suitable for a wider range of clients than is the case – since inappropriate cases are selected out prior to referral. When therapists fail to develop an adequate understanding with their referral network, they may receive inappropriate cases together with instructions to treat clients in a certain way; indeed, therapeutic arenas may be stipulated which are contra-indicated for certain clients. Therapeutic decision-making often takes place within political contexts, and where therapists are in subordinate positions they may jeopardize career advancement by exercising their own clinical judgement.

Third, the influence of consumer demand on 'therapeutic arena' selection needs to be borne in mind. In America, where private practice is so common, the demands are mainly for individual therapy as shown in Table 1.1. These demands reflect consumer interest and not necessarily the merits of this way of working. The impact of consumer interest on therapeutic practice in Britain awaits inquiry.

Finally, therapists may work in settings in which the nature of their clientèle, rather than client problems, may determine 'therapeutic arena' selection. A good example of this occurs in student counselling. I have sometimes considered that the most appropriate therapeutic arena for certain students would be family therapy. However, since their families often live hundreds of miles away, individual or group therapy was suggested as a second choice.

How psychological disturbance is construed

As is demonstrated throughout this book, different therapeutic approaches imply different perspectives on the nature of psychological disturbance. A related issue concerns the influence of therapists' views of such disturbance on the selection of appropriate therapeutic arenas. Therapists tend to differ in their views on whether psychological disturbance is mainly determined by intrapsychic or by interpersonal factors. Those who consider such disturbance to be determined mainly by factors within the disturbed person – intrapsychic determinants – are more likely to offer their clients the arena of individual therapy than other arenas. On the other hand, those who view 'the appearance of a symptom as reflecting an acute and/or chronic disturbance in the balance of emotional forces in that individual's important relationship systems, most particularly the family system' (Kerr 1981) – interpersonal determinants – are more likely to recommend the arenas of marital/couple or family therapy than that of individual therapy.

It is a pity that many therapists become polarized in their arguments about the determinants of psychological disturbance when a balanced view seems warranted. Sander (1979) has written that 'the separation of intrapsychic processes and interpersonal processes is quite artificial as these processes are always mutually influencing one another'. This principle of 'reciprocal influence' should preferably be borne in mind by therapists when carrying out assessments of their clients' problems, before making treatment recommendations. In my view, intrapsychic and interpersonal determinants of psychological disturbance can be viewed as separate continua presented orthogonally, as in Figure 1. Both intrapsychic and interpersonal determinants are deemed to have a large impact (high) or a small impact (low) – at the extreme points on each continuum – on clients' psychological problems. In the examples presented below (see Figure 1), cases are described where both sets of determinants are near the extreme poles.

Case A: intrapsychic – high/interpersonal – high In this case, the client's psychological disturbance is determined by both intrapsychic and interpersonal factors. The client's disturbance is chronic in nature and tends to be present in different contexts, situations and relationships; in all probability the client would still be disturbed even in more favourable interpersonal environments. However, an assessment reveals that the client's important interpersonal relationships are also disturbed. This analysis suggests that therapy for this person may well involve different arenas at different points in treatment.

Example A: Mr C had a chronic history of depression and long-standing relationship difficulties with his wife and co-workers. He basically hated himself and was, moreover, extremely sensitive to perceived constraints on his autonomy. He was first seen in individual therapy, where the focus was on helping him to adopt a more accepting attitude towards himself. A period of marital therapy followed where both Mr C and his wife were helped to negotiate mutually agreed periods of 'together time' and 'separate time'. Mr C was also helped to test out his

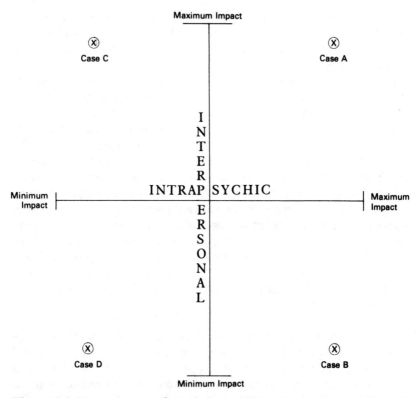

Figure 1.1 Determinants of psychological disturbance: intrapsychic and interpersonal continua

inferences that he was being constrained by his wife rather than assuming that his hunches were facts. Together the couple discovered a productive way for him to communicate his frustration when he was actually constrained and developed functional solutions when this problem arose. Finally, Mr C joined a therapy group where he was helped to assert himself constructively when he felt that he was being unfairly constrained by other group members.

Case B: intrapsychic – high/interpersonal – low   Here the client's disturbance is determined mainly by intrapsychic factors. Such disturbance is chronic in nature and tends to be present in different contexts, situations and relationships. However, important interpersonal relationships are not disturbed. The arena of individual therapy therefore seems particularly appropriate.

Example B1:   Miss L had suffered from long periods of morbid guilt concerning her perceived mistreatment of her deceased parents. She was happily married, and her husband was caring and supportive of her. She enjoyed good friendships and was well regarded at her job. She was seen in individual therapy where the focus of the work was on helping her to accept herself for her presumed 'sins'. She was then helped to place her 'sinful' behaviour in its proper context: as an understandable response to continued attempts on her parents' part to get her to make up, through academic achievement, for their own inadequacies in this area.

Group therapy may also be indicated if the person's problems involve specific disturbed secondary relationships, or if the person finds it difficult to develop and maintain such relationships.

Example B2:   Mr Y had long experienced anxiety about his 'weaknesses' as a male. He got along very well with his parents, with whom he lived, and was happily engaged to an understanding woman. He was popular with most of his co-workers, but did not get on with two of them who habitually teased him. A period of individual therapy where his dysfunctional attitudes towards himself were explored and corrected was followed by a period of group therapy. He was encouraged to disclose his 'weaknesses' to other group members and helped not to take the negative responses of one particular group participant too seriously. The group also gave him good advice on how to respond productively to teasing when it occurred.

When significant others (those in important interpersonal relationships with the client) are involved in therapy in such cases, it will be in the role of therapeutic aide.

Case C: intrapsychic – low/interpersonal – high In this case, the client's disturbance is determined mainly by interpersonal factors. One such client has functioned well in a variety of contexts, situations and relationships but becomes disturbed chiefly as a result of involvement in specific disturbed important relationship(s). Here, the salient therapeutic arena would be one that, if possible, dealt specifically and directly with the disturbed relationship(s): for example, marital/couple or family therapy.

Example C1:   Mrs G had led a happy life, but had recently become depressed when her husband became unemployed. Tension mounted and arguments increased as he continually failed to gain new employment. The treatment of choice was marital therapy, where they were both helped to express concern for each other in a non-defensive way and to develop new areas of mutual enjoyment. Mrs G subsequently helped her husband to prepare himself more thoroughly for his job search, and he felt that he was once again being supported by his wife.

In another case, although the client's relationship with himself is not disturbed, his *general* interpersonal relationships are disturbed. Here group therapy is indicated.

Example C2:   Mr T was a university student who liked his own company and enjoyed his work but could only develop superficial, fleeting relationships with other people. He joined a therapy group where he was given helpful feedback about the negative effects of his pervasively joking attitude. This helped him to re-evaluate his approach to others, and the group provided a forum for him to try out new and successful ways of relating to people.

Case D: intrapsychic – low/interpersonal – low   The client's disturbance is due either to an acute, context-limited 'crisis' which triggers problems, or to non-psychological factors. Important interpersonal relationships are good. Brief individual therapy or psychotropic medication seems indicated.

Example D: Miss R was a popular young woman who had many friends and had always enjoyed good relationships with her family. She lived alone, and became depressed a month after her flat had been burgled. A period of brief individual therapy in which she was both able to fully express her feelings about 'being invaded' by faceless intruders and to accept that she was not immune from the hazards of modern-day living was successful in alleviating her feelings of depression.

This schema, which can also be applied to different problems of a given individual, is not meant to be comprehensive. It constitutes one method of making sense of complex clinical material: an attempt to integrate intrapsychic and interpersonal determinants of psychological disturbance in a way that suggests the selection of appropriate therapeutic arenas. A similar view has been proposed by Aveline (1979): 'As a rule of thumb, when an individual's problem involves named people within their context then I work with that natural grouping, but if the problem is one of general social relationships, then a group is an appropriate medium, and if the individual's problems are essentially those of his relationship with himself or if a period of preparation is needed, I suggest one-to-one therapy.'

Therapist preferences

Most therapists have preferred ways of working, and this is often reflected in their choices of whom to work with in therapy. Some therapists, for example, find the complex interpersonal transactions that often occur in the arenas of marital/couple, family and group therapy too chaotic and prefer the order that the arena of individual therapy provides them (Sander 1979). On the other hand, other therapists prefer active intervention in a complex field and are consequently drawn to some schools of marital/couple and family therapy. Still other therapists prefer to avoid the intimacy and/or the emotional burden that individual therapy is likely to engender, or find such an arena unstimulating. Here, temperamental differences between therapists are apparent and have some effect on therapist decision-making. It is evident that therapists should become aware of their personal preferences for working in particular arenas and make attempts to minimize the potential bias that may result to the possible detriment of client care, perhaps by referring particular clients elsewhere.

In addition, adherence to certain therapeutic schools may bias therapists' thinking for or against therapeutic arenas. Transactional analysts, for example, may prefer to work in groups (Laurence Collinson), while Jungian therapists may prefer the arena of individual therapy (Kenneth Lambert). It is apparent, then, that therapists will have personal preferences concerning how to work with clients and that such preferences may have a biasing effect on their treatment recommendations. It is clear that the practice of psychotherapy will never become 'truly objective' in that it is practised by fallible human beings who have preferences, prejudices and biases.

The research literature

While psychotherapy will never become 'truly objective' in the scientific sense, it would be perilous for therapists to ignore such guide-lines as the research literature might provide. Psychotherapists are advised to read this literature with a critical eye and to familiarize themselves with the limitations of particular studies. Consistent research findings from several sources are, however, worthy of detailed study by practising psychotherapists who need to consider the implications that such findings may have for their work.

With respect to the appropriate selection of therapeutic arenas, the research literature suggests two major patterns:

(a) *Group therapy appears to be as effective as individual therapy.*

Orlinsky and Howard (1978) note that:

> In a sense this can be taken as favourable to group therapy since it produces equivalent results more economically. Yet it still seems plausible that some sorts of patients, or some sorts of problems might be treated more effectively on an individual basis while for others group therapy of some kind would be the treatment of choice. Ravid (1969), for example, found that patients who had already received a good deal of individual therapy, but who still needed further treatment, did better to have group therapy than to have still more individual therapy.

The above comment indicates the need for greater specificity in research on the appropriate selection of therapeutic arenas. Ideally, therapists need to know under which conditions, for which clients and at which times a particular arena would be the modality of choice. Unfortunately, we are a long way from this ideal. Perhaps the closest the research literature comes to making a firm recommendation is in the area of marital difficulties:

(b) *For marital problems, greatest benefit from therapy occurs when both partners are involved in treatment.*

When a client seeks therapeutic help primarily for marital problems, the research literature clearly indicates the importance of active spouse involvement in therapy. Individual therapy for marital problems when only one spouse is involved in treatment yields improvement in less than half (48%) of clients[3] (Gurman and Kniskern 1978). When both spouses are involved in treatment, improvement rates increase to two-thirds. Furthermore, it does not seem to make a great difference if partners are seen a) together (conjoint marital therapy); b) together in a group (conjoint group marital therapy); c) separately by the same therapist (concurrent marital therapy); or d) separately by different therapists who liaise with one another about the partners' treatment (collaborative marital therapy). The most significant factor, then, contributing to a successful outcome is that both partners are involved in therapy. Although, as most therapists who have worked with couples know, the involvement of both partners in therapy is not always possible, this should perhaps be the aim when marital problems are the focus for treatment. Of course, clients who come for help with marital problems often have other problems that are not directly related to their marriage, so some individual therapy may need to be provided in addition to marital/couple therapy. One cautionary note is in order here. In the research studies reviewed by Gurman and Kniskern (1978), it is not known to what extent the individual therapy for marital problems was actually maritally oriented. When such therapy has a distinct marital focus, improvement rates are enhanced (Bennun 1984).

Decision-making and therapeutic alliance issues

A consideration of the selection of appropriate therapeutic arenas inevitably leads to the issue of decision-making. Who is responsible for making clinical decisions – such as choosing a suitable therapeutic arena? Brian Thorne is in no doubt: it is the client. Not surprisingly, his ideas are in keeping with person-centred theory. His view is that it is unlikely that decisions about arena choice will be made before a relationship between therapist and client has been established. The therapist generally follows the client's lead and waits for signs to emerge from the client concerning the choice of an appropriate therapeutic arena. Thus, in Thorne's experience, most clients are seen by him initially in individual therapy, and when a change in therapeutic arena occurs the arena is selected by clients. The exception to this would be when the therapist had strong ongoing feelings concerning the greater appropriateness of a different therapeutic arena; here, the suggestion for an arena change would be initiated by the therapist, although the client would, in most situations, make the final decision.

On the other hand, there are therapists (not represented in this book) who hold strong opinions about the suitability of particular therapeutic arenas and will refuse to see the referred client in any other arena. For example, family therapists prefer to work with the 'identified patient' in the family setting and might well refuse to see this person alone in individual therapy. Here, again, the position is clear: the therapist is the primary decision-maker.

A different perspective is that decision-making in therapy is best viewed as a process in the development and maintenance of a therapeutic alliance between therapist and client. Bordin (1975, 1976) has argued that there are three major components of such an alliance: bonds, goals and tasks. Given that a good working relationship between therapist and client has been established (effective bonds), the therapist helps the client set realistic goals for change (shared goals). Therapist and client then come to a shared understanding concerning how best these goals can be met (meaningful tasks). It is acknowledged that each participant has tasks to perform in the therapeutic process. It is at this stage that the issue of therapeutic arena choice can be discussed: which arena is best suited to be the achievement of the client's goals? Therapist and client discuss the advantages and disadvantages of working in the various arenas and come to a joint decision concerning the most appropriate therapeutic arena. Both Fay Fransella and Faye Page have noted that such discussions will obviously be influenced by the way clients construe their problems; thus if clients see their problems in terms of difficulties in their relationship with themselves the direction of the ensuing discussions with their therapists concerning appropriate therapeutic arenas will obviously be different than it would if they viewed their difficulties as primarily involving their relationship with their partners. Sometimes the ways in which clients construe their problems help to perpetuate them, and consequently therapists should be aware that clients' preferences for particular therapeutic arenas might serve to maintain rather than ameliorate their problems. As Sander (1979) has noted, 'patients also defensively seek out modalities that may be more comfortable than therapeutic'.

There are other obvious dilemmas that emerge from an analysis of arena selection in terms of the 'therapeutic alliance' concept. First, clients' goals change during therapy; thus when should therapist and client make a decision about therapeutic arenas based on client goals? Second, if, for example, members of a family share the conviction that one of their members is sick ('the identified patient'), how does a therapist come to develop and maintain a therapeutic alliance with family members while refusing to work with just the 'identified patient'? Here, Dougal Mackay suggests that it is often necessary initially to involve family members or a spouse under the guise of inviting them to be therapeutic aides; later in treatment, these people can be involved as clients if necessary. Such matters involve ethical issues – which serve as another important source of influence on the choice of arena.

Ethical issues

Wherever the focus of clinical decision-making concerning choice of therapeutic arena may lie, it is important that both therapist and client are aware of the consequences of their decision. Sider and Clements (1982) view the decision as a question of ethics: 'Unrecognized is the fact that with the choice of modality also goes the relative valuing of certain therapeutic outcomes.' There may well be a tendency for therapists who work primarily in individual therapy to emphasize the interests of the individual and play down the interests of the other people with whom their clients are involved. Hurvitz (1967) has noted that even when a client comes to individual therapy for a non-marital problem, the act of seeking help outside the marital/family unit may have unintended, deleterious effects on the client's primary relationships: a spouse may feel excluded, or the situation may reinforce the view of family members that it is really the client who is the 'sick' member. They may well then treat the client as being 'sick', thereby possibly hindering the progress of individual therapy. These phenomena may not necessarily occur, but the possibility needs to be discussed with clients seeking individual therapy before therapeutic contracts are established.

Conversely, therapists who work with marital/couple or family units may tend to emphasize the interests of such units and downplay the interests of the individuals within them. Harper (1981) has outlined his view on the limitations of marital and family therapy. He points out that practitioners of these therapies tend 'to believe that an abstraction – a marriage or a family . . . is a realistic referent, a tangible and legitimate focus. Such practitioners are likely to come to think that they are working directly with these abstractions rather than with interacting individuals.' This raises the important issue concerning those with whom therapists make their contracts: is it with a 'marital/couple unit', 'the family', with each member in such units, with an individual, or with an individual with significant others as therapeutic aides (Weisz and Bucher 1980)? In addition, when more than one client is involved in therapy they need to realize and accept that the therapist is not going to side with any one individual in order for productive treatment to ensue.

Let me stress again that it is important for therapists and clients to discuss together the likely implications of each therapeutic arena under consideration. Sider and Clements (1982) have put this very well: 'we propose an honest exploration of individual and social level good in all such cases, an explicit statement of the therapist's loyalty when there is conflict between levels and a realization by both individual and social unit therapists that their choice of psychotherapeutic modality is not only a matter of personal preference or efficacy of technique. It is also a matter of ethics'.

Therapists' ethical decisions are also influenced by institutional constraints where matters of cost-effectiveness are likely to be relevant. Pressures may be exerted on therapists to see clients, for example, in group settings when waiting lists lengthen.

Choice of Therapeutic Arenas: One Therapist's View

I wish now to present one therapist's view concerning the choice of appropriate arenas for treatment. I have, for a number of reasons, chosen to present the view of Albert Ellis, founder of rational-emotive therapy (see Chapter 10). He has had about forty years' experience working as a therapist, works regularly in the four major therapeutic arenas – individual, group, marital/couple and family therapy – and is one of the world's most influential therapists. Although he works in America, I believe his views to be worthy of consideration by British therapists:

> In regard to your question about placing people in individual, marital, family, or group therapy, I usually let them select the form of therapy they personally want to begin with. If one tries to push clients into a form of therapy they do not want or are afraid of, this frequently will not work out. So I generally start them where they want to start. If they begin in individual therapy and they are the kind of individuals who I think would benefit from group, I recommend this either quickly after we begin or sometime later. People who benefit most from group are generally those who are shy, retiring, and afraid to take risks. And if I can induce them to

go into a group, they will likely benefit more from that than the less risky situation of individual therapy. On the other hand, a few people who want to start with group but who seem to be too disorganized or too disruptive, are recommended for individual sessions until they become sufficiently organized to benefit from a group.

Most people who come for marital or family therapy actually come alone and I frequently have a few sessions with them and then strongly recommend their mates also be included. On the other hand, some people who come together are not able to benefit from joint sessions, since they mainly argue during these sessions and we get nowhere. Therefore sometimes I recommend that they have individual sessions in addition to or instead of the conjoint sessions. There are many factors, some of them unique, which would induce me to recommend that people have individual rather than joint sessions. For example, one of the partners in a marriage may seem to be having an affair on the side and will not be able to talk about this in conjoint sessions and therefore I would try to see this partner individually. Or one of the partners may very much want to continue with the marriage while the other very much wants to stop it. Again, I would then recommend they be seen individually. I usually try to see the people I see in conjoint sessions at least for one or a few individual sessions to discover if there are things they will say during the individual sessions that they would refuse to bring out during the conjoint sessions.

On the whole, however, I am usually able to go along with the basic desire of any clients who want individual, marital, family or group psychotherapy. It is only in relatively few cases that I talk them into taking a form of therapy they are at first loathe to try. (Ellis, personal communication)

Indications and Contra-indications for Individual Therapy: Therapists' Views

Since this text is concerned with individual therapy I wish now to focus on the views of therapists (including those featured in this book) concerning indications and contra-indications for individual therapy.

Indications

(a) Individual therapy, by its nature, provides clients with a situation of complete confidentiality. It is thus indicated for clients for whom the opportunity to disclose feelings and personal meanings without fear that others may use such information to their detriment is important. It is an arena which is appropriate when clients want to discuss 'secret' material

(Fay Fransella). Individual therapy thus provides clients with an opportunity for greater openness than other arenas.

(b) Individual therapy, again by its dyadic nature, provides an opportunity for a close relationship to develop between therapist and client.
This may be important for some clients who have not developed close
relationships with significant people in their lives and for whom group
therapy may prove too threatening. It is especially important for more
disturbed clients who need to experience the order of an ongoing two-
person relationship in order to offset the chaos of the rest of their existence (Dougal Mackay). Moreover, in therapies where the development
and resolution of a transference relationship (see Chapter 2) is deemed to
be curative, individual therapy is probably the arena of choice.

(c) In the individual arena, therapy can proceed more at the client's pace.
The therapist can give the client his/her full attention (Francesca
Inskipp) and as much 'time and space' as the client desires (Fay Fransella)
– free from interruptions from other people. This is particularly
important for clients who are quite confused, who wish to explore value
dilemmas (Francesca Inskipp), and for those whose constructions of the
world are 'loose' and require tightening (Fay Fransella).

(d) Individual therapy is indicated when clients' major problematic
relationships are with themselves (Aveline 1979), or where others are not
centrally implicated (Sander 1979).

(e) Individual therapy may be indicated for a client who wishes to differentiate self from others, who has decided to leave a relationship (a
marriage, for example) and wishes to deal with the individual problems
that this may involve – although some conjoint sessions with the spouse/
partner may be helpful in matters of conciliation (Gurman and
Kniskern 1978).

(f) The arena of individual therapy provides therapists with opportunities
to vary their interaction styles with clients when this is called for, free
from the concern that such variation may adversely affect other people
present (Mackay).

(g) Individual therapy permits therapist and client to set a wider range of
goals than might be possible in the other arenas (Dougal Mackay), and is
particularly appropriate where a major reconstruction of the self is called
for (Fay Fransella).

(h) Individual therapy may be indicated when the client is not deemed
able to benefit from other therapeutic arenas: for example, where a person would monopolize a therapy group or be too withdrawn within it

(Yalom 1975), or when a person is deemed too vulnerable for family therapy.

(i) John Davis (personal communication) considers that individual therapy is particularly indicated for clients who: a) have severe problems trusting other people; b) will not 'open up' when other people are involved in the therapeutic arena; c) have difficulty sharing the therapist with other clients and d) are extremely anxious and/or depressed.

Contra-indications

(a) Individual therapy is contra-indicated for clients who are likely to become overly dependent on the therapist (Fay Fransella and Francesca Inskipp). Such dependency may become so intense as to be irredeemable. These clients may be more appropriately helped in group therapy, where any dependency that does develop may not be so pronounced.

(b) Individual therapy, by its dyadic nature, can often be a close interpersonal encounter, and thus is less likely to be indicated for clients who may find such intimacy or the prospect of such intimacy too threatening (Dougal Mackay).

(c) Drawing on the thesis that a group of people is less likely to be manipulated than one person, some therapists believe that individual therapy is contra-indicated for clients who are 'highly manipulative' (Faye Page) or who are diagnosed as 'borderline' personalities.

(d) Individual therapy may not be appropriate for clients who utilize intellectualization as a major form of psychological defence (Laurence Collinson). Such clients probably stand to benefit more from group therapy, where the corporate group membership is likely to be more successful in challenging this style of defence than is a single, solitary therapist and where there is a greater likelihood of the provision of an emotionally toned atmosphere which is deemed to be so beneficial for clients such as these.

(e) Individual therapy may not be appropriate for clients with sex problems where such problems are maintained by the partner's response (John Davis, personal communication).

(f) Finally, a number of therapists mentioned that individual therapy is contra-indicated when clients find this arena too comfortable. Based on the notion that personal change is facilitated in situations where there is an optimum level of arousal, individual therapy may not provide enough challenge for such clients. For example, Ravid's (1969) research, mentioned earlier, concludes that it may prove unproductive to offer individual therapy to clients who have had much previous individual therapy but still require further therapeutic help; although this may not hold when the previous individual therapy has been ineffectively conducted.

Individual Therapy as Part of a Comprehensive Treatment Strategy

Up to now the discussion has focused on the employment of individual therapy as the sole treatment arena. Some clinicians, however, see individual therapy as one phase in a comprehensive treatment approach or as an arena to be used concurrently with other arenas.

When individual therapy is used as a separate phase in treatment, it is often employed first. From a Kleinian perspective, Cassie Cooper considers the progression from individual therapy to group therapy a natural one, and one which corresponds to normal child development: from the intense dyadic interaction with the individual therapist (mother), the client learns in the next phase (group therapy) to work together with peers (siblings) and, where appropriate, to constructively challenge the authority of the therapist (father). Perhaps not surprisingly, Cooper considers this progression to be especially helpful for clients who have difficulty in forming and sustaining relationships with peers and with authority figures. Cooper's practice is to serve as therapist in both arenas, although the employment of different therapists in different arenas is a further option.

Fay Fransella considers that an initial period of individual therapy is important for most clients. The group therapy arena, however, can be introduced to clients early in treatment, and is seen as providing a context where they can experiment with new learnings derived from individual therapy. Individual and group therapy are here used concurrently, with the gradual phasing out over time of the individual sessions used for the processing of the data gleaned from the group therapy experiments.

The concurrent use of individual and group therapy arenas with different therapists is advocated by Ormont and Strean (1978). They argue that such concurrent treatment is helpful for a number of reasons:

(a) Clients' difficulties can be examined from different perspectives.
(b) Different aspects of clients' personalities are revealed in the different arenas.
(c) Clients who are 'inaccessible to influence in one setting become accessible in another'. However, such concurrent treatment is not applicable to certain clients, namely those who are pervasively anxious, severely depressed or experiencing delusions. According to Ormont and Strean, such clients tend to have an adverse effect on other group members and for this reason are better seen only in individual therapy.

Berman (1982) has written about the use of individual therapy sessions in conjoint marital therapy. Individual sessions may be indicated when: '1) therapy has not progressed for a significant period of time (three or four weeks); 2) the therapist senses a hidden agenda' – in one or both spouses – and '3) a client requests private time'. Berman notes that if a client 'requests such sessions, the issue of unbalanced alliances arises. The therapist must use his/her judgment to balance the possibility of manipulation against trust in the client's sense of what is necessary'.

Individual Therapy: One Client's View

This chapter would not be complete without the client's perspective; thus I asked one of my individual therapy clients to reflect on the question of therapeutic arenas as it related to her situation. Her account is meant to be illustrative rather than representative. Amy is a 41 year-old professional woman who sought help for stress problems arising from work and, to some degree, marital pressures. My assessment led me to conclude that her problems stemmed mainly from intrapsychic factors, although interpersonal (marital) factors were implicated to some extent. Amy decided to opt for individual therapy and remained in this arena throughout treatment. Although a period of conjoint marital therapy was discussed, Amy decided against this option. In conclusion to this chapter I present her account verbatim, since it is succinct and addresses a number of issues already discussed but from the client's perspective:

> As I only have had experience of individual therapy it is easier to comment on that. I can only surmise what it would have been like if my husband had come with me to counselling. Also as only part of my problems were caused

by my marriage we may not have dug so deeply into other areas of me that were of more value to me as an individual. The sessions would have been, I feel, more general about our marriage and our relationship and less about my own problems.

Maybe if we had come together I should not have felt I had become dependent on seeing you. I may have become more dependent on my husband and his understanding rather than having an awareness of my own problems. Having to overcome my feelings of dependence on you has made me overcome this problem, work it out, on my own.

I know that I gained more from our individual sessions than if we had come together. It would have been interesting to have been in a group session, at some point, to discover that other people have similar problems. As I am beginning to find as I now open up to people more. It is because I felt I wanted to find out how others feel that I have been more open; if I had had this experience in a group situation I may not have needed to experiment outside, and thus not have had the pleasure of deepening several friendships.

My seeing you in individual therapy was to me of enormous benefit. I feel I needed the very close understanding we developed to be able to open up to you, to trust you. There are several areas of my life that my husband knows nothing about and these I could not have discussed: the feeling of being trapped, because I know it would have hurt him, needed to be examined so I could come to terms with it; my going to bed with other men, he knows nothing of, also is part of me and the reasons for being unfaithful wanted talking about; the 'need' for love to feel attractive and wanted by someone and my feelings when these relationships ended.

Part of my problems, a large part I think, was covering up my feelings of inadequacy and shithood, by grandiosity, by proving I had to and could do it all. Also by having to please people, not upset them. To really uncover these feelings and work on them needed that session where I panicked. This was caused by me suddenly realising how much I cared what you thought of me. I don't think I would have such a crush on you if my husband had been there. The one-to-one emotional atmosphere could not have developed with three people there. I know I could not have opened up in front of my husband. The admitting of how I feel about you and the acceptance of those emotions as normal, if uncomfortable, and your acceptance of me, as I am, helped me a great deal. I felt less of a shit. If I had come with my husband I would probably been spared the uncomfortable, experience of sitting in your office being very physically aware of you as a male. These sensations interfering with my thoughts. The same also happened with the tapes; I was listening to you, your voice, rather than learning from them. But I would not have had it any other way, the individual sessions I mean, as by being attracted to you, I was made aware of feelings I did not think I still possessed.

On reflection individual therapy was best for me, even if I hadn't found you attractive, I wanted that close relationship that I feel can only develop in a one-to-one situation. If we had both seen you individually for a few sessions then perhaps seen you together this would have been the better solution. As we would both have had a chance to uncover things about ourselves we did not want the other to see.

Having discussed the issue of therapeutic arenas, we are now in a position to consider the different approaches to individual therapy.

Notes

1 This chapter will not deal with the finer decisions of selecting among different types of individual therapy. Readers who are interested in selecting among different brief forms of individual therapy should consult Clarkin and Frances (1982), who deal with selection criteria for crisis-intervention, psychodynamic, problem-solving and behaviour therapies. Readers who have a specific interest in psychodynamic therapies should consult Perry et al. (1984), who present selection criteria for four types of individual pschodynamically oriented psychotherapy: supportive, focal, exploratory and psychoanalysis.
2 This chapter will not deal with schizophrenic client populations. Readers who are particularly interested in the selection of appropriate therapeutic arenas in working with schizophenic clients should consult Mosher and Keith (1980).
3 To be strictly accurate, 48% improvement was obtained when American social workers in family service agencies acted as therapists. How far these results can be extended so as to apply to different therapists working in Britain remains to be seen.

References

Aveline M (1979) Towards a conceptual framework of psychotherapy: a personal view, *British Journal of Medical Psychology* 52: 271–275

Bennun I (1984) Evaluating marital therapy: a hospital and community study, *British Journal of Guidance and Counselling* 12(1): 84–91

Berman E M (1982) The individual interview as a treatment technique in conjoint therapy, *American Journal of Family Therapy* 10(1): 27–37

Bordin E S (1975) 'The generalizability of the psychoanalytic concept of working alliance', paper presented at the meeting of the Society of Psychotherapy Research, Boston

Bordin E S (1976) 'The working alliance: basis for a general theory of psychotherapy', paper presented at the meeting of the American Psychological Association, Washington DC

Clarkin J F, Frances A (1982) Selection criteria for the brief psychotherapies, *American Journal of Psychotherapy* 36(2): 166–180

Garfield S L, Kurtz R (1974) A survey of clinical psychologists: character-istics, activities and orientations, *The Clinical Psychologist 28*: 7–10

Gurman A S, Kniskern D P (1978) 'Research in marital and family therapy' in Garfield S L and Bergin A E (eds.) *Handbook of Psychotherapy and Behavior Change*, 2nd edition, Wiley, New York

Harper R A (1981) Limitations of marriage and family therapy, *Rational Living 16(2)*: 3–6

Hurvitz N (1967) Marital problems following psychotherapy with one spouse, *Journal of Consulting Psychology 31(1)*: 38–47

Kerr M E (1981) 'Family systems theory and therapy' in Gurman A S and Kniskern D P (eds.) *Handbook of Family Therapy*, Brunner/Mazel, New York, p. 234

Mosher L R, Keith S J (1980) Psychosocial treatment: individual, group, family, and community support approaches, *Schizophrenia Bulletin 6(1)*: 10–41

Norcross J C, Prochaska J O (1982) A national survey of clinical psychologists: characteristics and activities, *The Clinical Psychologist 35:* 1–8

Orlinsky D E, Howard K I (1978) 'The relation of process to outcome in psycho-therapy' in Garfield S L and Bergin A E (eds.) *Handbook of Psychotherapy and Behavior Change*, 2nd edition, Wiley, New York, pp. 310–11

Ormont L R and Strean H S (1978) *The Practice of Conjoint Therapy: Combining Individual and Group Treatment*, Human Sciences Press, New York, p. 35

Perry S, Frances A, Klar H, Clarkin J F (1984) Selection criteria for individual dynamic psychotherapies, *Psychiatric Quarterly* (In Press)

Prochaska J O, Norcross J C (1983) Contemporary psychotherapists: a national survey of characteristics, practices, orientations, and attitudes, *Psychotherapy: Theory, Research and Practice 20(2)*: 161–173

Ravid R (1969) Effect of group therapy on long-term individual therapy, *Dissertation Abstracts International 30*: 2427B

Sander F M (1979) *Individual and Family Therapy: Toward an Integration*, Jason Aronson, New York, pp. 203, 208

Sider R C, Clements C (1982) Family or individual therapy: The ethics of modality choice, *American Journal of Psychiatry 139(11)*: 1455–1459

Weisz G, Bucher B (1980) Involving husbands in treatment of obesity – Effects on weight loss, depression and marital satisfaction, *Behavior Therapy 11*: 643–650

Yalom I D (1975) *The Theory and Practice of Group Psychotherapy*, 2nd edition, Basic Books, New York

Chapter 2 Psychodynamic Therapy: The Freudian Approach

Michael Jacobs

Historical Context and Developments in Britain

Such is the influence of Freud's work on European and American thought and culture, even in the popular mind, that it is difficult to imagine that time when his ideas were so innovative and, indeed, shocking. Yet the mass assimilation of at least some of those ideas has also caused a mythology to spring up around Freud and Freudian psychotherapy which is perpetuated even by intelligent people who clearly have not read the original work. Caricatures are drawn of Freud as the dogmatic father-figure unable to tolerate opposition, or as the analyst who had a sexual answer to every thought, word or symbol. Perhaps the most inaccurate assessments of Freudian thought and practice are those interpretations which are based on his early writing alone and do not take into account either Freud's development of his own ideas or the vast amount of change that has taken place since his death nearly fifty years ago. Freudian psychotherapy is neither monolithic nor static.

Freud trained initially as a neurologist, and his scientific approach was welded – sometimes unhappily – to a philosophical and literary interest which formed part of the formal training of his day. Moreover, his science was heavily influenced by Helmholtz (through his mentor, Brücke): 'the billiard ball universe in which inert atomic structures were pushed around in space by an independent energy' (Guntrip 1968). Thus his early work stresses cause and effect in the mental as well as in the physical field, and uses a concept of mental energy as a potentially measurable entity which in the context of twentieth-century physics, philosophy and psychotherapy is less than adequate. Freud never completely relinquished the hope that his theories about the mind would one day be capable of description in physiological terms; yet his philosophical and literary interest led him to concentrate more upon the personality than upon his doctoral research on nerve cells, and a six-month visit to Paris to observe the work of Charcot enabled him to find evidence of 'the unconscious', a term which was already in use in fashionable literary circles in the nineteenth century. He returned to Vienna resolving to 'understand something of the riddles of the world in which we live and perhaps even contribute something to their solution' (Clark 1980). Neurosis – hysteria in particular – captured his imagination. Hypnosis, revealing as it did hidden layers of the mind which hitherto had been described only in philosophy and religion, provided him with his first technique: catharsis (originally a medical term for purging) was the process by which symptoms would be cured.

There was nothing particularly original in this. Working with Breuer, however, and open to the introduction of alternative techniques, he abandoned hypnosis as a questionable approach, replacing it with questions and orders to the patient to speak about the events leading to the onset of symptoms; then, following a rebuke by one patient, he adopted the technique of free association. The patient was to speak whatever came to mind, with all associations and side-issues, 'even if it is *disagreeable* to say it, even if it seems *unimportant* or positively *meaningless*' (Freud 1949). Resistance to free association, both conscious and unconscious, formed a second major strand of technique. The third major strand – and here Freud was not only innovative, but also brave enough to grasp an awkward nettle which Breuer found emotionally and intellectually too difficult – was to use the significance of the doctor-patient relationship (technically known as transference) as a means of clarifying other relationships of importance to the patient. These three strands remain central to analytic technique to the present day. In other respects technique has changed and developed – the use of the couch, for example, is not universal – and at all times the practice of analysis has served not only as therapy for the individual but as a tool for understanding the mind.

These techniques helped to release memories and fantasies which had been banished to the unconscious. It was a mark of Freud's originality that he used the details recounted by his patients to formulate new theories of the origin of neurosis. His teacher Charcot had emphasized the significance of heredity. Building upon chance remarks, first by Charcot and then by Breuer, with confirmation from his patients, Freud suggested that the secret to the cause of neurosis lay in sexual factors. To suggest that infantile sexuality was normal, and not just a sign of abnormality, was new. Already unpopular for espousing Charcot's methods, and against his own inner puritanism, Freud began to put forward his ideas, compounding the reaction to him by asserting that his patients (as children) were actually seduced by parents. He held to this hypothesis rather too tenaciously, until he withdrew it in favour of the theory of the Oedipus complex, and the *fantasy* of seduction. Freud suggested that wishes and fantasies (especially in children) are as powerful as if they had actually happened.

Psychoanalysis was born; but because of the cries of scandal over such intimate matters being talked about in the consulting room it received scant support in Vienna. Reviews of *Studies on Hysteria* were more favourable in England. Freud's analysis (at least until the formation of the small but dedicated Vienna Psychoanalytical Society) focused on himself, although apart from a few allusions (often disguised), the inner world of Freud the man remains elusive to this day, with much of his correspondence of that period of self-analysis still embargoed until the year 2000. With the publication of *The Interpretation of Dreams* in 1900, support for Freud slowly increased. As students visited him in Vienna and returned home, psychoanalysis expanded geographically through Europe and in America, but more importantly, as a discipline it extended further into the 'dark recesses of the soul'. As Clark (1980) observes, their work coincided with other discoveries which radically changed our view of the world: radioactivity, the nuclear atom, quantum theory, the rediscovery of Mendel's laws of inheritance, and the science of genetics: 'Freud and his followers had more in common with the leading spirits of the age than they may have realised'.

Britain was introduced to Freud's ideas particularly by Ernest Jones (Freud's biographer) and later by Melanie Klein. In 1938 Freud and his daughter Anna were given asylum in London from the Nazi threat which had already scattered German and Austrian analysts – most of them to America. The military hospitals in the Second World War provided opportunities for a much wider application of analytic ideas, promoting more general use of psychotherapy; although even by the thirties social workers and others were taking up Freudian theory. With Anna Freud and Melanie Klein as the figureheads of two distinct types of Freudian theory, there was nearly a split in the analytic movement in Britain. There had of course been secessions in the first generation (Jung and Adler), the second generation (Horney, Fromm, Perls, Reich and Rank when they went to the USA); and there have been since (Berne, Janov, Ellis, etc.); yet out of the ferment of ideas in Britain there emerged a psycho-analytic society which has generated considerable advances in theory (Fairbairn, Winnicott, Bowlby, Guntrip and Laing, to name the better-known) and in technique (for example, Balint's work with focal psycho-therapy, since carried forward by Malan). Refinement of technique in particular has helped adapt the length and depth of traditional analysis into a psychotherapy which is capable of wider application, and may therefore be of particular interest to the reader of a book such as this.

Theoretical Assumptions

The image of the person

Freudian theory, it should be remembered, arises from psychotherapy and not from formal research: 'It is more difficult for an analyst to be original than for anyone else, because everything we say truly has been taught us yesterday', i.e. by patients (Winnicott 1965). The theory has developed as the amount of data has increased, but also through changing perspectives. Many of Freud's original clinical observations remain valid, but as must be expected of any movement which pushes at the frontiers of knowledge, his theories have shifted in emphasis and in the language used to express them. The best-known Freudian model of personality (id, ego and super-ego) was neither the first nor the last in Freudian psycho-therapy. Deeper levels of therapy have given rise to different models, although the early ones still have some use, if only for their simplicity, in some applications of therapy, and with some clients.

One perspective that has changed has been the basic scientific back-ground. Freud started as a neurologist, and his first ideas reflect that dis-cipline. He moved fairly rapidly to a psychobiological theory with imagery akin to hydraulics. The focus of therapy was the relationship between the conscious and unconscious parts of the mind, seeking to undo the repression of sexual impulses or drives. Just as dammed-up (repressed) water has to find an alternative outlet, so sexual drives (libido) which are suppressed or repressed by the conscious mind have to find outlets, such as through neurotic symptoms. Conversion hysteria (psychogenic anaesthesia of limbs or senses) provided Freud with such examples. Catharsis and the freeing of memories enabled libido to be redirected into appropriate expression (adult sexuality) or sublimated expression (aim-inhibited sexuality, or love in a non-genital sense).

As a model it had drawbacks. It held out little hope that the majority of people could live in civilized society (in which instincts had to be curbed) without becoming neurotic, or criminal (acting out). Instincts themselves were questionable (appetites might be more appropriate), although they were carried forward into the later model of Freud's, a structural one of id, ego and super-ego. Here the id was still too readily identified with primitive drives seeking to discharge tension rather than being object- (or person-) seeking. From 1923 onwards, parallel with this new model, Freud was postulating an Eros (love) and a death instinct. The latter was a drive towards self-extinction, which was only secondarily turned outwards in aggression. Although the problem of aggression was an essential one to tackle, few of Freud's followers were able to accept his theory. They have preferred to view aggression itself as a drive, or more usually as a reaction to fear or vulnerability.

Yet implicit in Freud's later thinking were the seeds of ideas taken up by post-Freudian analysts, particularly the significance of objects (persons), both internal and external. The theory of the Oedipus complex is not simply about discharging sexual drives, but about the relationships in which such feelings arise: the relationship of the child to both parents. Freud's theory that the super-ego was formed in the child through the internalization of the idealized or feared parent of the same sex led the way to a more comprehensive theory of internalized objects in the 'inner world'. The internalization of either the whole person or part of the person (whole and part objects) was taken up by Melanie Klein, who continued to stress innate factors (see Chapter 3 and Segal 1973), and by Fairbairn (1952), who discarded the term 'id' and modified the 'super-ego' in favour of a theory of the ego which splits into three: the libidinal ego (seeking the exciting and fulfilling object), the anti-libidinal ego (the critical internal saboteur or persecutory object) and the central (observing and experiencing) ego.

Object-relations theory (as it is known in Britain rather than personal relations theory, the equivalent term in the United States) has become the major model for Freudian psychotherapists in Britain. Instincts are no longer seen as 'entities per se, but functions of the ego' (Guntrip 1968). Sexuality is seen as object-seeking, and (though in some people still a major difficulty) just one part of object relationships. Aggression is not an innate drive to hostile behaviour but a response to threat (particularly to the personality). The real drive is to become a person (Guntrip 1968). The ego at birth is largely unformed but unified (here modern Freudians differ from Kleinians), and develops through different stages (just as the body grows, and is indeed influenced by physical development) towards becoming a whole person. The relationship between the internal parts of the ego and their external relationship to others starts with the vital relationship of mother and baby. 'We are concerned with a living whole human being and how he can become a viable ego, a real self, a personal 'I' with all his inborn energies flowing together as an inwardly free and spontaneous capacity to enjoy, love and create' (Guntrip 1968).

The interplay between the inner world of the person and the external environment of that person continues throughout the developmental stages, with the internal and external worlds influencing each other. The original stages of Freud's theory (oral, anal and genital) were based upon pleasurable (or unpleasurable) areas of the body, although object-relations theory has expanded them to give more importance to the relationship with parents: first as the source of nurture, then as the authority figures, and thirdly as the first objects of love and sexuality. These early stages help form basic strengths for later stages of life. While Freud devoted attention to early childhood, others such as Anna Freud and Erikson have stressed the importance of adolescence. The impact of the cultural and social environment has been a feature of neo-Freudian writers.

Concepts of psychological health and disturbance

It is axiomatic to all Freudian thought that the neurotic or the psychotic person demonstrates (though writ large) the processes in the 'normal' person; indeed, it would be hard to find someone who is not in some way neurotic. Health might therefore be described as the absence of disturbance or the maintenance of an equilibrium, although many Freudian writers define normality in more positive terms.

These concepts have changed with the development of the basic model. Early writing defined the aim of therapy as to make the unconscious conscious, with the further aim of helping a person 'to love and to work'. The structural model described health in structural terms, and disturbance in similar language: 'The poor ego serves three severe masters . . . the external world, the super-ego and the id . . . If the ego is obliged to admit its weakness, it breaks out in anxiety – realistic anxiety regarding the external world, moral anxiety regarding the super-ego and neurotic anxiety regarding the strength of the passions in the id' (Freud 1964).

Although Freud described three stages of infancy (oral, anal and genital), it was the last two to which he devoted most attention, with the Oedipal situation seen as the most common cause of disturbance. Yet the Oedipus complex is a stage through which every child must pass: it is not in itself abnormal. Negotiated satisfactorily, the child suppresses sexuality until adolescence, when the formation of sexual identity and break with parental ties leads to his or her own partnership with another in adult life. At the same time the child identifies positively with the parent of the same sex, unless the super-ego identifies so strongly with negative features in that parent that it becomes a major inhibiting force. Freud paid less attention to pre-Oedipal, particularly to pre-verbal experience; it was the child psychotherapists (Klein, Anna Freud, Erikson and Winnicott), together with Fairbairn and Guntrip, who expanded awareness of the significance of the early months, although only Klein suggested that Oedipal manifestations were implicit at that age. From their various positions these analysts see the ego as being damaged in the first year of life, when defences against feelings of badness or weakness are formed to protect the frightened ego.

Knowledge of the primary development of the ego and of signs of early disturbance is important (particularly for knowing one's limitations as a psychotherapist), but the reader will be more concerned, in the practice of less intensive therapy, with subsequent stages. Erikson's (1965) model, the 'Eight Ages of Man', outlines the developmental tasks of each age, with the strengths which may be acquired in each, together with the weaknesses which arise from the unsatisfactory negotiation of any one period. The issue of the first stage is basic trust versus basic mistrust, in which the foundations of faith in self and the environment depend upon the quality of mothering (mothering representing the only world the infant knows). The second stage of autonomy versus shame and doubt depends upon the self-esteem built upon muscular (including anal) control and the encouragement (or criticism) of parents. Trust and autonomy help the child negotiate the third stage of initiative versus guilt, where the child's wish to stay close to one parent has to be reconciled with rivalry towards the other. The stages build upon each other like a series of building blocks until the final stage of life, where the issue is ego integrity versus despair (dependent on a person's verdict on their life) and where the virtues of old age include wisdom and renunciation. It is a very useful model, but a sketchy one (except perhaps in Erikson's work on adolescence, where he writes more fully about identity and identity crisis) and needs to be filled out from the studies of other analysts and psychologists (Piaget's work, for instance, has been well received and integrated with analytic theory). A great deal has been written about childhood and adolescence; somewhat less about the stages of adult life (but see Golan 1981).

Psychological health, in psychodynamic terms, is achieved by good object (person)-relations begun in early life, built up through the developmental stages (or through developmental lines, in Anna Freud's terms), leading to the ability to think, feel and act for oneself, to explore, to experiment, take risks, and above all to become one's 'self'. Such a person is sufficiently free from anxiety and guilt (though has acquired 'concern') to enter an erotic relationship with an extra-familial partner, and to form other important personal relationships in which there is a genuine meeting unaffected by erotic and neurotic elements (Guntrip 1968).

The acquisition and perpetuation of psychological disturbance

The previous section has described how weaknesses and failures in the parent-child relationship and in negotiating developmental stages can lead to disturbance or, in Freudian terms, to defences which may give rise to disturbance. Neuroses are maladaptive solutions, which may fail in the face of later crises. Defences to protect the ego are a normal part of adaptation, but if incomplete or tenuous they can fail under stress. Defences include splitting (in which ambivalent or contradictory feelings for the same person are split on to two or more objects to prevent negative feelings harming good ones); projection (disowning and often attacking parts of oneself put on to others); regression and fixation (respectively, retreating to a former developmental stage and not able to move beyond a particular stage); displacement (shifting feelings on to an object other than the person to whom they should be attached); denial (unconscious refusal to own feelings); reaction-formation (expressing the opposite emotion to that which is unconsciously felt). Underlying them all is the defence of repression (not permitting the access of painful feelings, or memories to consciousness – suppression describes a more conscious attempt to push down such feelings).

We can only truly speak of psychological disturbance when behaviour is inappropriate to a particular age. Appropriate behaviour at one stage (oral dependency in infancy, for example) only becomes a problem either if a child fails to move out of that phase or if an older person regresses to that stage (showing signs of dependency problems, for instance). People may function satisfactorily, at least on a conscious level, for many years unless circumstances, such as a reminder of earlier difficulties, cause defences to break down. It is rare for disturbance (as opposed to the normal fluctuation of feelings, even if intense such as grief) to be simply the result of current events; rather, it is connected with the significance of those events. Where a current crisis cannot be resolved through adaptation and the passage of time – a process that counselling can be helpful in assisting – the psychotherapist invariably looks for, although does not always quickly find, an event or more probably a series of events within earlier relationships which have predisposed the client to such a deep reaction. This is the revival of memories and feelings, albeit repressed, which make the current situation harder to resolve.

Defences serve another purpose, since they often express such repressed thoughts and feelings in a disguised form. They are essentially a compromise, a way of expression, but one that operates in a less than satisfactory way for psychological health. Symptoms and defences often provide clues to underlying difficulties, sometimes what is technically known as 'the return of the repressed'. Unsatisfactory defences not only perpetuate disturbance but may also provide disguised expression for repressed feelings, so that giving them up can be threatening: for instance, a young man who obsessively washes his penis after masturbation (feeling guilty) perpetuates the pleasure in the washing. Some people, of course, live in environments which cannot easily be changed, but many more choose or mould their environment to maintain their defences, even though they believe they are resolving former difficulties. For example, some people separate from a partner in order to escape conflicts, only to find that their new relationship shows similar characteristics. Neurotic relationships or patterns of behaviour are formed, and in those who come for psychotherapy they have frequently not only failed but repeatedly failed.

Freudian psychotherapy aims at undoing these unsatisfactory defences. Through a 'therapeutic regression' (Winnicott 1958) repressed and suppressed feelings, and wishes which have been frustrated in earlier life, can be re-experienced in safety, and expressed more appropriately in adult life.

Practice

Goals of therapy

Therapy seeks to help the client re-experience old conflicts but 'with a new ending' (Alexander and French 1946). The aim of the therapist is to analyse defences and conflicts. 'When we can help a disturbed personality to outgrow the blocking effects of its internal conflicts, we can trust the normal development process to take over' (Guntrip 1968). This unblocking includes making the unconscious conscious as well as acceptable and accessible to the ego (or central self). Another aim is to develop the client's ability to question and explore himself even when therapy has finished. Since self-analysis can never be complete the client, in developing good and equal relationships as a result of therapy, will use the insight and responses of others to supplement this task.

Such high aims are naturally limited by other factors. Goals are limited to what the client consciously wants to achieve, and to what the client is capable of achieving. Motivation, ego strength, the capacity for insight, the ability to tolerate the frustration of slow change, financial cost, the client's immediate environment and support, and the degree and length of any disturbance are all variables on the client's side; while the skills, experience, personality and time available to the client are variables on the therapist's side.

Psychotherapy therefore ranges from 'psychoanalytical first aid' (Guntrip 1968) or symptom relief to different levels of more intensive work, from sexual difficulties to dependency problems. Malan and his colleagues at the Tavistock Clinic have validated brief focal psychotherapy (about thirty sessions, once a week). In their view, the formation of a focus for interpretation is important. Limited and specific goals are set and results evaluated. Such goals, based upon the presenting problems, are defined by the therapist from a clinical assessment both of what might be possible, and of what is desirable to achieve in the time available. Even then, as in all psychotherapy it is the client who sets the pace by allowing only what he can cope with; and when a therapist goes too far ahead of the client, resistance (see later) occurs (Malan 1979). Freud's advice to a student remains as true today: 'I should advise you to set aside your therapeutic ambition and try and understand what is happening. When you have done that, therapeutics will take care of itself' (Roazen 1979).

The person of the therapist: therapeutic style

The words just quoted may confirm the image which some have of Freud as coldly intellectual. Intellectual he was (though also the uncoverer of strong repressed feelings); cold he was not. His wife and his patients describe his kindness; and he was not averse, despite writing of the therapist's 'abstinence' from all but interpretation, to giving money to at least one impoverished patient. If Freudian psychotherapy is rich in theory, Guntrip (1971) reminds us that 'to care for people is more imporant than to care for ideas'.

The Freudian psychotherapist aims at being neutral but not indifferent, patient but also persistent, firm but also flexible. He relates to the client in four ways. First there is a working alliance in which two adults co-operate to understand the 'child' in the client. The therapist's 'child', understood through his own therapy, is kept in check but contributes to his ability to empathize with or, in Freudian terms, 'identify with' the client. The therapist adopts a quiet, reflective style, intervening when in his judgement the client is ready to make use of a particular interpretation. Making interpretations is an art, and not the fitting of client to theory as some critics suggest.

There is a further reason for adopting this stance. Although today psychotherapy is more likely to be conducted face to face, the therapist's relative passivity and his abstinence from revealing much about himself (at least verbally) allow the client to develop perceptions about him which reflect the client's inner object world. This is the second aspect of the relationship, namely the way the client sees the therapist as if he were a parent or had parental qualities. The therapist interprets the transference relationship which develops and which is present not simply because of the therapist's neutrality but also because transference is a common phenomenon, such as when any 'authority figure' (however liberal he may be) is identified with a parent figure; this transference may include loving or dependent wishes/fears, anxieties about the 'judgement' of the therapist or struggles over authority and control. The personality of the therapist is held sufficiently in check to allow transference distortions from the past to be re-experienced in present relationships, not only within therapy but also in illustration of the way in which repetitive patterns from the past influence current relationships generally.

The therapist does not actually become a substitute parent. As Rycroft observes (1968) he should not consider himself 'the possessor of a store of agape or caritas so much greater than that of his patient's parents. Analysts who hold that their capacity to help patients derives from their ability to understand them, and that this ability depends on their knowledge of the unconscious are really being more modest'.

Indeed, the therapist is bound, by the nature of the therapeutic situation, to be a failure as a substitute parent. Hence Winnicott's graphic phrase that the function of the therapist is not to succeed but to fail 'because he can never make up to clients for what they have suffered in the past, but what he *can* do is to repeat the failure to love them enough . . . and then share with them and help them work through their feelings about his failure' (Malan 1979). This 'failure' applies not just to nurturing and the earliest levels of disturbance, but also to the 'failure' of the therapist to be the authoritarian person the client fears or desires or the 'lover' for whom the client with Oedipal problems wishes.

The third aspect of the therapist as a person is that he has his own neuroses, and his own counter-transference. He learns through his own analysis to be aware of his 'blind spots' and his own distorted perceptions. 'Counter-transference' is used in the literature in two senses: firstly to refer to his own distorted view of the other which interferes with therapist objectivity and secondly to describe feelings aroused in him by a client which may at times provide useful clues about that client's relationships to past and present significant others.

Fourthly, the therapist is a real person, and Guntrip (as opposed to Klein) believes that in therapy the client moves from unrealistic positive and negative transference relationships to discovering what kind of real relationship exists between them, and to an accurate perception of the therapist as a person in his own right. So, in Guntrip's (1971) words, the therapist must be a 'whole real human being ... and not just a professional interpreter ... Only then can the patient find himself and become a person in his own right'.

Major therapeutic techniques

One of Freud's first techniques, recorded in *Studies on Hysteria*, came at a patient's prompting. She said in a grumbling tone 'that I was not to keep on asking her where this or that comes from, but to let her tell me what she had to say'. Freud 'fell in with this', learned to be more patient, and so adopted the technique now known as 'free association' referred to in the first section of this chapter (Breuer and Freud 1955).

This was the fundamental rule, which he himself would often spell out in detail. It is a rule which is easier for a client to understand than fully observe. There are clearly thoughts, memories and feelings which clients are reluctant to expose, especially in early sessions. There are also thoughts and memories which clients are resistant to exposing, resistance being an unconscious defence, a way of preventing what is feared from emerging even into the client's consciousness. Therefore the first major aim of Freudian technique is to help free association to take place unchecked by suppression (conscious) or repression (unconscious). Interpretations by the therapist are often about resistance, aimed at freeing painful or feared thoughts and feelings so that they can be expressed openly. Only as this is achieved are the therapist and client in a position to understand the material in all its fullness, and to make the second and third major types of interpretation: those of the triangles of conflict and insight.

The encouragement of free association requires the basic skills of reflection, paraphrasing, minimal response, open-ended questions, the acceptance of silence, etc. that are shared with many of the counselling and therapeutic approaches described elsewhere in this book. Their value cannot be underestimated, but they can perhaps be taken for granted as basic techniques of Freudian psychotherapy also, facilitating the flow of the client's words and feelings. What is particular to psychodynamic psychotherapy is the interpretation of defences and the interpretation of transference.

These terms need some explanation. As stated earlier, transference is a feature common to all relationships, whereby others are perceived as likely to react or feel as significant people from past experience (particularly parents) might have done or as those towards whom similar feelings of fear, love, anger, jealousy, etc. may be felt as they were (if often suppressed or repressed) in the original family situation. Those whose personalities are chronically or acutely disturbed are inclined, because of their needs, to experience intense transference feelings. Add to this situation the 'symbolic love' (and also the actual deprivation) in what the therapist offers (unconditional acceptance, understanding, genuineness, warmth, but he is *non-possessive* too), and 'the patient's intense need and the therapist's response result in transference phenomena of extraordinary intensity' (Malan 1979).

Transference interpretation consists of linking two or more points of a triangle, called by Menninger the 'triangle of insight' (Ménninger 1958) or by Malan the 'triangle of person' (Malan 1979). These points are: first, parents or past significant persons (P); second, other or outside persons in current life (O) and third, the therapist or transference (T). It can also be expressed as 'back then', 'out there' and 'in here'. Typical links which might be made include: mother-wife (P/O); boss-father (O/P); tutor-therapist (O/T); parent-therapist (P/T); or that in a full transference interpretation, used in the following case 'You are finding it difficult to acknowledge the sadness you are feeling at leaving me (T) and others at university (O) because it might make you feel rejected by me (T) as you have so often felt the losses in your early years of mother and grandfather and Peter as rejection (P).' The transference interpretation, – which also permits the expression of real feelings – makes so much more concrete what would otherwise be an intellectual formulation concerned only with the past. It should also demonstrate the force with which the past influences the present.

The term 'triangle of insight' is confusing because insight is also the aim of the other major type of interpretation used in psychodynamic psychotherapy, namely the 'triangle of conflict'. The therapist does not confront repressed or suppressed feelings head on. He interprets the defence first, as the reason for avoiding feeling, and where possible frames such interpretations in a definite order (unlike transference interpretations where any two points may be linked); he interprets the *defence* against the *anxiety* of experiencing an *impulse or hidden feelings*. Ezriel (1952) expresses the same triad in terms of relationships: the required relationship (defence), the feared catastrophe and the avoided relationship. Thus the client in the case example *defends* by her bright and breezy manner against the fear (*anxiety*) of a more intimate relationship (*hidden feeling*) or, in Ezriel's terminology, requires a somewhat superficial relationship to defend against the loss (feared catastrophe) which would be felt should the close relationship (being avoided) develop. Similarly, her denial of the 'goodbye' at the termination is a defence against the pain (anxiety) of loss (hidden feeling).

There is clearly some overlap between these two triangles, of conflict and of person, with the P/O/T interpretation cited above using aspects of both. Defences are often erected against transference, and it is the defence which would be interpreted first. To move straight into transference interpretation (particularly in the case of defences that relate to the therapist) would be too threatening to many clients unless those defences, and the reasons for them, are first acknowledged. It needs to be said, and with some force, that transference interpretation and conflict interpretation are techniques which must be used with great care and sensitivity, and only by those possessing a deep understanding of their own counter-transference feelings and sufficient experience and supervisory skill to handle the intensification of the transference (positive and/or negative) which tends to follow the use of such interpretations.

Psychotherapy usually involves less frequent meetings than the traditional psychoanalytic four or five fifty-minute sessions per week: normally one or two sessions a week. Brief, or focal, psychotherapy, which will be more relevant to the potential practice of most readers, limits both the number of sessions and the focus of the therapy. The focus is different from the goal: objectives may be set as goals, but the focus is the means of trying to reach those objectives. This focus is on those areas of conflict and possible transference relations which form the major area of interpretation. It is formulated after the construction of a psychodynamic hypothesis, but is always open to refinement or change.

Brief focal psychotherapy, particularly as developed by Malan, concentrates upon the selection of clients whom it is felt will be able to benefit from the technique (using assessment interviews and, in Malan's work, projective tests). Positive indications are: (a) high, increasing motivation for insight; (b) rapport with the therapist; (c) response to interpretation;

(d) a current or recent crisis and (e) the delineation of a focus for inter-pretation. Trial interpretations are used in assessment interviews in order to see what the client's capacity is to use them.

As a result of two extensive studies, in which detailed content analysis was used, Malan (1976a) found that the techniques of major significance were thorough transference interpretation, particularly of negative transference, and the use of termination of therapy to work through grief and anger about endings. Loss of good 'objects' both in the external world and in the individual's inner world forms a major focus for many clients, in accordance with their particular life experience. Psychodynamic psycho-therapy uses loss of the therapist (in short, absences, breaks, holidays in his inability to be a substitute for past failed relationships and at the ter-mination of the contract) as one of the crucial aspects for interpretation. 'Where a major part of the patient's problem consists of loss, deprivation, or unfulfilled love, it is the therapist's task not to try and make this up to the patient – which is impossible – but to enable him to experience his true feelings about it, and to pass through them and come out on the other side' (Malan 1979).

The change process in therapy

Freudian psychotherapy, like psychoanalysis, is a treatment of choice and not, as some therapies appear to claim, a panacea for all ills. It is primarily the choice of the client, whose motivation for change needs to include the willingness to explore and tolerate the discomfort from the uncovering of more primitive parts of the personality. It is also a choice for the therapist, who needs to be able to discriminate between those for whom insight therapy is suitable and those for whom supportive therapy (in which valid defences may be strengthened rather than interpreted) or other forms of treatment may be more appropriate.

Freudian theory is of particular value to anyone who wishes to under-stand the dynamics of personal growth and development, especially the place of the unconscious, of fantasy and of object-relations. Freud indeed, perhaps too modestly, claimed more for his system as a research method (in depth rather than breadth) than as a cure for mental illness. He foresaw the time when chemotherapy would be sufficient for those who wanted symptom relief and pursued his methods as much to 'map' the inner world of the psyche as to 'cure' people. Freud was often pessimistic, not only in his theory but also about actual outcome in certain cases: those of psychotics and older people, for example. His followers have proved him wrong, but it needs to be restated that Freudian methods do not claim to be universally applicable, nor does any Freudian believe that theory can ever be complete. Bion (in fact a Kleinian) is right to remind us that by the time an interpretation has been carried out the universe has expanded beyond the analyst's own perception (Grinberg et al. 1977). The boundaries of inner space are as distant and mysterious as the boundaries of the universe.

Such a caution is needed in any understanding of the change process in therapy. There are many contributing factors, and no one is yet clear which are the most efficacious. Catharsis and abreaction, as in Freud's early work, are obviously important factors. The 'confessional' element is beneficial when events surrounded by guilt can be related to and accepted by the therapist and when the client, through seeing this acceptance and/or observing the sadism of the super-ego, is also able to accept them – as in the case which follows, where a story of seduction was told for the first time ever to another person. Repressed memories may be brought to light (again as happened in that case, though they are not mentioned in the account given here) and can clear the way for change.

The person of the therapist is vital. On a more obvious level, the client learns to identify with the observing, accepting and understanding (in both senses) attitude of the therapist, and then to introject (take inside) the person of the therapist. Clients frequently report conducting mental dialogues with the therapist between sessions, imagining what the therapist would say – and after a while often being very accurate! In successful therapy this introjection gradually changes so that the formerly sadistic super-ego in the client is replaced by an observing and insightful ego, as the central 'I' comes into its own. These are all aspects of the working alliance.

Then there is also the use of transference, for which Malan (1976a, 1976b) has some statistical evidence, suggesting that therapy tends to be more successful when transference links are made and can be worked through. Through his distorted and unreal perceptions of the therapist, the client is helped to see 'before his very eyes' the way relationships can be misinterpreted and expressions of feeling frustrated. For instance, the client who, having discovered the therapist to be an accepting person in reality, continues to fear his criticism, comes to recognize through continued interpretation that this fear is based rather upon real or imagined criticism by a parent and the subsequent internalized criticism of the super-ego (or anti-libidinal ego). Psychotherapy is a lengthy process because such an insight, once gained, needs working through time and time again – thus making therapy in some respects similar to the re-learning that is involved in behaviour therapy. Change which occurs dramatically or miraculously in psychotherapy is normally viewed with some suspicion: it may well be the defence of 'flight into health' or a re-action formation more than permanent change. Psychotherapists, perhaps because they have studied the complexities of personality, tend to be modest in their claims of success, particularly as far as deep change occurs. New solutions to problems are indeed found, but this does not mean that old 'neurotic solutions' have completely gone. We have to allow for those instances where clients, having apparently resolved issues, break down again. In such cases it is probable that the new structures were not strong enough to contain the re-emergence of old patterns. One analyst has suggested that complete dissolution of transference (pre-sumably used in its widest sense) is a myth (Sandler 1976).

Finally, the refusal of the psychotherapist to assume the mantle of the omniscient figure, which many would wish him to be, is seen also in the recognition that change occurs not only as a result of therapy but throughout life, with other people playing their part too, intervening in a person's life to positive as well as negative effect. Where change occurs in the client, it will frequently need to be accompanied by changes in others close to him. If this is not forthcoming the client, who might otherwise make significant changes, is prevented from doing so lest change breaks up the collusive relationships with another or others. The client who has a supportive environment, and people ready to look at themselves as well, can make the most use of translating what is learned and experienced in the psychotherapeutic relationship into life outside. In such cases individual therapy may be limited in its ability to bring about change, although Freudian theory and practice may also be used in working with couples, families and groups.

Case Example

Elizabeth came to see me at the start of her final year at university. She was attractive; one who might be called a 'blithe spirit'. She talked easily, somewhat blandly at times, but with a hint of tears held back. She said that she was lonely; she kept people at bay and was currently sleeping a lot and eating on her own. I felt very early on in the interview that she demonstrated schizoid features (withdrawal from any close human contact) and that I should offer her as much time as I could, given her final year and my work-load. She agreed to come weekly until the end of the year. After the first session I set down certain criteria for improvement: that she should be able to (a) tolerate the closeness involved in therapy; (b) get closer to others (perhaps being able to touch them, and talk to them about personal feelings); (c) recognize the ambivalence of love and hate felt towards her parents; (d) express some grief over the losses in her life and (e) finally pursue her career ambitions. (These were all matters which had come up in the first interview.) I realized that the short time available (thirty sessions in all) would not be sufficient to do more than move a little way towards these objectives. In the event she did stay in therapy (I anticipated she would want to run away, which she came close to doing at times), was able to allow herself to be touched by others (though only in play, and even then with some discomfort), and was able to share just a little more of her personal life with her friends. She was able to express some grief at her losses and to acknowledge ambivalent feelings towards her 'mother', particularly some positive feelings which were not initially present. She was also able to acknowledge some feelings of affection for me as therapist, without fearing she would lose me either for that reason or because I saw her as bad. She was able to express feelings of loss of me as therapist as termination approached, and even felt positive about being able to experience such feelings. I do not pretend that her schizoid problems were resolved, but I think that an opportunity was given and taken to use psychotherapy, and that she might have been able to contemplate further therapy once she got a job and was settled somewhere more permanently.

Such a summary only presents her initial problems and my assessment of the outcome. In the limited space available, only a fraction of the content of the sessions can be reported here, but enough to illustrate some of the points raised in the sections 'Theoretical Assumptions' and 'Practice' earlier in this chapter.

Elizabeth very quickly told me about her background in the first session. She had been born prematurely and rejected by her real mother, and spent the first few weeks of life in an incubator. Because of the circumstances of her birth she spent some months in hospital before going to a relative's family – where her new 'mother' was a fastidious person. When the children were upset, she would stuff a dummy or a jam sandwich into them. Her new 'mother' tried to get close to her, but Elizabeth would never allow this and resisted all such attempts. Instead, Elizabeth attached herself to the grandfather who lived with them, but he died when she was six and she then attached herself to her 'brother' Peter, who was nine years older. She worshipped and idealized him, following him around, sitting at his feet, enjoying his mere presence. She was taken completely by surprise when Peter ran away to sea when he was eighteen, to get away from 'nagging mother'. She was even more hurt when Peter rang up a year later to say he was getting married: she had lost him, too. Her 'father', from whom she seemed to have turned to the grandfather and Peter as being more accessible, was a remote person who enjoyed his hobbies but whose role in the family was limited. When Elizabeth was seven, a 'sister' was born whom for years she treated as 'her baby' despite resenting her favourite position with 'mother', which was naturally accentuated by her own refusal to allow 'mother' to get close.

It was on this information that I based my assessment of her as being psychologically damaged in early life, with further losses compounding the first rejection by and loss of her own mother. Her false self (the bouncy outward personality) disguised how shy and withdrawn she was underneath, with great dependency needs firmly pushed away. I commented that it must have been difficult to come and see me since she found it difficult to trust people, and she replied that she had chosen to do so because I was 'separate' and not involved: here was an example of her need to keep me, too, at a distance. I anticipated that this might happen with me; and indeed, she began the fourth session by saying that she had said it all, that there was nothing more to say.

The first break was at Christmas, and she returned from it to tell me about a previous Christmas when she was thirteen and Peter had come home with his wife. The family had gone out leaving her and Peter alone. They had begun by running down 'mother', but this led to Peter seducing her. Afterwards she lay in the bath for two hours, wanting to kill 'mother'. She had felt guilty about this incident for years, but now felt angry and wanted to punish men. She only felt safe with older, married men (though here we see the return of the repressed, since Peter was an older, married man). I observed that she felt able to trust me with what had happened. She replied that she had expected me to throw up my hands in horror – and was nonplussed that I had not. There followed an account of being forced by a young man, a year earlier, to have intercourse; of finding herself pregnant and inducing an abortion herself. She felt very lonely, in great pain, and thought that she would die. Following this the sessions concentrated upon her wish to be a baby and be cuddled and mothered, yet also fighting against such wishes. Peter had been a 'mother' to her in some ways; all she had wanted to do was hug him. She wanted to be cuddled by a man and given chocolate buttons; but she was too old for that, and men wanted more. With all this new material there were clearly Oedipal problems overlaying the original schizoid ones, and I often interpreted her fear of being close because of the threat of sexual intimacy, as when Peter made her feel so guilty; but also because she feared losing the person she wanted to mother her.

About half-way through the contract she started to come late, and again seemed resistant. She did, however, talk about herself as two people, the one Elizabeth, the outwardly charming person, and the other Lisa, the defensive, shy person who wanted to get close but was afraid to. She was beginning to feel Lisa coming out with me – and indeed, I was the first person with whom she had called herself Lisa since her grandfather died. It was he who had given her that name. It was the inner Lisa who had allowed Peter to get close but had then become frightened. Lisa liked teddies; Lisa felt five years old. It was the inner Lisa who was afraid of being turned on (perhaps in both senses?) and rejected. She acknowledged that depending on which person she was, she was no longer feeling indifferent to me.

Lisa had peeped out of her shell, but she was not sure where to go from there. She had sent mother some flowers – a gesture of reparation – but she still felt a brick wall round her, and felt it with me too. She was not only afraid of being hurt but of hurting others as well. She retreated, and as the last term started she felt she was back at square one. She talked of two friends breaking up, allowing me to introduce (ten sessions before it would happen) our own impending break and what that might mean to her. There was no obvious response to this, but she stopped sitting on the chair and sat further away on the floor; and over the weeks sat further and further away until she was almost at the door. There seemed to be three elements in this: first, she obviously wanted to put distance between us with the impending break (which I interpreted); secondly, she sat, rather childlike, at my feet, just as she had at Peter's feet; thirdly, there was (in counter-transference feelings too) a sexual element – she was wearing summer blouses which got more and more attractive, and said she had sexual fantasies – although later she responded to an interpretation of her sexual feelings (not made explicitly in relation to me) by sending a letter saying that she did not have sexual fantasies, only romantic ones. It was interesting that in her writing she used in places a small 'i' instead of the personal 'I', as if she were not yet a proper person.

She did, however, say in her letter that she hated feeling dependent on anyone, including me, but could not hate me as she did others. In the sessions which followed she spoke of her fear of rejection because it made her feel she was 'bad'. She recognized that the problems were in her, not in others; and this was a milestone, though it also brought despair. Different images of the end came into the sessions: a flag at half-mast, another couple who had split up – who would be the third, since it always went in threes? She cried at the song 'Puff the Magic Dragon' in which Jackie grew up and saw Puff no longer. I interpreted her feelings of sadness and her difficulty acknowledging them in case that made her feel 'bad'. There were other images of mothering: her fantasy of becoming a farmer's wife, looking after all the animals; making teddies for people she was leaving at the end of term. She brought a teddy to one session and cuddled and nursed it like a baby throughout – like her own wish to go on being held. She asked if I wanted her to make a teddy for me. I suggested that she had already given me more of herself than she had been able to give to others, and said I did not need a teddy to remind me of that. I also introduced the idea of her seeing someone else when she knew where she was going to live.

And so we came to the last session, when Elizabeth described meeting a person who had attached himself to her and poured out a story of trying to find his roots. He was not sure who his parents were and said he had inheritances which he could not get his hands on. She had taken him to a party in order to lessen the intensity of his talking to her, and there he had been eventually pushed out by the host because he had been making a nuisance of himself and talking about doom; if he had been talking about love, she felt, he would have been accepted. The man had said he did not want to go home.

I suggested that this man represented herself: unsure where to look for her roots, yet feeling there were other inheritances within herself which she wanted to get her hands upon. Like him, she was perhaps feeling pushed out by me (she nodded) and perhaps felt that I was pushing her out because she, too, had expressed at times her hate of the human race, and not love. She said that this thought had crossed her mind. I wondered if she too did not want to go home to 'mother'.

She talked about home, saying that if she changed perhaps her mother would change. She took up the suggestion I had made of seeing someone else – but she always needed to be pushed. It was difficult to make choices on her own. 'And difficult to say goodbye,' I said, as the time approached. 'I never say goodbye, because I don't know whether I will ever see anyone again or not,' she said as she got up to go.

Elizabeth/Lisa had told some of her story. Some aspects of it came to light again in the relationship between us, not only in trusting another with the burden of her guilt but in the transference as well. Her last words, like her first, indicated that she still had great difficulties with closeness, and with the threat of loss; but in the brief time available to her, therapy had begun to move the barriers, preparing the ground for longer psychotherapy later.

References

Alexander F, French T M (1946) *Psychoanalytic Therapy*, Ronald, New York

Breuer J, Freud S (1955) *Studies on Hysteria*, Hogarth, London, p. 63

Clark R W (1980) *Freud: the Man and the Cause*, Cape and Weidenfeld and Nicholson, London, p. 190

Erikson E (1965) *Childhood and Society*, Penguin, Harmondsworth

Ezriel H (1952) Notes on psychoanalytic group therapy II: interpretation and research, *Psychiatry 15*: 119–126

Fairbairn W R D (1952) *Psychoanalytic Studies of the Personality*, Tavistock, London

Freud S (1949) *An Outline of Psychoanalysis*, Hogarth, London, p. 38

Freud S (1964) *New Introductory Lectures on Psychoanalysis*, Hogarth, London, pp. 77–8

Golan N (1981) *Passing Through Transitions*, Collier Macmillan, London

Grinberg L (1977) Sor D de Bianchedi E T *Introduction to the Work of Bion*, 2nd edition, Jason Aronson, New York

Guntrip H (1968) *Schizoid Phenomena, Object Relations and the Self*, Hogarth, London, pp. 119, 124, 275, 356–7, 394, 404, 406

Guntrip H (1971) *Psychoanalytic Theory, Therapy and the Self*, Hogarth, London, pp. 27, 66

Malan D H (1976a) *The Frontier of Brief Psychotherapy*, Plenum Medical, New York

Malan D H (1976b) *Toward the Validation of Dynamic Psychotherapy*, Plenum Medical, New York

Malan D H (1979) *Individual Psychotherapy and the Science of Psychodynamics*, Butterworths, London, pp. 104, 141, 173, 193; Ch. 10

Menninger K (1958) *The Theory of Psychoanalytic Technique*, Basic Books, New York

Roazen P (1979) *Freud and his Followers*, Penguin, Harmondsworth, p. 151

Rycroft C (ed.) (1968) *Psychoanalysis Observed*, Penguin, Harmondsworth, p. 17

Sandler J. (1956) cited in Naiman J, Panel on the fundamentals of psychic change in clinical practice, *International Journal of Psychoanalysis 57*: 411–417

Segal H (1973) *Introduction to the work of Melanie Klein*, enlarged edition, Hogarth, London

Winnicott D W (1958) *Collected Papers*, Tavistock, London

Winnicott D W (1965) *Maturational Processes and the Facilitating Environment*, Hogarth, London, p. 182

Suggested Further Reading

Jacobs M (1982) *Still Small Voice*, SPCK, London (the application of Freudian techniques to counselling)

Malan D H (1979) *Individual Psychotherapy and the Science of Psychodynamics*, Butterworths, London (useful for technique, with many case illustrations.)

Rayner E (1978) *Human Development*, 2nd edition, Allen and Unwin, London (a psychodynamic account of the stages of growth from birth to old age)

Roazen P (1979) *Freud and His Followers*, Penguin, Harmondsworth (Freud's life and ideas, as well as those of his immediate followers)

Rycroft C (1972) *A Critical Dictionary of Psychoanalysis*, Penguin Books, Harmondsworth (a valuable reference for the terms used in Freudian, Kleinian and general psychodynamic writings)

Chapter 3   Psychodynamic Therapy: The Kleinian Approach

Cassie Cooper

Historical Context and Developments in Britain

Historical context

Melanie Klein was born in Vienna in 1882, the youngest of four children. Her family, the Reizes, were prominent members of the orthodox Jewish community: her mother was the daughter of a rabbi, her father a Talmud student. At this time the Jewish community in Europe was experiencing a heady period of 'emancipation', when age-old prejudices were receding and professional barriers crumbling with the arrival of new and radical political philosophies. Encouraged by the new professional opportunities that had opened up for Jews, Mr Reiz, then aged thirty-seven, abandoned his religious studies to read medicine; he was later to qualify and practise as a dentist. Melanie's recollection of these early years was that her family formed a loving and united group. Both parents were intellectuals, interested in literature and the sciences. She loved and admired her only brother, five years her senior, and at the age of fourteen decided that she, too, wished to become a doctor; with her brother's help and encouragement she was able to master the Latin and Greek necessary to enter a gymnasium, but her ambition to study medicine was to remain unfulfilled. Instead, three years later, she became engaged to Arthur Klein, an industrial chemist; and a year before her marriage in 1903, her beloved brother died, quite tragically, at the early age of twenty-five.

Throughout her life Melanie Klein continued to show a strong interest in medicine and medical research, frequently expressing her disappointment at not having pursued her ambition to become a doctor. For this reason and others the marriage was not wholly a happy one, although in due course she gave birth to three children, a daughter and two sons.

In 1911, prior to the outbreak of the First World War, the Klein family moved to Budapest, and it was here as a result of her continuing interest in medicine that Melanie was introduced to the writings of Sigmund Freud. She was excited and intrigued, finding in his theories some truths that she had always been seeking. In Budapest she met Sandor Ferenczi, the principal Hungarian analyst of that time. She became his patient, and in the course of her analysis he encouraged her emerging ideas on the use of psychoanalysis in working with young children. Melanie was now able to return to her interrupted career, albeit in a new form, and before the end of the war was already specializing in the analysis of small children. Her first published paper, *The Development of a Child*, was read to the Hungarian Psychoanalytic Society in 1921. The analysis of small children was considered 'inappropriate', – it had barely been touched upon, except by Freud in his work with 'Little Hans' – and the paper received a mixed reception from the strictly Freudian group.

However, Dr Karl Abraham, President of the Berlin Psychoanalytic Society showed great interest in the 'radical' ideas of Melanie Klein, which focused on a hitherto underdeveloped area of analytic practice. He extended an invitation to Melanie to move to Berlin and devote herself to further psychoanalytic research. She accepted and went to Berlin, taking her children with her: a move which precipitated the end of her marriage. Her husband chose to live in Sweden, where he had extensive business interests.

On her arrival in Berlin, Melanie continued her personal analysis with Karl Abraham. She was strongly influenced by his ideas and throughout her life acknowledged a deep and lasting admiration for his own work on the early stages of infantile development. Like Ferenczi, Karl Abraham inspired her to evolve new techniques for the analysis of children, and soon she was introducing startlingly innovative ideas into the field. He was her staunch supporter and advocate, but sadly this remarkable relationship lasted for only a year, for he developed a fatal illness and died in 1925. After his death she carried on regular daily self-analysis, a procedure which Freud himself had initiated. All her later works were based on this process, with daily analytic observations of her own and her patients' behaviour compared, examined and interpreted one against the other.

Continuing to explore and report on these new insights into the earliest years of a child's life, Melanie's contributions to the Berlin Society still evoked much controversy and acrimony; whilst in London, Ernest Jones, Freud's biographer and one of his original pupils, a doyen of British psychoanalysts, gave support to her views by inviting her to London to give a course of lectures to the British Society. These were followed, in 1926, by an invitation for her to stay and work permanently in London. Melanie was relieved to leave Berlin, and it was in London that her work flourished with her individual clinical and theoretical approach becoming widely accepted by other British analysts. She continued to live in London, writing, practising and teaching until her death in 1960.

The members of the British Psychoanalytic Society are often referred to as the 'English' school. This differentiated the work that was developing in London under Melanie Klein's influence from that of other centres of psychoanalytic teaching, notably that of the so-called 'Viennese' school.

Developments in Britain

The differences I am referring to were accentuated by the British analysts' view that the experiences of the first weeks of life were *significant* to the development of the individual. These analysts were also of the opinion that the anxieties, defences and unconscious fantasies of children under two years of age and the development of a transference relationship in such children could be explored and understood by the use of free association in a psychoanalytic setting.

In the early thirties, before the Nazi invasion of Europe, an attempt was made in an exchange of lectures with the Berlin and Viennese Societies (Rivière 1936; Waelder 1937) to clarify the different stances held by members of their respective groups on this and other issues. Its purpose was merely to allow them to agree to differ on the subject of the viability of child analysis. However, when in 1938 many German and Austrian analysts came to London as refugees from Nazi persecution, these conflicts became exacerbated, threatening to cause a split within the membership of the British Society. Melanie Klein was continuing her work and her teaching, and there grew up around her a large group of analysts and psychotherapists and an increasing number of students wishing to apply to her for training analyses and supervision. Susan Isaacs, D.W. Winnicott, Joan Rivière, Ernest Jones, T.E. Money-Kyrle and Hanna Segal all gave their support to her views. Unity was at last preserved among the British Society by the development of two separate streams of training within the main teaching course: the 'Continental' school of Anna Freud and the 'English' school of Melanie Klein.

The theoretical basis of Kleinian psychotherapy will be elaborated on further in this chapter, but it is worth while summarizing the Kleinian stance here.

First, Melanie Klein accepted the common themes of psychoanalytic theory which Farrell (1981) simplifies very well:

(a)   No item in mental life or in the way we behave is accidental. It is always the outcome of antecedent conditions.
(b)   Mental activity and behaviour is purposeful or goal-directed.
(c)   Unconscious determinants mould and affect the way we perceive ourselves and others. These are thoughts of a primitive nature, shaped by impulses and feelings within the individual of which he is unaware.
(d)   Early childhood experience is overwhelmingly important and preeminent over later experience.

Second, in addition to these basic assumptions, Melanie Klein threw new light on the hitherto unexplored regions of the pre-Oedipal stage. She went on to propose that:

(a)   Environmental factors are much less important than had previously been believed.
(b)   The beginnings of the super-ego can be identified within the first two years of life.
(c)   Any analysis which does not investigate the stages of infantile anxiety and aggressiveness in order to confront and understand them is necessarily unfinished.
(d)   The most important drives of all are the *aggressive* ones.

Theoretical Assumptions

The image of the person

It must be supposed that during the early months of life the child can make no distinction between himself as a personal entity and the bewildering world of light and darkness which surrounds him. An adult, on the other hand, can identify clearly the emotional responses elicited by external objects as purely personal feelings towards that object which comes from within his own mind. At this stage the child can only relate them to the object itself. His mother's nipple, a good feed, a soft cot or the touch of a hand which gives him pleasure are easily regarded as good objects; whilst something that gives him pain, such as hunger, cold and discomfort, can easily be converted into something that is bad. To the baby, hunger is a frightening situation: he is not able to understand the meaning of time, patience or frustration. He cannot appreciate that these situations are of a temporary nature and will soon be followed by a feeling of pleasurable relief as the warm milk goes down. A small change in the immediate situation can change feelings of anger and discomfort into blissful gratification. It follows, then, that the baby is able to love and hate one and the same object in rapid succession – there are no qualifications.

Melanie Klein (1937) writes: 'When the baby is hungry and his desires are not gratified, or when he is feeling bodily pain or discomfort the whole situation suddenly alters.' She continues:

> The baby becomes dominated by the impulse to destroy the very person who is the object of all desires, who is linked up with everything he experiences, good and bad alike. These feelings give rise moreover to painful states, such as choking, breathlessness, bouts of crying, and other sensations of the kind which are felt to be destructive to his own body, thus aggression, unhappiness and fears are again increased ... The temporary feeling of security which is gained by receiving gratification greatly enhances the gratification itself, and thus a feeling of security becomes an important component of the satisfaction whenever a person receives love. This applies to the baby as well as to the adult, to the more simple forms of love and to its most elaborate manifestations.

Concepts of psychological health and disturbance

Melanie Klein (1952b) introduced the concepts of ego-splitting and projective identification. This was a more complicated process than the theory of projection described by Freud. An understanding of the processes of introjection and projection is of major importance, and these terms can perhaps best be explained as follows.

Introjection For every human being, the outer world and its impact, the kind of life experiences he lives through and the objects he comes into contact with are not only dealt with externally but taken *into* the self to become part of his inner life. This inner world is a composite collection of sights, sounds and sensory experiences: complicated and secretive like the origin of life itself, and constantly dilating as we introject new experiences into our personalities. Any evaluation of our innermost selves must include an acceptance of this concept; the concept of an enduring self-image is based on this type of introjection.

Projection   This is a process which goes on simultaneously. It is a manifestation of the child's ability to place onto other people around him his aggressive and envious feelings, predominantly those of aggression, which by the very nature of their 'badness' must be got rid of either by the process of siting them within another person or by repressing the acknowledgement of their existence within the self, thus causing major disruptions in the process of establishing one's own identity and of feeling secure enough to establish other outward-looking relationships.

This two-way process of introjection and projection continues throughout every stage of our lives, twisting and turning, *interacting* and *modifying* in the course of maturation but never losing importance in relation to the world around us. Thus an internal world is built up in the child and the adult alike which is partially a reflection of the external one: the judgement of reality is never quite free from the influence of the boiling mercury that is in our internal world.

Splitting   Melanie Klein (1960) describes the situation which arises when the projected bad objects (those representations of the child's own ferocious and aggressive impulses) rebound upon him: take, for example, the desperate situation of a young mother who tries to please the baby who is literally biting the hand that feeds him. A child may refuse food and scream even when he is desperately hungry, and kick and push when he most longs for a caress. These stages, which thankfully are largely outgrown in the process of normal development, can be identified with the delusional sense of persecution sometimes found in the paranoid adult. Indeed, a residual persecutory element can always be found in the sense of guilt which is central to all civilizations. Persecutory anxiety reinforces the need to understand clearly how to separate the good object from the bad, the loved object from the dangerous one, and therefore to differentiate clearly between love and hate. Since the infant continues to need a good mother – his life depends upon it – by *splitting* the two aspects and clinging only to the good one, like a rubber ring in a swimming pool, he has evolved for the time being a means of staying alive. Without this loving object to keep him buoyant he would in fact sink beneath the surface of a hostile world which would engulf him.

The process of splitting continues throughout life, and in some forms it is never entirely relinquished.

The acquisition of psychological disturbance

The paranoid-schizoid position This combination of mechanisms and anxieties – feelings of great power over the parent contrasting with a sudden sense of persecution, the splitting of the good and bad parts of oneself and others – are very common indeed in the first years of life. These destructive feelings are of primary importance to the growth and development of the individual but can, in extreme cases, become the basis of later paranoia and schizophrenic illness. Melanie Klein (1957) singled out greed and envy as two destructive impulses, relating them first to the child's dominant relationship with the mother and later to relationships with other members of the family, and stating that they eventually become an intrinsic part of the individual's psychological make-up.

Greed is exacerbated by anxiety, the anxiety of being deprived, which gives rise to the need to take all one can from the mother and the family. A greedy infant may enjoy what he has for the time being, but this feeling is soon replaced by the feeling of being robbed by others of what he needs in the way of food, love, attention or any other kind of gratification. The baby who is greedy for love and attention is also afraid that he himself is unable to give to others, and this in its turn exacerbates his own situation. He needs everything, he can spare nothing – so what can he reasonably expect from others?

Envy is a spoiling pursuit. If milk, love or attention is being withheld for one reason or another, then the loved object must be withholding it and keeping it for his or her own use. The basis of envy is suspicion: if the baby cannot have what he desires, there is a strong urge to spoil the very object of desire so that no one can enjoy it. This spoiling quality can result in a disturbed relationship with the mother, who cannot now supply an unspoilt satisfaction. If feelings of envy are overpowering, this inhibits the ability to enjoy fully what has been offered and what can be offered.

In life it is a capacity for enjoyment and gratitude that make living pleasurable. Melanie Klein (1955) enlarged on these ideas, stating quite firmly that the aggressive envy experienced in infancy could inhibit the development of good object-relations and that this in its turn could affect the growth of the capacity to love.

Projective identification   Projective identification illustrates most clearly the links between human instinct, fantasy, and the mechanisms of defence. Sexual desires, aggressive impulses can be satiated by fantasy. Fantasy can be as pleasurable and as explicit as we wish to make it, but it is also a safety net: it contains and holds those bad parts of our inner self. The use of fantasy is obvious: in literature, in science, in art, and in all activities of everyday life.

The first good objects that the infant experiences centre round the aspects of mothering: feeding, caressing and helping the child. This is a fundamental factor in human development. A loving attitude on the part of the mother ensures that this good object can be introjected to become part of the inner self. If this is successfully accomplished an element of strength is added to the ego, which can then develop and flourish. Identification with the good characteristics of being 'mothered' will then form a strong basis for further helpful identifications; a child learns by copying the actions of its parents.

One aspect of identification is the rivalry which results from the male child's desire for the mother, his rivalry with his father and all the fantasies that are linked to this situation. The Oedipus complex (described in Chapter 2) is rooted in the baby's suspicion of the father, who takes the mother's love and attention away from him. The same applies to the female child for whom the relationship to the mother and to all women is always of supreme importance. To put a part of yourself into another person, to project a part of your impulses and feelings onto another, is to achieve an identification with that person. If an object is taken into the self (introjected), this involves acquiring some of the characteristics of that object and of being strongly affected by them, as in the case of the tortured convolutions of a family wherein no one is ever certain of who or what they are, child or parent, or whether or not they have ever or can ever be truly certain of what it is that others expect of them.

The depressive position The depressive position begins when the baby begins to recognize his mother. In the early months of life the baby is concerned with integration of the sights, sounds and stimuli, both pleasant and unpleasant, with which he is surrounded. Out of this dreamlike world sufficient integration is achieved for the baby to experience his mother as a whole object, not a succession of parts. She is no longer breasts that feed him, hands that hold him, a voice that soothes him, facial grimaces that either please or frighten him, but a complete entity on her own, separate, divided from him – someone who can choose to hold him close or stay away, kiss or neglect him. This gradual understanding of the separation process, this gradual awakening to the fact that it is one and the same person who is the container of both good and bad feelings, is then transposed internally to himself: he is as separate from her as she is from him; he can both love and hate this mother. His previous fears of being the frail objective of destruction extend subtly to an inner knowledge that he too can destroy the one person he loves and needs for his own survival. His anxiety has changed from a paranoid to a depressive one. In acknowledging the very existence of his separate being, he is exposed to the fear that he has made the cut. His aggression has destroyed the cord which linked him to his mother, leaving him with feelings of unutterable guilt, sadness and deprivation, a hurt that can never be healed, a pain that can never be assuaged. Separation is experienced as a kind of death – the death of that which was and can never be again.

Melanie Klein's (1948b) view of this process of separation and the depressive anxieties that it invokes was that, as a part of normal development, guilt feelings which develop because of the imagined harm done to the child's love object, actually enable the process of *reparation* to commence. Every child can show subtle tendernesses to those around him, anxieties and paranoid fears become modified during this period. These anxieties are painfully reawakened in the normal mourning processes of later life; adult depression involves a reactivation of this stage of infantile depression. Unlike therapists of other schools of psychotherapy, a Kleinian would consider the analysis of actual mourning situations a productive period. When the adult feels menaced and persecuted, the self-reproaches of the depressed patient are understood as a manifestation of the persecutory impulses which are directed towards the self.

The perpetuation of psychological disturbance

The impulses of destruction, greed, and envy are often cited as an example of how the persecutory and sadistic anxieties of early life can disturb the child's emotional balance and inhibit his ability to acquire and maintain good social relationships:

> If we look at our adult world from the viewpoint of its roots in infancy, we gain an insight into the way our mind, our habits and our views have been built up from the earliest infantile phantasies and emotions to the most complex and sophisticated adult manifestations. There is one more conclusion to be drawn which is that nothing that ever existed in the unconscious completely loses its influence on the personality. (Klein 1961)

Until Freud made his great discoveries, there was a need to think of childhood as a time of perfect happiness. While in the uterus, all babies exist in comparative safety; it is only when the baby makes its post-natal appearance – be it head or feet first or precipitately by Caesarian section – that it learns to draw new conclusions about the reality of existence. Loss of being an internal part of the mother gives rise to primary separation anxiety, which gives way to grief and then to the experience of mourning that which is lost. Aggression is also a major part of the mourning process. The infant tries, aggressively to re-enter the mother, to become at one with her again, to return to safety.

If these normal processes are disrupted in some way, if fantasy becomes reality and the loved object dies, leaves, neglects, batters, reacts too possessively or becomes obsessional, then it follows that these disruptions of normal interaction are likely to take a pathological course later in life.

Several empirical studies have appeared in the last twenty years (Robertson and Robertson 1967–72) which suggest that the incidence of psychiatric illness and personality problems is significantly higher for that proportion of the general population that shows an incidence of childhood loss. Bowlby (1979) states:

> Many of those referred to psychiatrists are anxious insecure individuals usually described as over-dependent or immature. Under stress they are apt to develop neurotic symptoms, depression, or phobia. Research shows them to have been exposed to at least one, and usually more than one, of certain typical patterns of pathogenic parenting, which include:
> a)   One or both parents being persistently unresponsive to the child's

care-eliciting behaviour and/or actively disparaging and rejecting him.

b) Discontinuities of parenting, occuring more or less frequently, including periods in hospital or institution.

c) Persistent threats by parents not to love a child, used as a means of controlling him.

d) Threats by parents to abandon the family, used either as a method of disciplining the child or as a way of coercing a spouse.

e) Threats by one parent either to desert or even to kill the other or else to commit suicide (each of them more common than might be supposed).

f) Inducing a child to feel guilt by claiming that his behaviour is or will be responsible for the parent's illness or death.

It is my opinion, however, that many of our beliefs concerning the influence of prevailing social conditions on the upbringing of children should be more flexible. The anger and aggressive feelings which the child can project on to the parent and others, renders the aggressive behaviour of parents ineffectual by comparison.

In a similar vein, Melanie Klein (1945) writes:

Repeated attempts have been made to improve humanity – in particular to make it more peaceable – and have failed, because nobody has understood the full depth and vigour of the instincts of aggression innate in each individual. Such efforts do not seek to do more than encourage the positive, well-wishing impulses of the person while denying or suppressing his aggressive ones. And so they have been doomed to failure from the beginning.

I make the point here that however well established is the desire of the child to be loved and to love and to be at peace with the world around it, aggressiveness and hate still remain operative. Segal (1973) calls this a 'tidy split' between good and bad impulses.

Practice

Goals of therapy

Melanie Klein never altered the technical principles which were the foundation of her early work, *The Psychoanalysis of Young Children* (1927). This work continues to form the basis of the psychodynamic work undertaken by Kleinian therapists and colours their distinctive concept of mental functioning.

A patient undertaking any kind of psychotherapy is bound to come to the first session full of hopes and fears, with deep-rooted fantasies and fears about himself and about his therapist. He presents material in the very first session which concern anxieties that are central to him at that moment in time. Colby (1951) suggests that predominantly the patient wants to feel 'better' to obtain relief from suffering, and is seeking, like an infant, immediate gratification of his needs. Wish-fulfilment is not confined to those who seek psychotherapy: people will always hope to obtain what they feel they need to make them happy and want to have it in the shortest possible time, with a minimum of effort.

The Kleinian therapist will not seek to gratify these wishes; nevertheless the anxieties which accompany them can, providing they are not excessive, act as a spur to development and personal achievement. This seeking of immediate gratification, thoughtlessness and demanding, extortionate behaviour further reflect the infant's relationship with the mother; they reflect a desire to exhaust and exploit her, to suck her dry, with all the guilt that this implies.

In starting work, the therapist will examine the patient's unconscious fantasies about himself and his relationships with other people: how do these fantasies relate to the reality of the outside world in the way it has been experienced in the past and in the present? This material is relevant to the current transference situation and to the private drama that is being played out at this moment in the therapist's room. Active interpretation of the transference situation is *central* to the work of Kleinian therapists:

(a) Early childhood projections and introjections become unconscious and are repressed, and it is the task of the therapist to encourage their emergence into the conscious everyday world, dealing in a positive, encouraging but direct way with the resistances to this process.

(b) Feelings and attitudes which were originally associated with important figures in early infancy have now become attached to other people who are part of our here and now. Thus, transference, a universal phenomenon, enters into *all* our relationships. An understanding of this process is central to the *therapeutic alliance* between therapist and patient.

(c) The Kleinian therapist will *not* focus on the mere translation of symbols or on interpretations which deal *only* with the symbolic representation of the material. He or she is primarily concerned with the *anxiety* and the sense of guilt which are associated with these presentations. It is the goal of the therapist to 'layer down' to those depths of early infantile behaviour which are being activated by the material and its associations, to touch upon the violent and painful places where the strongest latent resistances to growth and change are established.

Human relationships are purposeful, and develop and mature so that goals of one kind and another can be reached. If these goals are similarly perceived and interacted upon by both parties, their fulfilment will result in the achievement of some mutual satisfaction. To meet the goals of any relationship successfully and to satisfy the needs that are consonant with those goals a process of interaction must be activated which is uniquely suited to their accomplishment.

By the end of therapy it is hoped that the patient will be able to form these full and satisfactory personal relationships, that he will have gained insight into his personal situation and feel released from his early fixations and repressions. He will be less inhibited and more able to enjoy the good things of life while remaining sensitive, open and capable when problems arise. He will be able to assess his internal world, possessing a quiet reassurance and ego strength which stems from the knowledge that, even in times of stress, he will survive and, perhaps even more importantly, *he wants to survive.*

On the subject of terminating therapy, Melanie Klein (1948d) wrote:

> My criterion for the termination of an analysis is, therefore, as follows: Have persecutory and depressive anxieties been sufficiently reduced in the course of the analysis? Has the patient's relation to the external world been sufficiently strengthened to enable him to deal satisfactorily with the situation of mourning arising at this point? If these processes have been sufficiently experienced in the transference situation both the idealisation of the analyst and the feelings of being persecuted by him are diminished; the patient can then cope more successfully with the feelings of loss caused by the termination of the analysis and with that part of the work of mourning which he has to carry out by himself.

The person of the therapist

The training of a Kleinian therapist centres on the personality of the novice therapist; it is this understanding of the self which must be tuned to perfect pitch, like the finest violin. The person of the therapist is

encouraged to become an instrument which can interpret, colour and respond to the musical score, resonate and bend beneath the fingers of the
musician, constantly changing and developing his diagnostic sensitivities,
interpretation and technique. This tuning process will have been
undergone during a long term of personal analysis followed by a rigorous
period of training analysis and supervision at one of the formal institutes
for the training of psychotherapists.

Critics of psychodynamic theory suggest that the rigorous professional
training and analysis of a particular school is selective, and it follows then
that the therapist must inevitably become the prisoner of his own professional training, thus seriously impairing his capacity to compare and
assess the worth of a particular stance in contrast with other methods and
techniques. With some reservations, I would not entirely disagree with
this assessment. A therapist who believes dogmatically that only he –
together with a few other chosen spirits who adhere rigidly to his particular school or method – is correct, has *not*, in Kleinian terms,
advanced beyond the paranoid-schizoid position to acquire the capacity
for being depressed. Sensitivity to the depression within himself makes it
easier for the Kleinian therapist to doubt whether he himself or anyone
else has the key to understanding the complexity of a human being.

The concept of the paranoid-schizoid and depressive position will
naturally affect the way in which the Kleinian therapist will view his
patient's presentations. In dealing with the early anxieties which arise
from the relationship between the baby and the breast, and faced by the
harsher and more persecutory anxieties which lie in the deepest strata of
the mind, the more primitive the processes that are mobilized by this process, the more important it is for the therapist to remain unaltered in his
basic function: to refer the anxiety back to its source and resolve it by
systematically analysing the transference situation.

The therapist will need to be sensitive to those embryonic features of
emotional problems which are present in himself and which he sees
clearly reflected in his patients. He will need to be aware that possible
events in his own life, both those which occur in reality and those which
could have developed, are not denied and repressed. It requires of him an
understanding of the fact that within every human being lies the se-
ductive fantasy that he could have been something and someone else,
together with an ability to witness the flowering of this inner self in his
patients, whilst remaining for most of his own life in a profession where
self-expression is forbidden.

The calm, interested, helpful, accepting but neutral attitude of the Kleinian therapist differs from the manipulative and role-playing attitudes advocated by certain other strategies of intervention: power is acknowledged but interpreted. The Kleinian therapist, in the continuing interaction of the process, allows himself to be used as an *object*; in this way he may intrude but does not obtrude.

Use of the transference manifestations which develop during this process is the *primary* means by which the patient is helped towards better health and the maintenance of his continued psychic functioning. The process of giving full and minute attention to each detail of the patient's behaviour and language re-creates in the *therapeutic alliance* an opportunity to correct the infantile distorted view of object-relationships that have so constricted the patient's life. It provides incentive and reward in a benign relationship that encourages the patient to achieve the tasks that are imposed upon him by the discipline of therapy, and provides him with a model of strength and an identification with a reality, the 'real' person of the therapist.

Therapeutic style

If the patient gains control in psychotherapy, he will perpetuate his difficulties since he will continue to live his life constricted by the symptoms which have caused him to seek therapy. It follows, then, that however neutral and 'laid-back' the therapist may contrive to be, successful therapy can be described as a situation wherein the therapist maintains control of the kind of relationship he will have with his patient. In all forms of psychoanalytic psychotherapy, therapist and patient are confronted with a basic problem, the problem of object need: every patient regards the psychotherapist as real, regards all the manifestations of the treatment situation as real and strives to regard the therapist as a real object. The therapist, too, wants to regard the patient as real and to respond to the patient as a real object (Tarachow 1963). A primary urge in this relationship is the temptation to turn back the clock, to regress, to restore the symbiotic parental relationship that initially occurred with the mother, to fuse the boundaries and re-create the past as it was before and thus return to the time of ultimate dependency – replete, at one, inside the mother.

The therapist works assiduously to develop a therapeutic alliance characterized by the intimate, real and close working of two minds. The therapist and the patient undertake a controlled ego-splitting in the service of the treatment. The therapist and the patient work together in constructing a barrier against the need for a constricted object relationship. The therapist is not a breast, a hand, or a voice, a fragment, but a human being who is complete in every way.

Both therapist and patient have to struggle constantly against the array of temptations which lead the therapist to believe that he can allow himself to become closer to his patient, with the consequent dissolution and camouflaging of the existing ego boundaries – temptations which are further compounded because certain aspects of the therapeutic alliance are real. The therapist is concerned, caring in a real and human way for the patient. The patient is able to glean real things about the therapist: that he is single or married, goes on holiday, smokes, prefers one colour to another, shares accommodation with other therapists, etc. These clues lead to identification with the reality aspects of the therapist, *wordlessly* correcting transference distortions, supplying the motivation necessary for the therapeutic work of transference interpretation.

It is clear that every interpretation made by the therapist results in a loss or a deprivation for the patient. Interpretation frustrates him, denies him the opportunity of gratifying his fantasy wishes, placing him in the position of relinquishing some infantile object: 'It is a paradox that the interpretation – the act of the therapist that deprives the patient of the infantile object – also provides him with an adult object in the form of the sympathetic therapist' (Tarachow 1963).

Therapeutic models described in this book can all be defined in terms of how the transference as a resistance is exposed and treated. All schools of therapy are concerned with the extent to which the therapist imposes upon himself and his patient the task of setting each other aside as real objects, but a Kleinian therapist would explain it differently. The Kleinian method of treatment is one in which *at the beginning* it is the therapist's function to help the patient slowly but surely to surrender any hope of receiving gratification from the therapist as an *idealized* object. This happens even while the patient is encouraged to focus on his therapist as a possible source of other gratifications, gratifications which he is able in the real world to perceive and acknowledge: making good the injuries that were inflicted and received in unconscious fantasy and for which we still feel guilty and are making reparation, a fundamental element in love and in all human relationships.

Major therapeutic techniques

It is difficult to teach psychotherapy, and it is even more difficult to describe the techniques of psychotherapy. In an earlier paragraph I stressed that a Kleinian therapist will have learned his skill through the process of his own long-term psychoanalysis or psychodynamic psychotherapy: a process not unlike the age-old system of apprenticeship to a master or skilled craftsman of some repute and proven worth. The technique of psychotherapy is not a static process, and psychotherapists regularly attend case discussion groups, supervision sessions, seminars and study groups in order to meet and compare experiences and learn from each other in a lively fashion.

The setting The Kleinian therapist's room will differ only slightly from that of the strict Freudian. It will be comfortable, light and warm with an alternative choice of seating, namely a couch for the patient to lie on or a large reclining chair; in either case, the therapist will position himself at the side of and slightly behind the patient. The patient has the choice of sitting down and facing the therapist or of lying down on the couch; using the couch has certain meanings for certain patients, and some flexibility is allowed. However well prepared he may be for the rigours of psychoanalytic psychotherapy, the patient will find it easier to verbalize certain material when he is not facing the therapist.

The physical setting of the psychotherapy room remains constant and regular, the time and frequency of the session is not altered, and changes of time and holiday breaks are arranged well in advance of each session.

Selection of patients The Kleinian therapist would see himself as working best with a patient whose underlying conflicts were towards the *narcissistic* side; whose ego had undergone considerable deformation or weakening; who expressed an inability to love or be loved by others; who had conflicts over dealing with other people in a society, sexual or work setting; who complained about general intellectual and academic under-functioning; who had symptomatic phobias, anxiety states and minor perversions.

With some patients there may be a need to limit the period of treatment; it is useful, anyway, to indicate that the treatment will not go on indefinitely, that it will end at a certain time. In contrast to psycho-analysis, Kleinian therapy considers a realistic indication that the psychotherapeutic relationship will come to an end to be an important and necessary factor in working through the disorders of attachment, a process which is repeated when some aspect of the 'good object' is given up in this way. Sometimes the therapist will decide against taking a particular patient into treatment. This has serious implications for both patient and therapist alike and must be handled in such a fashion that neither disturbs the patient further nor causes him pain.

Transference interpretation   The work of the psychotherapist is centred on the transference situation and its interpretation. The therapist listens intently to the patient's material and endeavours not to be at all beguiled into giving practical advice, encouragement, reassurance or offering any active participation in the life of the patient or his family.

The concept of transference relates not only to an understanding of the 'here and now', the situation which is actually evolving between the psychotherapist and the patient, but to an understanding of the way facts and fantasies which relate to past relationships (especially those of internal figures from the patient's inner world) are transferred onto the therapist. This lively process is able to include current problems and relationships which are again interpreted and related to the transference as it develops. The Kleinian therapist is aware of the transference at the very *beginning* of therapy, but in making interpretations careful attention is given to the way they are handled, the timing, the order and language used, and especially the amount of interpretation.

The transference is used to investigate both positive and negative feelings directed towards the therapist. Interpretation of these feelings is kept sparse and succinct, using everyday language suitable for the patient and avoiding the use of technical and analytic terms which may give satisfaction to the therapist but are gobbledegook to the patient: if the patient cannot understand you, he may as well go home. Initial interpretations can only be simple restatements of the problem in dynamic terms.

In ways that are comparable with Freudian techniques and those of personal construct psychology the therapist keeps expressions of his own personality and life-style out of the consulting room. The patient is there to make contact with *his* expectations of *others* that relate more closely to the emotions he is experiencing as a result of his *therapy* than they do to what is happening in the external world.

In Kleinian therapy, the past is connected to the present *gradually*. Interpretations are given in a certain sequence:

(a) *Preparatory* interventions, interpreting resistances and defences, gauging the patient's readiness to accept the interpretation and wording it carefully;

(b) interpretations which *penetrate* from the surface to the depths, from what is known or imagined to occur in the present to what exists in the past which is less well known or unknown;

(c) layering slowly down to the earliest mental processes through to the later, more specialized types of mental functioning, the *unconscious* infantile archaic wishes and fantasies which focus on the therapist as a possible source of gratification.

A clear description of this process is provided by Loewenstein (1951), who refers specifically to psychoanalysis:

It happens frequently in the beginning of analysis that a patient describes a number of events which strike the analyst as having similarities. The analyst's task is then to show the patient that all these events in his life have some elements in common. The next step is to point out that the patient behaved in a similar way in all these situations. The third step may be to demonstrate that this behaviour was manifested in circumstances all of which involved competitive elements and where rivalry might have been expected. A further step, in a later stage of the analysis, would consist, for instance, in pointing out that in these situations rivalry does exist unconsciously, but is replaced by another kind of behaviour, such as avoiding competition. In all these stages of analysis the interpretation of mechanisms, as opposed to content, is significant. In a still later stage of the analysis this behaviour of the patient is shown to have originated in certain critical events of his life encompassing reactions and tendencies, such as, for example, those we group under the heading of the unconscious fantasies which have their origins in infancy. The interpretation extends in instalments throughout the analysis, and only in the last stages of treatment does an interpretation become complete. Thus there is a gradual interpretation from a preparation to an interpretation.

Working through   The patient is provided in the transference situation with an opportunity to work through his needs, wishes and his reactions to other people in the companionship of his therapist who, though acutely aware and sensitive to the nuances of the material, keeps continually to his neutral uninvolved role. He can then begin to examine more closely and in safety the mechanisms of projection and introjection which have led to the building of his inner complex world and distorted his perceptions of reality. Original fantasies come to light: fantasies of a crude and primitive nature. As Segal (1964) has noted, 'the mental correlate of the instincts – the phantasies of complete fulfilment. To the desire to love and eat corresponds the phantasy of an ideal love life and food giving breast; to the desire to destroy, equally vivid phantasies of an object shattered, destroyed and attacking'.

This view of fantasy colours the Kleinian therapist's technique in that all communications from his patient are viewed as continuing an element of unconscious fantasy – *even when they appear to be a presentation of absolute and undeniably factual material*. Splitting, introjection and projection are very active mechanisms of defence, and the interpretation of these persecutory anxieties and the way they are defended against is a focal point. When a therapist is idealized, he must look out for the projection of bad feelings that the patient has split off and verbalizes about the therapist himself. It may also be used to cover up the anxiety of separation and used as a reason to terminate the therapy before it is completed.

Klein (1961), writing on the process of working through, noted that

> Freud has postulated the process of working through as an essential part of psycho-analytic procedure. Enabling the patient to experience his emotions, anxieties and past situations over and over again both in relation to the analyst and to different people and situations in the patient's past and present life. To some extent, however, working through occurs in every normal individual development. Adaption to external reality increases and with it the infant achieves a less phantastic view of the world around him. The recurring experience of the mother going away and coming back again makes her absence less frightening and therefore his suspicion of her leaving him diminishes.

The change process in therapy

Hughes (1974) has given a particularly clear definition of the change process in Kleinian therapy:

> As the patient is helped to distinguish good experiences he can identify with the analyst as a person who cares for his own insight and well-being

and the way is open for the patient to do the same. As his envy lessens he can appreciate positive qualities in himself and others, acknowledged along with destructive qualities. Integration of split-off parts of himself is comparable to a process in the development of the normal infant who begins, at about three months of age, to tolerate loving and hating the same object with less splitting and projection. On the basis of a *repeated satisfying experience*, he is able to introject, that is to take into his own personality ideas and feelings of a good mother with less hostility and idealisation. He is then in a position to tolerate feelings of concern and responsibility towards his mother in whom the capacity to introject is crippled.

As treatment progresses, the patient comes to understand that his feelings of aggression and love are valuable, and so begins to value them. Early responses to interpretation which were felt by the patient to be prohibitive, unkind or unduly harsh, which tended either to frustrate desire or to punish – permitting him, even commanding him, to enter in fear and trepidation the forbidden areas of his primitive and passionate feelings – these regressive infantile expectations are overcome and replaced by a rationality he can accept. This can only come about if the therapist has been successful in helping his patient to become aware of this reality, with a strengthened ego and the ability to test out and expand on its realistic functioning.

Case Example

Maria, aged twenty-six years, was referred by her general practitioner and described as 'depressed'. She had separated from her husband, Gianni, after only seven months of marriage, following several serious incidents of assault. Maria had been prescribed a heavy dosage of tranquillizers and sleeping pills and now felt unable to manage without them, even though thoughts of suicide tempted her continuously and despite knowing that the availability of these tablets was a 'dangerous' thing. She had told the doctor that she was not sure if she 'could live out yet another week of her miserable life'.

Maria went on to tell me that she was an only child. The family had originated in Naples, but she had been born in London. Her father was dead, killed in an accident at work, and she had always lived with her mother. She had an excellent job as a courier for an Italian travel agency, and spoke Italian and French fluently. Her mother had part-time work helping in a restaurant owned by an uncle.

At this first session, Maria spoke in a lively and animated way. She was a tall, dark, attractive young woman dressed in elegant, fashionable clothes and with long hair carefully curled and nails carefully manicured. She presented herself as a person who took a great deal of care over her appearance, but perhaps this was only for our first meeting.

In the sessions that followed, Maria continued to look well groomed and smart. A great deal of her time was taken up with visits to the hairdresser and beauty parlour. These visits were expensive, but she explained that she had always needed special treatments for excessive facial and bodily hair. She had been a 'hairy' baby, and this had grown steadily worse as she grew older. At the age of eleven she had been hospitalized because of a hormonal imbalance, and for Maria this reinforced her suspicions that she was changing into a boy. She would masturbate and then look to see if this had encouraged the growth of a penis. She was not sure what she wanted to be, male or female. Menstruation did not help to ease her feelings of confusion; menstrual blood only convinced her that this was yet another symptom of 'damage' to her vagina. She was afraid to tell her mother that she was bleeding: she expected punishment for it.

The acquisition and perpetuation of psychological disturbance

Maria was born one year into her parent's marriage. After Maria's birth, her mother was unable to have more children. She was a breech baby; forceps were used after a long and protracted delivery, and a severe breast abscess later prevented her mother from breast-feeding. She had been put to the breast but had drawn blood instead of milk from the nipple. Maria had been handed around the family for others to feed; her mother did not want to have anything to do with her. She remembered her mother telling others that she would have preferred a son, even providing her unborn child with the name Paolo: 'A name that always haunted me. I could see and feel him around even though I knew that he wasn't really there. I made up brothers and sisters to defend me against Paolo. I always knew it was a terrible thing for an Italian Catholic family to have only one female child.'

She ended our first sessions by saying:

> I knew that my mother was frightened of me because I had sexual problems. My mother tried to change my boyishness and sent me for elocution,

ballet and piano lessons, lessons which we couldn't afford. She made me frilly dresses. In them I looked and felt strange, ostracised from other poor kids in the neighbourhood. The children thought my mother was mad and that I was a witch. My poor father worked like a dog, heaving heavy lumps of stone, leaving everything to do with the home to her; Italian fathers are like that.

What level of interpretation could I offer Maria at this stage? A patient undertaking a course of psychotherapy is bound to come into the therapist's room full of hopes and fears. Even before our meeting, that patient will begin to fantasize, and these fantasies will expand during therapy. These anxieties and wild imaginings are often exhibited more clearly in the first session than in later ones. Interpreting them – at a first level – can be reassuring to the patient, relieving him of some anxiety and showing him that he has had your full attention, your serious consideration, and that you mean to be helpful.

Maria clearly exhibited painful anxiety about her sexuality: the attention to detail in her dress covered her fantasized mutilation and her fear of causing mutilation to others. What could she draw from my breast – blood or milk? I asked Maria, 'What do you expect from therapy?' She replied, 'I've done so many terrible things. What will you say when you hear?' Maria needed to have me to hear these things, to witness her self-destructiveness; but this carried the fear of her destructive feelings for me.

In Kleinian therapy, the technique of transference interpretation is more central than it is to the classical Freudian method. Interpretation is given at the level of the greatest unconscious anxiety. My response to Maria about the possibility of drawing blood or milk from the nipple enabled her to express her guilt about drawing the life from her mother and in turn about effectively exhausting and exploiting her therapist.

At eighteen, Maria was sent on holiday to Naples. She was a virgin, but was persuaded to have sexual intercourse with a cousin. She was ignorant of the mechanics of intercourse and had felt nothing, pain or pleasure. On returning home she developed a slipped disc and was hospitalized, continuing to suffer chronic back pain.

Maria's several short-term relationships with men had been confined to masturbation and oral sex. She had allowed a man to penetrate her vagina with a glass bottle; she didn't like to think of it now, but she had done 'a lot of terrible things'. At twenty she had had 'proper' sexual intercourse at a drinking party and became pregnant: 'I could not believe it, my breasts began to fill with milk. I was shocked because I only had real intercourse once. I knew I must get rid of it, and the man arranged an abortion six years ago, but it still hurts inside.'

Two months after the abortion, Maria witnessed her father's death: a block of marble slipped and fell, crushing him beneath it. Maria accompanied her father in the ambulance to hospital. She was hysterical, insisting that she be allowed to resuscitate him, but he was dead on arrival. Maria blamed herself for the accident, feeling that she was evil and deserved punishment for her 'sins'.

Her father's death left them poor, and it was arranged that Maria should meet a prospective bridegroom (Gianni) at a family gathering. Gianni was handsome and came from a wealthy family, and Maria was in love for the first time:

> I am not lucky with men. Our engagement lasted three years, Gianni avoided getting married and did not want to have 'proper' intercourse. He just used to masturbate me in a crude, uncaring way like the others. Mostly he wanted me to watch him masturbate, telling me to look until he had finished. When I tried to make love to him, he would say 'Wait until we are married.' I still loved him. We had our wedding, then on our honeymoon night I felt I should confess to Gianni about my previous lovers and especially about the abortion. I thought it was right to tell your husband these things. I wanted him to forgive me, but he went mad. I remember him shouting: 'Load of filth, to start a family with you is to start a family on filth. *Putana* (prostitute)!' I was being hit, kicking and screaming. People came and pulled him away. I was so ashamed, swollen and bruised, black eyes, split lips.
>
> Next day his penis was red and sore. He insisted on going to a hospital, shouting that I had given him a disease. The doctor sniggered. He looked at me and said, 'Go out and look at the scenery' – implying that we had been having sex too frequently. We returned home, we were going to live with my mother. Mother was shocked to see us back, she saw my bruised face, but she gave me a look of hatred and fear. I knew then I would not tell her about the abortion or anything about Gianni and myself.

The next day Gianni hit Maria again. This time her mother came to their bedroom and pulled him away. Maria's mother stood her ground and ordered him out of the house. Gianni was now watching the house, telephoning her office; one moment insulting her and then begging her to return to him.

Therapy

Maria's mother defended her daughter, but for Maria this defence was suspect. In treatment Maria often spoke of the murderous anger she felt towards her mother – the mother who had 'handed her around to be fed' and now passed her on, via the family doctor, to a psychotherapist. Maria was totally unsure about what she could ever expect from any breast – blood or milk – but blood alone came from hers.

Maria's self-preservation was dependent on her trust in a good mother: splitting away the bad parts and clinging fiercely to the good, willing herself to love them, even to imagine that they were there so that she would be able to preserve her life. Maria was the baby who could not hold on to any of these good feelings and was exposed to a cruel, harsh world that she knew could destroy her.

This cruel and painful world built up inside Maria had continued throughout her life. She had no trust in her relationship with her mother or indeed with anyone else; she was still expressing the omnipotent, destructive anxieties and mechanisms that are predominant in the first few weeks of life. Maria's primitive, sadistic fantasies of being pulled from her mother by forceps and drawing blood from the proffered breast expressed her wish to destroy her mother, to mutilate and take over bits of her mother's body for herself – biting, cutting, tearing. These primitive feelings produced in their turn the strong sense of guilt which compounded Maria's unconscious fixation on her mother.

Trying to find a source of mother-love whilst at the same time containing these murderous feelings, and burdened with a sense of anxiety and guilt, Maria was unable to express any affection towards her mother. Her mother's behaviour had not encouraged the loving responses between mother and daughter which are normally followed by a turning away from the father. Even the mechanisms of idealization of the therapist were not being expressed: there was no one and nothing that Maria could identify as 'good'.

Major therapeutic techniques   I encouraged Maria to think again of her father; she was sure she could not. On only two occasions did he become important: he had given her life and he had died. Yes, her parents slept together, but she did not believe they had sex. Once she had seen a contraceptive floating in the toilet – her father may have used it.

She had not forgotten about it, but even now she would deny what it meant.

Maria was a difficult patient. Her twice-weekly attendances were intermittent; her apologies and excuses always came late after she had missed a session. These destructive attacks on me were aimed at negating the effect of the treatment. She often spoke of the meaninglessness of her life, the depression she felt at the loss of each part of herself as she spoke of these innermost 'monstrous' feelings. Feelings of want and helplessness and the collapse of her self-respect created a narcissistic wound. Therapy did not make her feel good: her continued hostility towards me and guilt about these feelings replicated the unrequited frustrations of her infancy.

Sadistic desires were also directed against her phantom brother, Paolo. Great jealousy and hate were directed against this non-existent child. Maria dreamed of mutilating her mother's womb, reaching up into it with a spoon to deface and castrate the male child it contained. This was a reflection of her real experience of cutting out her own baby, and of the poking and probing in her own vagina for the penis she had left behind in her mother's womb. Maria graphically described her omnipotent feelings when she had seen her father killed, but in her dreams she had rehearsed the death of her mother and practised her reaction to the event. With my help, Maria evoked repressed memories of seeing her mother in hospital recuperating from a hysterectomy and her grandmother dying of stomach cancer: scenes which reinforced both the malignancy within herself and her magic powers which were capable of destroying mother, father, brother, baby, grandmother and me.

The breakdown of Maria's omnipotent feelings was hard for her to bear. Giving up these fantasies caused her intense anxiety and fear of retaliation, followed by a period of intense depression. She began to talk of leaving therapy, leaving England, looking abroad for a job. She began spending wildly, using her credit cards and ordering clothes and perfume, sending the bills to her husband. After a 'lost weekend' of drugs, drink and violent sex, she entered a private psychiatric hospital as a voluntary patient, not contacting me for two weeks. When ECT was suggested by a psychiatrist, she discharged herself and telephoned for another appointment. This was a deliberate attempt to invoke counter-transference feelings: she was trying me out for reactions which would show her that love and/or hate still existed. This move, whereby interpretation is sought as a reassurance and an antidote to psychic pain rather than for insightful understanding, is one that Melanie Klein has illustrated many times.

The change process Maria's depressive guilt which followed this episode helped her ego to emerge mature and better integrated. She began to experience feelings of sorrow, responsibility and a genuine desire for object restoration. Maria received psychotherapeutic treatment for two years and three months. She made one attempt at reconciliation with her husband which ended disastrously: first in another brutal assault and finally in divorce. Maria emigrated to the USA with her mother and remarried within a year. Her second husband is a property developer; they have three children, two girls and a boy. She is no longer suicidal and appears in good health.

Psychotherapeutic experience has shown that even an intensive long-term therapy will only minimally decrease the power of the patient's persecutory anxieties and protective fantasies, and it can never remove them completely. These early anxiety situations are always internalized and rise to the surface when triggered by the day-to-day problems of living. This demarcates the limits of psychotherapy which cannot exclude the possibilities of future breakdown.

The final word will rest with Melanie Klein (1937):

> If in our earliest development we have been able to transfer our interest and love from our mother to other people and other sources of gratification, then, and only then, are we able in later life to derive enjoyment from other sources. This enables us to compensate for a failure or a disappointment in connection with one person by establishing a friendly relationship to others, and to accept substitutes for things we have been unable to obtain or to keep. If frustrated greed, resentment, and hatred within us do not disturb the relation to the outer world, there are innumerable ways of taking in beauty, goodness and love from without. By doing this we continuously add to our happy memories and gradually build up a store of values by which we gain a security that cannot easily be shaken, and contentment which prevents bitterness of feeling. Moreover, all these satisfactions have in addition to the pleasure they afford, the effect of diminishing frustrations (or rather the feeling of frustration) past and present, back to the earliest and fundamental ones. The more true satisfaction we experience, the less do we resent deprivations, and the less shall we be swayed by our greed and hatred. Then we are actually capable of accepting love and goodness from others and of giving love to others; and again receiving more in return. In other words, the essential capacity for 'give and take' has been developed in

us in a way that ensures our own contentment and contributes to the pleasure, comfort or happiness of other people.

In conclusion, a good relation to ourselves is a condition for love, tolerance and wisdom towards others. This good relation to ourselves has, as I have endeavoured to show, developed in part from a friendly, loving and understanding attitude towards other people, namely those who meant much to us in the past and those to whom our relationship has become part of our minds and personalities. If we have become able to some extent, deep in our unconscious minds, to clear our feelings of grievance towards our parents and have forgiven them for the frustrations we had to bear, then we can be at peace with ourselves and are able to love others in the true sense of the word.

References

Bowlby J (1979) *The Making and Breaking of Affectional Bonds*, pp. 136–7, Tavistock, London.

Colby K M (1951) *A Primer for Psychotherapists*, Ronald Press, New York.

Farrell B J (1981) *The Standing of Psycho-Analysis*, Oxford University Press, London.

Hughes A (1974) Contributions of Melanie Klein to psycho-analytic technique. In Varma V J (editor), *Psychotherapy Today*, Constable, London.

Isaacs S (1952) The nature and function of phantasy, in Riviere J (editor), *Developments in Psycho-Analysis*, Hogarth Press, London.

Klein M (1932) *The Psycho-Analysis of Children*, Hogarth, London.

Klein M (1937) Love, hate and reparation, in Rickman J (editor), *Psychoanalytic Epitomes*, Hogarth Press, London.

Klein M (1948a) The development of a child. *Contributions to Psycho-Analysis, 1921–45*, Hogarth Press, London.

Klein M (1948b) A contribution to the psychogenesis of manic depressive states. *Contributions to Psycho-Analysis, 1921–1945*, Hogarth Press, London.

Klein M (1948c) The Oedipus Complex in the light of early anxieties. *Contributions to Psycho-Analysis, 1921–1945*, Hogarth Press, London.

Klein M (1948d) Symposium on child-analysis. *Contributions to Psycho-Analysis, 1921–1945*, Hogarth Press, London.

Klein M (1952a) Notes on some schizoid mechanisms, in Riviere J (editor), *Developments in Psycho-Analysis*, Hogarth Press, London.

Klein M (1952b) On the theory of anxiety and guilt, in Riviere J (editor), *Developments in Psycho-Analysis*, Hogarth Press, London.

Klein M (1955) On identification, in Klein M, Heimann P, Money-Kyrle R E (editors), *New Directions in Psycho-Analysis*, Tavistock, London.

Klein M (1957) *Envy and Gratitude*, Tavistock, London.

Klein M (1961) *Narrative of a Child Analysis*, Hogarth, London.
Loewenstein R M (1951) The problem of interpretation. *Psycho-Analytic Quarterly,* *20*, 1–14.
Riviere J (1952) On the genesis of psychic conflict in earliest infancy, in Riviere J (editor), *Developments in Psycho-Analysis*, Hogarth, London.
Robertson J, and Robertson J (1967–72) *Young children in brief separation.* (Film series), Tavistock Institute of Human Relations, London.
Segal H (1964) *Introduction to the Work of Melanie Klein*, Heinemann, London.
Tarachow S (1970) *Introduction to Psychotherapy*, International University Press, New York.
Waelder R (1937) The problem of the genesis of psychical conflict in earliest infancy. *International Journal of Psycho-analysis*, 18, 406–473.

Suggested Further Reading

Klein M (1957) *Envy and Gratitude*, Tavistock, London.
Klein M (1960) *Our Adult World and its Roots in Infancy*, Tavistock Pamphlet.
Klein M, Riviere J (1937) Love, Hate and Reparation in Rickman J (ed) *Psychoanalytic Epitomes*, Hogarth Press, London.
Melzer D (1967) *The Psychoanalytic Process*, Heinemann, London.
Segal H (1964) *Introduction to the Work of Melanie Klein*, Heinemann, London.

Chapter 4 Psychodynamic Therapy: The Jungian Approach

Kenneth Lambert

Historical Context and Developments in Britain

Although C.G. Jung (1875–1961) did not at the outset wish to found an organized school of psychotherapy, he later encouraged the societies and training institutes that were set up all over the world to develop his ideas and methods. Today, the International Association for Analytical Psychology in Zurich comprises over a thousand analyst members. The main British body is the Society of Analytical Psychology, which trains candidates in adult and child analysis and psychotherapy and runs the C.G. Jung Clinic and the C.G. Jung Children's Clinic in London.

Analytical psychology is one of the main variants in psychodynamic psychotherapy to have emerged from the original Freudian background as a separate entity by comparison with movements led from within it by Klein, Winnicott, the school of object-relations theorists and others. Jung's break with Freud is by now well known to those who have read Jung's (1963) autobiography *Memories, Dreams, Reflections* or *The Freud-Jung letters* (1974). Between the two men there was not only a generational gap but temperamental and cultural differences that proved insurmountable, partly because as Winnicott (1964) has pointed out, it would not have been psychoanalytically possible at the time of the rift for anyone to have analysed the complications of Jung's nature. Today, however, many people feel that it is in terms of complementarity rather than incompatibility that those differences are best described.

Jung's background, as is shown in his autobiography, was medico-pastoral. His interests were more romanticist and empiricist than were Freud's. Archaeology, anthropology, medicine, psychiatry, psychoanalysis and religious studies, both Western and Eastern, were combined with a considerable knowledge of Gnosticism, alchemy and mythology. He was also steeped in the Teutonic philosophy of his time through Kant and Hegel; through Von Hartmann, Schopenhauer and Nietzsche; and the cultural studies of Burckhardt and Bachofen.

Krafft-Ebing and Freud met to an extent his empiricist needs, but to him their very large focus on human sexuality seemed limited. Thus it was that in 1911 Jung published *Symbols of Transformation* (1956) criticizing Freud's 'sexual' explanations of mother-son incestuous ties and proposing an understanding in terms of a universal human wish for renewal through a return into the mother as the primal source of life – a wish for death and rebirth. From then and on to the twenties, Jung began to formulate some general concepts for himself.

Central to these were the concept of the *self* conceived of as a dynamic energic system subject to the play of counterpolar opposites and the phenomenon of the *enantiodromia*, whereby a one-sided energy concentration tends to move into its opposite. This self consists of archetypes, this is to say potentialities or universal dispositions to experience existence in accordance with stereotypical patterns of expectation, to represent themselves to consciousness in terms of imagery and to express themselves within the particularities of flesh and blood, space and time. Further aspects of the self Jung (1971) described in the well-known terminology of the *persona* and *shadow*; the *anima* and *animus*; the *mana personalities* bearing parental authority; the *puer aeternus*, eternally fresh, young and self-renewing; the *wise old man* and the *wise old woman*. Added to these archetypes is a wide array of other patterns and themes referring to internal processes such as the pattern of *death and rebirth* already alluded to, the negotiation of the *liminal situation* in change and development, the undergoing of *initiation* and the *transformation* of primitive instinctual libido.

Over and against the *self* as a spontaneously functioning entity yet part of it and growing out of it, the *ego* is postulated to be the centre of its consciousness. The ego's function is to illuminate the development of internal relationships within the self and the latter's external relationships with the not-self. Thus Freud's notion of libido as mainly sexual is expanded by Jung to include the instinctual drives that lie behind relational, cultural and spiritual achievement.

As for clinical methods, Jung tended to favour the 'eyeball to eyeball' encounter between analyst and patient, both seated in chairs and in a dialectical relationship rather than in the type of relationship fostered by the use of the analytic couch, though he did not entirely foreswear the latter. For him the therapist's capacities for self-knowledge and integration were of prime importance – as were his capacities for personal involvement in, and response to, the personal challenge of his patient. He found that to understand his patient's dream material as an expression of his imaginative, primitive and holistic, though unconscious, response to life was often more helpful than Freud's (1900) view of the dream as composed of *manifest* material designed to mask the dreamer's *real* but latent wishes from his conscious ego.

We can now see that Jung was giving weight, in his opposition to Freud, to the feeling, intuitive, timeless and holistic imagery that finds its somatic basis in the right cerebral hemisphere. Not that he seriously denied the importance of the logical verbalization and rational aim-directed action of the left, at which Freud excelled: he had, indeed, come across both these opposites early in his life, in the personalities of his parents. It may well be that these experiences stimulated his concept of the *transcendent function* that can bring together opposites and generate new syntheses between them – with, no doubt, its somatic basis in the callosal bridge that links the left and the right. It is in the light of this that we can affirm that Jung was not so much denying Freud's language of *signs* as affirming the significance of the *symbol*.

The general formulations listed above came together by the twenties to be named analytical psychology. Jung, however, did not stand still but went on over four and a half decades to interest himself more and more in cultural processes. Indeed, during the last fifteen years of his life he produced a series of historical studies of an extraordinary brilliance. No more has analytical psychology stood still. There have been many developments (cf. Fordham 1978), and Samuels (1983) has attempted a case for discerning three tendencies within it.

One school, which may be called the 'Classical' school, has remained close to what are understood to be Jung's original methods. It is in evidence in Switzerland, New York, Los Angeles, Italy and Israel; and London, where there is a minority group formerly led by Gerhard Adler.

A second tendency has developed in England in the work of the Society of Analytical Psychology (Fordham et al. 1980). Here a reformulation of Jung's ideas on the self has been accomplished by a new focus upon areas somewhat neglected by Jung, such as early infantile development and the analysis not only of children but also of the infantile disturbances and potentialities so often repressed and left unintegrated within the adult patient. This has involved assimilating within a Jungian framework not only the classical psychoanalysis already known to Jung but also the work of later Freudian analysts such as Melanie Klein, Donald Winnicott, Harold Searles, Heinrich Racker, Heinz Kohut and many others. Out of this a creative synthesis is being achieved that has involved a more complete understanding of transference and counter-transference analysis, and also an understanding of the holding, object-presenting, mirroring, naming and reconstructing function of the analyst. A new interest in child analysis and psychotherapy has emerged under the stimulus of Michael Fordham; and in addition new light has been cast on the difference between more analytic and more psychotherapeutic aims. Analysis seeks to understand the present dynamics of the patient without pretending to 'know' what is good for him but rather becoming 'wise after the event'. Psychotherapy, however analytical, tends to attempt to help the patient to solve practical life problems and is inclined to 'know' what is good for him.

A third movement has arisen in the USA, under the stimulus of Hillman (1975) and counter to developments in London. It names itself 'archetypal psychology', and concentrates on the archetypally originated imaginative and mythic aspects of the human psyche. It attacks developmental psychology and considers that our culture is given over to the dominance of a 'heroic ego' that has turned the classical concepts of analytical psychology, namely self, integration and individuation, into objects of false aim-directed activity. How important this movement is in respect of practical psychotherapy no doubt remains to be seen; its influence in Britain is, in any case, minimal.

Theoretical Assumptions

The image of the person

My assumptions are, roughly speaking, shared by many members of the Society of Analytical Psychology. They are based upon thirty-five years of practice, during a period of great change, and represent a personal precipitation of experience for which I alone take responsibility (Lambert 1981b).

The basic image of the person is of an individual born into, and dependent upon, a community which nurtures (or hampers) the mother-child duo, the family, the school, the neighbourhood and the nation he belongs to (Odajnyk 1976). These concentric environmental forces may or may not support a wide range of predispositions to experience life in certain more or less stereotypical ways, called archetypes. The archetype is a postulated theoretical entity, the presence of which is inferred through patterns of imagery or behaviour that are typical and likely to be recognized, though with many variations, almost anywhere in the world. These, include the shadow, the anima and animus, mana personalities, the *puer aeternus*, the wise old man and wise old woman as well as the internal processes mentioned in the first part of the present chapter. Less abstract are the archetypal 'good' and 'bad' fathers, mothers, grandparents, siblings, priests, bosses, doctors, etc. which are presented to the psyche from within in terms of imagery.

When the archetypal expectation meets or projects itself upon objects corresponding to it in the real world, there nearly always occurs a clash: between the stereotypic aspects of the archetype and the particularity of the actual object. When the clash is not too great the archetype, say, of the mother, is modified and individualized by the actuality of the real mother; it may then be taken into the self and become an internalized archetypal object, to the immense benefit of the person concerned. On the other hand, if the sense of the outside object is weak, then the archetypal content can become dominant to the extent that the individual becomes swamped by internal imagery that cuts him off from the real world. An important theoretical advance in this field by Fordham (1957) postulates that some time after conception and while still *in utero*, let alone at birth, we are dealing with an original mainly undifferentiated self composed mainly of archetypal potential. As interaction with the environment takes place, beginning with intra-uterine life and onwards, the original self progressively deintegrates, that is to say archetypes become differentiated from the undifferentiated whole. For instance, in connection with the mother archetype, the de-integrations are of predispositions to experience, in feeling terms, parts of the mother in the first place as nipple, skin, warmth, teeth, eyes, etc. and then later the mother herself as a whole person. Naturally, however, these deintegrative experiences depend upon the presentation to the infant of a real mother or mother-person. If the fit between the two is good enough, then the deintegrate in question, now enriched by the experience of its correlate in the real physical world, can be re-integrated into the self as a whole. A marriage between the archetypal expectation and a real object has taken place, and the internalized mother has been individualized and is free to become an effective 'inner world' figure for the person concerned rather than a mere stereotypic image (Lambert 1981b).

Analytical psychology is thus concerned to facilitate deintegration-reintegration processes whereby the individual is enhanced by real-world experience in terms of flesh and blood and space and time and becomes all the more 'solid' as integration proceeds. Furthermore, while sharing in the common life the person progressively individuates and, as Jung (1971) puts it, becomes more 'in-divisible'. The process is essentially spontaneous and cannot be aimed at or contrived. It can provide its own meaningfulness for the individual and can enhance personal relationships as well as open him to religious experience, including that of death.

In this way the individual may become better rooted in himself and better related to the not-self. Interestingly enough, self-representations tend to express themselves in imagery that is parallel to religious symbolism. This phenomenon, however, needs careful analysis in order to distinguish between self experiences and the ground of the self which appears to be the object of religion. There may be a likeness between the two which is, nevertheless, not the same as an identity. Much experience suggests that a conviction of being in a state of identity with a god plays into illusions of infantile omnipotence and omniscience that can lead to states of inflation and psychotic omnipotence (but see Redfearn 1983).

Integral to the self processes just described is the development of ego-consciousness. Jung (1977), in his Tavistock lectures, dealt at some length with the notion of the development of the ego as a kind of skin: a function of adaptation to both the inner and the outer worlds, and vital to the survival of the individual organism. It can vary from a low level of awareness right up to that ego-consciousness of his situation and nature that is the mark of psychological man. Jung thought it developed spontaneously as small islands of consciousness capable of cohering into a sort of land mass – with a centre that he called the ego.

If we use Fordham's (1957) theory of deintegration and reintegration, we may understand that when each deintegrate tangles with its corresponding reality the fit is never perfect so that a clash occurs. It is out of the clash, provided that it is not shattering, that ego-consciousness is born. The latter is compounded, too, by experiences of joyous fulfilment of instinctual and relational need in connection with the mother, etc. Bits of such consciousness cohere, a centre develops, and the ego can develop and function as the conscious side of the self (cf. Lambert 1981a).

Concepts of psychological health and disturbance

In Jungian and other psychodynamic theories the concept of health is greatly enriched, sharpened and clarified as a result of the attempt to meet the complaints of suffering patients. Therapists are forced to distinguish between symptoms and the disorders they point to, and to avoid the temptation to alleviate symptoms save for first aid in times of crisis. This does not mean that great patience is not often required if patients are to be protected from traumatization by over-hasty or premature therapeutic interventions.

For Jungians, the concept of psychological health is bound up with the realization of the true self in terms of the level of integration and individuation that is appropriate to the point of development that has been reached in the here and now. The concept is concerned with dynamic change in relation to personal development and the capacity to respond creatively to changes in the environment within which the human organism exists. This involves the person in not being so split within himself and at odds with himself that he is unable to mobilize whole-hearted involvement and commitment to relationships and projects if that is required.

The wholeness or integration studied by Jungians is not to be confused with the Goethian concept of the many-sided or all-round man; an integrated man in the Jungian sense may even look one-sided and narrow in his range of interests and activity. Nevertheless, he can if necessary mobilize a wide range of abilities, considerations and feelings in a way that reduces unnecessary conflict and promotes rather than hampers his main and central aims. He may develop a persona or psychic 'clothes' that are appropriate to the many partial or more formal relationships of life; he can, to an extent, become aware of and integrate into his whole personality factors that he considers undesirable or less desirable, that is to say, the shadow. He may be able to relate to and develop contrasexual factors in his personality that are symbolized as female (anima) in a man and masculine (animus) in a woman, though it is now generally agreed that under certain circumstances the anima and animus may be discerned in a woman and a man respectively rather than the other way round (Lambert 1981b). Furthermore, as part of his individuation he will be all the more capable, if necessary, of respecting and coming to terms with authority and yet become an innovator and inaugurator of life. Sexually, too, when mature he will be capable of genital or creative sexuality, having integrated those earlier oral, anal and phallic developments as described by Freud.

Quite apart, however, from fostering such healthy developments of the first half of life as those listed above, Jungian psychology has also been concerned with psychological health in the second half of life and in old age. In the case of elderly people it is a not unusual therapeutic task to support attempts on their part to survey and come to terms with their life history as a whole. This often needs facing and may involve mourning the loss of that part of life, grieving over sins and mistakes, and discovering gratitude for its successes and happinesses – not alone, however, but in relation to a real person, the therapist, who in turn needs to mobilize on behalf of his patient empathy, imagination and understanding. This is a first stage in coming to terms with the ending of terrestrial life in death. The next task is to live as fully as possible the closing years of life: not by distracting attention from the situation or pretending to be young or through a schizoid withdrawal from the whole experience of life and death, but rather by combining a full experience of the present stage of life, in both its limitations and promises, with a developing philosophy of life. This is indeed a suitable occupation for the old when they have disidentified themselves from envy of the young and taken steps not to withdraw into isolation from others.

Enough has been written above to give indications of a concept of psychological health as a dynamic process rather than a static condition. The capacity to experience and handle dynamic change, deintegration and reintegration, loss, joy and personal relationships in all their vicissitudes requires a congeries of qualities the possession of which constitutes psychological health.

It is by comparison with such positive capability that ill-health may be defined; even though it is also through the stimulus of suffering, considered as a complaint and brought by patients to therapists, that a concept of health began to be developed. By comparison, yet again, any condition that hampers the positive processes just described may be classed as a *disturbed* one. Psychological disturbance may be described, in the first instance, in phenomenological terms. Such would be the classical psychiatric entities: depressiveness; schizoid, phobic, paranoid and manic states; hysteria; obsessionalism; narcissistic personality disorder, and so forth. To these in addition should be added the major psychoses, to the aetiology of which psychodynamics may supply some understanding – though, under present circumstances, not always therapeutic alleviation.

Psychological disturbance may further be identified and understood from a psychodynamic point of view under at least three main headings. First, there are disturbances that arise out of fixation, at earlier levels of development in the individual's life: in other words a hold-back of on-going process *at a deep level* has taken place. For instance, to give gross examples, the striving, over aim-directed and successful individual may begin to be overwhelmed by unlived or fixated adolescent wishes of a rebellious, sexually promiscuous, chaotic and defiant sort. They may demand to be acted out in a way that can sometimes be destructive towards his work, relationships and life-style; but this is not necessarily the case, for they can issue forth out of the chaos created into new and creative forms of life. At its most negative, however, the situation may be eased temporarily by a renewed process of denial and repression, thus causing a split within the self that is accompanied by energy loss and heightened anxiety. Another example would be of an adult man whose responsible and dedicated scientific life may be hampered by unconscious infantile, rage-filled, destructive envy of, contempt for and defiance of his scientific colleagues.

Secondly, serious disturbance may arise from the over-rigid and under-adaptable character structure that results from that excessive investment of libido in over-elaborated defensive systems that mark phobic, paranoid, obsessional and narcissistic personalities.

A third set of disturbances arises from the absence of any holding container, whether internalized or external, that might be forthcoming for the individual from a person, group or coherent life-style. In the case of such an absence we find great emotional lability, inconstancy, treachery and promiscuity of a sort that extends well beyond the purely sexual connotation of the word.

Finally, we should not forget the disturbance in the sense of reality of the schizoid individual who is always in danger of living in a world of archetypal images that is insufficiently modified by his sense of object relationships.

The acquisition of psychological disturbance

Most of the psychological disturbances of the state of health described sketchily above can be thought of as originating mainly from serious and traumatic distortions of the relationship between the individual and his early containing environment. That containing environment is, at first, provided mainly by the mother. She can give security through *holding* both physically and psychologically (Winnicott 1958a); to the secure child she can give parts of herself, and then herself as a whole, to be *an object or objects* that he can grapple with and experience as a real area of the not-self (Winnicott 1974). She can empathically *mirror*, in her demeanour and face, the varying moods or potential moods in her child, thus introducing him to his inner world (Winnicott 1974). She can *name* these as well as not-self objects and thus help him to control these experiences (Winnicott 1974). At first the father can hold the mother-infant duo; and it is important that the whole family is held by the wider groups within which it lives. It must be remembered how sensitive this whole transaction and interplay is and how easily it can be disturbed. The grosser disturbances, of course, spring from the absence of the mother through death, illness and other calamities. Subtler disturbances arise either from depression in the mother which cause in the child a sense of distance and isolation or, again, from her sheer ignorance, insensitivity, unreliability or uninstinctual nursery rules.

When these natural orders are disturbed, then the child in its immaturity can become overwhelmed by boundless greed, rage and fear, to the extent of disintegrating in a shattering way. The whole de-integrative and reintegrative process is knocked away, and the child, left alone, can only repress by mobilizing nearly cast-iron defences or move towards delinquency or madness.

The main clinical results of this type of dislocation are, generally, a great deal of repression coupled with fixations at early points in development, as for instance in the case of narcissistic personality disorder, where the infant attempts a do-it-yourself psychology coupled with a grandiosity that is hollow inside (Kohut 1971, 1977). Another description of this is Winnicott's (1958b), where the child develops a caretaker self, a mind-psyche, that attempts to care for his pain-racked psyche-soma. Other results can be listed as follows: intense difficulties in forming and sustaining relationships; over-anxiety when attempting to tackle change; fears of sexuality and aggression and their demands; fears of the inner world leading to manic and over-active extravert behaviour; fears of the outer world of people, relationships and things to the degree of schizoid withdrawal and a concentration upon internal archetypal imagery; underachievement, cynicism and feared loneliness or isolation; a feeling of meaninglessness even in the first half of life.

It ought to be added that such an incomplete but alarming picture of distress is to be understood mainly as a picture of pure psychological disorder, as distinguished from those problems that are connected with lack of opportunity, collision with the environment, or unemployment. Nevertheless, that pure psychological disorder can exacerbate the distress caused by such outer problems and militate against their solution.

It should also be added that many of the problems of the second half of life, of old age and of death can be rendered more difficult to solve as a result of early trauma and disturbance in the first months of life. As a result, the therapy of people in the second half of life may need to tackle the problems of infancy first.

The perpetuation of psychological disturbance

Psychological disturbance is perpetuated in people who generate little consciousness that they have any problems at all. Such unconsciousness may be based upon a hold-up in the process of maturation, or it may be the result of very serious damage sustained in the early life of the person concerned. This type of unconsciousness may extend to a noticeable inability to 'learn from experience' (Bion 1983); that is because such people are often overwhelmed by the need to discharge tension and find alleviation for their sufferings. To such a degree is this the case that they cannot bear the idea of generating sufficient understanding to be able to ascribe meaning to their plight – a difficulty that is met constantly during the early phases of analytical treatment and well known to analysts.

Other factors include the power of sheer habit, whereby patients often oppose change; it is not, however, only habit but also the product of archetypal factors working within the character structure of people whose object relationships are relatively weak. Archetypal patterns and themes are postulated to be timeless in themselves but may become modified to the extent that they tangle with flesh and blood and space and time. People who are over-dominated by archetypes do not easily change. Both the woman identified with the archetype of the Great Mother and the man equally so with one of the figures of the father may be observed to change very little in adaptation to reality as the years roll by; the same is true of the individual identified with the trickster archetype or with that of the *puer aeternus*, the ever-youthful boy. The individual needs to be able to struggle with these archetypal tendencies and to wrest value from them if he is not to be fixed in a negative way to them and by them.

A similar resistance to any change in psychological disturbance is sometimes found in the psycho-social environment within which the individual lives and, maybe, somehow survives. Such environments no doubt supply some of his needs and, no doubt, can claim his support; they do, however, sometimes develop patterns of social life and behaviour that persist through the years rather tenaciously, and hamper and control certain changes that might be developing in the individual.

Another potent cause of the perpetuation of psychological disorder in the individual is the quite natural response of a disturbed person's environment to the effects upon it of his behaviour. For instance, many types of defensive system can rob the defended individual of energy and diminish his capacity for sustained adult and responsible relationships. That leads to letting people down and disappointing them, actions which result in further misunderstanding and pain. Defences may be unnecessarily strong, and withdraw libido from real faith and hope and from perseverance, concentration and profundity in personal relationships. The result of this is to reinforce the defensive system out of which the disturbance originally emerged. Secondly, individuals who have been seriously disturbed by calamity, death or abandonment in their early lives may, quite unconsciously, so act in their social setting that they re-create the original situation. For instance, a woman who feels that her father abandoned her in childhood may be perceived to be either choosing the sort of men who are unable to sustain relationships or setting up situations of provocation which are likely to drive their male partners away. The result of this is likely to compound her half-conscious belief that all men are unfaithful scoundrels. For her, it can be almost a relief that her fundamental 'theory' is proved true. It is thus perpetuated, for too wide a gap between reality and her 'theory' produces a state of discomfort which the woman will unconsciously seek to alleviate in the way alluded to above.

Practice

Goals of therapy

Jungian therapy aims to analyse the personality of the patient within the therapeutic relationship in such a way that his ego-consciousness of self and others and their interrelationship is enhanced. Dynamic change and growth potential are thereby likely to be released, to the benefit of his personality and relationships. This generally involves the repair of past damage through reconstruction. Included also is the analysis of defences, blocks and inhibitions. Thus unsatisfactory personality structures can be reduced to their elements so that the patient can develop afresh on a basis that serves his needs better.

The accomplishment of such an endeavour often requires the analysis of the patient's inability and fear so that he allows himself to be in a dependent and contained situation and to trust another person, the therapist, to accept the verbal and emotional expression of the truth, often conceived of as the worst that is in him. Such an experience of trust is found, in clinical experience, to facilitate not only a transformation or modification of primitive feelings and emotions but also an integration of these elements into the more conscious and developed parts of the patient's personality, thus serving the needs of the patient's self as a whole.

In more specifically Jungian terms, the shorter-term goal often turns out to be the facilitation of the patient's ability to relate to archetypal material with increasing ego-consciousness in such a way that his spontaneous and instinctual life may be vivified in the broadest sense of that term: otherwise, if his ego-consciousness is weak and lacks cohesion, the archetypal images may seize him and isolate him from real life and real relationships in a stereotypic and de-individualizing way. The longer-term goal of Jungian therapy is to provide conditions that favour spontaneous movements within the self towards integration and individuation coupled with enhanced ego-consciousness (Lambert 1981b).

The person of the therapist

Jung claimed to be the first to insist that candidates training to be analysts should first undergo analysis themselves. Whether his claim is true or not, few people involved in psychodynamic analytical psychotherapy would disagree with him. Psychoanalysis would probably emphasize not only the personality enrichment involved but also the fact that it helps the would-be analyst to distinguish between the patient and himself at least in principle, while still appreciating the likenesses. Jungians would stress that the candidate's analysis needs to have sufficiently advanced in respect of his integration to make him a safe enough person for his patients to allow themselves to interact with, and trust and depend upon if necessary.

The presence of such integration must have influence upon the development of the candidate's analytic skills and his style of exercising them. There is little doubt, nevertheless, that wider horizons and objective skills are largely acquired in a training situation involving continuous reading and work in seminar groups taken by experienced analysts and through supervision by the latter of the trainee's analysis of at least two cases over an appreciable period of time.

The skills required for the practice of analytical psychotherapy are specialized ones, having their roots in, though distinguished from, the traditional medical and pastoral practice and care that lie behind the Hippocratic oath or the correct translation of St Paul's definitions of 'agape' in 1 Cor. 13. 1–6 (Lambert 1981b).

As for motivation, it goes without saying that genuine interest in and curiosity about human psychological dynamics is one essential. A second type of motivation can arise from the personal discovery of a certain ability to listen and to develop patience with and empathy and insight into the suffering of patients. A third is a willingness to tolerate with imagination the aggression that patients, in their long drawn-out movement into repair and integration, mobilize against those very analysts who are helping such changes to come about. Truax and Carkhuff (1967) have assembled a good deal of experience in this area with their emphasis upon the genuineness, accurate empathy and non-possessive warmth required. St. Paul's 'agape', to balance this, emphasizes the need to master and put to appropriate use the anger, hatred and temptation to exploit, that is the shadow of caring activity (Lambert 1981b).

It must be emphasized that grappling with inner talion (retaliatory) responses and using them for the benefit of patients rather than in a purely punitive way represents a difficult and testing requirement if analytic therapy is to be successful (Racker 1968). Furthermore, there is no way out of this by therapists' denying to themselves such feelings, for that introduces a dangerous falsity into the therapeutic relationship.

An even more important test for therapists centres round the handling of the way in which their patients treat them when they are (albeit unconsciously) attempting to establish object-relationships with their therapists and learning 'object-usage' (Winnicott 1974). Patients are trying out their therapists to see what they are made of. They seek to attack, intrude, dominate and cast their analysts away; they project upon them and transfer to them images that are sometimes wildly beside the mark and often insulting in a variety of ways. Sometimes patients draw their therapists into 'mirroring' qualities that are potential but not yet quite realized within them and are emerging as somewhat crude, primitive – and disconcerting (Winnicott 1974). Therapists under such pressure therefore need a firm sense of identity and boundaries if they are not to become deeply confused – though sometimes they need to live through just such confusion.

To feel able and willing to undergo the gruelling and testing process just described requires strong motivation, endurance, reliability, physical robustness and a capacity for a flexible adaptation in terms of deinte-gration and reintegration. Many therapists also feel that the release of gratitude within them towards their own analysts for their care and tolerance can provide motive power for the sustained work of therapy on behalf of their own patients in their turn. Also present in many therapists are reparative feelings. When in their own analysis therapists become aware of the destructive forces within them – particularly in relation to members of their own family, and their own analysts – they may discover within themselves intense drives towards therapeutic reparation.

A further motivation and reward is discovered in the intense interest of the many and varied experiences that come day by day within the pur-view of a therapist.

Finally, there is the question of the financial rewards. Fees are established on the piecemeal basis, i.e. payment per session within the context of a commitment on the part of therapists to work with patients for so many hours a week for as long ahead as the treatment requires.

The payment is for the provision of skill, care, patience, endurance, commitment and reliability, and also as some sort of compensation for the psychic erosion and damage that may be sustained by therapists as a result of the rage and destructive impulses of their patients. The corollary of that from the patient's point of view is that he is involved in summoning up his courage and mastering his compunction sufficiently to express emotionally and verbally such destructive or other wishes against the therapist upon whom he depends. The therapy becomes effective when the patient perceives that he has not destroyed his therapist; but this does not mean that the analyst may not sustain some damage.

Therapeutic style

From one point of view, therapeutic style is felt by Jungians to be what the individual finds he is comfortable with (Fordham et al. 1974). There may be discerned, however, certain general styles that are shared by groups of analysts who understand each other reasonably well.

At the beginning Freud and Jung shared a common style, therapy being shaped by the following factors: the use of the couch; the practice of free associative communication on the part of the patient; an absence of much in the way of directiveness on the part of the analyst, including a paucity of advice; interventions by the analyst being largely shaped by making analytical interpretations central to his communications; interpretations being largely of transference and resistance; dreams being understood as 'symbolic' or 'sign' expressions of unconscious processes; constructions or reconstructions being designed to demonstrate how complexes came into being in childhood; transferences being analysed as from childhood figures and interrelationships on to the analyst's person and the analytic relationship.

The style was quiet, in the main reasonable, non-directive and exploratory. Listening was an art to perfect. The analyst was to act mainly as a mirror or a screen on to which the patient spontaneously projected his unconscious contents. The patient was 'under' the analyst, according to certain traditional viewpoints in medicine.

When Jung separated from Freud, he tended to dissociate himself from many of Freud's practices in a kind of reaction against them. Thus he began to reject the couch, with its asymmetrical patient-therapist implications, and to use the chair according to an 'eyeball to eyeball' and symmetrical model of patient-therapist relationship. He neglected the 'reduction to early childhood' kind of interpretation more and more in favour of concentrating on adult archetypal patternings in the here and now (Jung 1953). He withdrew, to a degree, interest from the past in favour of a progressive interest in the future. He concentrated on the realization of the self as a dynamic bipolar system of opposites developing new levels of integration through the synthesizing effects of the *transcendent function*.

Later analytical psychology has found it necessary to develop Jungian studies in child development and to bring psychoanalytically originated methods, including a renewed use of the couch, into the service of Jungian therapy without seriously modifying Jung's spontaneity and interactional way of practising therapy (cf. Fordham 1978; Lambert 1981b).

To sum up this sort of development, a London Jungian would recognize more clearly than did Jung the essentially asymmetrical aspect of the therapeutic relationship in its nature. He would therefore feel responsible for the treatment and fully realize the patient's dependency need for another person to analyse what he spontaneously expresses. If he cannot thus depend on the therapist, the spontaneity of his free communication becomes cramped. Therefore, while the analyst's style needs to be alive, dialectical and interactional, it nevertheless needs to be expressed in terms of a 'low profile'. He needs to find a position which is not too intrusive for his patient but at the same time not too distant either. His responsibility towards his patient is shown in his generally reliable availability at the times arranged save at times of illness or crisis or necessary holidays. The latter, ideally, should be known by patients in advance so that they can arrange for their holidays to coincide with those of the therapist.

Other areas where the therapist takes responsibility include his indicating to the patient, if necessary, that he would like him to use the couch and his claiming the right to investigate and interpret if the patient feels unwilling. He is in a good position to know that, other things being equal, the physical position in which people find themselves on the couch promotes that looser, more associative flow of thoughts and feelings that is needed by many cramped and repressed people (Rubinfine 1967). Finally, in implementing by action his understanding of the importance to the patient of the regular physical presence of the therapist the latter may facilitate transference projections upon such elements of his many-sided personality as may be helpful.

Major therapeutic techniques

In view of the fact that the analysis of the psychodynamics of the patient is the central aim and that much of what happens emerges from unconscious levels in the patient, modern Jungian therapy uses free associative techniques of a mainly non-directive sort. During the opening sessions an assessment is made in connection with the number of sessions a week that would be necessary to make possible the appropriate depth of analysis. Thus evidence of serious privation, deprivation or damage sustained during early infancy makes it likely that four or five sessions a week are required, while problems of development in the context of a less unfavourable background can sometimes be managed on less.

The major techniques employed frequently include the use of the couch, free association and a close and detailed analysis of the patient-therapist interaction which involves, as a major factor, the analysis of the transference. Communication on the patient's part is not directed or interfered with. It is generally verbal communication about feelings, events, fantasies, dreams as they come to mind – concerning anything, including thoughts and feelings about the therapist. Sometimes useful communication can also be made through painting, drawing and modelling.

The whole process of freely associative communication may be understood as a skill that patients can slowly acquire. Often therapists are in a position to help by understanding and analysing fears, hesitations and resistances, and by naming the often inchoate feelings and thoughts that are beginning to manifest themselves in the patient's consciousness. This latter is especially important in cases where a privation of the 'mirroring' and 'naming' mother has occurred.

Dreams are interpreted within the context of the patient's life circumstances, including the therapeutic relationship and transference – but very seldom in isolation from that context (Lambert 1981b). Patients' reports of material occurring outside the session are assessed by comparison with what goes on inside the session. Direct advice is seldom given, though life problems, especially with younger people, are discussed and as far as possible related to the patient's psychodynamics. In understanding and interpreting the transference the analyst learns to use his own responses and counter-transferences as sources of information about the responses and transferences of the patient (cf. Fordham 1978; Lambert 1981b).

In the earlier phases of treatment, modern Jungians in London make use of reconstruction, the analysis of resistance and defences and an analysis of the patients' capacity for object-relationships and for internalizing objects (cf. Fordham 1978; Lambert 1981b).

The change process in therapy

That change processes in Jungian analytical therapy do take place, in a way that is a clear experience for the patient and easily discernible to the therapist and others, can by now be hardly doubted. For that to be predictable, however, much depends upon the problem of the selection of patients who are likely to benefit from the analytic process. They need to show signs of insight, interest in their inner world, some ability to communicate and not too calamitous and destructive a history (Edwards 1983). Granted this, plus the means to finance treatment, plus the time, opportunity and a geographical location which enables them to visit the therapist regularly, then something like a prediction that they will benefit and change is possible. The right conditions must nevertheless be provided by the therapist. A suitable environment is a room that is warm enough and quiet enough and, in principle, free from interruptions; in it there should be a couch with a rug and cushions and two armchairs. There must be an analyst who is able to listen and use words in an appropriate way and to gear into the patients' language in a benign and realistic way. If, however, the patient is not insightful, uninterested in his inner world and uncommunicative, all is not lost: in these cases what becomes essential is the therapist's analytic insight and understanding grasp of the situation. He does not communicate much of this to the patient, who is not yet able to be interested in meaning but interested mainly in the discharge of unbearable tension. A good example of this is the narcissistic personality disorder described by Kohut (1971, 1977). The patient has countered early privation by developing a do-it-yourself psychology whereby he develops a grandiose self, albeit with a hollow centre, and looks everywhere for idealized perfect parents who always turn out to be devils. Provided the therapist can understand the situation analytically and, so to speak, stay with the patient's rejection and hate-filled abuse of him, the time may come when the patient can become able to cope with analytic psychotherapy.

In the case of the neurotic patient who can benefit from analytical psychotherapy, some of the change processes often observed may be described as follows:

(a) Analytic repair processes may be applied to damage done to the child's sense of security in the early months and years of infancy as a result of the privation of the sustaining presence of the parental pair through the latter's illness, depression, or neglectful unreliability – to say nothing of death. The results of this issue forth as the destruction of basic trust; as crippling, rage-filled suspicion of the motives, even of people of good enough will; and as fear of change itself, even when it is for the better. There is plenty of evidence to suggest that each one of these distortions of good faith, and many more, can be considerably modified in time through the analysis of how they came about and the provision of reliable care on the part of the therapist. The changes involved are those that arise out of *repair*.

(b) Blocks in the development of talents of, for instance, an artistic or administrative or business sort, or, on the other hand, of capacities for friendship and relationship, may be modified or diminished through the analytic and validating work of the therapist. These releases are often accompanied by feelings of joy never before experienced by the patient.

It is possible to affirm that the changes just outlined belong to the processes of *individuation*.

(c) Changes connected with the conscious realization and understanding of the counter-polar processes of the self and the way in which persona and shadow, good and evil, male and female, youth and age, consciousness and unconsciousness may transcend their opposites through the operation of the transcendent function. There are also internal archetypal changes, such as death and rebirth, that may be hinted at by symbolic dream imagery. In this case we are dealing with *integrative* changes whereby the person involved experiences subjectively a new sense of sureness and balance, while, objectively, his self may be perceived to be more whole and integrated.

These sorts of change are fostered in a safe therapeutic situation in which the patient develops through his transference relationship with the therapist and through their relationship as real persons. The understanding, the naming and the interpretations of the analyst all assist the growth and strength of the patient's ego-consciousness. This enables the patient to become better able to modify the archetypes, the defences, the resistances and the internalized archetypal objects within his psyche. The ego becomes the self on its conscious side and can even become strong enough to stand aside at times, to relinquish its controlling and organizing function and let the creative innovations through from the centre of the personality as, indeed, notably happens in the case of great artists – such as, for instance, Mozart and Beethoven.

Case Example

A literary-minded woman in her forties entered analytic psychotherapy feeling unfulfilled, though married with grown-up children and successful in a small business run on very personal lines. In it she combined flair and energetic boldness with a ruthless clarity of mind while maintaining good relations with both staff and customers. Underneath a bright and cheerful front, however, and at a deeper level, she could occasionally sense an anxiety that was frighteningly pervasive.

My patient had married young – to get away from home – a husband more overtly anxious and, to her mind, obsessionally cautious about details. Babies had seemed messy and boring, but though she had felt too young, she had brought up three children who lacked academic interest but became successful at business. As the children grew up, she found within herself increased capacities for social extroversion and acquired male friends who could be intellectually stimulating and sympathetic but who irritated and frustrated her by tentative and unfulfilled personality traits.

Further communications to me suggested the development of strong defences against depression and anticipatory fear of bankruptcy and poverty. She was plagued by these when she was alone. To counter that depressive anxiety she had succeeded in generating feelings of endless 'vitality' and 'activity'. In the company of some she could become 'the life and soul of the party'; in that of others, she fell into dead boredom. Sexually, she could swing between quiet, loving relationships that nevertheless threatened boredom on the one hand, and on the other, terrified sado-masochistic fantasies of a male sexual brutality that, in practice, she mainly avoided. In general relationships as well, a new awareness was developing that behind her conscious, interested care of others she was dominated by an intense need to please others and be loved by them; at the same time, however, she was apt to be seized by short-lived outbursts of really murderous rage against anyone who crossed her need for admiring validation and love.

The manic defences described above, together with her high estimation of intellectual interests and her philosophical disapproval of depression, began to become more and more understandable as information about her home background and childhood emerged and could be pieced together. She had been raised in a family that was, in fact, economically and culturally inadequate to meet the expectations and needs of this able, intelligent child. There had been emotional inadequacy, too. Her mother was kindly, but failed as a responsible adult to spend the housekeeping money wisely or manage meals in time for her daughter during the lunch break at school; she had had to borrow her daughter's pocket money and had landed her into a great deal of shopping and cooking at a time when she was already stretched by school and homework. As a result, the daughter had become more and more incensed with rage and ran distinctly short on compassion. As for the father, he had seemed to her mean, opinionated, angry and disgruntled – ugly, a thorn in her flesh – always disagreeing with her ideas and frustrating any plans to put them into action. In addition, her brother had died and her sister had had a breakdown over the death. The sum of these relationship difficulties and the family depression and calamities supported the 'omnipotence' and 'omniscience' of my lively patient, who became 'the able one' of the family while longing passionately to escape from its cramp and depression.

My patient had felt instinctively that it would be by means of her intelligence and intellect that she would succeed in getting away, and so lived an isolated, studious life while at school. Under the important inspiration of an able woman teacher she had managed to win a scholarship to a good university. There, after faltering a bit at first, she had obtained a good degree – with the encouragement this time of an admired and distinguished professor. After this she had gone on to teach, to marry, to go abroad, to bring up children and to succeed at business.

In all this it was clear that history was repeating itself. The emotions of depression and belligerence that had marked her experience of her primary family were being reactivated by marriage and her new family. This time, however, the depression, boredom and anger were more successfully defended against and kept at bay. She could avoid being 'swallowed up' or cramped by them: she could expand outwards in her business life and the manic atmosphere of the 'market-place'. The cost, however, was considerable, for she became more manically over-controlled and more extroverted than was really suited to her nature.

Her treatment involved a reconstruction of the relationships and attitudes of her history and the way in which she had been pushed into a heroic do-it-yourself psychology. She was helped to realize how much the uncomfortable and unhappy feelings needed to be acknowledged and understood. For a long time she treated me as if I were an idealized 'good' figure that might counter her unfavourable family matrix: a kind of guru, teacher or professor, and yet unobtainable. The negative side of the transference showed itself in her difficulty in making use of my attempts to point out and interpret her aggression, her disapproval of depression, her perfectionist criticism of herself and others, and the degree of the violence of her rage against weak, cautious and tentative men – especially if they crossed her or dared to criticize her. Deeper down, the transference to me was of her unhelpful, critical father.

In general she hated the way in which the underside of her manic efficiency plagued her with its depression, floating guilt, general malaise, fear and irritability. During this period also she began to experience consciously a much more frightened and prudish attitude towards sexuality than she had previously allowed her conscious, sexually liberated self to feel. On one occasion she and her sister became disproportionately critical in destructive ways and angrily repressive of the sexual verbal expressions and sexual pop songs loved by the adolescents of the family. I had fairly firmly pointed this out and had drawn attention to the disproportionate intensity of the feelings involved. Soon afterwards, she had the following dream, replete with archetypal imagery:

> I come to a round pool on the surface of which a mackintosh had been laid out and was floating. Seated on the mackintosh was a beautiful young boy. I thought it would be very nice to sit next to the boy, and I felt sure I could

snuggle up beside him without getting my dress wet and spoilt in the water. At that moment I saw an enormous woman standing behind the boy. Apparently, this huge lady was a therapist and was bringing the boy up perfectly by means of her skill and insights, and had warned me against spoiling her work by talking to the boy. She now criticized me for having spoilt all her work with the boy by what I had done. I became furiously angry with the woman, yelling at the top of my voice how horribly unfair and cruel she was when I had done nothing to the boy and had said nothing to him. I could have killed her.

She realized that the image of the huge lady so skilful with the boy must represent an idealization and magnification of me in archetypal terms. She also realized that the anger against the big woman represented how angry she was with me for interpreting her sexual fears in a way that seemed critical. The fear of getting her dress wet links with her fear of the mess and disorder in sexual life; but the fear, the dream suggests, hampers the growth of the beautiful boy, who surely represents her newly potential masculine self hitherto projected on to men. My patient could see the pool as herself and her depths; as a place of transformation and change; as a mandala. The incongruous mackintosh turned out to be the name of a conservative, timid, orderly and safety-seeking branch of her family – it 'protects' her from the depths. The therapist is made female through fear of man, through homosexual feelings and a need for an improved mother image. In her next dream, a brutal soldier was about to rape her daughter whom she saved by taking him on herself. He led her away and then vanished: was the male threat overestimated, or did she magic him away? In the next dream, she found a woman in a coffin lying in shallow water. The woman was wrapped in a mackintosh. It fell away from her, and she could see that the woman was still alive. Two or three sessions later she told me she had become convinced that all her life she had unconsciously believed that she had killed her father, and that this belief lay behind most of her depressions, anxieties, guilt feelings, demoralization and craving to be loved and accepted.

In her treatment, my holding function involved the provision of plenty of time and breathing space, and demanded from me listening, the facilitation of growth, and a relating to her that avoided intrusiveness. I reconstructed the origins of her attitudes and object-relationships in the context of the transference. This enabled her to understand the ruthless, if not murderous and enraged, feelings behind her emotionally isolated life and how that isolation in turn left her at the mercy of archetypal images and themes.

It was the provision of myself as a flesh and blood therapeutic companion that modified and personalized the archetypes. This modified her manic defences, anxiety and depression, deepened her personality and improved her relationships.

References

Bion W R (1983) 'Learning from experience' in Bion W R *The Seven Servants*, Jason Aronson, New York

Edwards A (1983) Research studies in the problems of assessment, *Journal of Analytical Psychology* 28: 299–311

Fordham M (1957) *New Developments in Analytical Psychology*, Routledge and Kegan Paul, London

Fordham M (1969) *Children as Individuals*, Hodder and Stoughton, London

Fordham M (1978) *Jungian Psychotherapy*, Wiley, Chichester

Fordham M, Gordon R, Hubback J, Lambert K (eds.) (1974) *Technique in Jungian Analysis 2*, Academic Press, London

Freud S (1900) *The Interpretation of Dreams*, standard edition 4 and 5, Hogarth, London

Hillman J (1975) *Revisioning Psychology*, Harper & Row, London

Jung C G (1953) *Two Essays in Analytical Psychology*, Collected Works 7, Routledge and Kegan Paul, London

Jung C G (1954) The practical use of dream analysis in Jung C G *The Practice of Psychotherapy*, Collected Works 16, Routledge and Kegan Paul, London

Jung C G (1956) *Symbols of Transformation*, Collected Works 5, Routledge and Kegan Paul, London

Jung C G (1959) *Aion*, Collected Works 9:2, Routledge and Kegan Paul, London

Jung C G (1963) *Memories, Dreams, Reflections*, Routledge and Kegan Paul, London

Jung C G (1971) *Psychological Types*, Collected Works 6, Routledge and Kegan Paul, London

Jung C G (1977) 'The Tavistock lectures: on analytical psychology in theory and in practice' in Jung C G *The Symbolic Life*, Collected Works 18, Routledge and Kegan Paul, London

Kohut H (1971) *The Analysis of the Self*, International University Press, New York

Kohut H (1977) *The Restoration of the Self*, International University Press, New York

Lambert K (1981a) Emerging consciousness, *Journal of Analytical Psychology* 26: 1–17

Lambert K (1981b) *Analysis, Repair and Individuation,* Academic Press, London

McGuire W (ed.) (1974) *The Freud-Jung Letters,* Hogarth, London

Odajnyk V W (1976) *Jung and Politics: The Political and Social Ideas of C G Jung,* New York Publishing Press, New York

Racker H (1968) *Transference and Counter-Transference,* Hogarth, London

Redfearn J W T (1983) Ego and self: terminology, *Journal of Analytical Psychology* 28: 91–106

Rubinfine D I (1967) Notes on the theory of reconstruction, *British Journal of Medical Psychology* 40: 195–205

Samuels A (1983) The emergence of schools of post-Jungian analytical psychology, *Journal of Analytical Psychology* 28: 345–362

Schwartz-Salant N (1982) *Narcissism and Character Transformation,* Inner City Books, Toronto

Truax C G, Carkhuff R R (1967) *Towards Effective Counselling and Psychotherapy,* Aldine, Chicago

Winnicott D W (1958a) 'The observation of infants in a set situation' in Winnicott D W, *Collected Papers: Through Paedriatrics to Psychoanalysis,* Hogarth, London

Winnicott D W (1958b) 'Mind and its relation to the psyche-soma' in Winnicott D W *Collected Papers: Through Paedriatrics to Psychoanalysis,* Hogarth, London

Winnicott D W (1964) Review of Jung C G *Memories Dreams Reflections International Journal of Psychoanalysis* 45: 450–455

Winnicott D W (1965) 'The theory of the parent-infant relationship' in Winnicott D W *The Maturational Processes and the Facilitating Environment,* Hogarth, London

Winnicott D W (1974a) 'The use of an object and relating through identifications' in Winnicott D W *Playing and Reality,* Penguin, Harmondsworth

Winnicott D W (1974b) 'The mirror-role of mother and family in child development' in Winnicott D W *Playing and Reality,* Penguin, Harmondsworth

Suggested Further Reading

Fordham M (1974), Gordon R, Hubback J, Lambert K (eds.) *Technique in Jungian Analysis,* Academic Press, London

Fordham M (1978) *Jungian Psychotherapy,* Wiley, Chichester

Jung C G (1953) *Two Essays on Analytical Psychology,* Collected Works 7, Routledge and Kegan Paul, London

Jung C G (1954) *The Practice of Psychotherapy,* Collected Works 16, Routledge and Kegan Paul, London

Lambert K (1981) *Analysis, Repair and Individuation,* Academic Press, London

Chapter 5 Person-Centred Therapy

Brian Thorne

Historical Context and Developments in Britain

Historical context

Dr Carl Rogers, the American psychologist and founder of what has now become known as person-centred counselling or psychotherapy, has always claimed to be grateful that he never had one particular mentor. He has been influenced by many significant figures, often holding widely differing viewpoints; but above all he claims to be the student of his own experience and of that of his clients and colleagues.

While accepting Rogers's undoubtedly honest claim about his primary sources of learning, there is much about his thought and practice which places him within a recognizable tradition. Oatley (1981) has recently described this as 'the distinguished American tradition exemplified by John Dewey: the tradition of no nonsense, of vigorous self-reliance, of exposing oneself thoughtfully to experience, practical innovation, and of careful concern for others'. In fact, in 1925, while still a student at Teachers College, Columbia, Rogers was directly exposed to Dewey's thought and to progressive education through his attendance at a course led by the famous William Heard Kilpatrick, a student of Dewey and himself a teacher of extraordinary magnetism. Not that Dewey and Kilpatrick formed the mainstream of the ideas to which Rogers was introduced during his professional training and early clinical experience; indeed, when he took up his first appointment in 1928 as a member of the child study department of the Society for the Prevention of Cruelty to Children in Rochester, New York, he joined an institution where the three fields of psychology, psychiatry and social work were combining forces in diagnosing and treating problems. This context appealed to Rogers's essentially pragmatic temperament.

Rogers's biographer, Kirschenbaum (1979), while acknowledging the variety of influences to which Rogers was subjected at the outset of his professional career, suggests nevertheless that when he went to Rochester he saw himself essentially as a diagnostician and as an interpretative therapist whose goal, very much in the analytical tradition, was to help a child or a parent gain insight into his own behaviour and motivation. Diagnosis and interpretation are far removed from the primary concerns of a contemporary person-centred therapist, and in an important sense Rogers's progressive disillusionment with both these activities during his time at Rochester marks the beginning of his own unique approach. He tells the story of how near the end of his time at Rochester he had been working with a highly intelligent mother whose son was presenting serious behavioural problems. Rogers was convinced that the root of the trouble lay in the mother's early rejection of the boy, but no amount of gentle strategy on his part could bring her to this insight. In the end he gave up, and they were about to part when she asked if adults were taken for counselling on their own account. When Rogers assured her that they were, she immediately requested help for herself and launched into an impassioned outpouring of her own despair, marital difficulties, confusion and sense of failure. Real therapy, it seems, began at that moment, and it was ultimately successful. Rogers (cited in Kirschenbaum 1979) commented:

> This incident was one of a number which helped me to experience the fact – only fully realized later – that it is the client who knows what hurts, what direction to go, what problems are crucial, what experiences have been deeply buried. It began to occur to me that unless I had a need to demonstrate my own cleverness and learning, I would do better to rely upon the client for the direction of movement in the process.

The essential step from diagnosis and interpretation to listening had been taken, and from that point onwards Rogers was launched on his own path.

By 1940 Rogers was a professor of psychology at Ohio State University, and his first book, *Counseling and Psychotherapy*, appeared two years later. From 1945 to 1957 he was professor of psychology at Chicago and director of the university counselling centre. This was a period of intense activity, not least in the research field. Rogers's pragmatic nature had led to much research being carried out into person-centred therapy. With the publication in 1951 of *Client-Centred Therapy*, he became a major force in the world of psychotherapy and established his position as a practitioner, theorist and researcher who warranted respect. In an address to the American Psychological Association in 1973, he maintained that during this Chicago period he had for the first time been giving clear expression to an idea whose time had come. The idea 'was the gradually formed and tested hypothesis that the individual has within himself vast resources for self-understanding, for altering his self concept, his attitudes, and his self-directed behavior – and that these resources can be tapped if only a definable climate of facilitative psychological attitudes can be provided' (Rogers 1974).

From this 'gradually formed and tested hypothesis' non-directive therapy was born as a protest against the diagnostic, prescriptive point of view prevalent at the time. Emphasis was placed on a relationship between counsellor and client based upon acceptance and clarification. This was a period, too, of excitement generated by the use of recorded interviews for research and training purposes, and there was a focus on non-directive techniques. Those coming for help were no longer referred to as 'patients' but as 'clients', with the inference that they were self-responsible human beings, not objects for treatment. As experience increased and both theory-building and research developed, the term 'client-centred therapy' was adopted, which put the emphasis on the internal world of the client and focused attention on the attitudes of the therapist towards his client rather than on particular techniques. The term 'person-centred' has won Rogers's approval in the last decade because it can be applied to the many fields outside therapy where his ideas are becoming increasingly accepted and valued and because in the therapy context itself it underlines the person-to-person nature of the interaction where not only the phenomenological world of the client but also the therapist's state of being are of crucial significance. This 'I-Thou' quality of the therapeutic relationship indicates a certain kinship with the existential philosophy of Kierkegaard and Buber, and the stress on personal experience recalls the work of the British philosopher/scientist Michael Polanyi (whom Rogers knew and admired). In recent times, too, Rogers himself has reported his own deepening respect for certain aspects of Zen teaching and has become fond of quoting sayings of Lao-Tsu, especially those that stress the undesirability of imposing on people instead of allowing them the space in which to find themselves.

Developments in Britain

Although Rogers's influence percolated spasmodically into Britain in the post-war years – mainly through the work of the National Marriage Guidance Council, and then often in an unacknowledged form – it was not until the mid-1960s that his ideas came to be studied in depth in British universities. Interestingly enough, the reason for this development was the establishment of the first training courses in Britain for school counsellors. These programmes (initially at the Universities of Keele and Reading) were largely dependent in their first years on American Fulbright professors of psychology or counselling, many of whom were steeped in the client-centred tradition and introduced their British students to both the theory and practice of client-centred therapy. It is therefore with the growth of counselling in Britain that Rogers's work has become more widely known, and it is probably true to say that the largest recognizable group of person-centred practitioners currently working in Britain are counsellors operating within the educational sector. It is also significant that when Rogers started working in the 1920s psychologists in America were not permitted to practise psychotherapy, so he called his activity 'counselling'. British practitioners have tended to use the word 'counsellor' and to eschew the word 'psychotherapist', for perhaps different reasons: they have seen the word 'psychotherapist' as somehow conducive to an aura of mystification and expertise which runs counter to the egalitarian relationship which the person-centred approach seeks to establish between therapist and client. In the last decade, thanks partly to the growth of the Association for Humanistic Psychology in Britain, there are many signs that the person-centred approach is moving out of the educational arena and making its impact felt more widely. The work of the British Centre of the Facilitator Development Institute (founded in 1974 on the initiative of Rogers's close associate, Dr Charles Devonshire) has introduced person-centred ideas to a wide variety of psychologists, social workers, psychiatrists and others; while the establishment in 1980 of the Norwich Centre for Personal and Professional Development has given Britain its first independent therapy and training agency committed to the person-centred approach.

Theoretical Assumptions

The image of the person

The person-centred therapist starts from the assumption that both he and his client are trustworthy. This trust resides in the belief that every organism – the human being included – has an underlying and instinctive movement towards the constructive accomplishment of its inherent potential. Rogers (1979) has often recalled a boyhood memory of his parents' potato bin in which they stored their winter supply of these vegetables: this bin was placed in the basement several feet below a small window, and yet despite the highly unfavourable conditions the potatoes would nevertheless begin to send out spindly shoots groping towards the distant light of the window. He has compared these pathetic potatoes in their desperate struggle to develop with clients whose lives have been warped by circumstances and experience but who continue against all the odds to strive towards growth, towards becoming. This directional (actualizing) tendency in the human being can be trusted, and the therapist's task is to help create the best possible conditions for its fulfilment.

In recent years the person-centred approach has been criticized by many who see the emphasis on the trustworthiness of the human organism as too optimistic, even naive. Theologians amongst others have suggested that the person-centred view of man does not deal with the problem of evil or with the dark side of human nature. Rogers (1979) has attempted to counter this accusation by pointing to a formative tendency in the universe – and in support of this he draws on some of the latest advances in biology – which in no sense denies the fact of entropy, the tendency towards disorder and deterioration. The universe, it seems, is always building and creating as well as deteriorating and dying. The same process, Rogers maintains, is at work in the human being; and it is therefore altogether legitimate to trust the actualizing tendency without thereby closing one's eyes to or attempting to obscure the fact of the life-negating forces in human development.

The elevated view of human nature which the person-centred therapist holds is paralleled by his insistence on individual uniqueness. He believes that no two persons are ever alike and that the human personality is so complex that no diagnostic labelling of persons can ever be fully justified. Indeed, the person-centred therapist knows that he cannot hope to

It is easier to talk about your feeling
towards others than feeling
~~to~~ about yourself. Yet it's
easier
~~to talk~~ to criticise yourself
than others. (Peru)

Mail Distribution LHR

uncover fully the subjective perceptual world of the client and that the client himself can do this only with great effort. Furthermore, the client's perceptual world will be determined by the experiences he has rejected or assimilated into the self-concept.

Concepts of psychological health and disturbance

The self-concept is of crucial importance in person-centred therapy and needs to be distinguished from the self. Nelson-Jones (1982) has made the helpful distinction of regarding the self as the real, underlying organismic self – that is, the essentially trustworthy human organism which is discernible in the physiological processes of the entire body and through the growth process by which potentialities and capacities are brought to realization – and contrasting this with the self-concept which is a person's conceptual construction of himself (however poorly articulated) and which does not by any means always correspond with the direct and untrammelled experiencing of the organismic self.

The self-concept develops over time and is heavily dependent on the attitudes of those who constitute the individual's significant others. It follows therefore that where a person is surrounded by those who are quick to condemn or punish (however subtly) the behaviour which emanates from the experiencing of the organismic self, he or she will become rapidly confused. The need for positive regard or approval from others is overwhelming and is present from earliest infancy. If therefore behaviour arising from what is actually experienced by the individual fails to win approval, an immediate conflict is established. A baby, for example, may gain considerable satisfaction or relief from howling full-throatedly but may then quickly learn that such behaviour is condemned or punished by the mother; at this point the need to win the mother's approval is in immediate conflict with the promptings of the organismic self, which wishes to howl. The result may be a cessation of howling or a continuation of howling which is now, however, experienced increasingly as reprehensible by the howler. The organismic self which enjoyed howling is under censure and is therefore no longer fully to be trusted. Instead, the individual begins to construct a self-concept which may eventually transmit the message that howling is wrong and the desire to howl a sign of weakness or even malevolence. If the message 'I am weak and evil because I want to howl' is too intolerable, it may even be converted into 'I do not wish to howl because I am a good boy (or girl).' Whatever the outcome, the original promptings of the organismic self are now no longer a trustworthy guide to acceptable behaviour and may indeed gradually cease to be accessible to consciousness.

If individuals are unfortunate enough to be brought up amongst a number of significant others who are highly censorious or judgemental, a self-concept can develop which may serve to estrange them almost totally from their organismic experiencing. In such cases the self-concept, often developed after years of oppression of the organismic self, becomes the fiercest enemy of the self and must undergo radical transformation if the actualizing tendency is to reassert itself.

The person-centred therapist is constantly working with clients who have all but lost touch with the actualizing tendency within themselves and who have been surrounded by others who have no confidence in the innate capacity of human beings to move towards the fulfilment of their potential. Psychologically healthy persons, on the other hand, are men and women who have been lucky enough to live in contexts which have been conducive to the development of self-concepts which allow them to be in touch for at least some of the time with their deepest experiences and feelings without having to censure them or distort them. Such people are well placed to achieve a level of psychological freedom which will enable them to move in the direction of becoming more fully functioning persons. 'Fully functioning' is a term used by Rogers to denote individuals who are using their talents and abilities, realizing their potential and moving towards a more complete knowledge of themselves. They are demonstrating what it means to have attained a high level of psychological health, and Rogers has outlined some of the major personality characteristics which they seem to have in common. The first and most striking characteristic is openness to experience. Individuals who are open to experience are able to listen to themselves and to others and to experience what is happening without feeling threatened. They demonstrate a high level of awareness, especially in the world of the feelings. Secondly, and allied to this characteristic, is the ability to live fully in each moment of one's existence. Experience is trusted rather than feared and is therefore the moulding force for the emerging personality rather than being twisted or manipulated to fit some preconceived structure of reality or some rigidly safeguarded self-concept. The third characteristic is the organismic trusting which is so clearly lacking in those who have constantly fallen victims to the adverse judgements of others. Such trusting is best displayed in the process of decision-making. Whereas many people defer continually to outside sources of influence when making decisions, fully functioning persons regard their organismic experiences as the most valid sources of information for deciding what to do in any given situation. Rogers (1961) put it succinctly when he said, 'doing what "feels right" proves to be a ... trustworthy guide to behavior'. Further characteristics of the fully functioning person are concerned with the issues of personal freedom and creativity. For Rogers, a mark of psychological health is the sense of responsibility for determining one's own actions and their consequences based on a feeling of freedom and power to choose from the many options that life presents. There is no feeling within the individual of being imprisoned by circumstances or fate or genetic inheritance, although this is not to suggest that Rogers denies the powerful influences of biological make-up, social forces or past experience. Subjectively, however, the person experiences himself as a free agent. Finally, the fully functioning person is typically creative in the sense that he or she can adjust to changing conditions and is likely to produce creative ideas or initiate creative projects and actions. Such people are unlikely to be conformists, although they will relate to society in a way which permits them to be fully involved without being imprisoned by convention or tradition.

The acquisition of psychological disturbance

In person-centred terminology, the mother's requirement that the baby cease to howl constitutes a *condition of worth*: 'I shall love you if you do not howl.' The concept of conditions of worth bears a striking similarity to the British therapist George Lyward's notion of contractual living (Burn 1956). Lyward believed that most of his disturbed adolescent clients had had no chance to contact their real selves because they were too busy attempting – usually in vain – to fulfil contracts, in order to win approval. Lyward used to speak of usurped lives, and Rogers, in a similar vein, sees many individuals as the victims of countless internalized conditions of worth which have almost totally estranged them from their organismic experiencing. Such people will be preoccupied with a sense of strain at having to come up to the mark or with feelings of worthlessness at having failed to do so. They will be the victims of countless introjected conditions of worth so that they no longer have any sense of their inherent value as unique persons. The proliferation of introjections is an inevitable outcome of the desperate need for positive regard. Introjection is the process whereby the beliefs, judgements, attitudes or values of another person (most often the parent) are taken into the individual and become part of his or her armamentarium for coping with experience, however alien they may have been initially. The child, it seems, will do almost anything to satisfy the need for positive regard even if this means taking on board (introjecting) attitudes and beliefs which run quite counter to its own organismic reaction to experience. Once such attitudes and beliefs have become thoroughly absorbed into the personality they are said to have become internalized. Thus it is that introjection and intern-alization of conditions of worth imposed by significant others whose approval is desperately desired often constitute the gloomy road to a deeply negative self-concept as the individual discovers that he can never come up to the high demands and expectations which such conditions inevitably imply.

Once this negative self-concept has taken root in an individual the likelihood is that the separation from the essential organismic self will become increasingly complete. It is as if the person becomes cut off from his own inner resources and his own sense of value and is governed by a secondary and treacherous valuing process which is based on the internal-ization of other people's judgements and evaluations. Once caught in this trap the person is likely to become increasingly disturbed, for the negative self-concept induces behaviour which reinforces the image of inadequacy and worthlessness. It is a fundamental thesis of the person-centred point of view that behaviour is not only the result of what happens to us from the external world but also a function of how we feel about ourselves on the inside. In other words, we are likely to behave in accordance with our conception of ourselves. What we do is often an accurate reflection of how we evaluate ourselves, and if this evaluation is low our behaviour will be correspondingly unacceptable to ourselves and in all probability to others as well. It is likely, too, that we shall be highly conscious of a sense of inadequacy, and although we may conceal this from others the aware-ness that all is not well will usually be with us.

The person-centred therapist recognizes, however, that psychological disturbance is not always available to awareness. It is possible for a per-son to establish a self-concept which, because of the overriding need to win the approval of others, cannot permit highly significant sensory or 'visceral' (a favourite word with Rogers) experience into consciousness. Such a person cannot be open to the full range of his organismic experiencing because to be so would threaten the self-concept which must be maintained in order to win continuing favour. An example of such a person might be the man who has established a picture of himself as honourable, virtuous, responsible and loving. Such a man may be progressively divorced from those feelings which would threaten to undermine such a self-concept. He may arrive at a point where he no longer knows, for example, that he is angry or hostile or sexually hungry, for to admit to such feelings would be to throw his whole picture of himself into question. Disturbed people, therefore, are by no means always aware of their disturbance; nor will they necessarily be perceived as disturbed by others who may have a vested interest in maintaining what is in effect a tragic but often rigorous act of self-deception.

The perpetuation of psychological disturbance

It follows from the person-centred view of psychological disturbance that it will be perpetuated if an individual continues to be dependent to a high degree on the judgement of others for a sense of self-worth. Such persons will be at pains to preserve and defend at all costs the self-concept which wins approval and esteem and will be thrown into anxiety and confusion whenever incongruity arises between the self-concept and actual experience. In the example above the 'virtuous' man would be subject to feelings of threat and confusion if he directly experienced his hostility or sexual hunger, although to do so would, of course, be a first step towards the recovery of contact with the organismic self. He will be likely, however, to avoid the threat and confusion by resorting to one or other of two basic mechanisms of defence: perceptual distortion or denial. In this way he avoids confusion and anxiety and thereby perpetuates his disturbance while mistakenly believing that he is maintaining his integrity. Perceptual distortion takes place whenever an incongruent experience is allowed into awareness but only in a form that is in harmony with the person's current self-concept. The virtuous man, for instance, might permit himself to experience hostility but would distort this as a justifiable reaction to wickedness in others: for him, his hostility would be rationalized into righteous indignation. Denial is a less common defence but is in some ways the more impregnable. In this case, the individual preserves his self-concept by completely avoiding any conscious recognition of experiences or feelings which threaten him. The virtuous man would therefore be totally unaware of his constantly angry attitudes in a committee meeting and might perceive himself as simply speaking with truth and sincerity. Distortion and denial can have formidable psychological consequences and can sometimes protect a person for a lifetime from the confusion and anxiety which could herald the recovery of contact with the alienated self.

For some people it is ironical that the very concept of the fully functioning person serves indirectly to perpetuate their disturbance. It is as if they catch glimpses, in therapy or in their everyday lives, of what it might mean to trust the organismic self but they almost immediately reject this possibility because the established self-concept informs them that to trust themselves in this way would be to move towards a state of total selfishness and self-indulgence. It is as if at such a moment the judgemental voices of parents, teachers and others whose imposed conditions of worth have led to the self-concept in the first place are joined by the full choir of those forces in church and state (and in psychology!) which tell the individual that he can have no confidence in his own capacity for growth.

The suggestion that the fully functioning person is no more than a selfish and self-indulgent hedonist with no sense of a caring, responsible relationship to others and to society is a travesty of the person-centred viewpoint. It is axiomatic for the person-centred therapist that the human organism, when it is trusted, longs for relationship with others and for opportunities to serve and celebrate the wider community. Once again, one is reminded of the experience of George Lyward and his adolescent clients at Finchden Manor. The boys and young men who sought help from Lyward had often been abandoned by orthodox psychiatry and frequently had lengthy records of violence and disruptive behaviour. Once they were welcomed into the community and given the chance to relax and to discover their acceptability, their violent behaviour simply disappeared – sometimes within hours. Gradually it was replaced by a responsiveness to others which indicated an essential gentleness at the core of the personality that had never previously been allowed to find expression. Lyward's experience, which was constantly reinforced over a period of forty years, is a striking example of the truth contained in Rogers's (1964) statement: 'I believe that when the human being is inwardly free to choose whatever he deeply values, he tends to value those objects, experiences, and goals which make for his own survival, growth and development, and for the survival and development of others.' Unfortunately, there are many forces in our society which operate powerfully against the acceptance of such a statement.

Practice

Goals of therapy

The person-centred therapist seeks to establish a relationship with a client in which the latter can gradually dare to face the anxiety and confusion which inevitably arise once the self-concept is challenged by the movement into awareness of experiences which do not fit into its current configuration. If such a relationship can be achieved, the client can then hope to move beyond the confusion and gradually to experience the freedom to choose a way of being which approximates more closely to his or her deepest feelings and values. The therapist will therefore focus not on problems and solutions but on communion or on what has been described as a person-in-person relationship (Boy and Pine 1982). The person-centred therapist does not hesitate therefore to invest himself freely and fully in the relationship with his client. He believes that he will gain entrance into the world of the client through an emotional commitment in which he is willing to involve himself as a person and to reveal himself, if appropriate, with his own strengths and weaknesses. For the person-centred therapist a primary goal is to see, feel and experience the world as the client sees, feels and experiences it, and this is not possible if he stands aloof and maintains a psychological distance in the interests of a quasi-scientific objectivity.

The theoretical end-point of person-centred therapy must be the fully functioning person, who is the embodiment of psychological health and whose primary characteristics were outlined above. It would be fairly safe to assert that no client has achieved such an end-point and that no therapist has been in a position to model such perfection. On the other hand, there is now abundant evidence, not only from America but also, for example, from the extensive research activities of Reinhard Tausch and his colleagues at Hamburg University (Tausch 1975), that clients undergoing person-centred therapy frequently demonstrate similar changes. From my own experience, I can also readily confirm the perception of client movement that Rogers and other person-centred practitioners have repeatedly noted. A listing of these perceptions will show that for many clients the achievement of any one of the developments recorded could well constitute a 'goal' of therapy and might for the time being at least constitute a valid and satisfactory reason for terminating therapy. Clients in person-centred therapy are often perceived to move, then, in the following directions:

(a) away from facades and the constant preoccupation with keeping up appearances;
(b) away from 'oughts' and an internalized sense of duty springing from externally imposed obligations;
(c) away from living up to the expectations of others;
(d) towards valuing honesty and 'realness' in oneself and others;
(e) towards valuing the capacity to direct one's own life;
(f) towards accepting and valuing one's self and one's feelings, whether they are positive or negative;
(g) towards valuing the experience of the moment and the process of growth rather than continually striving for objectives;
(h) towards a greater respect for and understanding of others;
(i) towards a cherishing of close relationships and a longing for more intimacy;
(j) towards a valuing of all forms of experience and a willingness to risk being open to all inner and outer experiences, however uncongenial or unexpected

(Frick 1971)

In his most recent writings Rogers has spoken of a new type of person who, he believes, is emerging in increasing numbers in all cultures and in all parts of the world. This person of the future bears a striking resemblance to the fully functioning person described in his earlier work, and there is little doubt that for the person-centred therapist his work with individual clients is linked to the belief that the survival of the human species may well depend on mankind's increasing ability to be open to experience and to trust the deepest promptings of the human organism. For Rogers himself, this has meant in recent years a willingness to be open to, amongst other things, the world of the paranormal and to engage with the discoveries of modern-day theoretical physics which could leave room for an over-arching spiritual force. To the person-centred therapist all forms of experience warrant attention for they may have concealed within them the meaning and goal of an individual life. Increasingly, too, I myself have come to feel that the more I am able to help my clients explore and validate their own experience the more I may be co-operating with an evolutionary process where the attainment of individual uniqueness and the realization of corporate membership of the human race are part of the same activity.

The person of the therapist

It has often been suggested that of all the various 'schools' of psychotherapy the person-centred approach makes the heaviest demands upon the therapist. Whether this is so or not I have no way of knowing. What I do know is that unless the person-centred therapist can relate in such a way that his client perceives him as trustworthy and dependable *as a person*, therapy cannot take place. The person-centred therapist can have no recourse to diagnostic labelling nor can he find security in a complex and detailed theory of personality which will allow him to foster 'insight' in his client through interpretation, however gently offered. In brief, he cannot win his client's confidence by demonstrating his psychological expertise, for to do so would be to place yet another obstacle in the way of the client's movement towards trusting his own innate resources. To be a trustworthy person is not something which can be simulated for very long, and in a very real sense the person-centred therapist can only be as trustworthy for another as he is for himself. The therapist's attitude to himself thus becomes of cardinal importance. If I am to be acceptant of another's feelings and experiences and to be open to the possible expression of material long since blocked off from awareness, then I must feel a deep level of acceptance for myself. If I cannot trust myself to acknowledge and accept my own feelings without adverse judgement or self-recrimination, it is unlikely that I shall appear sufficiently trustworthy to a client who may have much deeper cause to feel ashamed or worthless. If, too, I am in constant fear that I shall be overwhelmed by an upsurging of unacceptable data into my own awareness, then I am unlikely to convey to my client that I am genuinely open to the full exploration of his own doubts and fears.

The ability of the therapist to be genuine, accepting, and empathic (fundamental attitudes in person-centred therapy which will be explored more fully later) is not developed overnight. It is unlikely, too, that such an ability will be present in someone who is not continually seeking to broaden his own life experience. No therapist can confidently invite his client to travel further than he himself has journeyed, but for the person-centred therapist the quality, depth and continuity of his own experiencing become the very corner-stone of the competence which he brings to his professional activity. Unless I have a sense of my own continuing development as a person I shall lose faith in the process of becoming and shall be tempted to relate to my client in a way which may well reinforce him in a past self-concept. What is more, I shall myself become stuck in a past image of myself and will no longer be in contact with that part of my organism which challenges me to go on growing as a person even if my body is beginning to show every sign of wearing out.

Therapeutic style

Person-centred therapists differ widely in therapeutic style; nevertheless, they all have in common a desire to create a climate of facilitative psychological attitudes in which the client can begin to get in touch with his own wisdom and his capacity for self-understanding and for altering his self-concept and self-defeating behaviours. For the person-centred therapist his ability to establish this climate is crucial to the whole therapeutic enterprise, for if he fails to do so there is no hope of forming the kind of relationship with his client which will bring about the desired therapeutic movement. It will become apparent, however, that the way in which he attempts to create and convey the necessary climate will depend very much on the nature of his own personality.

The first element in the creation of the climate has to do with what has variously been called the therapist's *genuineness*, realness, authenticity or congruence. In essence, this realness depends on the therapist's capacity for being properly in touch with the complexity of feelings, thoughts and attitudes which will be flowing through him as he seeks to track his client's thoughts and feelings. The more he can do this the more he will be perceived by his client as a person of real flesh and blood who is willing to be seen and known, and not as a clinical professional intent on concealing himself behind a metaphorical white coat. The issue of the therapist's genuineness is more complex, however, than it might initially appear. Although the client needs to experience his therapist's essential humanity and to feel his emotional involvement, he certainly does not need to have all the therapist's feelings and thoughts thrust down his throat. The therapist must therefore not only attempt to remain firmly in touch with the flow of his own experience but he must have the discrimination to know how and when to communicate what he is experiencing. It is here that to the objective observer person-centred therapists might well appear to differ widely in style. In my own attempts to be congruent, for example, I find that verbally I often communicate little. I am aware, however, that my bodily posture does convey a deep willingness to be involved with my client and that my eyes are highly expressive of a wide range of feeling – often to the point of tears. It would seem therefore that in my own case there is frequently little need for me to communicate my feelings verbally: I am transparent enough already, and I know from experience that my clients are sensitive to this transparency. Another therapist might well behave in a manner far removed from mine but with the same concern to be genuine. Therapists are just as much unique human beings as their clients, and the way in which they make their humanity available by following the flow of their own experiencing and communicating it when appropriate will be an expression of their own uniqueness. Whatever the precise form of their behaviour, however, person-centred therapists will be exercising their skill in order to communicate to their clients an attitude expressive of their desire to be deeply and fully involved in the relationship without pretence and without the protection of professional impersonality.

For many clients entering therapy, the second attitude of importance in creating a facilitative climate for change – *total acceptance* – may seem to be the most critical. The conditions of worth which have in so many cases warped and undermined the self-concept of the client so that it bears little relation to the actualizing organism are the outcome of the judgemental and conditional attitudes of those close to the client which have often been reinforced by societal or cultural norms. In contrast, the therapist seeks to offer the client an unconditional acceptance, a positive regard or caring, a non-possessive love. This acceptance is not of the person as he might become, a respect for his as yet unfulfilled potential, but a total and unconditional acceptance of the client as he seems to himself *in the present*. Such an attitude on the part of the therapist cannot be simulated and cannot be offered by someone who remains largely frightened or threatened by feelings in himself. Nor again can such acceptance be offered by someone who is disturbed when confronted by a person who possesses values, attitudes and feelings different from his own. Genuine acceptance is totally unaffected by differences of background or belief system between client and therapist for it is in no way dependent on moral, ethical or social criteria. As with genuineness, however, the attitude of acceptance requires great skill on the part of the therapist if it is to be communicated at the depth which will enable the client to feel safe to be whatever he is currently experiencing. After what may well be a lifetime of highly conditional acceptance, the client will not recognize unconditionality easily; when he does, he will tend to regard it as a miracle which will demand continual checking out before it can be fully trusted. The way in which a therapist conveys unconditional acceptance will again be dependent to a large extent on the nature of his or her personality. For my own part, I have found increasingly that the non-verbal aspects of my responsiveness are powerfully effective: a smile can often convey more acceptance than a statement which, however sensitive, may still run the risk of seeming patronizing. I have discovered, too, that the gentle pressing of the hand or the light touch on the knee will enable a client to realize that all is well and that there will be no judgement, however confused or negative he is or however silent and hostile.

The third facilitative attitude is that of *empathic understanding*. Rogers (1975) himself has written extensively about empathy and has suggested that of the three 'core conditions' (as genuineness, acceptance and empathy are often known), empathy is the most trainable. The crucial importance of empathic understanding springs from the person-centred therapist's overriding concern with the client's subjective perceptual world. Only through as full an understanding as possible of the way in which the client views himself and the world can the therapist hope to encourage the subtle changes in self-concept which make for growth. Such understanding involves on the therapist's part a willingness to enter the private perceptual world of his client and to become thoroughly conversant with it. This demands a high degree of sensitivity to the moment-to-moment experiencing of the client so that the therapist is recognized as a reliable companion even when contradictory feelings follow each other in rapid succession. In a certain sense, the therapist must lay himself aside for the time being with all his prejudices and values if he is to enter into the perceptual world of the other. Such an understanding would be foolhardy if the therapist felt insecure in the presence of a particular client, for there would be the danger of getting lost in a perhaps frightening or confusing world. The task of empathic understanding can only be accomplished by a person who is secure enough in his own identity to be able to move into another's world without the fear of being overwhelmed by it. Once there, he has to move around with extreme delicacy and with an utter absence of judgement. He will probably sense meanings of which the client is scarcely aware and might even become dimly aware of feelings of which there is no consciousness on the part of the client at all. Such moments call for extreme caution, for there is the danger that the therapist could express understanding at too deep a level and frighten the client away from therapy altogether. Rogers, on a recording made for *Psychology Today* in the 1970s, has described such a blunder as 'blitz therapy', contrasting this with an empathic response, which is constructive because it conveys an understanding of what is currently going on in the client and of meanings that are just below the level of awareness, but does not slip over into unconscious motivations which frighten the client.

Empathic understanding of the kind that the person-centred therapist seeks to offer is the result of the most intense concentration and requires a form of attentive listening which is remarkably rare. In my own experience, I am still startled and saddened when a client says to me, 'You are the first person who has ever really listened to me' or 'You really do understand what I feel and nobody else ever has.' And yet I am forced to acknowledge that I am offering something which is infinitely precious and which may well be unique in the person's experience.

If the communication of genuineness and acceptance presents difficulties, the communication of empathic understanding is even more challenging. In this domain there can, I believe, be less reliance on non-verbal signals. Often a client's inner world is complex and confusing as well as a source of pain and guilt. Sometimes he has little understanding of his own feelings. The therapist needs therefore to marshal the full range of his own emotional and cognitive abilities if he is to convey his understanding thoroughly. On the other hand, if he does not succeed there is ample evidence to suggest that his very attempt to do so, however bumbling and incomplete, will be experienced by the client as supportive and validating. What is always essential is the therapist's willingness to check out the accuracy of his understanding. I find that my own struggles at communicating empathic understanding are littered with such questions as 'Am I getting it right?' and 'Is that what you mean?' When I do get a complex feeling right, the effect is often electrifying, and the sense of wonder and thankfulness in the client can be one of the most moving experiences in therapy. There can be little doubt that the rarity of empathic understanding of this kind is what endows it with such power and makes it the most reliable force for creative change in the whole of the therapeutic process.

It is Rogers's contention – and one to which he has held firm for over forty years – that if the therapist proves able to offer a facilitative climate where genuineness, acceptance and empathy are all present, then therapeutic movement will almost invariably occur. In such a climate, a client will gradually get in touch with his own resources for self-understanding and prove himself capable of changing his self-concept and taking over the direction of his life. The therapist needs only to be a faithful companion, following the lead which his client provides and staying with him for as long as is necessary. Nothing in my own experience leads me to dispute Rogers's contention that the core conditions are both necessary and sufficient for therapeutic movement, although I have recently argued that when a fourth quality is present, which I have defined as tenderness, then something qualitatively different may occur (Thorne 1983). This fourth quality is characterized chiefly by an ability on the part of the therapist to move between the worlds of the physical, the emotional, the cognitive and the mystical without strain and by a willingness to accept and celebrate the desire to love and to be loved if and when it appears in the therapeutic relationship. I cite my own thinking as evidence for the fact that person-centred theory and practice is in no sense a closed system and is constantly being refined and developed, both by Rogers himself and by other practitioners.

Major therapeutic techniques

There are no techniques which are integral to the person-centred approach. Person-centred therapy is essentially based on the experiencing and communication of attitudes, and these attitudes cannot be packaged up in techniques. At an earlier point in the history of the approach there was an understandable emphasis on the ebb and flow of the therapeutic interview, and much was gained from the microscopic study of client-therapist exchanges. To Rogers's horror, however, the tendency to focus on the therapist's responses had the effect of so debasing the approach that it became known as a technique. Even nowadays it is possible to meet people who believe that person-centred therapy is simply the technique of reflecting the client's feelings or, worse still, that it is primarily a matter of repeating the last words spoken by the client. I hope I have shown that nothing could be farther from the truth. The attitudes required of the therapist demand the highest level of self-knowledge and self-acceptance, and the translation of them into communicable form requires of each therapist the most delicate skill which for the most part must spring from his or her unique personality and cannot be learned through pale imitations of Carl Rogers or anyone else.

The change process in therapy

When person-centred therapy goes well a client will move from a position where his self-concept, typically poor at the entry into therapy and finding expression in behaviour which is reinforcing of the negative evaluation of self, will shift to a position where it more closely approaches the essential worth of the organismic self. As the self-concept moves towards a more positive view so, too, does the client's behaviour begin to reflect the improvement and to enhance further his perception of himself. The therapist's ability to create a relationship in which the three facilitative attitudes are consistently present will play a large part in determining the extent to which the client is able to move towards a more positive perception of himself and to the point where he is able to be in greater contact with the promptings of the organismic self.

If therapy has been successful, the client will also have learned how to be his own therapist. It seems that when a person experiences the genuineness of another and a real attentive caring and valuing by that other person he begins to adopt the same attitude towards himself; in short, a person who is cared for begins to feel at a deep level that perhaps he is after all *worth* caring for. In a similar way, the experience of being on the receiving end of the concentrated listening and the empathic understanding which characterize the therapist's response tends to develop a listening attitude in the client towards himself. It is as if he gradually becomes less afraid to get in touch with what is going on inside him and dares to listen attentively to his own feelings. With this growing attentiveness there comes increased self-understanding and a tentative grasp of some of his most central personal meanings. Many clients have told me that after person-centred therapy they never lose this ability to treat themselves with respect and to take the risk of listening to what they are experiencing. If they do lose it temporarily or find themselves becoming hopelessly confused, they will not hesitate to return to therapy to engage once more in the process, which is in many ways an education for living.

In Rogers and Dymond (1954), one of Rogers's chapters explores in detail a client's successful process through therapy. The case of Mrs Oak has become a rich source of learning for person-centred therapists ever since, and towards the end of the chapter Rogers attempts a summary of the therapeutic process which Mrs Oak has experienced with such obvious benefit to herself. What is described there seems to me to be so characteristic of the person-centred experience of therapy that I make no apology for providing a further summary of some of Rogers's findings.

The process begins with the therapist's providing an atmosphere of warm caring and acceptance which over the first few sessions is gradually experienced by the client, Mrs Oak, as genuinely *safe*. With this realization the client finds that she changes the emphasis of her sessions from dealing with reality problems to experiencing herself. The effect of this change of emphasis is that she begins to experience her feelings in the immediate present without inhibition. She can be angry, hurt, childish, joyful, self-deprecating, self-appreciative; and as she allows this to occur she discovers many feelings bubbling through into awareness of which she was not previously conscious. With new feelings there come new thoughts and the admission of all this fresh material to awareness leads to a *breakdown of the previously held self-concept*. There then follows a period of disorganization and confusion, although there remains a feeling that the path is the right one and that reorganization will ultimately take place. What is being learned during this process is that it pays to recognize an experience for what it is rather than denying it or distorting it; in this way the client becomes more open to experience and begins to realize that it is healthy to accept feelings, whether they be positive or negative, for this permits a movement towards greater completeness. At this stage the client increasingly comes to realize that *she can begin to define herself and does not have to accept the definition and judgements of others.* There is, too, a more conscious appreciation of the nature of the relationship with the therapist and the value of a love which is not possessive and makes no demands. At about this stage the client finds that she can make relationships outside therapy which enable others to be self-experiencing and self-directing, and she becomes progressively aware that at the core of her being she is not destructive but genuinely desires the well-being of others. Self-responsibility continues to increase to the point where the client feels able to make her own choices – although this is not always pleasant – and to trust herself in a world which, although it may often seem to be disintegrating, yet offers many opportunities for creative activity and relating (Rogers 1954).

Case Example

Colin, a student studying history, presented himself at the university counselling service towards the end of the first term of his final year. He was small and somewhat frail in appearance, and carried himself stiffly and lopsidedly. His head was held to one side and appeared to be too heavy for his body. He had a fixed and inappropriate smile.

During the first session Colin stumbled a great deal over his words but was able to convey that some two weeks previously he had 'ground to a halt' and was now incapable of studying or even of reading a book. He felt frightened and paralysed, and confessed to a sense of desperation and helplessness. He had not experienced such a total sense of paralysis and 'frozenness' before, and wondered if he were going mad. I listened attentively and reflected the fear that so clearly characterized his state of mind. It appeared that my acceptance of his deep agitation and my willingness to track him rather than probe for information gave him reassurance. The person-centred counsellor does not seek information unless it seems crucial to an understanding of the client's inner world; and in Colin's case, although it might have been helpful, amongst other things, to know something about his academic standing in the university, I posed no question. Listening, tracking and communicating my understanding of Colin's inner turmoil served to establish very quickly a climate in which my acceptance and my empathy were clearly present. Within myself I felt great warmth towards Colin and compassion for his troubled state of mind, and I have little doubt that he was directly aware of this. About two-thirds of the way through this first session of fifty minutes he appeared to relax somewhat and unexpectedly began on a new tack. He became increasingly articulate as he told me that with his inability to study there had come a flood of insight about himself. He had finally acknowledged to himself that he was homosexual and was struggling with the implications of this for his future development. He talked of his working-class home where he lived both during the term and the vacation with his parents and two sisters. He felt that his mother would be highly condemning if she knew of his sexual orientation. He saw his father as potentially more accepting, but with him there were strong differences of political viewpoint, and this made for tension.

This first session was particularly rich in content but is chiefly notable for the way in which Colin, given a facilitative climate, was able to talk about a mass of new feelings and perceptions about himself which up to that point had paralysed him. It was as if his self-concept had been in turmoil when he entered the counselling room but that gradually during the session he was able to reorganize to some extent a whole host of feelings and experiences which had initially terrified him but then became more manageable as he experienced my acceptance and understanding.

When he appeared three days later (for we had agreed to meet twice a week for at least the next six weeks) he was still unable to study, but in many other respects his paralysis had loosened its grip. He reported that he had rung an acquaintance and that a third student had contacted him because he was concerned that Colin was overworking. Furthermore, Colin had decided that he must leave the parental home and that he would need to gather strength for this move.

During this second session Colin was still concerned about his inability to function as a student, but already there were signs that anxiety about this situational problem was giving way to a much more general preoccupation with his total life situation. The session was less emotional than the first encounter, and it seemed as if Colin was checking out that the acceptance and understanding he had received previously were authentic and continuing.

The third session was remarkable for a totally unexpected reason: within minutes of beginning Colin was expressing deep emotion about his cat. The cat was ill, and Colin had had the stressful experience of taking it to the vet. In a significant way, it seemed that as he thought of his cat he was able in my presence to get in touch with a well of sadness and compassion which had not been tapped before. Whereas he had previously told me *about* his feelings, he was now able to experience feelings with me – and as a result our relationship became closer. This movement from talking *about* situations and feelings to the actual *expression* of feelings experienced in the moment is typical of person-centred therapy, although with Colin the movement from the one to the other was enormously rapid. Even more remarkable was the fact that in the closing minutes of this session Colin suddenly announced that he had decided (and I suspect he meant at that very minute) to intermit his studies and to ask the university to give him leave of absence for the rest of the academic year. The expression of feelings often gives rise to the emergence of new thoughts.

Colin arrived for the fourth session with an altogether more confident air. His body seemed less stiff, although the fixed smile was still very much in place. He announced that he had put in a formal application for intermission and that he would like my support for this with the university authorities. Now for the first time I learned that Colin was a very able student and was tipped to get a good degree. It seemed that the brain which was currently refusing to apply itself to academic work had more than proved its intellectual capacities. Towards the end of the session Colin's smile vanished for a few minutes. 'I'm going to give myself time to grow up,' he said.

For Colin, the implementation of his desire to intermit his studies and to 'give himself time to grow up' was of great significance. Up to that point his life had been very much determined by events and by the educational conveyor belt. At his first session he had appeared as the victim of formidable forces which were paralysing him, and he had talked of his fear of the judgements and attitudes of his family. Nobody could have presented more graphically the image of a person trapped by forces and people outside his control. Now, only a fortnight later, he was able to see the possibility of self-direction and to realize that even the great institution of the university could be persuaded to conform to his wishes.

The following session was a mixture of powerful feeling and decision-making. Colin confessed to a high level of exhaustion and then spoke of bodily tension. He was also full of foreboding about the forthcoming interview with his general practitioner, whom he both feared and to some extent despised. He needed to persuade the GP to give him a month's sick leave because this would ease his financial situation in terms of receiving social security, and yet at the same time he felt caught in his fear of authority figures. We explored together how he might best present himself to the doctor, and as he gathered courage he also announced his intention of beginning the task of finding himself new accommodation.

This session was significant for two reasons. In the first place, Colin's growing concern about his tension and his body in general was a further indication of his desire to move towards greater completeness. Secondly, his openness to the negative feelings about the interview with his doctor enabled him to work constructively on his difficulties with authority figures. The person-centred therapist, by welcoming the whole person, offers the possibility in a principally verbal encounter of exploring physiological issues, and this was to prove of great importance to Colin. Furthermore, the essentially egalitarian relationship between therapist and client allows the client to share his fears about authority figures even when these, as in this case, are also members of the helping professions. For the person-centred therapist the fear of authority is often an area of critical importance: such fear is frequently reinforcing of the conditions of worth which underpin a damaging self-concept and the chance to work with a client on a specific relationship of this kind can have valuable outcomes for the reorganization of a client's conception of himself.

Colin returned for his next session full of anger about his GP. He reported a bad interview, and told of the doctor's class-conscious attitudes and arrogant assumptions about university students. This was the first time I had witnessed Colin's anger; it was the first time, too, that I had received the full force of his political convictions and sensed his passionate concern for the deprived and the underprivileged. For the second time in our sessions Colin wept, and for the first time he actually commented on our relationship: 'It's nice to be able to say what I want here – I always feel safe.' In the closing minutes of the session he delighted me by admitting that despite the GP's impossible attitude he had in fact got his month's sick leave, had turned down the offer of tranquillizers and wanted my help next time to explore relaxation training!

As I reflect now on this session I am struck by the fact that in many ways Colin and I were unlikely companions. A married, middle-class, middle-aged, heterosexual, liberal, Christian, person-centred therapist would not naturally seek the company of a young, homosexual, working-class, Marxist, agnostic, history student. And yet I am convinced that our very differences may well have been an important ingredient in the therapeutic relationship. I sense that because I was so different Colin's experience of my acceptance and understanding was the more powerful and enabled him in the following months to cross other boundaries which had previously seemed beyond his capacity. It is significant, too, that in this sixth session he was able to allude directly to our relationship and that within a short time, as seems so often to occur in person-centred therapy, his relationships outside therapy markedly improved.

Colin continued in therapy for a further thirty-nine sessions, on a fortnightly basis after the initial six-week period (his own choice, which he not infrequently extended to three weeks and on one or two occasions reduced to one week). He also joined a therapy group convened by a colleague for a period of ten weeks. I believe, however, that the essential work was done in these first six interviews. In that brief period he moved from a position where he saw himself as paralysed, hopelessly immature, weighed down with sexual conflicts and terrified of the judgements of others to one where he had discovered that it was possible to allow apparently negative feelings into awareness without catastrophic consequences, that he could risk experiencing deep feelings in the presence of another person, that he did not need to be trapped by the judgements of others and that he could actually take over the direction of his own life. This he then proceeded to do, and I remained his supportive companion in the enterprise until he needed me no longer. By then he had a first class degree, a home of his own and a sexual partner. He could also smile when he wanted to, and his head seemed to sit squarely on his shoulders.

References

Boy A V, Pine G J (1982) *Client-Centered Counseling: A Renewal*, Allyn and Bacon, Boston, p. 129

Burn M (1956) *Mr Lyward's Answer*, Hamish Hamilton, London

Frick W B (1971) *Humanistic Psychology: Interviews with Maslow, Murphy and Rogers*, Charles E Merrill, Columbus, Ohio

Kirschenbaum H (1979) *On Becoming Carl Rogers*, Delacorte, New York p. 89

Nelson-Jones R (1982) *The Theory and Practice of Counselling Psychology*, Holt, Rinehart and Winston, Eastbourne

Oatley K (1981) 'The self with others: the person and the interpersonal context in the approaches of C R Rogers and R D Laing' in Fransella F (ed.) *Personality*, Methuen, London, p. 192

Rogers C R (1954) 'The case of Mrs Oak: a research analysis' in Rogers C R and Dymond R F (eds.) *Psychotherapy and Personality Change*, University of Chicago Press, Chicago, p. 106

Rogers C R (1961) *On Becoming a Person*, Houghton Mifflin, Boston, p. 190

Rogers C R (1964) Toward a modern approach to values: The valuing process in the mature person, *Journal of Abnormal and Social Psychology 68*: 160–167

Rogers C R (1974) In retrospect: forty-six years, *American Psychologist 29*: 115–123

Rogers C R (1975) Empathic: an unappreciated way of being, *The Counseling Psychologist 5*:2–10

Rogers C R (1979) 'The foundations of the person-centered approach', unpublished manuscript

Rogers C R, Dymond R F (eds.) (1954) *Psychotherapy and Personality Change*, University of Chicago Press, Chicago

Tausch R (1975) Ergebnisse und Prozesse der klientenzentrierten Gesprächspsychotherapie bei 550 Klienten und 115 Psychotherapeuten, Eine Zusammenfassung des Hamburger Forschungsprojektes, *Zeitschrift für Praktische Psychologie 13*: 293–307

Thorne B J (1983) 'The Quality of Tenderness', unpublished manuscript

Suggested Further Reading

Boy A V, Pine G J (1982) *Client-Centered Counseling: A Renewal*, Allyn and Bacon, Boston

Kirschenbaum H (1979) *On Becoming Carl Rogers*, Delacorte Press, New York

Rogers C R (1951) *Client-Centered Therapy*, Houghton Mifflin, Boston

Rogers C R (1961) *On Becoming a Person*, Houghton Mifflin, Boston

Rogers C R (1980) *A Way of Being*, Houghton Mifflin, Boston

Chapter 6 Personal Construct Therapy

Fay Fransella

Historical Context and Developments in Britain
Historical context

Philosophers have argued about the nature of science and of man throughout the centuries, but never more vehemently than in the seventeenth and eighteenth. During this period two streams of thought were developing about the nature of man: one points us in the direction of twentieth-century behaviourism and Skinner, and the other towards the whole humanistic movement and the theoretical formulations of George Kelly (1955).

In the seventeenth century, Isaac Newton was also developing Galileo's methods of inquiry into the form we recognize today as scientific method. The entire cosmos was regarded as functioning like a perfect machine with precise laws governing its movements, so science was defined as the discovery of these laws by experiment.

Immanuel Kant (1724–1804) rebelled against the prevailing ideas of seventeenth-century philosophers such as Hobbes and Locke. In particular, he was against their emphasis on the essential passivity of the individual and the view of science that truth could be found 'out there' by applying the experimental methods of physics. Kant argued that man is active upon the world and has at least some control over his actions; also, that he is never able to perceive reality directly (the noumena) but only to see things filtered through *mental categories* (the phenomena). Thus Kant offers us the model of a person who is active rather than passive, and incapable of making direct contact with reality. The person cannot therefore be studied by the use of the scientific method as in physics but can only be understood through an examination of consciousness.

Many of Kelly's ideas can be seen as springing directly from those of Kant, but there is an additional and very important source of influence: Vaihinger's 'as if' philosophy (1924). Vaihinger suggested that since we have no way of gaining direct access to truth we should look at God and reality in a hypothetical way, 'as if' they were true. This appears as a fundamental idea in Kelly's own philosophy of *constructive alternativism* and his *psychology of personal constructs*.

Behaviourism dominated psychological thinking for the first sixty years of the twentieth century, and it is in this context that the development of Kelly's ideas should be considered. Immanuel Kant was a philosophical revolutionary; George Kelly was a psychological one. Just as Kant rebelled against the prevailing view that human beings are passive and powerless over their own destinies, so Kelly came to psychology at a time when the establishment view was behaviourism, with its doctrine of the essential passivity and powerlessness of humanity. Kelly (1969a) describes how he sat through endless lectures in his psychology course watching innumerable 'Stimulus→Response's being written on the blackboard. He waited patiently for someone to discuss the nature of the arrow. They never did – at least, not to Kelly's satisfaction.

Kelly received his Ph.D. in psychology – with particular emphasis on physiology – in the early 1930s. He became Professor and Director of Clinical Psychology at Ohio State University in 1946. However, in order to gain a fuller insight into the context in which his ideas developed it is important to know something of his earlier studies: in 1926 he obtained a BA degree in physics and mathematics, later a master's degree in educational sociology, and in 1930 a Bachelor of Education degree in Edinburgh.

Knowing now of his training in physics and mathematics, it comes as no surprise to find that Kelly's model of the person is couched in the language of science, as is his whole theory. He also introduced a new method of measurement (the repertory grid) and wrote a method of non-parametric factor analysis to go with it (see Fransella 1984 for a more detailed discussion of the influence on Kelly of his training in physics). But it is important to bear in mind that his is a science based on the philosophy of *constructive alternativism*: a science in which there are no 'facts', only support for current hypotheses. These hypotheses may lead to others, which encompass new events, and so on. At some infinite moment in time we might learn all there is to know about the universe, for there *is* a reality 'out there'; but this is unlikely since the universe, like the person, is in a constant state of motion.

The person is also a form of motion. Kelly's whole approach is about action, prediction and change. The client, for instance, may 'test out' alternative ways of making sense of the world in the relative safety of the consulting 'laboratory', using role-play or enactment. Here we find the influence of Moreno, who was developing his ideas on psychodrama when Kelly was formulating his theory.

Although certain threads running through Kelly's work bear a close resemblance to existentialist thinking, there is no evidence that translations of the works of Sartre and others were available in the United States in the late 1930s and 1940s; in fact, it is very difficult to find out what precisely did influence Kelly, the man, in his formulation of one of the most comprehensive theories known to psychology.

Developments in Britain

Kelly, an American, found receptive readers first and foremost in Britain, and there are many reasons why this should have been so. Only in the 1980s has there been a quickening of interest in his work in its country of origin. Neimeyer (1983) has described its development in the context of the sociology of science. He uses Mullins's (1973) model of the socio-historical development of new theory groups, which focuses on the changing patterns of communication.

Before and for some time after the publication of Kelly's *magnum opus, The Psychology of Personal Constructs*, in 1955, he and others interested in his ideas worked largely in isolation. However, by 1966 workers in Britain had attained *cluster* status: that is, the development of local groups with a minimum of seven people plus a publication explosion. Neimeyer finds that by 1972 the major clusters in Britain were beginning to dissolve and that personal construct theory was steadily establishing itself as a mature speciality; by contrast, America and the rest of Europe are only now, more than ten years later, beginning to enter the *cluster* stage of development.

Up to 1978 there was surprisingly little work published on psychotherapy – surprising, since this is the 'focus of convenience' of personal construct psychology. But things have now changed, and interest is developing rapidly, both in the theory and in its application to psychotherapy. Evidence of this growth of world-wide interest is the establishment in 1982 of the first centre devoted solely to the teaching and applications of personal construct psychology. As Neimeyer's analysis would lead one to predict, the Centre for Personal Construct Psychology has been established in the capital city of Great Britain – London.

Theoretical Assumptions

The image of the person

Kelly suggests we might look at the person 'as if' you and I were scientists: by this he meant that we could all be seen as doing the same sorts of things that scientists traditionally do. We have theories about why things happen, erect hypotheses derived from these theories, put these hypotheses to the test and see whether the predictions based on our hypotheses are validated or invalidated. We test our predictions by behaving. Viewing all behaviour 'as if' it were an experiment is one of Kelly's unique contributions to our understanding of the person.

Kelly's (1955) formulation of the 'psychology of personal constructs' relates to this image of the person. He suggests that we might come to understand ourselves and others *in psychological terms* by studying the personal constructs we have each evolved in order to help us predict events in our personal worlds.

We approach the world not as it *is* but as it appears to be: we gaze at it through our construct *goggles*. We make predictions about events constantly and continually – there is no let-up. We are active beings, 'forms of motion'.

Construing is not all going on in the head; we construe just as much with our bodies as with our minds. Kelly considered dualistic thinking a hindrance to understanding. At any given moment it is just as appropriate to ask what a person is feeling as what he is thinking, for many constructs (discriminations between events) have either been formed before we have formulated the words to express them or else the discriminations have never acquired verbal labels.

For example, a child may discriminate between types of voice: a harsh, grating voice and a soft, smooth one. The harsh, grating voice is related to feelings of reassurance, a large body to snuggle up to, and is there before the child goes to bed. The soft, smooth one gives conflicting messages: sometimes it is comforting like the harsh, grating one, but at other times – often when it is *particularly* soft and smooth – there are feelings of unease, of all not being well. Later, as an adult, that person may never be able to put into words exactly why he cannot abide women who have soft, smooth voices and why he himself has developed a harsh, grating one: his pre-verbal constructs are thus being applied in adult life.

Concepts of psychological health and disturbance

Kelly argued fiercely against the use of the medical model in the field of psychological disorder. Like many others, he felt that those with psychological problems were not 'ill' and did not need to be 'treated' by 'medical doctors'. He believed that the use of the medical model hampers our attempts to understand people and to help them deal with whatever it is that is troubling them: if there is no 'illness', there can be no 'health'.

Instead, he suggests that we might use the concept of *functioning*. A person who is functioning fully is one who is able to construe the world in such a way that predictions are, for the most part, validated. When invalidation *does* occur, the person deals with it by reconstruing. For example, you are at a party and go up to a stranger whom you construe as likely to be friendly. You start a general conversation and, before a few moments have passed, that 'friendly' person is arguing fiercely with you and being quite unpleasant: he is certainly not 'friendly'. You have been invalidated. If you are fully functioning, you will accept this invalidation and reconstrue the person, perhaps as someone who has a very deceptive façade that you were stupid not to have seen through earlier. You leave the incident behind you, and put it down to *experience*: that is what is meant by reconstruing.

But someone else, who is incapable of dealing with invalidation, may not come out so unscathed; she might become more and more embarrassed, flustered and bereft of words. She would then become increasingly anxious since she was confronted by an event which she finds difficult to construe at all. Not only is she unable to predict the outcome of this event, but she finds she is increasingly unable to predict herself. The situation is a traumatic one: hopefully, either someone will soon come to her rescue, or the stranger will move off. The person who experiences a considerable number of such predictive failures will often consider herself to have a 'problem'.

Another way of dealing with invalidation is to 'make' things work out the way we predicted. When we do this we are being 'hostile' (extorting validational evidence for a social prediction that we have already seen to be a failure). For example, having construed that stranger as 'friendly', you might behave in such a way that he thought you were going to faint. He might put his arm under your elbow to support you, guide you towards the drinks table, and so on. Now you can say to yourself: 'There you are! I told you he was really a friendly person!' Such hostility as this is well known in counselling and therapy, and will be discussed later. Yet there is nothing essentially 'bad' about hostility: it is a way of dealing with events when our construing lets us down.

Nevertheless, the person who functions reasonably well is one who does not use too much hostility to deal with invalidation, does not find himself too often confronted by events he cannot construe (and so become overwhelmed by anxiety), and whose system for construing the world has had potentially troublesome preverbal constructs 'updated'. This means that he has been able to explore, at some level of awareness, those early childhood discriminations. For instance, is it valid, in adult life, to take an instant dislike to people who have soft, smooth voices? Perhaps the construction does not now lead to useful predictions.

The acquisition of psychological disturbance

Kelly argued theoretically that the person is an integrated, indivisible whole; but that does *not* mean that individuals necessarily see themselves that way. Many of us are dualists in the way we understand ourselves. Likewise, it makes no theoretical sense to ask how a disturbance in construing is acquired; since personal construct theory takes the position that we act upon the world and construe (predict) events in the world, we cannot 'acquire' something as if we were buying it in a shop or having it imposed upon us, like measles.

Yet a client may construe his vomiting, for instance, as a 'bodily symptom' which he 'acquired' as a result of some stressful psychological event. It is the client's construing that the therapist has to understand.

To the therapist, however, the vomiting is as much construing as is the way the client describes it. As he examines the client's construing system (in verbal and non-verbal terms), he will be examining the context within which the vomiting arose.

It is important to remember here that *behaviour is the experiment*. So we look at the event as if the child's first vomit was his way of asking a question of his world. It might have gone something like this: 'As far as I can see, if I go on as I'm doing, I will grow up and be successful like my father. But I don't want to be successful like my father. He is aggressive and weak, like all men. Perhaps if I'm sick I won't grow up and can remain a child.' He vomits; he is now treated differently. Has he 'acquired a disturbance'? I think not. He has tried an experiment which, according to the way in which he construes the world, works. He is successful, but not like his father.

I must add that, although I have spelt out a possible process in words, this does not mean that the thoughts go consciously through the child's head in this way; his experimentation was taking place at a pre-verbal level.

The perpetuation of psychological disturbance

The vomiting is perpetuated because 'it works'. The child's predictions are validated. He has succeeded in stopping the process of maturation. It now takes on a meaning of its own: 'I'm someone who is sick. I cannot lead the sort of life which, were I able to, would make me a highly successful person.' When as an adult this person comes for help to overcome his problem of vomiting, we find that he has hedged his bets: the opposite of being successful is not, as one might expect, being unsuccessful but is being 'not yet successful'. This means he may still be a potential genius. He sought help because he was getting some invalidation of this construing. He began to see it as rather ludicrous to be forty years old and still a potential genius – something had to yield.

Problems persist until the person is able to find acceptable alternative ways of dealing with the world. Many long-standing problems, such as stuttering, become enmeshed in the person's core-role construing: in the superordinate ways in which individuals construe themselves. Sometimes this ends in the individual seeing himself as 'a stutterer', 'a vomiter', 'a useless person'. The longer a problem exists for a person, the more likely it is to become part of the construing of the self and the more likely it is to persist – for to change the essence of the self is no easy undertaking.

It is not only core-role construing that takes place at a superordinate level. The *organisation corollary* states that constructs are organized into a system and that a superordinate construct is one that includes another as one of the elements in its context. Hinkle (1965) demonstrated that the more abstract (superordinate) the constructs were the more implications (other constructs) they implied and, incidentally, the more resistant they were to change.

Hinkle also described 'implicative dilemmas' in construing. These may occur because the person has not worked out the meaning of (or lines of implication for) a particular superordinate construct. The subtle changes in meaning in different contexts are unclear, and with such a lack of clarity, few useful predictions can be made or, if they are made, lead to invalidation. Alternatively, the lines of implication are there, but in conflict. This aspect of 'implicative dilemmas' has been elaborated by Tschudi (1977): see page 143. An example of such a dilemma can be seen in the case study at the end of this chapter.

The reasons for problems persisting must be sought within a person's construing of himself and his world. He behaves in a particular way because that is most meaningful to him; it is in that way he is able to achieve maximal control over events – and over himself. The problem becomes enmeshed in his core-role superordinate construing system. The longer the problem persists, the more difficulty the person is likely to have in changing.

Practice

Goals of therapy

The person with a psychological problem is 'stuck': he keeps repeating the same old behavioural experiments over and over again. Since personal construct psychology views the person (amongst other things) as a form of motion, enabling the person to 'get on the move again' becomes the goal of therapy. As Kelly (1969b) puts it:

> the task of psychotherapy is to get the human process going again so that life may go on and on from where psychotherapy left off. There is no par-

ticular kind of psychotherapeutic relationship – no particular kind of feelings – no particular kind of interaction that is in itself a psychotherapeutic panacea

The person of the therapist

Although no one has yet tried to relate the qualities of personal construct therapists either to success or failure with clients or to the qualities of other types of therapist, Kelly specifies a number of skills that they need to acquire. These are outlined below.

A subsuming system of constructs   Above all, therapists must have a 'subsuming construct system' and be skilled in its use. Every therapist needs a set of professional constructs within which to subsume a client's own personal system of constructs. For the analyst, it is spelt out in psychoanalytic terms; for the rational-emotive therapist, in RET terms; for the personal construct therapist it is spelt out in terms of the theoretical constructs stated in the psychology of personal constructs. Kelly (1955) describes it thus:

> Since all clients have their own personal systems my system should be *a system of approach* by means of which I can quickly come to understand and subsume the widely varying systems which my clients can be expected to present.

A therapist should be able to specify precisely what constructs are being used whenever a therapeutic decision is made: for example, if he systematically uses the writing of a self characterization (see 'fixed role therapy', page 141) with clients, he should be able to state precisely what this procedure is designed to do.

In personal construct therapy, the subsuming system is that which defines the theory itself. Those constructs most commonly used in psychotherapy are referred to as 'professional constructs'. One such is *loose* versus *tight*: is the client using constructs in a way that leads to varying predictions (loosened construing) or to predictions which state that events will definitely be one way or another (unvarying or tight construing)? Bannister (1962) based his theory of the origins and maintenance of schizophrenic thought disorder on this construct.

Another commonly used construct is *dilation* versus *constriction*. Very often those in psychological distress have narrowed their perceptual field in order to minimize apparent incompatibilities (constricted). If this were part of the therapist's formulation, a therapeutic goal would be to encourage aggression (in Kelly's sense) through a broadening of the range of daily activities.

Yet another is *propositional* versus *constellatory*. Construing propositionally means, for instance, looking at a client 'as if' anxiety were a problem and seeing where that leads. If the client is being looked at in a constellatory manner, the therapist is effectively saying such things as, 'Since this client is suffering from anxiety, then it is important to look at his dependency on his mother.'

Therapists who lack an adequate subsuming system of constructs may fail to help a client change. Once the therapist allows his *own* construing to intervene between himself and the client, he may find himself being used by that client and have difficulty extricating himself.

Construing the client's constructions   The skill to use the professional construct system depends on the therapist's ability to subsume the client's personal system. Kelly spells this out in his notion of *role*. When we attempt to construe another's construing system we are playing a role in relation to that person. We may get it wrong, but the fact that we are trying to put ourselves in another person's shoes and to look at the world through that other's eyes means that we are playing a role in relation to that person, subsuming the other's construing system. Without this skill, the therapist cannot start.

Creativity and aggression   Given the focus on the client and therapist as personal scientists, the therapist needs to be creative, versatile and aggressive. Kelly (1955) comments that 'Every case a psychotherapist handles requires him to devise techniques and formulate constructs he has never used before.' Such creativity means the readiness to try out unverbalized hunches; and a willingness to look at things in new ways:

> Creation is therefore an act of daring, an act of daring through which the creator abandons those literal defenses behind which he might hide if his act is questioned or its results proven invalid. The psychotherapist who dares not try anything he cannot verbally defend is likely to be sterile in a psychotherapeutic relationship.

To be creative the therapist must be able to adopt a variety of roles and be aggressive in testing out hypotheses (aggression being the active elaboration of one's construing). In psychotherapy, both client and therapist must be prepared to be aggressive and to take risks.

It must always be borne in mind that an unwritten basic tenet of personal construct psychology is that we have created ourselves and can therefore re-create ourselves if we so wish.

Verbal ability The therapist must be skilled both verbally and in observation. A therapist must be able to speak the client's language in addition to having a wide-ranging vocabulary. By understanding the meanings that word-symbols have for the client the therapist can minimize the risk of misunderstandings.

Therapeutic style

The personal construct therapist's style can best be understood by looking once again at the model of the 'person as scientist': both struggle to understand the same problem and so find a solution to it. The therapist, like a research supervisor, knows something about designing experiments, has experience of some of the pitfalls involved in any type of research and knows that, ultimately, only the research student can carry out the research. This supervisor-research student model may sound cold and calculating, but it is not: anyone who has ever been in one or both of those positions knows only too well how totally involving and challenging is the task.

One of the most important aspects of such a relationship is that both client and therapist must have a personal commitment to solving the problem and to the necessary work and experimentation that this involves. Within this research framework, the therapist initially adopts the *credulous approach*: all personal evaluation is suspended; there are no judgements. Everything the client says is accepted as 'true'.

As the therapist gains access to the client's world and begins to formulate hypotheses about the nature of the problem, the former begins to put these to the test. However, being active in therapy does not mean that the therapist necessarily adopts a directive role; he may, in fact, be very quiet and give the client absolute freedom to do, say or think whatever he wishes. Nevertheless, the role is decided on by the therapist. His construing of the client's constructions leads him to consider that this 'quiet' role is something the client can use *at this stage of therapy*. The personal construct psychologist therefore *acts as validator or invalidator of the client's construing*.

One implication of construing the therapist as a validator of the client's construing, is that he uses the relationship as another valuable 'tool' for helping the client's reconstructions. For instance, 'transference' or 'dependency' is not a general problem to be 'dealt with'. At a particular stage in therapy it may be useful, such as when attempts are being made to verbalize pre-verbal constructs; at another time, or with other clients, dependency on the therapist may prevent the client from conducting useful experiments outside the therapy consulting room.

The therapeutic style is thus dictated by the ways in which the therapist construes the needs of the client, always remembering that client and therapist are *both* in the experimenting and reconstruing business.

Major therapeutic techniques

Kelly (1969b) expresses his view on techniques thus:

> There is no ... particular set of techniques of choice for the personal construct therapist. The relationship between therapist and client and the techniques they employ may be as varied as the whole human repertoire of relationships and techniques. It is the orchestration of techniques and the utilization of relationships in the on-going process of living and profiting from experience that makes psychotherapy a contribution to human life.

The self characterization   Kelly is reported as saying that if he were to be remembered for one thing, he would like it to be his first principle: 'If you do not know what is wrong with a person, ask him, he may tell you.' A working model for this is the self characterization, for which instructions are carefully worded, as follows:

> I want you to write a character sketch of (Mary), just as if she were the principal character in a play. Write it as it might be written by a friend who knew her very *intimately* and very *sympathetically*, perhaps better than anyone ever really could know her. Be sure to write it in the third person. For example, start out by saying, 'Mary is ...'

There is no formal method of analysis. However, one might look at the first sentence as if it were a statement of where the person is now and at the last as a statement of where the person is going. One might look for themes running through the whole piece. What one tries to do is to go beyond the words and glimpse inside where the person lives. These character sketches can be written from a variety of standpoints: 'Mary as she will be in ten years' time', '. . . as she will be when her problem has disappeared', or any other form which seems to offer the person a way of exploring her constructions of the world. An example of the use of the self characterization as a therapeutic instrument can be found in Fransella (1981).

Fixed role therapy   Kelly based his one detailed example of the theory in action on the use of the self characterization. In his description of fixed role therapy, he also gives an implicit account of the way we invent and create ourselves.

The therapist writes a second version of the client's initial self-characterization. This is not a replica of the first, since that would only lead back to where the client is now; nor should it be a complete opposite, since no one will readily turn his life on its head – instead, the client's *fixed role sketch* is written so as to be 'orthogonal' to the first. For instance, if the client is using the construct *aggressive* versus *submissive* in relation to his boss, the sketch might talk of being *respectful*.

When the sketch has been written, client and therapist pore over it together. They modify it until it describes a person who the client feels it is possible for him to be. The client now lives the life of that person for a few weeks: he eats what this new person eats, dresses as he would dress and relates to others as this person would relate. During this period of fixed role enactment the therapist has to see the client fairly frequently. The sessions focus on what the client sees as going on, which ventures were successful and which were not, what messages he is getting from others and so forth.

The purpose of this fixed role enactment is to get over the idea that we can, indeed, change ourselves; that even the client can change, though he seems so stuck at the moment. He learns about self-inventiveness: he learns what happens when he alters a particular item of behaviour, and whether it is useful to explore this line of inquiry further or whether he should try something else. He discovers how the way we construe others and behave towards them influences how they behave towards us. He learns to read new messages from others. This is particularly important since the person we have invented is, in large part, the result of the way we have construed the reactions of others to us.

Fixed role therapy is certainly not suitable for everyone; it can, however, be very useful in modified form. For instance, the client and the therapist may choose to work out just one experiment for the former to carry out during the period before the next appointment: this might be to experiment with being respectful to his boss on just one occasion and see what difference it makes to how the boss reacts, to how the client feels about himself. These 'mini' fixed roles need to be worked out carefully with the client, but can give useful insights into the direction in which both client and therapist think he might profitably travel.

Repertory grid technique   This technique has been modified a number of times since Kelly described it in 1955 (see Fransella and Bannister 1977). Its uses are many and its analyses often complex. It is basically a technique which enables the therapist to obtain some degree of quantification of the relationships between the constructs of clients and those of the individuals who people their worlds. Though it has a place in the psychotherapy setting, it is not essential; it is only useful if the therapist sees it as such. It can be used to validate therapists' hunches, in monitoring change over time, or in helping clients explore their construing of events more fully. In the last-named context, it becomes part of therapy if the results are fed back to the client.

Laddering, pyramiding and the ABC model   These are all methods for exploring construct relationships without getting into the complexities of statistical analysis that are often necessary with repertory grids.

Laddering helps the client explore the relationships between constructs at more and more abstract levels (Hinkle 1965). For instance, if the client uses the construct *dominant* versus *submissive*, the therapist would ask which he would prefer to be. If the answer were *submissive*, the client would then be asked: 'Why? What are the advantages of being a submissive rather than a dominant person?' The client might answer that submissive people do not get attacked, whereas dominant people do. The client is again asked why he has this preference: 'What are the penalties of being attacked?' The reply might be that he would not know how to respond; if one were dominant and were attacked, one would be in a fight. And so the questioning goes on, until the construing has reached such a superordinate level that it has nowhere else to go (in this example, it might be something to do with self-preservation).

Laddering is an art and one that is not easy to learn; but having learned it, most people find it an invaluable tool in psychotherapy. Not only does it enable the therapist to learn a great deal about the client within a very short time, but frequently it also enables the latter to gain considerable insight into his own world.

Pyramiding aims at identifying the more concrete levels of the construing system (Landfield 1971). Instead of asking 'Why?', the client is asked: 'What?' or 'How?'; 'What sort of person is a submissive person?'; 'How would you know that a person is being submissive?' This method can be useful when planning behavioural experiments.

The ABC model involves finding out the advantages and disadvantages to the client of each pole of a construct (Tschudi 1977). This can be used to advantage with constructs connected with 'the problem'. In the case of a woman whose 'problem' was being overweight, the client would be asked first to state an advantage of being the desired weight (perhaps she would be able to wear nice clothes); then for a disadvantage of being overweight (perhaps she gets out of breath when going upstairs). Next, she is asked for a disadvantage of being the normal weight (perhaps she would find there was too much choice around and so get confused), and finally for an advantage of being overweight (perhaps men do not bother her). These answers are regarded not as 'truths' but as guide-lines for further exploration.

Techniques from other therapies   The choice of technique is always determined by the current formulation of the problem, which is couched in the language of the professional theoretical constructs. Personal construct therapists find the use of dream material, guided fantasy, systematic desensitization and many other techniques of great value for specific purposes, but it must be emphasized that the choice of technique is guided by theory; this is very definitely not an empirical approach.

The change process in therapy

Since part of the model of the person in personal construct psychology is that we are a form of motion, the process of change is built into the theory.

Its theoretical base   The *fundamental postulate* states that 'a person's processes are psychologically channelized by the ways in which he anticipates events'. Three of the elaborative corollaries are specifically concerned with change.

The *experience corollary* states that 'a person's construction system varies as he successively construes the replication of events'. Merely being in a situation does not, of itself, mean that one has had experience; it is only experience if one has cause to construe some aspect of it in a way that differs from the way one construed before. An agoraphobic woman placed in a situation at some point in her behaviour therapy hierarchy will only have experience of that situation if her construing of the world is in some way different from what it was before. Kelly (1955) equates experience with learning:

> The burden of our assumption is that learning is not a special class of psycho-
> logical process; it is synonymous with any and all psychological processes.
> It is not something that happens to a person on occasion; it is what makes
> him a person in the first place.

The *choice corollary* states that 'a person chooses for himself that alternative in a dichotomized construct through which he anticipates the greater possibility for extension and definition of his system'. This is a basic motivation construct. As living beings we strive to make our world a more predictable and personally meaningful place. We may not like the world in which we are living, but it is preferable to live in it than to launch ourselves into a vast sea of uncertainty.

In a certain sense, the client is 'choosing' to remain as he is rather than change. The person who has stuttered since early childhood sees no alterna-tive but to continue stuttering in adulthood: that is the only world he knows. By communicating with other adults in that way he can make sense of the interaction – it is personally meaningful to him. If he were to suddenly become a fluent speaker, he would be launched into chaos (Fransella 1972). In much the same way, smoking is meaningful for the smoker, obesity for the obese and depression for the depressed.

A personal construct approach involves helping the client construe what he or she is going to become and not simply eliminating the undesired behaviour directly.

The third corollary to do with change – *modulation* – states that any variation within a construing system 'is limited by the permeability of the constructs within whose range of convenience the variants lie'. Construing new events is difficult if many of a person's constructs are not open to receive them; they are pumice rather than sponge. Someone who stutters and knows too precisely how people respond to his attempts at communication will find it difficult to employ new constructions of those interactions. He will not 'see' different responses.

The *creativity cycle* (from tight to loose to tight construing) is central to all change. A client may have to be shown how to loosen his construing so that he can allow ideas to 'float around'; only after this can they be tightened up again in some new way. Guided fantasy and dream analysis are both ways in which loosened construing can be encouraged and explored.

The accompaniments of change   As any psychotherapist and any client knows, change is not easy and can be uncomfortable. To help the client to understand this, the personal construct therapist uses constructs to do with transition, such as *anxiety, threat and guilt*. This is where emotion is built into the theory.

In personal construct theory, *anxiety* is an ever-present feeling as we explore our world, for we are continually being confronted by events we find difficult or impossible to construe. Any change is therefore accompanied by anxiety, and thus therapy is a very anxiety-provoking time for the client – and, on occasion, for the therapist.

We experience threat whenever we are aware of imminent change in how we construe the essential essence of the 'self'. Therapy may move too fast; it may be too successful. The client realizes that, if things go on at the present rate, some really radical changes will have to be faced. It becomes too much for him to contemplate, and he returns to where it is safe, to the previous behaviour. The client has 'relapsed', but he is doing something very positive and useful *in his own terms*. It can be a signal to the therapist that an alteration in therapeutic strategy is called for. Relapse is not necessarily 'bad': it can be a safety-valve.

When a client is asked to change ways of construing the self, he may experience guilt. Most people who stutter define themselves as stutterers: this is an essential aspect of their being. As therapy progresses and they communicate more and more like fluent speakers, some may experience guilt since they are being dislodged from their core role: that of being a stutterer. Hence the focus on elaborating construing of where the client is *going* rather than on where he is now.

Case Example

Hilda is a plump, attractive 21-year-old with a mop of long hair with which she plays a great deal. She was happy at home and now often visits her mother, father and older sister. She works in the family business.

She is nine and a half stone in weight, five feet two inches tall, and has asked for help because of being overweight. Her mother is 'slim' and her sister 'very slim'. Father is very keen on keeping fit and takes a lot of exercise. Food is an important issue at home.

Hilda started to put on weight when doing her O level examinations. During the last five years she has been able to get down to her desired weight of seven and a half stone, but always puts the weight back on again. Although attractive, she has always been shy. She never had boyfriends at school, and has had few since.

The problem, as she sees it, is that her bedroom at home is close to the kitchen – which has no doors on it. She binges at night but can control her eating during the day. Her aim is to stop bingeing and so get down to seven and a half stone and to stay that weight.

At the initial interview the personal construct approach was explained to her and she was given the opportunity to go away and think it over. But she made up her mind then and there, agreeing to come on the course of eight one-hour weekly sessions. She was asked to bring along a self characterization and a food diary for her appointment the following week.

Elaborating the complaint

The therapist uses the 'credulous approach' all the time data are being collected and construing explored. The data include everything the client offers.

Her 'me now' self characterization was about 800 words long, written partly in pencil and partly in ink. It starts off by saying:

Hilda has a sweet face and she has a sweet nature. If she likes you she will make the effort to get to know you by asking all sorts of curious questions covering your background. If she doesn't like you because she may feel you're overpowering, then she clams up.

Towards the end, she says:

She doesn't like to be pushed around and be forced upon, though sometimes she is a little forceful with her friends . . . She likes her own company. She keeps a diary which she writes when she feels like it . . . She is vain and vain about her weight. Her vanity is important to her. Her clothes are important to her.

Her 'slim me' self characterization was only half a page long. It read:

She's very attractive: she has a good figure and she's quite sexy. She's attractive in that she catches the eye of a lot of people and appeals to some but not all. She seems shier and not as jovial and giggly as she was when she was more overweight. She has less confidence in herself but more confidence in being able to attract men. She could probably be a bitch to men if she had to be.

Hilda had some difficulty in dealing with the laddering of her constructs, and seemed to like her construing to be clear-cut and 'neat'. This had implications for therapy, suggesting that some 'loosening' exercises might be needed. Examples of her constructs are as follows:

expect people to come to them versus *vivacious*; *lazy* versus *motivate themselves to do things*; *indecisive* versus *decisive* and *adventurous* versus *close-minded*. The laddering of this last construct led to *learn about life* versus *sit at home and do nothing*, then on to *take opportunities as they come along* versus *do not do so*.

In the second session, Hilda said she had been reading her diary of a year ago, when she had got down to eight stone, and handed me this extract:

I feel so low, but all of a sudden out of the blue I'm getting chased. I can't handle it. For the first time I can choose who I like. But I feel I'm wanted for one thing only.

I was with someone I really shouldn't have been with. I'm so callous, childish and adventurous. I felt guilty. I was used. I don't feel safe. I'd rather not have these people. I'm suddenly scared. Since I've lost those pounds I feel like every guy is trying to grab me and I have this fear, I cannot trust them.

They make me sick. I love it yet I hate it.

After I've been out, or with a guy, why do I come home and eat? Don't I like myself then? Is the fat a protection? I feel now that I'm more attractive that I have this power over men but once I've reached its manifestations I lose: then they gain in control.

Initial hypotheses

An initial formulation of the complaint is made, based on the above data and other indications of how the client construes the world. Kelly (1955) describes diagnosis as 'the planning stage of treatment'. There is no great pressure to complete this since reconstruing usually starts during the construct elicitation and writing periods.

The personal construct therapist is not usually concerned with how the problem is acquired, unless this is an issue for the client; for, as Kelly says, no person need be a victim of his biography but may become a victim of the way he *construes* that biography. The therapist focuses on what it is that prevents change. Hilda can lose weight, but 'always puts it back on again'. Why should this be so?

Femininity in general seems poorly construed, and her own in particular. This is hypothesized partly from her writings, from the fact that, at the age of twenty-one she appeared very much the girl and not the woman; and from the fact that her 'slim me' was not well elaborated compared with the present self and contained several negative implications.

From her laddering we learn that being adventurous relates to learning about life and taking opportunities when they come along. Yet from her diary notes we find that being adventurous is not all good: it can lead to promiscuity. Her implicative dilemma here seems to be that if you are not adventurous you sit at home and do nothing.

Part of Hilda's overall problem seemed to be a difficulty in saying 'no'. In the meantime, being overweight solves the problem for her: men are not interested in fat girls.

The therapy

The aim of therapy, based on the initial formulation of the problem, was to help Hilda elaborate and put into words the sort of person she would be and the sort of world she would live in if she were permanently 'slim'.

Subsidiary aims were to encourage her to loosen her construing (the creativity cycle cannot operate without that) and to help her say 'no'.

To help her loosen her construing we used enactment, dreams and guided fantasy. Hilda was happy to play absurd games, such as talking to and being a refrigerator. In one dream, she was at a party ringing up a plastic surgeon to ask how much it would cost to make her nose smaller (it is too large, particularly if she were slim). However, her slim and lovely sister says it is lovely as it is.

Hilda made full use of the discussion of this less attractive aspect of her 'slim' self and enjoyed the role-play of being her nose talking to her. In one fantasy session, she was in the South of France having a long, cool drink under coloured umbrellas: I'm wearing a bikini—T-shirt—men are not particularly noticing me—I want them to—but if they do I feel uncomfortable—I'm not used to it—I don't know what to do.'

We examined the implication that one *should* do something if men look at one. Men were the ones who dictated. Why should this be? Hilda was intrigued by the idea that *she* could be in control of the situation. She concluded that her problem was not a matter of will-power to say 'no' but of an attitude of mind. Her homework was to observe what attractive women do when men make advances to them: how many are 'grabbed'?

In the first four weeks Hilda lost half a stone. She felt slim, was happier and more talkative, had had easier interactions with people (especially at two parties) and felt generally freer in herself. But this weight loss proved too fast: she was not yet ready to be fully a 'slim' Hilda. She became depressed, and lost no weight in the fifth week, having been at the peanuts. She was preparing herself for another failure.

This was dealt with by focusing on her constructs of being decisive and in control: it was *her* treatment programme, and she was only to do what she felt capable of. She decided to lose three pounds in the coming week, to have no binges, to have small helpings and to enjoy each mouthful. We negotiated that she was not to feel a failure if all these were not possible to achieve – but they were, and she felt very pleased with herself.

She then went away on holiday for two weeks. During this time she lost three pounds and reported feeling 90% in control of her eating habits. She described being amazed that the weight loss had been so painless, but she felt that she now understood what her weight was all about. She was confident that she would continue to lose weight and would not relapse.

She believed that there might be the odd time when she would 'let go' but that would be all right, since she was in control. Perhaps the most important thing was that she said: 'If a man looks at me now, I see it as a compliment' – she could take them or leave them.

Comments

It is not my intention here to give the impression that all psychotherapy along personal construct lines goes so well – I wish it did. But Hilda is an example of how the personal construct therapist uses a variety of tools, dictated by the client's problem at a particular point in time. Over the eight-week period we used eliciting and laddering of constructs, the self characterization, controlled elaboration of construing, role-play and enactment, fantasy and some behavioural analysis.

Hilda was able to use these exercises and find a way of getting out of her dilemma. She was 'on the move again': the goal of all personal construct psychotherapy. Two years later, she has not quite got to her now desired eight stone in weight, but she is most content with her eight stone seven pounds and really wonders what all the fuss was about.

References

Bannister D (1962) The nature and measurement of schizophrenic thought disorder, *Journal of Mental Science 108*: 825–842

Fransella F (1972) *Personal Change and Reconstruction: Research on a Treatment of Stuttering*, Academic Press, London

Fransella F (1981) 'Nature babbling to herself: the self characterisation as a therapeutic tool' in Bonarius H, Holland R and Rosenberg S (eds.) *Personal Construct Psychology: Recent Advances in Theory and Practice*, Macmillan, London

Fransella F (1984) 'What sort of scientist is the person-as-scientist?' in Adams-Webber J R and Mancuso J C (eds.) *Applications of Personal Construct Theory*, Academic Press, Ontario

Fransella F, Bannister D (1977) *A Manual for Repertory Grid Technique*, Academic Press, London

Hinkle D (1965) 'The Change of Personal Constructs from the Viewpoint of a Theory of Construct Implication', unpublished Ph.D. thesis, Ohio State University

Kelly G A (1955) *The Psychology of Personal Constructs* 1 and 2, Norton, New York pp. 75, 595, 600–1

Kelly G A (1969a) 'The autobiography of a theory' in Maher B (ed.) *Clinical*

Psychology and Personality: The Selected Papers of George Kelly, Krieger, New York

Kelly G A (1969b) 'The psychotherapeutic relationship' in Maher B (ed.) *Clinical Psychology and Personality: The Selected Papers of George Kelly*, Krieger, New York p. 223

Landfield A W (1971) *Personal Construct Systems in Psychotherapy*, Rand McNally, New York

Mullins N (1973) *Theories and Theory Groups in Contemporary American Sociology*, Harper & Row, New York

Neimeyer R A (1983) Uneven growth of personal construct theory, *Constructs*, 2: 5

Tschudi F (1977) Loaded and honest questions' in Bannister D (ed.) *New Perspectives in Personal Construct Theory*, Academic Press, London

Vaihinger H (1924) *The Philosophy of 'as if': A System of the Theoretical, Practical and Religious Fictions of Mankind*, translated by Ogden C K, Routledge and Kegan Paul, London

Suggested Further Reading

Adams-Webber J R and Mancuso J C (eds.) (1983) *Applications of Personal Construct Theory*, Academic Press, Ontario

Bannister D and Fransella F (1980) *Inquiring Man*, 2nd edition, Penguin, London

Epting F (1984) *Personal Construct Counseling and Psychotherapy*, Wiley, New York

Landfield A W (1980) Leitner L M *Personal Construct Psychology: Psychotherapy and Personality*, Wiley, New York

Maher B (ed.) (1969) *Clinical Psychology and Personality: The Selected Papers of George Kelly*, Krieger, New York

Chapter 7 Existential Therapy

Emmy van Deurzen-Smith

Historical Context and Developments in Britain
Historical context

Existential psychotherapy is, more than any other current therapeutic approach, solidly rooted in a philosophical background. This background is the phenomenological and existential traditions of twentieth-century Western Europe. A familiarity with existential philosophical thinking is an essential prerequisite for practising existential therapy. Most of the theory of this approach is primarily philosophical and concerned with the description of the nature of being – the exploration of the meaning of human existence.

The existential movement in psychotherapy proposes a philosophical process of reappraisal of values and assumptions. It encourages an active attitude of wonder and questioning; it initiates a radical reappraisal of reality in a fundamental way. It refuses to attempt to merely repair the cracks in the adaptation to this usually taken for granted 'reality'. In this sense, the approach is a direct application of general philosophy and thus represents not only much of Western thinking, from as early as some of the pre-Socratic philosophies, but also much of Eastern thinking, particularly that of Zen Buddhism.

In the interest of simplicity, I shall limit this discussion of the origins of the existential approach to the consideration of the more directly observable roots.

Soren Kierkegaard (1941) Kierkegaard can be considered the initiator of a renewed interest in this kind of essential philosophical reappraisal of human experience. A philosopher at work in Denmark at the beginning of the nineteenth century, he struggled his own lonely struggle to reach clarity on man's position in the universe. His writings are particularly relevant today, when most people seem to have reached the same level of doubt and uncertainty about living that Kierkegaard dared experience in all its fullness, one hundred and fifty years ago.

Friedrich Nietzsche (1969) This German philosopher of the second half of the same century voiced for the first time both disbelief in a divine power transcending humanity and belief in a human ability to become godlike or superhuman. He exhorted mankind to rise above itself. A large section of today's so-called human potential movement has similar underpinnings in atheism and humanism.

Kierkegaard and Nietzsche are sometimes referred to as the philosophers of freedom (Warnock (1970). Their contribution has been to challenge Christianity and to prepare humanity for a world where science has replaced religion, where new values must be established and a different meaning to living must be found in order to overcome a phase of doubt and even despair. Man has been affirmed as standing alone and free; the old protections have been removed, and new challenges have to be faced.

Edmund Husserl (1952) The next step in this philosophical movement towards re-examination was one that was no longer centred around emotion and experience but based on a thoroughly intellectual and, indeed, on an alternative scientific approach. The phenomenological movement started by Edmund Husserl, German philosopher and pupil of Brentano, aimed at purifying academic thinking about our experience of the world.

Phenomenologists introduced the idea that ultimately all knowledge can only be subjective and that therefore all science that strives for objectivity in a purely numerical fashion separates us from the truth which must include subjective experience. Husserl proposed that we should go back to the things themselves and re-experience the sense of wonder that things simply 'are' rather than take them for granted or use them. This initiated the method of phenomenological reduction, which consists of clearing our path of perception and experience by examining our preconceptions and assumptions about the world first, so that we are able to consider things in a way that is pure and fresh.

The existentialist thinkers   Existentialists such as Heidegger, Sartre, Merleau-Ponty, Camus and others have all been greatly inspired by this original phenomenological work – as well as by the innovations of Kierkegaard and Nietzsche.

Existentialism became a very popular philosophical movement in Europe between 1940 and 1950, and was concerned with establishing a theory of human experience and knowledge through the application both of the methods of phenomenology and the philosophies of freedom. Salvation was no longer seen as obtained from God or any other external source, but always through the act of existence itself.

Sartre's (1948) ideas were particularly instrumental in transforming philosophical theory into a practical philosophy and a psychology of living. His descriptions of mankind's struggle to exist and to be in the face of nothingness, his analyses of the internal processes involved in this constant struggle, his insights into the nature of imagination and human emotions, and his account of human relationships are all in the domain of philosophical psychology and together form a strong body of reference to the understanding of human experience as opposed to the mere description of that experience which is provided by conventional psychology (Sartre 1949, 1951).

The early existential therapists   Binswanger in Switzerland and Minkowski in France were among the first to apply phenomenological and existential thinking to working with patients. Both emphasized the importance of understanding the entire structure of existence of the patient. They opened the door to a new kind of psychotherapy, which is still even now in its formative stages (Valle and King 1978). Medard Boss is currently one of the foremost representatives of this movement in Europe (Boss 1963, 1975).

In the United States, Rollo May (1958) and Irving Yalom (1980), among others, have popularized some of the existential therapeutic ideas, while those such as Rogers, Perls and Ellis have also put certain of these ideas into practice. There has not been a radical existential approach in the United States based firmly on the continental European ideas, and much work still needs to be done if a complete existential method is to take its place in the world of psychotherapy.

Developments in Britain

While existential ideas were gradually losing some of their direct impact as a fashionable philosophy on the Continent, and while they were applied in a diluted form by some practitioners in the USA, Britain became the breeding ground for a renewed, vigorous interest in the existential approach. A radical British psychiatrist based his reconsideration of the schizophrenic experience of the world on a combination of object-relations theory and Sartrean existentialism (Collier 1977). R.D. Laing (1970a; Laing and Esterson 1970) took the world by storm with his writings which for the first time in Britain emphasized the importance of understanding the subjectivity of experience of the patient, and in particular that of the schizophrenic experience.

This emphasis on experience and understanding, breaking away from prejudice, diagnosis and objectifying forms of treatment, led to the creation of the so-called therapeutic communities: private homes where previously labelled schizophrenics could find asylum to journey through the authentic experience of madness (Berke and Barnes 1973).

This new approach which seemed based on freedom, choice and individual responsibility, appealed greatly to the sixties generation. Many people came to England to taste this alternative way of life. Laing was idealized by those who wanted recognition for the truth of their inner experience, for the pain they felt in living in a scientific and technological, objectifying world. He was the person who seemed to take the next practical step forward from the earlier successful, Continental existential philosophy movement; not surprisingly, his ideas were more popular on the Continent than in his own country. However, this original pull became less strong once the movement seemed to have no concrete, original therapeutic strategies to propose other than life in a household and a referral to usually quite psychoanalytic or eclectic forms of psychotherapy.

The Philadelphia Association (PA) of R.D. Laing eventually moved in various other directions of interest, such as Zen Buddhism, rebirthing and Lacanian psychoanalysis. The Arbours Association, which derived from the PA and was founded by Joe Berke and Morty Schatzman, eventually moved more and more into a psychoanalytic direction with definite Kleinian undertones.

The existential method of therapy as such has not been further developed explicitly by R.D. Laing or his followers. Several individuals in Britain are, however, each developing their own particular brand of existential therapy: some after a phase of involvement in or training with the Philadelphia or Arbours Associations; others following more directly the psychoanalytic trail that leads towards existential analysis. Of special interest are the contributions of Aaron Esterson (1970) and David Cooper (1972) to the original resurgence of the approach in this country. More recently, Peter Lomas (1981) and F.A. Jenner (1982) have made noteworthy contributions to the field. In association with the PA, John Heaton (1982) and Steve Gans (1984) also have published relevant articles on the application of existentialism and phenomenology to psychiatry. The *British Journal of Phenomenology* also regularly publishes articles on the impact of existentialism and phenomenology on psychotherapy.

The author has developed her own method of existential praxis, which she teaches both in Antioch University's London-based master's programme in the psychology of therapy and counselling and on the South-West London College's counselling courses (van Deurzen-Smith, in preparation).

Theoretical Assumptions

The image of the person

Human nature is versatile: people are intrinsically different from objects or concepts in that they cannot be defined other than by their basic lack of essence. A house is a house, a table is a table, a tree is a tree, but a person is not the same person every day or even every second. Humans define themselves not by essence but by existence: it is only in the way in which I choose my actions and my existence that I define myself as I become. The being of humans is therefore closer to nothingness. It can only come into existence by choosing a particular way to fill the nothingness which exists both inside the person and between people.

If I grow passive, I will be reduced to nothingness; for example, even if I have gained a reputation for myself in the past, this does not guarantee my ongoing essence as reputable – it can be lost at any moment. I can never rest on my laurels; nothing can be taken for granted; everything is to be reinvented, moment after moment. I am only what I actively exist as now. Humans are therefore ever changing, and much is possible for the person who affirms this active selfhood positively.

The uniqueness of each individual is also determined by this capacity of humanity to change and adapt to multiple circumstances and situations. Each person is a completely different version of a 'human'; no person can therefore ever have complete knowledge or understanding of another's character or experience – subjectivity is all. Classifications of character or personality can only make sense if they focus on the active mode of being of each person, rather than objectively categorizing some intrinsic and externally observable qualities. People can indeed exist in various modes. Some of the tasks of living are predetermined; and although the way in which people address themselves to those tasks cannot be pre-classified – and indeed, the way in which any one individual addresses herself to that task is not necessarily the same in a predictable manner – at least the tasks and modes of being themselves can be classified.

Binswanger (1963) was the first to introduce the concepts of *Umwelt*, *Mitwelt* and *Eigenwelt* (the concept of *Uberwelt* will be added for completeness).

The relation to the Umwelt or 'world around us'   This refers to *the physical dimension*: the relation we have to the earthly, material world; the way in which we relate to our bodily self; the way in which we relate to objects and the physical realities of space, climate, weather, health, disease, sexuality and procreation.

The relation to the Mitwelt or 'world with others'   This is *the social dimension*, the relation we have to other people around us, or to animals if they, too, represent the 'other'. It includes our attitude towards culture, society, co-operation, rivalry, friendship, hate and love; our awareness of sameness and difference, unity and plurality, withdrawal and expansion.

The relation to the Eigenwelt or 'own world'   This, *the inner dimension*, is the relation we have to our inner self, the way we view and imagine our being as uniquely affirming itself. The relation to our own creativity and authenticity, strengths and weaknesses, activity and passivity, feelings, thoughts, imagination, reflection, ideas, and aspirations. It also includes the relationship we have to our own past, present, and future.

The relation to the Uberwelt or 'world above' This, *the cosmic dimension*, is the relation to the universe, to life in its transcendental manifestation and to infinity. This includes our attitude towards time and death, our religious beliefs and our spirituality.

Concepts of psychological health and disturbance

The healthy individual is the one who embraces life fully and moves ahead actively and courageously in growing awareness of the four modes of being, increasingly capable of negotiating life's obstacles and perils successfully with spirit and enjoyment in spite of, or possibly thanks to, ups and downs. The person who lives in this way will be on the way to authentic existence. 'Authentic' means 'genuinely proceeding from its own source', in other words, in close co-operation with the inner truth and spirituality. This implies that the authentic human being, rather than following external facts or opinions, is capable of living in a way that is true to a more intrinsic value-system and to an awareness of universal reality. Being authentic, which is the existential synonym of psychological health, does not necessarily mean being ruthlessly frank with fellow human beings, being 'up-front' and often cruel; neither does it consist simplistically of obeying the rules of free choice and 'doing your own thing' regardless or 'taking responsibility' or 'owning up' for certain words or acts.

Authenticity can only be reached through a long and arduous process of relentless and sincere introspection. It can only come forth as a side-effect from an active commitment to truth. Becoming authentic is about facing life and self. It is about welcoming the laws of the universe, including death and pain, destruction and despair as well as life and pleasure, creation and joy. It is about coming to terms with human limitations and possibilities by coming to terms with one's own experience of these things. It includes the constantly renewed recognition of one's answerability to one's inner self – thereby increasing one's ability to make positive choices and to initiate action and change.

Psychological disturbance, therefore, is defined as the blocking of this authenticating process. In Sartre's (1951) terms, disturbance is life in 'bad faith' (*mauvaise foi*) or self-deception; it is being inauthentic (Heidegger 1949). Those who live inauthentically pursue goals that are not essentially their own; they take on roles and believe – or nearly succeed in convincing themselves that they believe – in the necessity of such roles or attitudes. Thinking of oneself as a milkman or a Master of Arts or a madman rather than apprehending the contingency of these roles is part of the trap of becoming inauthentic.

The disturbed (inauthentic) person performs acts that have no personal meaning or value. She acts without awareness of self and in the exclusive context of duty, opinion, or some other sort of externally determined factor. Neuroses or psychosomatic disorders can be the consequence of such false-self-based living. Psychoses, on the other hand, are the manifestation of the nothingness we can fall into when we try without a firm starting point or without appropriate maps of life to venture into authenticity by denying external pressures and realities altogether.

Authenticity can not be reached by living exclusively according to convention; neither can it be reached by breaking with convention before an inner stability has been found and authentic strength built up.

The acquisition of psychological disturbance

It should be clear from the above that psychological disturbance from the existential position is seen as being acquired by each and every one of us through the simple realities of conformism and discipline. The instruments of this learning to be inauthentic are education and family life (Laing 1971). As Kierkegaard had already pointed out in the early nineteenth century in his book *Fear and Trembling and Sickness unto Death* (Kierkegaard 1954), mankind attempts constantly to deny the reality of nothingness. From this constant attempt to deny the unavoidability of death and disease, to deny the limitations of living and being human, the person construes a false life on the unstable foundation of a belief in comfort and pleasure. This false life is lived by false selves: inauthentic layers of character or personality that obscure the reality of life and silence the voice of the inner self and aspirations to truth.

Most people learn very early on in life that it seems profitable to go with the system, to join the opinion of the strongest group or to build up the outer appearance that is most acceptable. Most people very soon become duped into believing in the external values they have conformed to, burying deep down their own aspirations to truth and reality of being. Most people therefore experience shocking gaps in the meaning and full-ness of their lives at crucial times such as adolescence, mid-life and old age or in moments of crisis such as bereavement, marital breakdown, unemployment and so on. Certain other people never attain sufficient social status to want to compromise their inner values: the incentive is just not strong enough. When, in a family, no place is given to one of the members, when her right to exist or to be a person in her own right is constantly denied – be it by explicit references to her as 'immature' and 'incapable' or by implicit collusion in making this person an extension of another member (in symbiotic relationship with the mother, for instance) – then this person will build up a false self. This untenable situation will not last very long as this false self is making no contact with inner reality (Laing and Esterson 1970). Psychotic withdrawal from the whole social 'battle' will ensue sooner or later when the 'no win' situation has reached a climax.

This same situation may occur in later life, not necessarily as a result of early parental destructive influence but possibly as the outcome of the impact of a school, social group, work-place or a partner. It could happen in any case where the person's confidence in being able to gain from adaptation to inauthentic reality is undermined. If at any point in life, through any event or social dynamic, a person's hope for the possible success of a false-self adaptation is shattered, one of two things may occur. If the person has already established a core sense of self with the ability to face the world and life with a minimum of authentic ontological security[1], then the precipitating event will only become a stimulus to pull oneself together and build a life more on real, inner foundations than on false, external ones. This is a step towards authenticity and genuine health. However, if the person's sense of inner reality, of self, has not had a chance to establish itself firmly, a total breakdown may occur. The de-spair accompanying this breakdown could become fertile ground for a beginning of authenticity; indeed, the struggle towards existential health necessarily includes this aspect of despair and doubt.

It is of course particularly to those in this phase of existence that exis-tential therapy is geared: as a process of reflection and taking stock, of examination of priorities and inner values, and ultimately of making de-cisions about further direction in life.

The perpetuation of psychological disturbance

It should be obvious by now that the existential concept of psychological disturbance is not a static one: one does not acquire a disturbance or a symptom once and for all; one is also never safely out of reach of disturbance. The polarity health-unhealth is a continuum on which we move back and forth in one direction and the other, according to the degree of clarity and integrity we enact and realize in ourselves at any point in time. As soon as I take myself for granted in any role or any way of being – for instance, as 'basically healthy' – the danger of obscuring my own intention towards health is at hand.

Nothing is more easy than the perpetuation of inauthenticity or self-deception: possessions, jobs, friends, partners and children can all be used to hold up the illusion of my invulnerability. The illusion of my external reality can be temporarily secured by the right sort of clothing, social skills or status. The better I am able to establish these walls and this armour around me, the more will I become identified with the illusion, with the false self, and the more weak and unreal will my inner reality become. In times of crisis, those people who function with the best-defended false selves suffer most if the crisis successfully breaks down the outer deception. Those who are most in touch with their inner reality will succeed in crossing these crisis situations. The intermediate position of having rejected false-self adaptation without having firmly established inner reality may be preferable to inauthenticity. Indeed, Frankl (1959) has shown how those who have schizoid (i.e. inwardly turned) tendencies may have more ease in surviving in an extremely harsh situation like a concentration camp.

However, under normal conditions society encourages the perpetuation of false-self adaptation and therefore of psychological disturbance. Our Western economy is based on the craving for falsehood and illusion: machines and appliances, houses and clothes, are over-produced in order to satisfy the urgency of escape from reality, escape from our inner freedom (Fromm 1942). None of us are entirely free of this pressure, and the question can be raised whether we wish to be or indeed whether we would be capable or strong enough to live life in total earnestness and honesty. Without a basic awareness of our own compliance with this falsehood we would be unable to deal with its consequences: for instance, the nuclear problem, wars, pollution, drugs, an amoral society with a high crime rate, and so on.

The psychological disturbance of individuals is a reflection of the psychological disturbance that we perpetuate as a group in the lie we live today. Those of us who break down or face a crisis are usually amongst those closest to sanity or authenticity. But only if there is strength and support enough to face this crisis will the breakthrough towards health occur.

Practice

Goals of therapy

The goals of existential therapy are: first, to encourage the client to become authentic and relinquish self-deception; second, to assist the client to clarify and grasp the inner value-system and mode of existence in the world; third, to enable the client to come to terms with life, by building up confidence in and reliance on inner self and reality; and fourth, to explore with the client what her priorities are and to eventually determine a new direction for living.

The emphasis in therapy is always on understanding of the subjective experience of the client. Authenticity can only be reached after the client has decided to investigate honestly what her life is all about at present. Transparency can only come about very gradually while a basic shift in attitude towards existence is achieved.

The goals of therapy are therefore very general. They only point in the direction of progress towards truth and meaning, as any serious philosophical investigation would. The more specific goals are directly related to the client's particular problems in living. Existential therapy is unlikely to focus on certain aspects of behaviour or symptoms that the client wants to be free of. In such cases where the client does have such concrete worries, these are considered as one manifestation of a particular attitude towards the world. It is this attitude that will then be examined. The assumption is that a change in attitude will, as a side-effect, eliminate any symptoms or undesirable behaviour connected with it. By definition, focusing upon specific problem-solving or symptom elimination reinforces a mechanical attitude to life experience in the client's awareness; in other words, if bad faith is emphasized, bad faith will flourish. Only by searching for the inner kernel of truth and sanity will real change for the better eventually be effected. Although there are many forms of therapy that may offer 'quick cures', they rarely involve the client's basic belief system or general mode of living.

The client's ability to become answerable to herself is the basic, first requirement of all lasting and ongoing improvement. This commitment to being true to oneself and aware of one's ability to reinvent the past, the present and the future through a basic change in attitude towards life is what will generate new subjective meaning to existence.

The person of the therapist

If therapy is to be on the level of essential examination of life and the meaning of life, the therapist will clearly have to be a person who has a deep interest in philosophy. The professional attitude of the existential therapist must be in line with his personal life and commitments, and could in no case be purely technological or skill-based. In this approach, the person of the therapist is indeed more important than the role of the therapist; it is the quality of understanding, awareness and clarity that the therapist can provide as a fellow human being that will light up the darkness in which the client is likely to be groping for new direction.

In terms of training, the implications are rather unusual. The existential therapist will preferably have a thorough knowledge not only of psychology but of philosophy and an ongoing involvement in philosophical investigation and questioning. The therapist's personal life is of great importance, as a journey towards becoming truthful and authentic will probably have led the trainee through various crises that have been dealt with inventively and creatively. Times of despair, anxiety and loneliness must be a living reality that she can struggle through successfully. Alongside the firm interest and training in philosophy, the existential therapist should first and foremost be committed to the practice of living.

Only a person who has come to terms with the major aspects of existence will be ready to be a consultant to those who have difficulty coming to terms with life; in other words, the therapist needs to be a person who is actively on the way to authenticity. The road to authenticity is that of self-examination and critical thinking about the meaning of existence. It is not, as is sometimes believed, that of becoming more and more spontaneously honest or congruent with one's feelings, but that of reflection and discovery of such essential principles of truth as can be found in one's deepest self. This discovery of self can only occur when the comfort of deceptive living is exchanged for a personal struggle with at least the following aspects of being human:

(a) To face *finitude*: to have an open attitude towards death and an ability to envisage one's own part in the cycle of life and death.

(b) To envisage *suffering* as an intrinsic part of existence rather than trying to escape from it. This is the idea that incurable crisis is essentially part of life and will predictably return, as will also relief and joy (Anderson 1978). Part of this involves accepting anxiety and seeing difficulties as a challenge and part of the adventure of being human.

(c) To be receptive to *awareness* in all available ways (through sensory experience, feeling, intuition and reflection) and to be able to experience this more and more fully.

(d) To be aware of the subjectivity of the experience of *time*. To view past, present and future as a continuum that one is a creative part of ('I am what I make for the future of the givens of the past').

(e) To come to terms with the reality of *transformation* as it happens both in us and in the world around us; to build confidence in this sense of flux as well as to succeed in actively navigating the stream of life.

(f) To investigate the basic *values* that may be the best guide-lines and safeguards of right direction.

(g) To build a sense of *self* that is strong and capable enough to withstand harsh conditions, a sense of self based on inner truth and strength rather than on a false self.

(h) To be capable of *autonomy*, which is different from independence in that it is the recognition of one's ability to function as a unit which is part of the larger unit of relationships in society; it is the capacity to affirm one's individuality and ability to face oneself alone.

(i) To grasp the possibility of *affirmation of life*, the ability to say 'yes' and embrace existence fully and joyfully (Tillich 1977).

(j) To be responsible, which means answerable to oneself about the choices one makes and the actions one takes. This also implies the active living of one's *inner freedom*, which is of course different from an omnipotent fantasy about total control over the world and one's living conditions (Frankl 1973).

(k) To affirm that this freedom will necessarily lead to choice of direction which will involve a *commitment* (meaning cannot be found randomly). This commitment will involve the capacity to overcome the limitations of one's originally necessary self-centredness in the direction of care for other humans. This will manifest itself as *I-Thou* relating to others, which is about full respect and acknowledgement of the other's subjective experience (Buber 1958). This comprehensive attitude towards others cannot be learned as a skill, for it is not mere empathy or unconditional positive regard; it surges up naturally when all the above are becoming living realities.

The existential position on training therapists is therefore about a process of apprenticeship first through life and then in a supervisory relationship with an accomplished therapist. The therapist who learns this trade in this way will most likely be capable of a special kind of flexibility. She will be particularly sensitive to the dialectical dimension of problems in living. Conflicts will be seen in terms of polarities that can be overcome usefully only if the strength of both extremes is included in the synthesis of opposites.

The attitude of wonder that is so essential in phenomenology will extend beyond wonder about self, others, and the world to wonder about and reverence for the universal principles that organize our lives and the cosmos. This transcendence of pure humanity will be the horizon for any existential work. This brings us full circle to the first point above, in that, facing our finitude ultimately means facing the infinite (Jaspers 1954). Clearly, the existential therapist needs to bring to her professional work ongoing clarity on her philosophical position to help her towards a greater recognition of the client's current philosophical position in life, thus encouraging the examination of its gaps, contradictions and possible destructive effect on the client's current life-style.

Therapeutic style

Existential therapy has the reputation of advocating a non-technological, relationship-oriented therapeutic style. Although in principle this is correct, it is often interpreted as giving licence for anyone to do anything with anybody. In fact, the existential mode of working, while focusing on relationship rather than technique, is nevertheless a therapeutic method with an explicit framework. This framework consists of a clear arrangement concerning the time and place of the (usually weekly, sometimes twice-weekly) meetings. Client and therapist are both seated in comfortable chairs, probably at a ninety-degree angle. The business arrangement is that the client pays a standard fee in return for the therapist's assistance in clarifying the basic problems in living that preoccupy the client at present as well as in exploring the general attitudes towards existence that she operates with. The focus of the 55 minute session will be exclusively on the client's experience and self-examination – not (according to a popular misconception) on a sharing of experience.

The relationship between therapist and client is that of two partners who together investigate the existence of one of them. The differences between them are that the one has to pay money while the other receives it and that the one receives the service of full attention that the other provides. Also, the one is an expert on her own experience while the other will proceed carefully in the exploration and understanding of this experience; and the one is, for the moment, lost on the seas of life, while the other has attained a certain mastery in sailing with the winds and around the rocks and has some basic sense of direction. These differences between them are thus complementary and should make fruitful co-operation possible and desirable for both.

An existential therapist is a lay version of the spiritual guide that exists in most religions. The obvious need for such 'guidance' in our present day and age, where religion has faded and fails to satisfy many, has generally only been responded to with help based on the medical model, which usually aims at the alleviation of pain and dissolution of pathology. The existential model proposes the return to an ethical exploration and support system that is capable of addressing the issues that have been neglected in twentieth-century Western society. The existential style of therapy will reflect this function of mentorship in the discussion-oriented session where the therapist will regularly stimulate thought on certain important issues or encourage the client to explore her subjective experience in all its meanderings. Also, she will encourage the client to examine the exact meaning of the concepts that constitute her picture of the world, and will from time to time probably question prejudices and preconceptions.

All this is done in a co-operative atmosphere closer to that of a private tutorial than to that of a medical consultation. The target of the relationship between therapist and client is that of the I-Thou interaction, which acknowledges the 'other' in her essential individuality and uniqueness. This posits the right of the individual to be recognized in her own genuine selfhood rather than be subject to preconceived notions of what a person is or should be (Buber 1958). This respect for the client includes a respect for her present need or habit of being inauthentic, or her right to remain so if so desired.

Major therapeutic techniques

Classically speaking, the existential approach does not favour technique. It works specifically against the danger of reducing the human therapeutic relationship to an objectifying experimental situation. It is important that this remains the central statement on technique in the existential way of working, especially in the face of increasing pressure to standardize, quantify and objectively assess methods of psychotherapy.

This does not, however, absolve us from the need to answer the question: How do I apply all the above in practice? Each existential therapist will, of course, employ her own style and personality and will have the licence or even the duty to do so more than in other approaches. One could even posit that to the extent to which any therapist of any conviction dares to enter into the therapeutic relationship as a person rather than exclusively as a technician, to this extent is she also an existential therapist.

Encounter To make that personal encounter the very basis of therapy is to opt for a fundamentally existential approach. This attitude can be found for instance in person-centred therapy (Rogers 1951). It is the event of real communication between two human beings that is the crux of the matter. For the client, what will transpire from this is not only the experience of being recognized as real by the therapist, but in turn the experience of recognizing the reality of the therapist. This is why the emphasis is on the I-Thou relationship and why there is no way in which this can be turned into a technique. No amount of listening skills or reflecting skills is going to replace or constitute the reality of a genuine openness and truthfulness.

Exploration of the subjective world-view This openness and truthfulness will manifest itself in the way in which the therapist will,

together with the client, identify and address the issues that are important for the client to face. It is in the active exploration with the client of
the client's ideas and assumptions about life that the existential therapist
will be able to live up to her status of mentor. It is in the action of inves-
tigating the client's inner experience and searching for the values and
meaning that she believes in that the client will be able to find not only
insight but the experience of having a companion in the struggle for survival. Some of the leading questions used during this phase are: 'What is
this like for you?', 'How do you experience this?' and 'How do you con-
ceive of this?'

Enquiry into meaning   Once we have a clearer picture of the client's
subjective view of the world and are able to grasp its outward limitations,
an exploration of its internal structure is initiated with a deeper enquiry
into the actual meaning of the words and concepts that the client uses. It
is all too easy to mime understanding and convince oneself in the process
that one hears the client and feels empathy towards her. The therapist
does not take her understanding for granted, but asks for definitions. A
real comprehension of the client's world can only come forth (both for
the therapist and the client) from a constant questioning of the obvious or
taken for granted. An apparently empathetic therapist may be on a totally
wrong track: what is worse, the client may follow the therapist in that
track and end up believing that she has been understood and has
understood herself without any real questioning of the lies that continue
to obscure the inward light. It is indeed only if and when the therapeutic
process reaches those depths of the client's experience where light shines,
where the client recognizes her own truth, that the enquiry has reached
its aim. This will be instantly recognizable by the immediate upsurge of
strength, potency and will to live. There will be a strong emotional
resonance similar to the experience one has when listening to a favourite
piece of music, a resonance that is the experience of being moved, of finding oneself at once part of the stream of life. One can only come to this
re-experience of oneness with oneself and existence by systematically
scraping off the surface layers of prejudice, falsehood and self-deception.
    This is done through a careful process of scrutiny. The therapist dur-
ing this phase of therapy will remind the client continuously of the
importance of the suspension of assumptions. The leading questions during this phase will be: 'What does this mean to you?', 'What does this

remind you of?', 'What is the purpose of this?' and 'Where does this lead you?'

Strengthening the inner self   Once the outer prejudice has been loosened up by this process, the inner self becomes more directly involved in the therapeutic encounter. The client will start to be able to experience the sense of 'I am the one who experiences this, that way', 'I am the one who moves through life in this manner', 'It is I who approaches people in that way' and 'It is I who craves for this reality of mine to be recognized.' This is the time when inner self-reliance is discovered and strengthened. Personal values can now be uncovered. It is these base-line values that were probably buried under heaps of bad faith and external values and that will now become the guide-lines for new direction. The therapist encourages this focus on the inner self by reminding the client to answer her own questions, rather than by asking the client any further questions.

Establishing priorities   It is when the client comes to grips with those inner values – that is, when she is starting to ask the question, 'What really matters to me in living?' – that little by little priorities for choices will be established. The client is likely to say things like, 'If this is what matters most, then the sacrifice of that is not really such a sacrifice.' It becomes possible to see clearly where the future lies: first to imagine, then to choose, then to construct a road towards a new sort of life.

Of course, during this time there will be many instances of sinking back into old habits and surface living – in fact, there will always be –but the initiative of the client to question the relapse gradually becomes more frequent and certain. The client learns to recognize her illusions, and will need less and less prompting in climbing back to the inner self. The therapist will now use gentle reminders of what was worked through earlier in therapy and will encourage the client to think imaginatively and creatively about future possibilities.

Making a commitment   It is in this ongoing adventure of constant discovery, exploration and reappraisal that the self eventually becomes strong and determined enough to implement priorities. The time is ripe for the making of a consciously chosen commitment to this truth-seeking way of life. It is now often possible to recognize a place, an action, a person or an idea which warrants full engagement; now learning is put into practice, and concrete changes are made. The therapist now more than ever becomes the mentor who reminds the client of the importance of an easy pace, of the need to keep on exploring and questioning rather than run straight into a new complacency. The client may be encouraged to picture possible difficulties and obstacles. The therapist assists the client in preparing for total self-reliance, which can only be based on constant self-examination and realignment with inner values. The therapist's main task now is to monitor this self-evaluative process.

Living   Once the client is convinced that she is able to manage this ongoing process alone, no matter what the external circumstances are, the sessions are ended. Often a follow-up meeting will be arranged three months later, or a regular check-up point may be decided on (say, every six months for the next two years). In many cases, however, the client will have gained sufficient self-confidence to want to find this opportunity for regular recapitulation of priorities and authenticity in some other way, usually in an intimate relationship.

After all, paying money for guidance that one is able to find in one's self and with someone one cares for becomes a superfluous luxury. The therapy ends naturally in this way, probably within a span of three months to a year from its beginning. The task of the therapist is to allow this separation to happen as early as possible; the temptation is usually to hold on to the client for rather too long. The technique is now that of reminding oneself and the client that problems are never solved and that life will always remain full of obstacles and crises. If the client can face that, the client is ready.

The change process in therapy

Change is arrived at through self-comprehension, a comprehension that is attained through careful scrutiny. This happens through a process of defining external reality as it is subjectively experienced. Reality is then redefined as inner priorities emerge.

The emphasis throughout is on internal rather than external change. The therapist inspires the client to reclaim her capacity to live authentically. The client re-experiences a sense of inner strength when the base line and essential quality of existence are envisaged. The courage of being true to oneself is then discovered. A *sine qua non* of permanent authenticity is the permanent self-evaluation that constitutes the nucleus of the therapeutic process

The indispensable counterpart of the client's learning this self-evaluative method is, of course, the therapist's commitment to exactly the same process (van Deurzen-Smith 1983). The criterion for this evaluation is obviously the inner value-system; what one evaluates is the extent to which one succeeds in being authentic, not only with the client but in one's personal life. The evaluation of one's interventions in the therapeutic situation will be seen in the light of the goal of *becoming* a therapist rather than in imagining one ever can *be* just that. The existential therapist therefore checks interventions in the following ways.

The first is by incessantly checking back the effect of the intervention and by taking the client's reaction to it most seriously. Only if my words make sense to you and connect with your inner experience am I on the right road towards understanding your world. This does not necessarily mean that I have to use the same words as the client; the words themselves have far less power than the meaning I express by the way I respond and pick up the essence of what matters to the client at that moment in time rather than some triviality or other, in whatever perfect technical way. As long as the client signals to me that I am making sense to her and that together we are throwing light into those corners that were darkest, the intervention was right.

Second, by a continuous questioning of my own prejudice. If I do not ask myself repeatedly whether by a particular word or concept I really understand the same thing as the client does, I will easily lapse into complacency. So I ask myself how I came to the conclusion that 'freedom', say, is an important value for the client: did I think up the concept first and adjust my hearing of the client's words to suit my intentions, or did I only formulate that word slowly after searching for a concept that would appropriately translate these descriptions of the client's world, these definitions, these images.

Finally, by asking myself after each session how truthful I was in my attitudes to both myself and the client. The ultimate criterion for the evaluation of my therapeutic work is whether I was applying myself in accordance with my values, my philosophy of life and my ethics of therapy (van Deurzen-Smith 1984).

Case Example

Marie-Louise is a 24-year old Frenchwoman. In the first interview she presents herself as a small, but sturdy, colourfully dressed and generously made-up young lady. She works in England as an au pair and has done so for the last nine months. She left France because she did not know how to solve some of the situations she was involved in. She had broken off a three-year relationship with her boyfriend because he wanted her to marry him and move with him to another town where he had just been promoted. She felt this was a trap and that she would be unable to maintain her independence if she went along with him; independence is one of the main concepts that Marie-Louise's choices are apparently based on. Of her three sisters (all older than she) two are married and installed in 'bourgeois' family life. Marie-Louise has obvious contempt for this.

The third sister has an alternative life-style but is unable to manage her life satisfactorily. The parents are divorced after many years of fighting. Marie-Louise's picture of marriage is that of a battlefield where no one can win. Her picture of her own and her sister's alternative life-styles is that of a romantic voyage into nowhere.

She has fled to England to escape from the impossible choice between marrying her boyfriend and becoming like the two elder sisters and her mother, or opting for a bohemian life-style and ending up like her other sister. She now works for an upper-middle-class family in Richmond and spends all her time off with a group of free-floating people of her own age, around Hammersmith.

The problem she experiences is that of not knowing what to do with her life; every possible option seems to carry potential destruction. She thought she could solve things by starting a new life in England; now she realizes everything is still the same, or worse. The French ex-fiancé has taken up a relationship with another woman. In the gang she hangs out with in England, there is a total denial of the value of a personal relationship. While she was pregnant a few months ago, the other women in the group supported her in obtaining an abortion while using the occasion to cut her off from her privileged relationship with one of the men in the group. They call her 'Marylou' and do not seem interested in hearing about her past life in France. She is able to talk quite freely about her French life with Mildred, her employer, but she senses Mildred's pressure on her to conform and settle down in a 'mature marriage'. At this point in time there is no one she trusts implicitly: everyone is out to make her give up something, and nobody really knows her. This theme recurs many times throughout the weekly therapy sessions that take place over a four-month period. Her trust in me is based chiefly on the fact that I at least admit what I want from her: a fee for the session and a commitment to working towards total frankness. What I offer in return seems most attractive to her: a joint building up of an understanding of her experience in all its many facets and complexity; permission for her to explore the completeness of self that has been lost between her fear of being reduced to a conventional, 'maturely' marrying, dependent Marie-Louise and a fear of being doomed to become Marylou, an outlaw and desperately lonely. We agree on a once-a-week arrangement, with a review after three months.

In the second session, Marie-Louise talks about a letter she has had from François, her ex-fiancé. He tries to make her feel jealous and offers her marriage again, more on his terms than ever. To Marylou it seems like a last chance to become 'mature' and 'dependent': if she refuses this time to go straight, she will have to be a 'punk' ever after – that is how she views the dilemma. And most of the session is spent on exploring the definitions and fantasies that constitute the dilemma in her mind. What does it mean to be married? What does it mean to be a punk? What is her own world like inside, beyond those definitions of a way of life? What essential qualities of life are not to be found in either of those accounts of reality?

Slowly, Marie-Louise starts to talk about what life 'should be like' or 'could be like' instead of focusing on the two thus far impossible realities she has envisaged. It transpires that what matters most is to sometimes find a life where she will be with people who can listen to her and talk about those things that matter: independence *and* romantic love for instance, rather than either/or. We talk about her image of independence and dependence. She discovers that what she really values is autonomy, i.e. the ability to be a person in her own right, strong enough to remain true to herself while relating deeply to others.

Her Hammersmith group is, of course, in favour of 'independence', but then it follows that love cannot exist: to maintain independence one has to reject commitment to anything or anybody. That is not what Marie-Louise wants, although it has often seemed the only way out of smothering relationships. She is starting to disidentify with the ideas of Marylou. She is starting to identify her own personally meaningful ideas and aspirations. She is afraid it will not be realistic to live according to her own ideas, following her own conscience rather than the norm of some existing group in society; she does not think anyone will understand or agree. She wonders where I will want to push her: will I stand by her side when she makes her real self known, or will I come down in judgement, in favour of independence or dependence?

The next session she challenges me. She breaks down in despair and cries for nearly half an hour uninterruptedly. There is no direct cause other than her expectation of me letting her down and trying to perk her up in spite of herself. She fears I may propose a solution, announcing my bias by choosing the 'right life-style' for her. It is only because I do not do this and instead relate to her isolation and despair, to her fear, by letting her know that I respect it and will allow it, it is only because I show her this respect, first by saying these things and then by letting her cry her own sorrow through, that she starts to feel some confidence – not only in my understanding of her reality but chiefly and for the first time in her own right to be just exactly the way she is.

The next session is different. Marie-Louise does not wear make-up. 'It only messes up when I cry anyways.' She comes in to sort out her part in the relationship with François. She has still not replied to the letter he sent her two weeks ago; she is still overflowing with resentment for his treatment of her, his expectations of her fitting in with his life. I remind her several times of the importance of examining her active part in the relationship rather than focusing on her feelings about what he does to her. She discovers that by doing this she not only gets insight into her own character and actions, but also builds up a stronger image of herself as an active human being who does not exclusively respond, react and feel but also creates, initiates and acts.

This new way of viewing her relationship inspires her to write a letter to François the following week. She is pleased with herself for having formulated for the first time what she wants out of a relationship. She considers the relationship ended because she now knows what she does want to experience with a man.

During those weeks the sessions focus on her slowly building up self-esteem. My interventions are all geared to help us explore her inner frame of reference. The Catholic values are much more intrinsically present than she ever wanted to acknowledge herself. She is only able to acknowledge her own rights once she has been able to acknowledge her own 'guilt' in terms of the Catholic Church. Sleeping around and having an abortion are not things that she can easily forgive herself for; in order to live that life of 'freedom' she has had to disown her conscience; she has had to live in 'bad faith', with the created image of the independent Marylou. She lost her substance in the process. Gradually, she is now rebuilding her own sense of substance and identity. Some time during these two months she receives a letter from Bernadette, her actress sister, who informs her of the attempted suicide of one of their mutual friends. Marie-Louise understands that act as the only possible way out of the emptiness that follows the flight away from one's own inner reality. She is determined to not flee any more. She has several open disagreements with both her friends in Hammersmith and Mildred, her employer. She concludes that she cannot any longer 'play the part' in either case. She decides towards the middle of the third month in therapy that the time has come for her to explore a more creative future; and she plans a trip to France to investigate training courses in social work. Her idea is to find a place in the world where she will be able finally to be herself and help other people to do so too.

She has now been in England for exactly a year and thinks she is ready to go back and face her sisters, her parents, even François if she happened to meet him. She is determined to stick to the values she has discovered as her own. To be autonomous rather than dependent or independent is the most crucial decision in terms of her relationship to her family. She fears, however, that no one will understand her new self, although she finds that Mildred has been more respectful of her since she applied for the social work courses.

We have already arranged for the last review session before her trip to France when she phones me in a panic one day. François has arrived in England without giving her any notice. He has come to see her in order to persuade her to come back and marry him. He affirms that he will respect her new sense of self, but he does not want to listen to her plans for study. Marie-Louise fears that her new autonomy will melt in front of this new proposal, which for the first time includes her as a person important enough to make a trip to England and abandon his current girlfriend for. She is sure it will not last if she gives in now, but she is also sure, suddenly, that she loves him and wants him to love her. In that phone call, she decides to tell François all of that and then go off on the trip as planned, alone. The review session is spent considering her growing sense of direction in the midst of all the distractions and disappointments that she fears she will meet on her way. We discuss the middle way between turning her back on people or situations because they have not allowed her sense of self and merging into other people's opinions or ways of life for the sake of it, giving up inner reality. Marie-Louise decides that her commitment to a course of study is of essential importance to her because she needs time to establish her new reality more concretely and substantially. She still fears it will mean a choice away from the relationship with François. She leaves with doubts, anxiety and guilt about walking out on François a second time, albeit this time for positive reasons.

When she comes back to England a few weeks later, it is only to fetch her luggage and say her goodbyes to Richmond, Mildred, Hammersmith and me. We have two sessions during this time. Marie-Louise looks very different from the way she did four months ago: she has found her own image somewhere between the classic woman and the punk girl styles. She has obtained a place on the desired course, but is already disappointed with the curriculum. We examine her expectations and her attitudes towards the course. At the end, she seems clear enough about what it is she wants from the course without having to expect it to provide her with the ultimate answer.

We talk less about her parents and François than might have been useful. It would have been good to be able to have some more sessions now that the new way of life is being established. Marie-Louise herself is pleased she is leaving me behind in England. She wants to do it on her own now. She wants to have her disappointments and fears and live through them without assistance.

That seems a healthy attitude. Though I am aware of the limitations of the metamorphosis, a good deal seems to have been accomplished and I have a basic confidence in her positive attitude towards life: she will find her way.

A letter, fifteen months later, indicates that Marie-Louise has had all the disappointments she expected. Her views on social work are certainly less idealistic than at the outset. She has, however, continued with her course of study and is finding satisfaction in her own ability to do so. She sees François at weekends and holidays, and there is a possibility of his obtaining a post near Marie-Louise's college. She says she would feel ready to live with him and commit herself to him if he were prepared to make his commitment clear by that move towards her.

It is very possible that the shortness and intensity of the therapy, combined with the urgency of the situation, was as important a factor in making this case a successful one as the focus on crucial existential issues. I suspect that in this case a long-term dynamic therapy might have been destructive, as would any therapy that had implied a specific future outcome.

Note

1 Ontological insecurity is defined by Laing (1970) as the experience of 'the individual (who) in the ordinary circumstances of living may feel more unreal than real; in a literal sense, more dead than alive; precariously differentiated from the rest of the world, so that his identity and autonomy are always in question'.

References

Anderson T G (1978) 'Existential Counselling' in Valle R S and King M (eds.) *Existential-Phenomenological Alternatives for Psychology*, Oxford University Press, New York

Berke J H, Barnes M (1973) *Two Accounts of a Journey Through Madness*, Penguin, Harmondsworth

Binswanger L (1963) *Being in the World*, translated by Needleman J, Basic Books, New York

Boss M (1963) *Psychoanalysis and Daseinsanalysis*, Basic Books, New York

Boss M (1975) *Existential Foundations of Medicine and Psychology*, Jason Aronson, New York

Buber M (1958) *I and Thou*, Scribners, New York

Collier A (1977) *R. D. Laing: The Philosophy and Politics of Psychotherapy*, Pantheon, New York

Cooper D (1972) *The Death of the Family*, Penguin, Harmondsworth

Esterson A (1970) *The Leaves of Spring*, Tavistock, London

Frankl V (1963) *Man's Search for Meaning*, Washington Square Press, New York

Frankl V (1973) *Psychotherapy and Existentialism*, Penguin, Harmondsworth

Fromm E (1942) *Fear of Freedom*, Kegan Paul, London

Gans S (1984) *Levinas and Pontalis: Meeting the Other as in a Dream*, Parousia Press, London

Heaton J (1982) 'A discussion on phenomenology, psychiatry and psychotherapy' in Jenner F A (ed.) *Phenomenology and Psychiatry*, Academic Press, New York

Heidegger M (1949) *Existence and Being*, Henry Regnery, Chicago

Husserl E (1952) *Ideas*, Collier, New York

Jaspers K (1954) *Way to Wisdom*, Yale University Press, New York

Jenner F A (ed.) (1982) *Phenomenology and Psychiatry*, Academic Press, New York

Kierkegaard S (1941) *Concluding Unscientific Postscripts*, Princeton University Press, Princeton

Kierkegaard S (1954) *Fear and Trembling and Sickness unto Death*, translated by Lowrie W, Princeton University Press, Princeton

Laing R D (1970) *The Politics of Experience*, Penguin, Harmondsworth, p. 42

Laing R D (1971) *The Politics of the Family*, Penguin, Harmondsworth

Laing R D (1974) *The Divided Self*, Penguin, Harmondsworth

Laing R D, Esterson A (1970) *Sanity, Madness and the Family*, Penguin, Harmondsworth

Lomas P (1981) *The Case for a Personal Psychotherapy*, Oxford University Press, Oxford

May R, Angel E, Ellenberger H F (1958) *Existence: A New Dimension in Psychiatry and Psychology*, Basic Books, New York

Nietzsche F (1969) *The Genealogy of Morals*, translated by Kaufmann W, Vintage, New York

Rogers C R (1951) *Client-Centered Therapy*, Houghton-Mifflin, Boston

Sartre J-P (1948) *Existentialism and Humanism*, translated by Mairet P, Methuen, London

Sartre J-P (1949) *The Psychology of the Imagination*, Methuen, London

Sartre J-P (1951) *Being and Nothingness*, translated by Barnes H, Methuen, London

Tillich P (1977) *The Courage to Be*, Fountain, New York

Valle R S, King M (eds.) (1978) *Existential-Phenomenological Alternatives for Psychology*, Oxford University Press, Oxford

van Deurzen-Smith E (1983) 'The function of self-evaluation in training counsellors', BPS Counselling Psychology Section Annual Conference, London

van Deurzen-Smith E (in preparation) *Existential Counselling*

van Deurzen-Smith E (1984) Counselling philosophy: an exploration, *Self and Society*

Warnock M (1970) *Existentialism*, Oxford University Press, Oxford

Yalom I D (1980) *Existential Psychotherapy*, Basic Books, New York

Suggested Further Reading

Collier A (1977) *R. D. Laing: The Philosophy and Politics of Psychotherapy*, Pantheon, New York

Lomas P (1981) *The Case for a Personal Psychotherapy*, Oxford University Press, Oxford

May R, Angel E, Ellenberger H F (1958) *Existence: A New Dimension in Psychiatry and Psychology*, Basic Books, New York

Valle R S, King M (eds.) (1978) *Existential Phenomenological Alternatives for Psychology*, Oxford University Press, New York

Yalom I D (1980) *Existential Psychotherapy*, Basic Books, New York

Chapter 8   Gestalt Therapy

Faye Page

Historical Context and Developments in Britain
Historical context

Gestalt therapy was developed by Frederick (Fritz) Perls and his wife Laura (Posner) Perls. There is no precise English translation of the German word *gestalt*, which can mean 'configuration', 'organized whole', 'a pattern' and so on. The context, environment or background in which an entity, object, element or need exists is the 'ground'. This entity, object, element or need which stands out or is attended to is the 'figure' or 'foreground'.

Perls trained as a psychiatrist and psychoanalyst in the Freudian tradition during the 1920s and 1930s, and began analysis with several orthodox analysts; he was, however, dissatisfied with their passivity and rigidity. On the advice of Karen Horney he entered analysis with Wilheim Reich, whose theory that the body was as important as the mind in the development and maintenance of resistances was to prove an influence on his holistic approach and ideas concerning neurosis.

Perls persisted in the field of psychoanalysis and in 1935 founded the Institute of Psychoanalysis in South Africa. Kogan (1976) commented that 'psychoanalytic theory was for Perls the major foundation upon which he built his understanding of human behaviour'.

In the early 1920s Perl's thinking was greatly influenced by the philosopher Sigmund Friedlander, especially by his ideas of differential thinking (the process of thinking in opposites rather than in terms of cause and effect) and creative indifference (the mid-point, zero point or balanced point from which the opposites or polarities are viewed or considered: cf. Perls 1969a). These can be seen in Perls's use of polarities such as successful/failure and top dog/underdog to identify, exaggerate and clarify personal splits (differential thinking). This then leads to resolution: acceptance of both as part of the person (the mid-point, creative indifference).

While working at the Institute for Brain Damaged Soldiers in 1926, Perls came into contact with Gestalt psychology. Here he met Laura, also a Gestalt psychologist, and they worked together for the next quarter of a century. (Laura's contribution to the development of Gestalt therapy has only recently begun to be acknowledged.) It was from Kurt Goldstein and the writings of Wertheimer, Koffka, Kohler, Lewin and others that Perls found valuable ideas for developing Gestalt therapy; he was also influenced by the existentialist concepts that a person must take responsibility for her own existence and live in the present. From Gestalt psychology he borrowed the concept of 'the incomplete gestalt', which he called 'unfinished business' and saw as the corner-stone of personal responsibility (Emerson and Smith 1974). Perls (1973) said: 'the basic premise of Gestalt psychology is that human nature is organised into patterns or wholes, that it is experienced by the individual in these terms, and that it can only be understood as a function of the patterns or wholes of which it is made'.

Although Fritz and Laura Perls organized the first Institute of Gestalt Therapy in New York in 1952, it was not until the mid-1960s, when Perls moved to the Esalen Institute in California, that Gestalt therapy became well known and recognized as an important aspect of the human potential movement. There are now training institutes in many Californian cities, in Cleveland, Boston, Chicago, Miami, Dallas, Hawaii and elsewhere, as well as in Germany, Holland and Italy.

Developments in Britain

There was an upsurge of interest in the human potential movement in Britain in the late 1960s and early 1970s: 'growth centres' sprang up in various places, especially in London. These centres tended to invite visiting leaders from North America so as to facilitate seminars and workshops, which were usually experientially based and not designed to provide training. Certain individuals obtained training whenever and wherever it was available, usually with these visiting Gestalt therapists from other countries; and some followed this up by attending one or more training institutes in the United States.

In 1972/3 Dr Ischa Bloomberg was asked to lead some Gestalt workshops in Britain. Dr Bloomberg had received his training at the New York Institute, under the supervision of Laura Perls, and worked with Fritz Perls and others in the early 1950s. While leading these workshops he found there was a need and a demand for Gestalt training in Britain, and a small group of people thus began their training with him (Bloomberg, personal communication).

From these early beginnings a number of courses have been established in various parts of the country. The following training opportunities are currently available: the Gestalt Centre in London offers a four-year training programme divided into four phases consisting of personal growth, method, philosophy, seminars and supervision and having an individualized and flexible system based on credits; Donna Brandes, who trained in the United States, offers a programme in Newcastle; in the south-west, Liz Shaper organizes training in staff development for those in the caring professions; Malcolm Parlett, who is also on the staff of the Gestalt Centre, is planning with Dr Richard Tillett and Liz Shaper a training programme for NHS staff to be held in the West Country in 1984; and Barry Hinksman, in the Midlands, offers introductory training in Gestalt therapy and supervision for professionals working in the Gestalt mode and is currently involved with the Scottish Association for Gestalt Education (SAGE) in organizing a training group. SAGE, established in 1976/7, is affiliated to the Gestalt Training Service. This is a co-operative of trainers including, among others, Ischa Bloomberg and Roger Trenka-Dalton, who are based in Europe, Wendla ter Horst from Holland, and Hilda Courtney and John Whitney who were instrumental in setting up SAGE. This co-operative offers a three-year training course. SAGE has completed three training programmes and is initiating a fourth. About two hundred hours of training are offered during the three years, plus follow-up supervision.

Many therapists found, as I did, that the needs of people in different cultures can vary greatly, especially in terms of support. The hard-hitting, highly confrontative and sometimes discounting style of some Gestalt therapists from the west coast of America is inappropriate to Britain, and it has taken some time for Gestalt therapists and trainers in Britain to make the necessary cultural adaptations.

As there is no central organization to give or deny accreditation, the choice of a training scheme tends to be based on personal preference. Gestalt therapists, in general, do not advocate the process of formal accreditation and diplomas. This affords both limitation and freedom to training, the limitation being that the possibility exists that unsuitable or ill-trained people will practise Gestalt therapy and the freedom being that training can be adjusted to suit the needs of an individual and the culture in which she works.

Theoretical Assumptions

The image of the person

Gestalt therapy is based on a holistic view of the person and her relationship to her environment. Its tenets are derived from those of biological form and process. The person functions as a unified organism, with mind and body viewed as inseparable; her modes of activity, such as thinking, feeling, breathing, behaving, etc. are interrelated, and she is capable of being aware of these.

As is true of all organisms, a person interacts with her environment in order to live and grow, and can only be seen in terms of this interaction; she cannot be self-sufficient. The nature of this relationship between person and environment determines her behaviour (Perls 1973). The environment, too, makes demands on an individual which require attention. A person is, like all organisms, self-regulating, and any imbalance is experienced as a need to correct this imbalance. She has the ability to adjust creatively to these requirements and to make choices concerning the way she does this. She determines her own responses and is thus responsible.

Perls (1969b) stated that 'every individual, every plant, every animal has only one inborn goal – to actualize itself as it is'. Being involved in her striving for self-actualization, a person has many needs: biological, physical, social and spiritual. She is not inherently good or bad; she is who, what and how she is, in accordance with what best suits her capabilities at a particular moment and in a particular situation. A person lives in the present and can only experience, respond, feel and think, etc. in the here and now: change only occurs in the present.

Concepts of psychological health and disturbance

In Gestalt therapy, psychological health and disturbance are not mental but organismic (Latner 1974). A person's mind is not healthy or disturbed; the whole of her is healthy or disturbed. In healthy functioning, a person adjusts creatively to her environment by the clear formation and destruction of Gestalts. The processes involved in this require some elaboration.

Organismic self-regulation   All organisms have a natural, balanced state which must be maintained within certain limits for survival: this is the principle of homeostasis. An organism has an inherent drive to maintain this equilibrium in order to grow and develop to its full potential. The organism does this simply by being what it is: it knows what it needs by being what it is. A person strives to maintain this balance, which is continuously disrupted by her needs or by the demands of the environment. She regains equilibrium through gratifying or eliminating these needs and demands (Perls 1969a, 1969b). If unhindered, a person will know what she needs by being who she is; she will rely on her own nature to know what is healthy.

Contact   For healthy functioning it is necessary for the person to be fully engaged in the process of transacting with her environment. It is through healthy contact that she is able to assimilate those aspects of her environment that she requires. With poor contact, assimilation is prevented and integration does not occur. These transactions take place at the contact boundary where the differentiation between self and environment is made; where self stops and 'not self' begins. This is where psychological events take place.

Awareness   'Awareness develops "with" and is integrally "part of" the organismic environmental transaction' (Enwright 1972). Awareness is how a person knows of herself, of her environment, and of her conception of these two. Perls (1969b) described awareness as covering three zones: 'awareness of self, awareness of the world, and awareness of what's between'. This intermediate zone is a person's representation of her internal reality, how she understands; and it includes thinking, planning, worrying, day-dreaming, anticipating, remembering and so on. In healthy functioning, by accurately representing her internal and external reality a person is able to integrate the two in a creative adjustment; awareness develops spontaneously at those points of the contact boundary that are relevant to ongoing need and/or demands. Awareness, therefore, can only occur in the here and now.

Figure and ground in the formation and destruction of Gestalts When an imbalance occurs within the person, or in her relation to her environment, this is experienced as a need. If there is no disturbance in awareness this need emerges as a figure in the ground of the person's awareness. At any given time there will be several imbalances or needs; that which is most important to the person's survival or self-actualization will emerge as the figure in the overall background. In healthy functioning, the person differentiates this dominant need clearly as the figure from the ground of her total experiencing. This meaningful whole, of figure and ground, is a Gestalt. As the need increases, excitement or tension is generated, activating the person to satisfy the need. The Gestalt is then destroyed, the figure merging back into the ground. Balance is restored, energy is released, and the next most important need emerges, forming a new Gestalt. In healthy functioning, this emerging and receding is a continuous, rhythmic process. The resulting formation and destruction of Gestalts is a functional definition of health and growth.

Disturbed functioning The person interrupts her continuous formation and destruction of Gestalts by trying to take over and control her self-regulatory process in order to change herself or her environment to fit a preconceived image of how she or it 'should be'. She distorts her awareness of herself and her environment, thereby confusing the interaction between the two. She does not know what she needs as she does not differentiate clearly between figure and ground, thus preventing the formation of strong Gestalts. Not knowing what her needs are or what the environment demands she is unable to make good contact with the outside world. She is bored, confused, anxious, rigid and/or self-conscious (Perls et al. 1974). She tries to manipulate herself and/or her environment to satisfy needs in unhealthy ways; her behaviour becomes fixed, rigid and polarized. She stifles her growth and limits her potency. As needs are not met, Gestalts are not destroyed and accumulate, thus binding energy. Perls called this 'unfinished business'. Instead of using her natural aggression to move towards objects or people that are necessary for need satisfaction, she may use it pathologically against objects, others or self (Harman 1974a).

The acquisition of psychological disturbance

In general, disturbed functioning is acquired when there is a persistent interruption in the natural ongoing person/environment interaction resulting in unmet needs which, in turn, result in an accumulation of uncompleted Gestalts.

Sometimes certain needs cannot be met due to a lack of environmental support, as happens in the case of famine, war, and so on. At other times, people in the environment will refuse to meet a person's needs. The younger the person, the more she depends on environmental support for survival. It is inevitable that a child should at times be frustrated in the satisfaction of her needs, and a certain amount of frustration is necessary to the development of her potential to grow. However, if she is continually prevented from expressing and meeting her needs, she suppresses the excitement that accompanies her emerging needs and uses this energy to hold back and control them. This interferes with her self-regulatory process, even though this is the best way she has of coping within her capabilities at the time. The emerging figure is unclear, and Gestalt formation is blocked. This creates distortions in her perception of herself, others and their interaction, resulting in disorders of development. She is unable to differentiate clearly between her own needs and the demands of the environment, and thus her ability to obtain what she does require is impaired. There is a lack of integration, and polarities or splits may result which disrupt her functioning as a systematic whole. These disturbances take place at the contact boundary, basically where she stops and the environment begins, and where differentiation and awareness of what is self and not-self take place. Perls (1973) described four mechanisms through which these boundary disturbances are acquired.

Introjection   This is an uncritical acceptance of concepts, attitudes, beliefs, morals, etc. imposed by significant others in a person's life. She takes in 'whole' bits of her environment rather than biting off a portion, chewing it and assimilating it or spitting it out if it is not good for her. She takes in parts that are not self. These take the form of 'shoulds' or 'should nots': for example, 'I should be helpless' or 'I should not get angry.' She then behaves 'as if' she were helpless or not angry (Ward and Rouzer 1974). The contact boundary is moved so far inside herself that little remains of self (Perls 1973). She makes herself responsible for what is part of her environment.

Projection   Those aspects of a person that do not fit in with her self-image are disowned, and others are made responsible for them. She thus avoids taking responsibility for her own feelings, needs and even parts of her body. The contact boundary is moved too far outside herself.

Retroflection   When a person cannot direct her behaviour (often aggressive) outwards towards others, she will often direct it back at herself, usually in physical ways – such as hitting her knee with a clenched fist. This might also be what she wanted or needed from others but could not get. If this were affection, she might hug herself, or reassurance might be reflected in statements like 'I told myself.' The contact boundary is down the middle of her, so she manipulates herself as though she were her environment.

Confluence   This is when a person feels no boundary between herself and her environment. She cannot make good contact with others, nor can she withdraw from them. She either always acquiesces to others or attempts to change the other person and make them be like her by persuasion, bribery or force. There is a demand for likeness to 'self' and an intolerance of that which is 'not self'.

These mechanisms can be seen in terms of 'doer' and 'done to'. The introjector does as others would like her to do, the projector does unto others what she accuses them of doing to her, the reflector does to herself what she would like to do to others or what she would like others to do to her, and the confluencer does not know who is doing what to whom' (Perls 1973).

Everyone uses these mechanisms from time to time; it is with their continued and inappropriate use, which blocks awareness and prevents good contact, that disturbances are acquired. One or all can be functioning in rapid succession. Perls (1973) did not assume that any behaviour (with the exception of traumatic neurosis) is an example of only one of the mechanisms.

The perpetuation of psychological disturbance

Even though a person's disturbed functioning may have been acquired in the past, she actively perpetuates her disturbance in the present. The accumulation of unmet needs, of unfinished Gestalts, is forever demanding attention so that she finds it difficult to function fully in the present (Perls 1973). Her self-regulatory process is not working properly, so there is no hierarchy of needs; they all seem equal and are thus confused with environmental demands.

In a person's middle zone of awareness – awareness of what is between her and the world, what might be called 'mind' or 'consciousness' – is a large area of 'fantasy activity' that takes up much excitement and energy and leaves little left to allow her to be in touch with reality (Perls 1969b). This results in anxiety or 'stage fright': the gap between now and later (Perls 1969b, 1972). She is preoccupied with the future, about what might happen or how she will perform. The future is seen as threatening because her catastrophic expectations might be fulfilled or her overly optimistic ones might not be (Perls 1969b). She holds back her healthy aggressive energy which is required for assimilation, integration and growth; thus she inhibits her awareness of internal and external reality as they actually are in the present. She does not make good contact with her authentic self or with her environment as it is, and disorients her sensory and motor processes through which she makes contact.

The person keeps trying to actualize her self-image rather than her self by projecting, introjecting, retroflecting and remaining in confluence. She wants to maintain the *status quo*, and continues to behave as though nothing has changed or will change. Areas of her past may have been threatening, painful or unpleasant, and she coped the best she could; but she is functioning 'as if' she were still existing in the past.

The person wants herself or the environment to be different than they are, so she feels dissatisfied. She should be different, so she plays controlling games: 'I should be nicer', 'I ought to be able to do this', 'I ought to be happy', etc. She behaves 'as if' she is important, strong, weak, etc. Perls (1969b) refers to this as the 'phoney' or 'role' layer of neurosis of growth disorder. If an individual becomes aware of these inauthentic roles and attempts to be more honest, then she encounters her fears which Perls called the 'impasse' (Perls 1969b). These could be of rejection, pain, embarrassment, despair, regret or inadequacy. She is afraid of her fear and does not want the frustration and suffering, so she becomes phobic and avoids them. Archaic responses are maintained as though they were necessary in the present, and she predicts how she will feel in the future. The person remains immature and continues to manipulate in unhealthy ways rather than grow up (Perls 1969b). There is a reliance on memories of how she used to feel and does not want to feel again, and she is unwilling to take the risks to find her true self. She denies the possibility of tears, laughter, rage or joy for that might re-establish the Gestalt she has not finished (Latner 1974).

Practice

Goals of therapy:

Maturation The process of maturing in Gestalt therapy is seen as a transcendence from environmental support to self-support (Perls 1969b, 1972). This is not depending on others for what a person is capable of doing for herself; it does not, however, exclude experiencing interdependency needs, as no one can be completely self-sufficient in our society. The therapist will help the person learn how she manipulates the environment in unhealthy ways. The therapist avoids doing for the person what she is capable of doing for herself.

Integration This refers to the person functioning as a systematic whole: sensory, cognitive and motor processes are interrelated. It has to do with the identification of disowned fragments or opposites. When parts of a person are competing, the energy is dissipated; when integrated, energy is available to deal with new Gestalt formation. The therapist works towards this integration.

Awareness Perls (1969b) believed that awareness by and of itself could be curative: with awareness, a person can establish conditions under which she can solve her own difficulties. The therapist will direct the person's attention to the way she blocks her awareness.

Responsibility Being willing and able to say 'I am I' and 'You are you' is having response-ability rather than having duty or obligations. To be aware that I respond, think, feel, and do is to take responsibility for who I am and what I do. Taking responsibility does not entail taking the blame or blaming other people or situations. The therapist assists the person a) to become aware of how she avoids taking responsibility and b) to assume responsibility.

As with most therapeutic goals, those of Gestalt therapy extend into one another; if the therapist is directing attention to the person's awareness, this tends to enhance development in one or all areas. A focus on integration may increase the person's awareness. Perls (1969b) noted that these goals are never attained once and for all, since they are ongoing processes: 'Integration is never completed ... There is always a possibility of richer maturation – of taking more and more responsibility for yourself.'

The person of the therapist

In general, effective Gestalt therapists are comfortable with improvisation rather than a set pattern or programme to follow. They are at ease with emotional intimacy and expressions or explosions. They strive to be aware of themselves and of their feelings and observations of people. They invest little in cognitive or intellectualizing processes, and even less in making interpretations. They make observations, but do not 'read minds'. They are generally more active than passive or reflective, and tend to be firm and self-confident in their approach. By accepting that a person cannot be other than she is at the time, therapists respect the individual and her integrity. Although caring for the person, therapists do not try to take away that person's responsibility for herself. Rather than attempting to solve the person's problems, effective Gestalt therapists are concerned with helping the person discover and develop her own capacity for solving her own problems. (Fagan and Shepherd 1972; Greenwald 1972; Latner 1974; Page 1977).

Therapeutic style

A competent Gestalt therapist employs different styles depending on the particular person and the situation. In all instances she needs to be flexible and effective. When working with severely disturbed people, her approach is slower and more cautious than when dealing with less disturbed individuals. She would tend to use the methods aimed at improving the person's contact with reality rather than fantasy, dreamwork, or role-playing for example.

There are examples of Gestalt therapists' work with severely disturbed people (for instance, Close 1972; Lederman 1969, 1972) which point out 'that the therapists or educators competence with certain populations is much more important than the technique as such' (Simkin 1976). However, many Gestalt therapists would tend to agree with Shepherd's (1972) assessment that

> Gestalt Therapy is most effective with overly socialised, restrained, constricted individuals – often described as neurotic, phobic, perfectionist, ineffective, depressed, etc. – whose functioning is limited or inconsistent, primarily due to their internal restrictions whose enjoyment of living is minimal. Most efforts of Gestalt Therapy have, therefore, been directed towards persons with these characteristics.

Bearing this in mind, the style of a therapist is based on an 'I-Thou' relationship with the person. This might entail a high level of confrontation or frustration in order to focus on how the person is attempting to manipulate the therapist or holding the person's hand to establish a channel of support. The therapist responds to what she is aware of at a particular moment. As several things may be observed by the therapist simultaneously, she does make choices in her responses. Her choices are based on her skills and experience, and her therapeutic responses depend on her creativeness in finding a way to increase that particular person's awareness in that particular situation.

In general, the style of Gestalt therapists varies: I have seen effective Gestalt therapists whose styles ranged from soft-spoken, gentle and patient to noisy, highly confrontative and pushy. I myself have on occasion moved slowly from an upright position to lying on the floor while listening to a person 'talk about' how bored and fed up he was feeling. Another time I might get up, start singing and hop around to the back of someone who is expressing his fear of being ignored while never once looking at me. In the case of someone who has been identifying with an extremely frightening and threatening experience, I have held onto him and rocked him.

I have found that being a woman therapist has many advantages. Some women think another woman is more likely to understand their difficulties; others may feel easier and be more open when expressing emotions such as anger, or their fantasies or frustrations. They see a difference between 'confiding' in me and 'confessing' to a man. We have or have had certain similar experiences. There is also the value of my being different in other ways and thereby offering other 'possibilities of being-a-woman' (Polster 1976).

Some men have an expectation of greater caring and concern from a woman; they do not feel as threatened or concerned with their self-image, and are more likely to express feelings and needs that they might not readily express to a man. Those who have other expectations find an opportunity to test out those expectations in a safe situation. In both instances, they are afforded other possibilities of contact with another person and especially with a woman.

Major therapeutic techniques

The techniques of Gestalt therapy are used in conjunction with the therapist's own style of expression in the therapeutic situation. There is no 'right' way or time to employ them. The 'ground rules' are made explicit from the start. Other techniques are introduced or suggested by the therapist when she thinks it appropriate. Some of the techniques can be powerful in contacting emotions and facilitating their expression. Emotion is one of the major forms of energy and excitement in the process of Gestalt formation. It is therefore an intricate part of therapeutic intervention to contact emotion in the here and now and move towards developing more integrated and healthy ways of expressing emotion.

The ground rules are a set of guide-lines devised in order to facilitate change. They are not a list of 'shoulds', 'dos' and 'don'ts' but are intended to promote an atmosphere and opportunity that will encourage greater awareness of 'self' and of 'other'. They are usually described at the beginning of therapy.

Awareness   Awareness is essential in Gestalt therapy. The unblocking of awareness and the drawing of attention to awareness is involved in most of the methods employed by the therapists. Awareness allows choices; it is not a 'should' or 'must'. If a person is not aware, then her choices and responses are limited.

The here and now   In Gestalt therapy, all encounters concern present experiences: the only contact with reality is in the present. Past and future are considered memories and expectations which the person is experiencing in the present. The therapist works with what is available, obvious, with what is in front of her.

Statements instead of questions   A person is required to make statements instead of asking questions whenever possible. Through the use of questions the person tends to avoid making meaningful contacts and interactions. Questions are usually an attempt to ask the therapist to explain or justify herself or her existence. They are often a means of manipulating a therapist into giving the person support, advice, information, etc. that the person could obtain from herself. They are also a way of maintaining dependency on others and the therapist which prevents the person from moving from environmental support to self-support.

No gossiping   This means not talking about those who are not present. 'Talking about' is often a way of avoiding feelings that a person thinks she cannot cope with at the time, and no gossiping is a way of encouraging a direct confrontation of those feelings (Levitsky and Perls 1972). In a group, the person would be asked to speak directly to the individual she was talking about; in a one-to-one situation, the therapist would use the 'empty chair technique' (discussed in the next section) to talk to the absent person.

'Can't' and 'won't' statements   The person is required to change statements by using the words 'I won't', 'I don't want to', or 'I am not willing' instead of 'I can't'. (This is unless it is a realistic statement, such as 'I can't fly an aeroplane' or 'I can't do quadratic equations'.) This encourages the person to face her own unwillingness to do or change certain things. She takes responsibility for her own actions or inactions rather than blaming others or circumstances.

Responsibility   The therapist tells the person that it is her responsibility to say 'yes' or 'no' to the therapist's suggestions. The person is encouraged not to pressurize herself into doing something she really objects to. She is expected to take responsibility for what she says or does, and for what she does not say or do.

'I' language   The person is discouraged from using depersonalizing language such as 'it', 'one' or 'you' when 'I' is the meaning. Using 'I' encourages involvement in responsibility rather than distance and non-responsibility, and enables a person to view herself as active rather than passive.

I and thou   The person will often be asked to speak to the therapist while looking directly at her and using the therapist's name. This increases the person's awareness of the difference between talking 'to' and talking 'at' and can emphasize incongruities between what the person says and how she says it. This also encourages the person to face her avoidance of communicating directly and unequivocally to another person, to the 'other' (Levitsky and Perls 1972).

Many of the techniques in Gestalt therapy are used in both individual and group therapy. The variety and number are limited only by the skill and ingenuity of the therapist. Certain techniques are used more frequently than others. The concentration here will be on those used in individual therapy.

The empty chair technique: to encourage dialogue   The therapist asks the person to move back and forth between two chairs or seats. The chairs can represent a conflict between the person and someone else in which she moves from the chair in which she is herself to the other chair, where she speaks as the other person and creates a dialogue. The chairs may represent splits *or* polarities within the person such as weak-strong, joyful-sad, right hand-left hand, stomach-throat, and so on; there is practically no limit to the number of splits that can be identified. This enables the person to see the polarities or splits more clearly and to contact and integrate aspects of herself that she avoids or disowns. On the surface, this would seem to be a fairly simple therapeutic task; yet a great deal of skill, perceptual sensitivity, experience, ability and understanding of the Gestalt process are required of the therapist. Without these, accurate focusing by the therapist is difficult and resolution is unlikely to be obtained (Fagan et al. 1976).

Unfinished business This is an analogy of the incomplete Gestalt. Unfinished business is unresolved feelings. When the therapist notices unresolved feelings, the person is asked to 'finish' the situation. The person may enact the situation in the present, and finish 'it' off by saying what she wanted to say, and the empty chair may be employed. This 'finishing off' involves a 'letting go' of feelings that the person has been 'hanging on' to, for perhaps a very long time. Just saying the words does not finish off a situation or unresolved feeling; the feeling needs to be expressed along with the words. The therapist needs to be capable of dealing with intense emotions which can and do occur.

Reversals The therapist asks the person to role-play characteristics that she claims she does not or could not possess. This is to promote a realization that a person's behaviour can often cover up the opposite type. She may then contact parts of herself that have long been held down.

Exaggeration or repetition A gesture or movement unnoticed by the person may be seen as significant by the therapist, such as tapping fingers. She would ask the person to exaggerate the movement in order to make the meaning behind it more apparent and accessible to the person. The person may be asked to repeat a statement made in a casual way that seems important in content. She may be asked to repeat it several times, perhaps in a louder voice. This is to promote an integration of what a person says with how she says it, and to contact feelings she has submerged or avoided.

Offering a sentence 'Will you try this on for size?' or 'May I feed you a sentence?' is used when the therapist notices an implicit attitude or statement while listening to or observing the person either in the content of what is said or how the person says it (the process). The therapist will offer a sentence to the person to repeat, usually prefaced by one of the above questions. The person is encouraged to be aware of and test out her reactions when saying it. The emphasis here must be on the person experiencing what she has said through her own involvement, rather than on the intuitive or interpretive ability of the therapist.

Staying with a feeling   The person is encouraged to deliberately 'stay with' a feeling and to elaborate on the what and how of her experience so as to promote a confrontation of what was previously avoided. The therapist helps the person distinguish her fantasies, expectations and imaginings from her perceptions. When a person makes a clear contact with what she is really feeling, then there is the possibility for change to occur.

Owning a projection   When a person talks about other people, she is frequently using projections. If the therapist thinks this is the case, she will ask if any of the descriptions or characteristics could also belong to the person. She might ask the person to try 'owning up' to her projections by using 'I am' or 'I have' before the descriptions. In this way the person is able to look at possibilities she has refused to see before. These attributes can be desirable and pleasant ones as well as undesirable and unpleasant ones.

Dreams   Gestalt therapy views a person's dream as that person: every detail of the dream is a part of her and an expression of her in the here and now. The person is asked to tell her dream, or a portion of it, in the present tense, as though she were in the dream. She is then asked to 'be' or give a voice to the people or things in her dream. The therapist might encourage her to carry on a dialogue between two bits of her dream, two people or objects, or an object and a person. Recurring and old dreams are seen as 'unfinished business'. The interpretation of dreams is not used; the experience is unique to the person, whether it is frustrating, frightening, exciting, boring or beautiful.

Therapists use these techniques and others, and develop them in different ways. They are not necessarily appropriate for all therapists or all people. To rely solely on techniques means you are a technician, not a therapist (Harman 1974b).

The change process in therapy

Most people go to see a therapist because they want to be changed. A tenet of Gestalt therapy is that change occurs when a person becomes what she is, not when she tries to become what she is not. Beisser (1972) calls this 'the paradoxical theory of change'. Awareness enables a person to identify her needs and use the excitement generated by them to mobilize her behaviour in contacting the environment appropriately (either to assimilate or reject). This then completes the Gestalt, 'Gestalt formation always accompanies awareness' (Perls et al. 1974); and it is through awareness that change occurs. It is by being aware that a person can be who she is. Perls believed that the basic difficulty in unhealthy functioning is that a person has lost awareness of how she prevents herself from being who she is (Perls et al. 1974). The change process in Gestalt therapy involves her learning how she stops herself from being aware. The therapist's own awareness, expertise and skill enable a person to increase her own awareness in this one-to-one relationship.

'Gestalt therapy is being in touch with the obvious' (Perls 1969a), and assisting the person to do this is a primary focus of the therapist. By the appropriate use of the therapeutic techniques discussed earlier the therapist focuses on the different aspects of the person's awareness or non-awareness. This is done in order to encourage the person to be in contact with, and stay in, the present and to take responsibility for herself at this particular time and place. Awareness develops with, and is integrally part of, this therapeutic relationship and is based on a present perception of the present situation (Enwright 1972).

The development of awareness of the 'obvious' usually follows the person taking a risk in her interaction with the therapist. She feels a sense of moving into unfamiliar areas without being able to predict the outcome. A merging feeling of discovery and/or rediscovery is experienced which leads to a positive effect for the person. Enwright (1972) calls this 'emotional' insight and contrasts it with the 'intellectual' insight in psychoanalysis which lacks a 'crucial rootedness in the actual'. This process is a reorganization of self and environment, a figure and ground, and thus a new Gestalt. This is often called the 'Aha!' experience: a rediscovery of something lost or a discovery of something new. At that moment the person has changed the structure of herself and her environment and will feel, think and behave differently (Latner 1974). Many people have said, 'I feel like myself, I feel right,' after experiencing this process.

To assimilate this, repetition is necessary in order for the person to feel comfortable and familiar with the new experience. It is similar to the first time a person balances on a bicycle by herself when she wants to learn to ride. She does not stop there; she continues until she can ride easily, smoothly and comfortably. The great amount of concentration and effort then recede into the background, and a new interest emerges. Latner (1974) called this 'closure and satisfaction'. When this is achieved, the person who was supporting her lets go at the point when the rider gains her own balance.

The therapist's task is to help the person discover the habitual ways in which she controls her awareness and prevents herself from being self-directive and self-supportive, and then to allow the person to continue on her own. The therapist cannot change a person; she can, however, provide the opportunity and be available as a catalyst to facilitate change (Yontef 1976; Perls 1977). 'Therapy is seen as a microcosm of everyday life as it is the interaction, person to person, which forms the basis for and process through which the therapeutic change occurs' (Levin and Shepherd 1974).

Case Example

The client

Jane is a popular GP, married with two children. She said she was tired, lacked enthusiasm and was vaguely unhappy much of the time. Jane could not think of any reason for her lack of energy as she had no physical problems, liked her work and loved her family. I had met Jane several times at meetings and social functions. She had attended a talk I had given and decided to refer herself.

In Gestalt therapy there is less emphasis on the cognitive aspects of diagnosis and assessment than in many therapeutic approaches. Gestalt therapists do have, however, a background of experience, knowledge and skill and their own awareness and intuition from which they respond to the person in therapeutic interactions. Making use of these, therapists form a understanding of the person's interactions with her environment. Fagan (1972) called this process 'patterning'. This is part of the understanding I formed of Jane during our sessions over a three-month period.

The acquisition and perpetuation of disturbance

Jane was the eldest of four children. From early in her life she had been required to please her parents by being a 'good girl', denying her own wants and needs and adopting those of her parents. She suppressed the excitement accompanying her needs and used this energy to hold back and control them. She felt embarrassed and a 'bad girl' if she expressed herself in a clear manner such as saying 'no', being demanding or making a fuss. She then had difficulty differentiating her own needs and wants from those of other people. She introjected the attitudes of her parents in order to deal with her environment to the best of her capabilities at the time. Jane was vague about her wants, and feared refusing to comply with those of other people; she was burdened with 'shoulds' and 'shouldn'ts'.

To perpetuate this, Jane projected her needs outwards and became a doctor. She disowned those aspects of herself that wanted to be looked after, given time and attention; still wanted by others when she was not 'good' and/or 'perfect' or if she said 'no'. She then projected these onto others, especially her patients: 'They need looking after,' or 'They need my time and attention,' and so on. Jane rarely said 'no' to the demands of her job; she behaved as though she were required to do this in order to justify her own existence, as she had had to do when younger. Spending a great deal of time and energy playing the 'perfect' doctor left her little time and energy for herself or her family. Jane behaved 'as if': she were her mother; her family were not as important as her work; she needed little from others; she always wanted to say 'yes'. When confronted with her own feelings, needs or wants, she experienced conflict. To avoid this she became tired and vague, or felt uncomfortable and inadequate.

Initially, Jane looked tired and without energy. She would usually sit or stand with her arms wrapped around her waist or crossed and with her hands rubbing her upper arms. As her parents had discouraged physical displays of affection, Jane had learned not to hug people or ask to be hugged and even to deny these wants. Instead, she did to herself that which she wanted others to do to her or wanted to do to them. Again she perpetuated this by behaving 'as if' she did not want to hug or be hugged: she 'kept her distance', did not look at people, was too busy or tired, did not have the time.

Jane's contact with herself and with others was restricted by her limited awareness. She had difficulty dealing effectively with interactions in the present as she was functioning with outdated behaviours and values from the past. There was so much unfinished business (incomplete Gestalts) around that the energy needed for forming new, strong Gestalts

was dissipated. Her self-regulating system was unable to function appropriately. She used so much energy stopping herself experiencing and
expressing her needs and 'hanging on' to her self-image that she had little
left with which to participate in new situations or with life in general. She
was continually attempting to actualize her 'image' rather than her 'self',
and feared there was nothing to her beyond this; that there was only
pain, rejection, humiliation, being unloved – a void.

Therapy

In the first session Jane and I discussed the ground rules and clarified
what she wanted from the therapy sessions. Her goals were to: feel more
energetic; have more enthusiasm about life in general; like herself.
Throughout therapy I was encouraged by Jane's trust in me and my
work. This, in many ways, facilitated her progress.

Major therapeutic techniques   Jane had difficulty saying 'no' to people
and therefore to me in the therapeutic situation; she wanted to please,
suppressed her defiance and became vague and tired instead. The distress
of her possibly refusing and her fantasy of what might follow were too
unpleasant. She interrupted her awareness by avoiding: staying in the
here and now; taking responsibility for her feelings; and interacting with
me directly. To discourage this in our sessions together I:

(a)   stayed in the here and now, and insisted she did as well;
(b)   did not give advice and frustrated her attempts to manipulate me
       into giving her the kind of support she could obtain for herself;
(c)   requested she use 'won't' instead of 'can't', encouraging her to face
       up to her unwillingness to accept responsibility;
(d)   requested her to replace 'it' with 'I' to enhance personal involvement
       rather than distancing herself;
(e)   used exaggeration and repetition with certain statements that
       seemed important so as to promote an integration of the content of
       her statements with the way she uttered them;
(f)   required her to make contact with me as a person by looking directly
       at me when speaking.

She identified and risked confronting her 'stubbornness'; and instead of
her catastrophic expectation of reprimand, distress or whatever, she

found she was able to feel good in her defiance. Her 'aggression' was directed appropriately in the therapeutic situation, and she adjusted to it creatively. One important awareness for Jane was that I did not ignore her, get angry with her or go away. I was pleased and happy for her.

Jane practised by noticing how she was feeling in various situations requiring a 'yes' or 'no'. She became more aware of her feelings and wants and of her choices, not only to say 'yes' or 'no' but to negotiate as well.

During therapy Jane became increasingly aware of her posture, particularly her tendency to 'hug' herself (retroflection). Gradually, she began to turn her energy (aggression) outwards (with me and with her family especially). She was encouraged to 'check out' her feelings and what she wanted when she was aware of retroflecting, and to hug or be hugged. This included her perception of appropriateness which she tested out for herself in situations where she felt safe.

Using the 'empty chair' technique enabled Jane to clarify the polarities of many conflicts. By expressing and experiencing both the limitations and values of each side of the conflicts she resolved them. For example: she expressed and accepted her anger towards her parents, as well as her love for them, by identifying with the sad and angry child who was not allowed to be who she was; she took responsibility for some of her aspects she had disowned, such as being defiant, soft, competent, fearful, sexy, maternal, frivolous, cruel, loving and so on.

By taking risks with me in the therapeutic situation Jane faced some of her fears and moved through these to contact herself as she was in the here and now. She became more capable of experiencing, differentiating and expressing her feelings and needs.

As Jane improved, her awareness of how she prevented herself from taking responsibility became more acute; she became more able to respond appropriately to different situations; her ability to respond was greater, and she increased her choices of responses. As she identified with the competing fragments of her self which she had disowned, she became more able to integrate these and function better as a systematic whole. Jane became more self-supportive and found she could do more than she had ever imagined possible.

As Jane's awareness expanded, so did her expression, differentiation, responsibility and self-support. Her energy increased, and her vagueness and tiredness decreased. She was able to assimilate and feel more comfortable with her new experiences and with herself.

At the termination of therapy Jane looked energetic and said she felt more enthusiastic and joyful about herself and her life. She realized that three months of therapy would not solve all her problems and that she would experience the old feelings at times. She said she would contact me if she were unable to do something about this on her own.

References

Beisser A (1972) 'The paradoxical theory of change' in Fagan J and Shepherd I (eds.) *Gestalt Therapy Now*, Penguin, Harmondsworth, p. 88

Close H T (1972) 'Gross exaggeration with a schizophrenic patient' in Fagan J and Shepherd I (eds.)*Gestalt Therapy Now*, Penguin, Harmondsworth

Emerson P, Smith E W L (1974) Contributions of gestalt psychology to gestalt therapy, *The Counseling Psychologist 4*: 8–12

Enwright J (1972) 'An introduction to gestalt techniques' in Fagan J and Shepherd I *Gestalt Therapy Now*, Penguin, Harmondsworth pp. 136, 138

Fagan J (1972) 'The task of the therapist' in Fagan J and Shepherd I *Gestalt Therapy Now*, Penguin, Harmondsworth p. 102

Fagan J, Lauver D, Smith S, Deloach S, Katz M, Wood F (1976) 'Critical incidents in the empty chair' in Hatcher C and Himelstein P (eds.) *The Handbook of Gestalt Therapy*, Jason Aronson, New York

Fagan J, Shepherd I (eds.) (1972) *Gestalt Therapy Now*, Penguin, Harmondsworth

Greenwald J A (1972) The ground rules in gestalt therapy, *Journal of Contemporary Psychotherapy 5*: 3–12

Harman R L (1974a) Goals of gestalt therapy, *Professional Psychology 5(2)*: 178–184

Harman R L (1974b) Techniques of gestalt therapy, *Professional Psychology 5(3)*: 257–263

Hatcher C, Himelstein P (eds.) (1976) *The Handbook of Gestalt Therapy*, Jason Aronson, New York

Kogan J (1976) 'The genesis of gestalt therapy' in Hatcher C and Himelstein P (eds.) *The Handbook of Gestalt Therapy*, p. 239

Latner J (1974) *The Gestalt Therapy Book*, Bantam, New York p. 81

Lederman J (1969) *Anger and the Rocking Chair: Gestalt Awareness with Children*, McGraw-Hill, New York

Lederman J (1972) *'Anger and the rocking chair'* in Fagan and Shepherd *Gestalt Therapy Now*

Levin L and Shepherd I (1974) The role of the therapist in gestalt therapy, *The Counseling Psychologist 4*: 27–30

Levitsky A, Perls F S (1972) 'The rules and games of gestalt therapy' in Fagan J and Shepherd I (eds.)*Gestalt Therapy Now*, Penguin, Harmondsworth

Page F (1977) 'Gestalt group therapy with severely anxious out-patients: a pilot study', unpublished dissertation for the British Psychological Society diploma in clinical psychology

Perls F S (1969a) *Ego, Hunger and Aggression*, Random House, New York p. 54

Perls F S (1969b) *Gestalt Therapy Verbatim*, Real People Press, Lafayette, Cal., pp. 19, 49, 64–5

Perls F S (1972) 'Four lectures' in Fagan J and Shepherd I (eds.) *Gestalt Therapy Now*

Perls F S (1973) *The Gestalt Approach and Eye Witness to Therapy*, Science and Behaviour Books, Ben Lomond, Cal., pp. 3, 40–1

Perls F S (1977) 'Gestalt therapy and human potentialities' in Stevens J O (ed.) *Gestalt Is*, Bantam, New York

Perls F S, Hefferline R F, Goodman P (1974) *Gestalt Therapy*, Penguin, Harmondsworth, p. 15

Polster M (1976) 'Women in therapy: A gestalt therapist's view' in Hatcher C and Himelstein P (eds.) *The Handbook of Gestalt Therapy*, Jason Aronson, New York p. 562

Shepherd I (1972) 'Limitations and cautions in the gestalt approach' in Fagan J and Shepherd I (eds.) *Gestalt Therapy Now*, Penguin, Harmondsworth p. 265

Simkin J S (1976) *Gestalt Therapy Mini-Lectures*, Celestial Arts, Millbrae, Cal., p. 36

Wallen R (1972) 'Gestalt therapy and gestalt psychology' in Fagan J and Shepherd I (eds.) *Gestalt Therapy Now*

Ward P, Rouzer D L (1974) The nature of pathological functioning from a gestalt perspective, *The Counseling Psychologist 4*: 24–27

Yontef G M (1976) 'The theory of gestalt therapy' in Hatcher C and Himelstein P (eds.) *The Handbook of Gestalt Therapy*, Jason Aronson, New York

Suggested Further Reading

Downing J, Marmostein R (1973) *Dreams and Nightmares: A Book of Gestalt Therapy Sessions*, Harper & Row, New York

Fagan J, Shepherd I (eds.) (1972) *Gestalt Therapy Now*, Penguin, Harmondsworth

Perls F S (1969) *Gestalt Therapy Verbatim*, Real People Press, Lafayette, Cal.

Perls F S (1973) *The Gestalt Approach and Eye Witness to Therapy*, Science and Behaviour Books, Ben Lomond, Cal.

Stevens J (1976) *Awareness: Exploring, Experimenting, Experiencing*, Bantam, New York

Chapter 9   Transactional Analysis

Laurence Collinson

Historical Context and Developments in Britain

Historical context

Transactional analysis originated in California, which was also the place of some of its earliest and richest growth and development. Its founder, indeed its creator, was Eric Berne (1910–1970). He had been born in Montreal; his father was a general practitioner and his mother a writer and editor. His family, like many other Jewish families, had come to 'new' and libertarian worlds (Canada, in the case of the Bernsteins) from Russia and Poland, probably to escape the anti-Semitism and pogroms of Eastern Europe.

Like his mother and father, he graduated from McGill University. He followed his father's profession, receiving his MD and his Master of Surgery in 1935 at the age of twenty-five. A year later he moved to the United States, where for two years he was a psychiatric resident at the Psychiatric Clinic of Yale University School of Medicine. Before joining the US Army Medical Corps, he became an American citizen, shortening his name from Eric Lennard Bernstein to Eric Berne in the process.

From 1941 he began training as a psychoanalyst at the New York Psychoanalytic Institute, becoming first an analysand of Paul Federn and later, after his war service, of Erik Erikson in San Francisco, near where he had settled in the seaside town of Carmel. Despite Berne's many years of training the title of 'psychoanalyst' was, to his disappointment, refused him on the grounds that he was not yet ready; but he was told that he might apply again after three or four years. None the less, this refusal seemed to spur him on to work even more intensely on the new approach to psychotherapy that he was developing in his ambition to add something of substance to psychoanalysis. He had already written several important papers on intuition and on what would turn out to be the beginnings of structural analysis, the first of what later became the four major divisions of TA; the others, in order, are transactional analysis proper (the specific use of this term refers to the analysis of transactions), game analysis and script analysis.

By the end of 1958 Berne had developed TA as an almost complete system. His progress was aided particularly by his establishment in 1950–51 of a weekly clinical seminar which attracted an exciting group of people, many of whom have since made major contributions to the theory and practice of TA. Their discussions, ideas, and interactions also helped Berne to advance his concepts and make them into a coherent whole. During this time this group, which became known as the San Francisco Social Psychiatry Seminars, started the publication of the *Transactional Analysis Bulletin*; with Berne as editor, the first issue appeared in January 1962. Nine years later, in January 1971, the *Bulletin* was replaced by the quarterly *Transactional Analysis Journal*, a lively publication containing articles ranging from hints about handling groups to comprehensive, academic descriptions and discussions of new theory and practice. The first issue took the form of a memorial to Eric Berne, who had died of a massive attack of coronary thrombosis in July 1970.

Developments in Britain

British TA emerged in three broad and somewhat overlapping stages. Although there may have been, before 1962, scattered individuals who were aware of and used TA, having either read about it or visited California, it was not until that year that John Allaway, the Vaughan Professor of Adult Education at the University of Leicester, got together with a Northamptonshire primary school headmaster, Joe Richards, to create an evening course in transactional analysis for mature students at the University of Leicester in both Leicester and Northampton. Using their knowledge of group dynamics and Berne's *Transactional Analysis in Psychotherapy* as a textbook, they provided an introductory course that incorporated both cognitive and affective elements. News of the value that participants gained from the course soon spread, and Allaway and Richards were shortly giving similar courses at the Universities of

Nottingham and Loughborough. When *Games People Play* appeared as a 'private' publication in 1963, it also was absorbed into the course and added to its insightfulness and delight. The course became so popular that it was extended into weekends and the summer vacation. The course, which had been spread over one term, was extended to two terms so that participants could obtain a group experience at an advanced level. Allaway and Richards between them trained over a thousand students, some of whom took their new knowledge abroad – a few to Europe, and, in the case of one person, as far as Tanzania! One of their students was Adrienne Lee, now founder and director of NECTA, the Nottingham Institute for Transactional Analysis.

After I became interested in TA I contacted every source I could think of to find out if anyone was studying or using TA in or near London and heard eventually of a librarian, David Porter, who was on a similar quest. I contacted David, and at our first meeting we agreed to form some kind of TA discussion group; his role was to contact interested people and mine was to provide the accommodation and refreshment. This group, which became the London TA Study Group, had its initial meeting at my flat in the Barbican on the evening of 17 April 1972. Later it became the North London Study Group; and although its membership has fluctuated, it is still, at the time of writing, meeting regularly at the homes of its members.

In November of the same year Alan Byron, a Sheffield psychiatrist of whose existence I had been unaware during my hunt, organized Britain's first 'official' TA Introductory Course (known as the '101') in his home town. It was attended by myself and several other members of the study group, including a general practitioner, Margaret Turpin, who took out a contract to train for clinical membership of the International Transactional Analysis Association (ITAA) with the course tutor, Warren Cheney, a psychotherapist from Berkeley, California, and a prominent member of the ITAA until his recent death.

With the return to London, late in 1972, of Michael Reddy, a counselling psychologist who had been training with Robert and Mary Goulding in the States, the history of TA in Britain entered its third stage. In addition to John Allaway and Joe Richards, who had no direct contact with the international organization, there were now three people, Michael Reddy, Alan Byron and Margaret Turpin, leading TA groups and workshops with the authorization of the ITAA. Reddy, a clinical member who later became Britain's first teaching member, began in 1973 to train others who wanted to use TA in their own work and/or become certified members of the ITAA. I was, as far as I know, the first person wholly trained in this country to obtain ITAA certification. The study group was even more active than it had been, attracting a comparatively large participatory audience to its functions. The number of people engaged one way or another with TA was several times greater than it had been a year earlier.

It was Michael Reddy who, with the support of Margaret Turpin, Alan Byron and some others less immediately concerned with TA, founded the Institute of Transactional Analysis in Britain, the country's first direct 'official' link with the ITAA. He had previously established an advisory committee, which lasted about a year, to draw up plans and to work on a constitution for the Institute. The ITA's first annual conference was held at Heythrop College, London, on 27 October 1974, since when an ITA conference has been held annually with ever-increasing success in terms of attendance and events.

To my mind, the pioneer efforts of seven people have been primarily responsible for the establishment and steady, if not speedy, growth of TA in this country. These seven are: John Allaway, Joe Richards, Margaret Turpin, Michael Reddy, Alan Byron, David Porter as a publicist and the first editor of the ITA *Bulletin*, and myself as a publicist and the second editor of the *Bulletin*. Michael Reddy must also be given credit for the considerable amount of work he did in the establishment of TA in the rest of Europe and for his initiatory role in the formation of the European Association for Transactional Analysis (EATA).

As I have previously indicated, the gradual progress of the ITA in involving itself with training standards and ethics, and in certification processes for its own members, is for me part of its valuable growth toward independence from its hitherto reliance on the rules and regulations of other national and international TA organizations. If our standards are acceptable to other TA associations, so much the better; if not, we would do well to ignore the symbiotic relationship that might otherwise arise if we collude in being Child to their Parent.

Theoretical Assumptions

The image of the person

Almost all that follows refers to the theories and concepts of transactional analysis as written about and practised by its founder, Eric Berne. Several 'schools' of TA have arisen since his death, and as each school has both added to and departed from some of Berne's ideas, detailing the different standpoints would require more space than I have available.[2]

Berne's image of the person was, in a sense, contradictory. He saw each person as capable of being in charge of his own destiny, of, almost instinctively, wanting to attain autonomy – or, rather, *re*attain autonomy, for autonomy is the province of the uncorrupted child, before its life is invaded by the 'trash'[3] of negative parental influences. Autonomy, according to Berne (1968), 'is manifested by the release or recovery of three capacities: awareness, spontaneity and intimacy'. Awareness, Berne goes on to say, requires living in the here and now, and not in the elsewhere, the past or the future. Spontaneity, in contrast to its popular definition, does *not* mean impulsive behaviour; it means recognizing that each of us has options of feelings and behaviour and the freedom to choose the option most suitable to the occasion. Intimacy means loving the other for *being*, not doing; it means loving without the expectation of reciprocation. It is the intent of the natural child and therefore requires an act of will on the part of the programmed ('scripted') grown-up. It is, in consequence, rare in our society.

Believing that each of us is capable of autonomy, and being at the same time only too conscious that 'people are born princes and princesses, until their parents turn them into frogs', Berne came to the conclusion that most people were unwilling to transcend their negative attitudes to life, expressing it in the sad view that there may be no hope for the human race 'but there is hope for individual members of it' (Berne 1968).

Berne regards each person as having three ego states. He uses the word 'ego' here in the Freudian sense: as the conscious part of the personality, in touch with and capable of dealing with reality, as opposed to the (mostly) unconscious parts: the id and the super-ego.

In defining 'ego state' as a consistent pattern of feeling and experience directly related to a corresponding consistent pattern of behaviour (Berne 1961), he names these three parts of the structure of the human personality Parent, Adult and Child and draws them as three equal circles touching vertically (see Figure 1); he uses initial capitals so as to make a distinction between an ego state and a real parent, adult, or child. The Child ego state within us still carries the feelings, thoughts and behaviours of the child we once were; the Parent holds all the messages, both positive and negative, that we accepted from our own parents and other 'authority figures', as well as the behaviours they modelled for us and the moral, ethical and other attitudes and opinions they held toward themselves, other people (including their children) and the world. The Adult is that part of us which assesses the reality of a situation and chooses how to respond to the available data. Unlike Freud's ego, super-ego and id, Berne's ego states possess observable behaviours and recognizable inner feelings. With practice, it becomes a simple matter to diagnose which ego state another person or oneself is in.

Concepts of psychological health and disturbance

Implicit in Berne's view of autonomy is the TA existential position 'I'm OK – you're OK', which is possibly the most basic assumption of trans-actional analysis. At the core of all our behaviour is the desire to love and to be loved, and an inner knowledge that this is a natural part of our

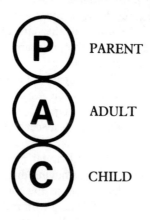

A COMPLETE PERSON

Figure 9.1

humanity. It is our treatment by our parents and other significant people in our childhood that leads us to question whether we deserve so to be regarded or so to regard ourselves. And when we almost invariably come up with the answer 'No', we have to work out ways of obtaining what we believe we lack. We find out over a period of time which methods work and which do not, and thus we decide to repeat, over and over again, those methods that seem to get us what we want, no matter what psychological pain accompanies them. We may make these *decisions* about behaviour either in awareness or outside of awareness.

Unfortunately, these repetitive thought/feeling behaviour patterns were only minimally successful, even in childhood; but we keep repeating them in later life because they have now become habitual, and the consequences are at least uncomfortable, at worst disastrous. They have become the psychological games and the scripted behaviour in which we indulge to obtain love of one kind or another. Occasionally through their use we seem to be getting what we want; ultimately we never do. Only by choosing a different and often risky behaviour to replace the conditioned one do we stand a chance of becoming the person we want to be. Thus autonomy, which can never be total anyway, may also be defined as being game-free and script-free.

Functionally, the three ego states need to be subdivided for more precise analysis (see Figure 9.2). Berne divided the Parent ego state into the Critical Parent and the Nurturing Parent; and the Child into the Adapted Child and the Free (sometimes called Natural) Child. The Adapted Child is itself divided into two parts: the Compliant Child and the Rebellious Child. Contrary to some adolescent opinion, rebellion and freedom are not the same thing: rebellion and compliance are both adaptations to a given situation.

In addition each of the subdivisions, which could be considered as six separate ego states, is divided into two. TA theory holds that all ego states are valuable: 'problems' arise because there is a conflict between what the person's Child wants and what his Parent says he *should* want. It is at this point that the person develops either wish-fulfilment fantasies or catastrophic ones of rejection, when he would be better off referring to his Adult, which would make a realistic and unemotional appraisal of what is and is not possible if he takes the risk he is scared of taking. It may be necessary, even wise, for him to adapt to the situation; but over-adaptation to it is a form of what TA calls 'passive behaviour', which ultimately results in even greater conflict.

Each ego state may be diagnosed in four ways and in the following sequence (as described by Paul McCormick):

(a)   Behavioural (observing whether the behaviour is parental, adult-like, or childlike);

(b)   Social (observing others' responses to the behaviour, – for example, if the responses are disapprovingly parental, the behaviour is probably Child);

(c)   Historical (verifying the origin, in time, of the ego state in question, as by 'Yes, I'm in my Parent, all right. I sound just like my father did when I was ten');

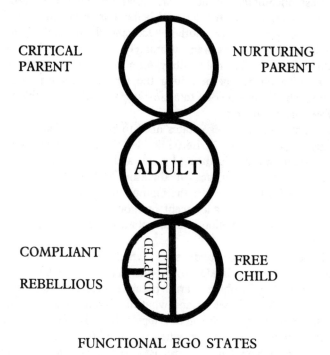

CRITICAL
PARENT

NURTURING
PARENT

ADULT

COMPLIANT

REBELLIOUS

ADAPTED
CHILD

FREE
CHILD

FUNCTIONAL EGO STATES

Figure 9.2

(d) Phenomenological (re-experiencing – not just remembering – 'in full intensity, with little weathering, the moment or epoch' (Berne) when the ego state was originally experienced.

It is necessary, according to Berne, to correlate these four methods before the diagnosis can be validated. This may seem a lengthy process, but practice speeds it up; in any case the process is – with the exception of therapeutic situations – rarely so fully explored. Someone skilled at the process can usually 'hunch' another's ego state on the basis of (a) and (b) above. Checking out with the other person is, however, always necessary for confirmation.

In TA, physical and psychological health is said to be directly proportionate to the number and intensity of strokes a person receives; a stroke being defined as a unit of recognition given to infants in the form of touching, holding, cuddling and to grown-ups by verbal and non-verbal transactions, a transaction being defined as the unit of social action. Berne believed – basing his conclusion on work done in 1945 by René Spitz on the lack of sensory stimulation in infancy – that the human need for strokes is as much a biological hunger as our basic hungers for air, food and shelter; and that stroke deprivation in grown-ups as well as infants leads to psychological and physical difficulties. He coined the phrase that if we try to exist without strokes we are in danger of having 'our spinal cords shrivel up', which led him to the further conclusion that if a human being is unable to obtain positive strokes (for being and doing), he or she would rather have negative strokes than no strokes at all. This provides a rationale for the fact that many, if not most, human beings engage in unhealthy and unrewarding behaviours like 'rackets' (painful internal dialogues) and 'games' (painful external transactions) to satisfy their hunger for strokes of excitement and recognition.

The acquisition and perpetuation of psychological disturbance

TA theories on the acquisition and perpetuation of psychological disturbance have already been dealt with partially, since the material is inextricably bound up with previous subject-matter. It might be helpful, however, to recast some of that material, thus allowing the reader a more objective view and myself more space for necessary additions.

There are four different kinds of analysis involved in the theory and practice of transactional analysis:

(a) Structural analysis or the analysis of ego states;
(b) Transactional analysis proper, which includes the study of some basic communication skills (or the lack of them);
(c) Game analysis (or, more colloquially, how to mess up relationships);
(d) Script analysis, or the analysis of the life dramas that people act out compulsively.

Ego-state pathology results from one of several causes. The most common is probably contamination of the Adult by the Parent or Child or both (see Figure 9.3). Contamination of the Adult by the Parent can result in prejudice, or by the Child in delusions or hallucinations. An example of a Parent-contaminated Adult would be the belief that certain races,

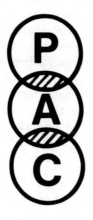

DOUBLE CONTAMINATION

Figure 9.3

nations or even religions are 'genetically' inferior to others; while an example of a Child-contaminated Adult would be the paranoid belief (with fear and anger) that the two people over there, who may not even be aware of my presence, are talking about *me*.

Another type of ego-state pathology is exclusion, whereby the psychic energy that is usually available to cathect[4] all ego states does not do so. When the energy is shared by only two ego states, we say the person lacks a Child or an Adult or a Parent. If the energy is available to only one ego state, we say that the person is in constant Adult; or it may be constant Child; or constant Parent.

Berne regarded TA as a social psychiatry, that is, a form of psychotherapy in which the difficulties being treated occur because the clients' exchange of strokes, either in transacting with other people or between their own ego states (in the form of dialogue or fantasy), is unsatisfactory or inappropriate. The strokes that clients get may be sufficient to ensure survival but insufficient to enhance their lives. Thus it becomes necessary to determine the client's stroking patterns, which can be done by the observation of the interchanges between the client and others or which the clients may tell the therapist indirectly by the manner in which they present themselves.

Berne suggested that there are two kinds of transaction in 'ordinary' conversation: complementary and crossed (see Figures 9.4 and 9.5). In complementary transactions, the transactional stimulus and the transactional response involve the same two ego states. In crossed transactions, the stimulus and response may involve three or four ego states. The way in which the client deals with crossed transactions is probably stereotyped, and will yield a great deal of information to the therapist. Similarly, the manner in which the clients talk about themselves will indicate the extent to which the client opts for self-punishment. As a general rule, the intensity of the self-punishment is directly proportionate to the client's refusal to accept responsibility for creating his other problems; it is likely to be proportionate also to the clients' involvement in rackets, games and scripted behaviour.

A third kind of transaction is ulterior (see Figure 9.6); and it is at this point that TA moves into game analysis. Berne defines a game as a set of ulterior transactions, repetitive in nature, with a well-defined psychological payoff. In practical terms, game analysis deals with what goes on between people beneath surface level. The analyst must be alert to incongruities of speech and behaviour; he must learn to 'read the Martian': to see people (and situations) exactly as they are, and without making value-judgements. People play games because there is an enormous exchange of strokes; unfortunately, the strokes are mostly negative, and leave the players with 'bad' feelings (the 'payoff'). Playing a game is not only exciting and stimulating but also represents an attempt to be right, to win over the other, to try to make the other do what *you* want. The very nature of a game precludes winning, because we do not play with the person or persons we think we are playing with; whatever the current issue may seem to be, such as a spouse continually coming home drunk, or having affairs on the side, or even something as apparently trivial as a person failing to do the washing-up when it is his or her turn to do so, we are playing with the parents or parental figures of our own childhood in

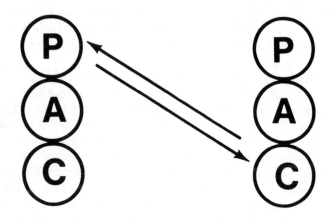

COMPLEMENTARY TRANSACTION

LILA (Child): I'm scared.
JOAN (Parent): So you should be.

Figure 9.4

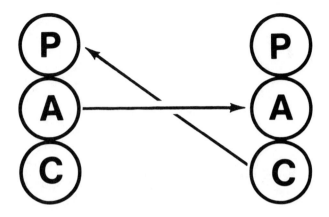

CROSSED TRANSACTION

LILA (Child): I'm scared.
THERAPIST (Adult): Are you smiling?

Figure 9.5

an impossible attempt to get the other person(s) to give us the respect, understanding, attention, affection or love that they failed (or, rather, our belief that they failed) to give us in childhood. We want to force the other game-player to resolve an issue from the past that can never, in reality, be resolved in the present. The only person who can resolve those left-over issues is oneself.

Similarly, and in response to our perception of what was going on, we made decisions in infancy and childhood about what seemed to us the best way of being taken care of by our parents or parental figures. Those decisions may or may not have worked then (what is certain is that they do not work now); none the less we are determined to stick to those decisions and to *make* them work (known as 'being right'). It is those decisions that indicate to us how we should programme our lives; it is those decisions that form the basis of what is known in TA as the script, defined by Berne as 'a life plan based on a decision made in childhood,

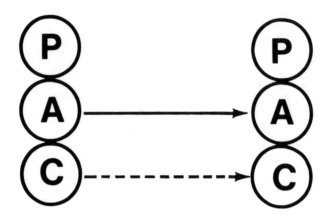

ULTERIOR TRANSACTION

A — A: I'm not one to talk . . .
C — C: . . . but I do enjoy a bit of gossip!

Figure 9.6

reinforced by the parents, justified by subsequent events, and culminating in a chosen alternative'. For the script analyst, once a client becomes aware of having made a negative early decision, it is then within the client's power to 're-decide' and thus take tentative steps toward autonomy, or at least to change a 'losing' script into a 'winning' one.

Practice

Goals of therapy

I have not been able to find a simple answer to the question: What are the goals of transactional analysis as a form of psychotherapy? This may have something to do with my own mythical belief that there *ought* to be a perfect answer and that I *ought* to know what it is. There is, however, no such simple answer; each client brings his or her own goal into the therapeutic partnership.

Clients' goals are usually expressed in the form of contracts, and drawing up contracts is regarded by transactional analysts as an indispensable first step in treatment. The four basic requirements of a therapeutic contract are:

Mutual consent A clear explicit and specific offer is made to the client, who, perhaps after some discussion, understands and accepts the offer.

Valid consideration The therapist agrees to ameliorate or cure; in return the client agrees to pay money – or barter – to attend the therapy sessions regularly, to participate actively in therapy and to do whatever else may be necessary, such as the completion of certain tasks, 'homework' and so on.

Competency Both therapist and client must be competent: the first to be able to give proper treatment, the other to be able to accept it.

Lawful object The contract must not violate either local law or consensually accepted moral and ethical principles.

Clients' goals are generally expressed in the form of specific changes they want to make in their lives: for example, to lose weight, to make more friends, to stop playing games with my spouse. Therapists will ask, 'How will I know that you've made this change?' and will also want to ensure that clients have a real investment in making such changes. They will therefore insist that the changes include observable behaviours, that the clients' ego states agree that such changes will be valuable, and that the changes offer a satisfactory alternative to the clients' 'safe' but uncomfortable ways of life at present.

Therapists' goals, on the other hand, will consist of the process or processes they need to use in order to help the clients fulfil their contracts. They may see this in such terms as 'decontaminating' the Adult, re-cathecting the Child, discarding outworn Parent tapes, improving listening skills, understanding the different options available before, during, or after a game and/or analysing the clients' scripts so that the latter becomes fully aware of the early decisions they made and can re-decide about the best way of handling old troublesome issues that they attach to current relationships.

The person of the therapist

In my experience, there is no set of well-defined personal qualities that transactional analysts must have in order to be effective therapists. There are some people practising TA whose personal qualities (in my opinion) have left me in some doubt as to their likely effectiveness as therapists, and yet I hear from their own clients and from knowledgable sources that they are 'good'. The opposite also applies, in that some people whose personalities seem to me such that they would make ideal therapists turn out to be 'poor' therapists.

I am therefore left with my own semi-fantasy about what personal qualities are likely to help make a person an effective therapist – and these would apply irrespective of whether the practitioner's model were TA or anything else. First, the therapist must be fully accepting of his or her client, no matter what the latter's problems or personalities may be; this is what the expression 'I'm OK – You're OK' means. Second the therapist must care about his or her clients but must not rescue them, the term 'rescuer' in TA being one of the three roles played out by a person involved in a game (the other 'drama' roles are 'persecutor' and 'victim'). Rescuers are those who, because they have a compulsive need for approval, do things for others that they do not want to do (which involves trying to read the others' minds) or do more than 50% of the 'work' of starting or maintaining a relationship.

Third, however inadequate therapists may consider themselves to be in their bleaker periods (therapists are human, too), they must be able to model the kind of behaviour they want their clients to adopt. Fourth, therapists need not only to be skilled in their own therapeutic model but also knowledgeable of other models and able to use them when appropriate; they must also be willing to be in therapy or to accept continual supervision, or both.

Finally, and not least importantly, they must be able to use and develop the Free Child parts of their personality, especially those faculties concerned with enjoyment, fun and intuition. If there is one talent essential to the practice of effective TA, it is the intuitive ability of therapists. In addition, therapists need to give themselves permission to let that ability grow and even to take over from 'reason' when they have unexpected insights that are threatened by what seem to be more rational and commonsensical viewpoints.

Therapeutic style

From my observation, each TA therapist has his or her own unique style. This is dependent basically on the personality of the therapist, who will adopt or grow into the style best suited to him or her, although at first he or she may have the beginner's problem of believing that there is a 'right' style for TA.

The therapist's style will also have to do with the fact that there are now a number of TA 'schools' that diverge to a greater or lesser degree from the Bernean or 'classical' school. There is, for example, the Re-decision School[5], where the therapist's approach is fairly directive but one which leaves the client to reach an awareness of his or her choices and to discover other possible options. In the 'Classical' School, itself subdivided, the therapist aims to get the client to accept responsibility for his or her own predicament, and in general does this, as Barnes (1977) points out, with the 'use of humour, imagery, imagination, intuition and hyperbole'. The Cathexis School's[6] approach to TA differs considerably from that of other schools in theory and method in that – particularly for clients in residence – it is strongly directive, negatively critical and includes what those enthusiastic about Cathexis methods might call 'regressive reparenting' and the caring confrontation of passivity with the aim of setting limits that the original parents failed to provide, and those less enthusiastic have described as 'punishment', such as standing the regressed 'child' in a corner for hours on end until he or she begins to 'think' about the 'problem' in accordance with the Cathexis model, or tethering him or her to a bedpost until he or she decides to behave 'properly'.

In addition, the therapist's style is influenced by the facility with which TA combines with other therapies. For instance, a therapist receptive to psychoanalytic theory is likely to be more silent than the 'average' TA therapist and to offer fewer (but 'deeper') interpretations. A therapist who integrates TA with Gestalt therapy is likely to keep the client firmly within a 'here and now' framework, a therapist attracted by bioenergetics is likely to incorporate bodywork with TA, and so on.

Major therapeutic techniques

Techniques used by transactional analysts can be roughly divided into two categories, and this applies whether the techniques are regarded as major or minor. Firstly, there are those derived from other modes of therapy – and TA therapists usually have little if any hesitation in using them. When TA therapists use a non-TA technique it is often with the intention of highlighting some aspect of TA theory that they believe will be helpful to the client. For example, the Gestalt technique of talking to an empty chair, which for the Gestalt therapist would be a means of helping the client towards 'here and now' awareness and the completion of a Gestalt probably related to someone who is for the client a 'top dog' figure, might be used by the transactional analyst as a method of demonstrating to the client some of his or her games or as a means of starting or furthering script analysis.

TA itself is primarily (in my opinion) an educational therapy: that is, one in which awareness and understanding lead to behavioural change. This is not to deny the emotional and cathartic elements that clients experience when they begin to understand what happened that led them to this present difficult point in life, nor to deny the importance of emotions in therapeutic work. Another way of putting it is: feelings are not necessarily primary in TA therapy, as they sometimes are in such modes as encounter, Gestalt therapy and bioenergetics.

Secondly, there are many techniques derived solely from TA theory. An article by a well-known TA practitioner (Erskine 1973) suggests that there are six therapeutic stages 'that can serve as a guide in shaping the course of treatment and in making termination decisions'. These six stages follow closely the historic progression of TA itself, starting with structural analysis (the diagnosis of ego states), transactional analysis proper (the diagnosis of communication), game analysis (the diagnosis of negative repetitive patterns and racket – as opposed to authentic – feelings) and script analysis (the uncovering of early decisions).

Stage 1 is marked by defensive behaviour, the therapy for which involves clearing up clients' ego-state pathology, such as contaminations and exclusions.

Stage 2 is marked by anger arising from clients' awareness that they have engaged in repetitive behaviour for many years; some basic but not extensive script analysis will have been provided here, because clients, in becoming aware of the way their ego states function, are likely to be angry also with their parents for not meeting their childhood needs. The ways in which clients transact with others will help the identification of ego state pathology.

Stage 3   is marked by clients' feeling hurt: they may, with the use of regressive exercises, come to believe that it was their own fault that their parents acted as they did.

Stage 4   is when clients begin to recognise that whatever the difficulties were with their parents, they chose 'to incorporate only selected messages'. However vulnerable they as children may have been to parental pressure, they as grown-ups now realize that they alone are responsible for their own behaviour. Erskine (1973) says that at this stage clients may attempt to terminate treatment because they are unwilling to give up the Parent-Child symbiosis or cannot face rewriting their own scripts.

Stage 5   requires a treatment contract involving and satisfying three ego states: the Adult, the Free Child and the Nurturing Parent. A treatment contract denotes a commitment to change. All the steps so far have involved the potency of the therapist, potency being defined as a quality of a therapist who has 'a personal sense of authenticity, credibility, trustworthiness, and responsiveness'. They also, according to James, are skilled at their work and want to keep on learning. Potency is one of TA's 'three P's': potency, permission, and protection. Clients need permission from their therapist (and ultimately from themselves) to make the moves away from negative scripting and protection in doing so, since changing behaviour involves taking fundamental and unfamiliar risks.

Stage 6   Here clients become aware that they have many options in choosing the ego state with which to offer – or to respond to – a transactional stimulus. This means that all ego states have been decontaminated and that clients can cathect (put psychic energy into) whatever ego state seems to them most appropriate in the circumstances. In this state of autonomy or near-autonomy they are capable of forgiving their parents and understanding that they did the best job they knew how to. This is what Werner Erhard, in one of his *est* seminars describes as 'completing your relationship with your parents'.

Berne (1962) summarizes the process of therapy thus: 'using the therapist as an intermediary, the patient's Child shifts his allegiance from his inner Parent to his own Adult. For a large percentage of cases, this is sufficient therapeutic goal in itself. If desirable and practical, further psychoanalytic deconfusion of the Child can be advantageously undertaken under these improved dynamic conditions'.

No matter how many treatment stages are postulated, all three ego states of the therapist need to be involved. Berne (1966) divides the Adult therapeutic operations that form part of TA technique into eight categories:

a)   Interrogation: asking questions to get important information.
b)   Specification: giving relevant information clearly.
c)   Confrontation: crossing transactions to point out inconsistencies.
d)   Explanation: what the therapist's Adult thinks is going on.
e)   Illustration: using an anecdote, figure of speech, or comparison to reinforce a confrontation or an explanation.
f)   Confirmation: using new confrontations to confirm the same issues.
g)   Interpretation: showing ways of understanding a situation so that the client's distortions may be corrected or past experiences regrouped.
h)   Crystallization: summarizing client's position to facilitate redecision.

Berne (1961, 1966, 1973a) also suggests a number of Parental and Child therapeutic operations to help the clients to cathect Adult. Among the Parental operations he includes support, reassurance, persuasion to follow the therapist's advice, exhortation to take care of themselves and the three P's mentioned above. Interventions from the therapist's Child, Berne says, should be carefully and rarely used. Such interventions, he writes, add humour to the procedures, and can also facilitate the client's openness: Readjustment and reintegration of the (client's) total personality require an emotional statement from the Child in the presence of the Adult and the Parent. In *Principles of Group Treatment*, Berne (1966) is even more liberal about laughter:

> The therapist should remember that while death is a tragedy, life is a comedy ... Curiously enough, many patients reverse this dramatic principle, and treat life like a tragedy and death like a comedy ... Human beings, according to the existentialists, are in a predicament all the time; and even those who subscribe to other philosophies must admit that they are in a

predicament a good deal of the time. The biological or survival value of humour is to deal summarily with predicaments, thus releasing the individual to go about the business of living as effectively as he can under the circumstances. Since most psychogenic problems seem to arise from self-deception, Adult humour has a most rightful place in the materia medica of the psychotherapist.

Berne speaks of 'the bull's eye' as being an ideal intervention. This is a statement from the therapist which has a therapeutic effect on a client's Parent, Adult and Child simultaneously. The following is an example from my own work with a client. Joan is a career woman who wants to marry. She has a man friend who is abroad many months each year. She is anxious that he should propose to her, but scared of taking the initiative herself. She believes that her only option is to be compliant and over-nurturing, in the hope that he will guess how much she 'loves' him (see Figure 9.7).

THERAPIST   JOAN

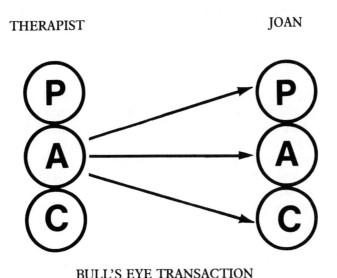

BULL'S EYE TRANSACTION

Figure 9.7

JOAN:	It was nice when he came back for a while. He stayed with me. He had nowhere else to stay. Of course, he could have stayed with his mother, but he decided not to.
LAURENCE:	Are you sure he didn't stay with his mother?
JOAN:	(*A long pause, then bursts out laughing*) Oh, shit!

In addition to 'talking therapy' and 'intuitive therapy' there are innumerable exercises, games (in the ordinary sense of the word), structured fantasies and other methods of eliciting thoughts, feelings, and behaviours which are available to the transactional analyst to help the clients to become aware of what is going on for them. And of course there is nothing to prevent a therapist devising exercises with a TA content for the purpose of diagnosing ego states or analysing transactions, games, scripts and dealing with related issues such as strokes and how clients structure time. As with other therapies, TA therapists also ask the clients to do 'homework' exercises related to their contracts, and to concern themselves with 'here and now' situations in the course of the session.

The change process in therapy

The transactional analyst is likely to view the concept of 'change' in a variety of ways, most of which overlap. At the most basic level, clients are changed when they have reached and are able to maintain the goals of their treatment contracts. For example, giving up smoking, acting assertively in situations in which they were previously – or at least 'felt' like – passive victims, cathecting Adult in the presence of 'authority figures', learning to exchange positive and acceptable strokes with spouse or lover or someone else important to the clients.

Another aspect of positive change occurs when clients recognize that all their ego states are available to each of them and that they can use them flexibly and appropriately.

A third kind of change occurs when clients finally realize that they are responsible for their own lives and stop playing games and engaging in scripted behaviour. This implies a number of other factors: stopping the inner dialogue between Parent and Child (this is usually experienced as a conflict between the client and his/her current *bête noire* in an attempt to win victory over the other, at least in fantasy); finding ways – usually through more fun and enjoyment – of increasing the strength of the Free Child; taking up the existential position 'I'm OK – you're OK' much more frequently; both intellectually and emotionally disproving their basic myths, such as 'I'm inadequate', 'I'm not lovable' or 'It must be my fault'; deciding to alter their losing scripts to winning ones. In TA, winning means achieving self-directed goals, which of course have to be possible of achievement; otherwise, clients, in setting out to be winners, remain losers.

'Redecision' is another way of looking at change. The clients in infancy made decisions that would help them to survive the seemingly overpowering parental pressures. Whatever was decided, said Berne, can be redecided. Script analysis helps clients to uncover those early decisions that were a protective device when they were small but which do not work so well, if at all, in adult life.

Berne (1973b) had an antipathy towards what he called 'making progress', which, he suggested, went on in most 'mental health' institutions and in much therapy: 'The slogan of "Making-Progress Therapy" is "You can't get better until you are fully analysed", while the slogan of "Curing-Patients Therapy" is "Get well first and we'll analyse it later if you still want to." '

In transactional analysis, the process of change is accompanied by an understanding of what Berne, in several of his books, refers to as 'Martian', defined as the observation of earthly happenings without preconceptions. This is similar to the well-known Zen saying: 'Before studying Zen, men are men and mountains are mountains. While studying Zen, things become confused. After studying Zen, men are men and mountains are mountains.' It is also similar to the *est* 'proverb': 'What is, is; and what isn't, isn't.' As much, if not most, psychological conflict arises because people persist in the belief that life should be or should have been different from what it is, Martian can be of immense value to both client and therapist (and certainly has been to the present writer) in helping them to let go of difficulties that they have unnecessarily created for themselves.

All the theory and all the practice of TA, all TA therapy, teaching and training, all contracts, all processes and all goals are simply different expressions for and different methods of directing the client (and always, to some extent, the therapist) from a losing script to a winning script, or from scripted to autonomous behaviour.

Total autonomy seems to me to be an unattainable ideal; autonomy for brief periods is not, and may perhaps grow with practice. Let Berne (1973b), with his wry pessimism, have the last word:

> Life is simple. All you have to do is figure out the most probable outcomes of various courses of conduct, and then pick the most attractive or the least troublesome. Only if you want certainty does it become difficult, because that you cannot have. Sometimes it amounts to deciding which of the things you don't want to do you should go ahead with. For example, each day a man may have to decide whether he would rather have his testicles cut off or his brain washed.

Case Example

The client

Bernard is a big, slow, lumbering man in his mid-fifties. Now divorced, he is the father of two sons: one in late adolescence, the other aged twenty and attending university. Bernard has been living for two years with a woman of his own age, a teacher and former group client of mine. Bernard is a highly respected freelance journalist good at the work he does, which brings in a regular satisfactory income, but continually doubtful of his talent and his personal adequacy. He is alcoholic in bursts: able for months at a time to engage in social drinking, but then, at a time that he perceives as a crisis, drinking heavily for a week or two, ending up in a stupor and having to be dried out, full of remorse and self-pity. In doing script analysis with Bernard, I find that the chief factors that emerge are his still-present resentment at what the small Bernard took to be his mother's indifference towards him and his determination not to fail, as she told him his father failed, to be a good husband and provider. His parents were also inconsistent in their requirements of and attitudes towards him so that, then and now, he uses confusion and indecision as both an avoidance of doing the 'wrong thing' and a cover for his frustration and anger.

It was not easy to make a satisfactory treatment contract with Bernard. He claimed to feel helpless, depressed, sad and, not least of all, not to know what he wanted. He had two major worries: first, that his lover would leave him and second, that he procrastinated with his work so much that his various editors would no longer commission him. We settled finally for an autonomy contract – that is, one with which over a period he would learn that he was not helpless but able to take charge of his own life and to accept responsibility for his own behaviour. There were sub-contracts: to stay in touch with his emotions so that he would know what he wanted; to learn ways of communicating with his lover so that they would better understand and accept each other; and to curb his Rebellious (Adapted) Child when he realized he was using it against himself in a destructive manner (for that was what his procrastination was about).

Myths and decisions

Bernard gives (or used to give) the impression of being lethargic; he speaks ponderously, with long pauses between words and phrases as if he has to be careful that whatever he says next is the right thing to say. This might be of some advantage in writing, but not in verbal communication. In my work I allow my own senses and emotions – my reactions to the client – to give me psychological feedback which I then check with the client and, if he is in a group, the other members. I found myself at first participating in Bernard's efforts to convey what he wanted to me, and then my silent sympathy turned to impatience because I was using too much psychic energy to little or no avail. When I began to understand the Martian of our relationship, I realized that while I was attempting to rescue Bernard, he was persecuting me; when I then switched to persecutory anger, he became victim – a role he must have felt comfortable in, since it was the one he usually ended up adopting. Another way of analysing the experience is to regard Bernard's halting speech as a way of both clinging to and repudiating the other person at one and the same time: a contradictory method that Bernard had developed in order to control others but which inevitably led to his 'feeling' that others were controlling him.

It took me a number of sessions to appreciate fully why I was feeling helpless and inadequate to treat him. He was passing his own 'hot potato' on to me. He was doing what in TA is called 'episcripting'; one of the few ways his subconscious knew to enable him to feel powerful was to try to make those around him feel powerless. His favourite rackets are guilt and confusion (a mixture of frustration and suppressed anger), and his favourite game is 'Why don't you – Yes, but,' the purpose of which is for someone coming on in the victim role to end up feeling triumphant at the inability of those from whom he asked for help to help him. The need for such behaviour on the part of a grown-up person (in this instance, Bernard) is often related to the parents setting the child contradictory limits for the same kind of behaviour. For example, when a mother is feeling OK, she may encourage her child to go out and play with his friends; yet at other times, when she is feeling not OK, she may violently lose her temper with him for engaging in the same behaviour (going out to play with his friends) that she has sometimes previously supported.

While the myths (in TA, beliefs that a person accepts as true) that go to make up a person's frame of reference must inevitably contain their opposite extremes at a hidden level, the polarities engendered in Bernard's childhood by his interactions with parental figures and presently incorporated into his system of thinking, feeling, and behaving are more overt than is usual for people coming into therapy.

During the process of script analysis, Bernard and I agreed that the decisions he had made in infancy and early childhood – mostly unconscious and unformulated – could be expressed verbally as follows:

(a) 'I won't rock the boat, but I'll make sure people know I'm around.'
(b) 'If I try hard enough I'll win – once, anyway.'
(c) 'I'll prove myself even if it kills me (by alcohol?).'
(d) 'I won't expect anything from anybody, but people had better know what I want.'
(e) 'I'll keep them together, even if I have to tear myself apart in doing so.'
(f) 'I'll let them know somehow that I'm hiding my feelings.'
(g) 'I won't leave them, but I'll manage to push them away.'

TA theory makes a distinction between such aspects of the script apparatus as decisions, myths, injunctions, and counter-injunctions (or permissions), but the differences are often arbitrary. The decisions f) and g) above, for example, contain two injunctions: 'Don't be close' and 'Don't leave me'; and two myths: 'I know what they're thinking,' and 'They ought to know what I want.' My separation here of myths and decisions is for the sake of demonstration and convenience rather than as a pointer to the realities of Bernard's situation. Some of the myths that can be derived from the decisions – and vice versa – are:

(a) 'Nobody knows the trouble I've seen.'
(b) 'Life ought to be fair, but they're to blame if it's not.'
(c) 'Some day my princess (and Santa Claus) will come, but not for me.'
(d) 'Nobody loves me.'
(e) 'They're out to get me, so I'd better get them first.'

The crux of Bernard's various dilemmas seems to be: If I succeed, I'm spurious; if I fail, I'm humiliated?

Treatment plan and therapy

There are (at least) three factors involved in Bernard's unsatisfactory manner of relating to other people and to the world. The first is his game process which follows a pattern something like this:

Appear to be helpless;
Demand (by tantrums or other forms of meaningful silence) to be helped;
Express relief (and hide resentment) that they agree to help you;
Make sure they don't help you;
Your payoff: triumph (temporary); theirs: angry despair.

Games are played in order to get survival strokes – and as many as possible; no matter how negative they might be, they are still to be preferred to none at all. It is necessary therefore for Bernard to start getting positive strokes, and in as straight a manner as possible. He has to learn Claude Steiner's (1974) 'stroke economy', which postulates that people hold the same false belief (there isn't enough to go around) about strokes as about money: 'don't ask for strokes; don't give strokes; don't accept strokes; don't reject strokes you don't want; and don't stroke yourself'. It is important that Bernard risks asking directly for what he wants, or says clearly what he does not want (he may well be rejected); on the other hand, he may well be accepted; or he may compromise.

The second factor is guilt. Guilt is an attempt to punish oneself or others psychologically for behaviour disapproved of by one's Parent ego state; it is also the overt expression of covert anger or resentment. In order to deal with this, Bernard will not only have to understand the nature and function of guilt, but also to let go of it, particularly in the form most favoured by Bernard: blame. This requires the practice of two new behaviours: to disclose his feelings of anger at the time he has them *or* to stay in touch with them and to trace their origin, which will have little to do with what is happening at present. The other behaviour is to be assertive: to say 'yes' when he wants to say 'yes' and 'no' when he wants to say 'no', and to make sure that the 'yes' is not spoken out of a need for approval or the 'no' out of a need to be obstinate.

The third factor is autonomy, which is something that cannot be incorporated into behaviour either by the process of learning or the process of catharsis. It is a concept that needs first to be intellectually understood, incorporated into one's philosophy of life, and then practised consistently in as many areas of life as possible. Bernard has to become aware that he himself is responsible for setting up most of the unsatisfactory situations in which he finds himself. Responsibility, however, cannot be achieved until one accepts oneself as one is right now. Only thus can one move toward being the self one wants to be (not the same as being what one *ought* to be). When Bernard first consulted me he was almost entirely concerned with how he ought to be with others; conversely, others ought to know how to behave with him.

Our work is directed towards Bernard's learning to give and receive positive strokes according to the 'stroke economy'; towards expressing his feelings, particularly anger, which is difficult for him, at the time they occur; towards being assertive; and towards accepting responsibility for colluding in creating the kinds of situation that he claims to find problematic.

After about five years, Bernard's treatment has been successful to the extent that he has largely stopped blaming others, kept his job, firmly established his relationship to the point where he and the woman have bought a house to live in together; is more, although not totally, in touch with his feelings; is clearer about what he does and does not want.

He still has alcoholic episodes, but is sober for months on end. He has trained and obtained certification to practise as a counsellor using transactional analytic methods. He has, additionally, taken a course in psychoanalytic psychotherapy, so that if he decides he wants to practise psychotherapy full time, or if the recession makes it necessary for him to do so, he has the required qualifications.

Notes

1   I would like to give thanks and acknowledgement to *ITA News*, the journal of the British Institute of Transactional Analysis, in which the first section of this chapter, in modified form, first appeared.

2   Such information can be found in Barnes, G (ed.) (1977) *Transactional Analysis After Eric Berne: Teachings and Practices of Three TA Schools*, Harper and Row, New York.

3   'Trash' is one of Berne's favourite 'philosophical' words. He defines it as 'the things people are doing to each other instead of saying hello'.

4   Berne (and Freud) use this word to mean the investment of libidinal energy in a person, object or idea.

5   The Redecision School, of whom Robert and Mary Goulding are the best-known exponents, uses a combination of TA and Gestalt to help clients examine their early childhood decisions and to redecide about those that are no longer appropriate.

6   The Cathexis School was founded by Jacqui Lee Schiff with the aim of helping severely disturbed clients create a new Parent ego state for themselves to replace the malfunctioning Parent while engaging in artificial developmental stages akin to those undergone by a child in the course of 'normal' development.

References

Barnes G (ed.) (1977) *Transactional Analysis After Eric Berne: Teachings and Practices of Three TA Schools*, Harper and Row, New York, p. 16

Berne E (1961) *Transactional Analysis in Psychotherapy*, Grove, New York, p. 246

Berne E (1962) Clinical notes, *Transactional Analysis Bulletin 1(1)*: 10–11

Berne E (1966) *Principles of Group Treatment*, Grove, New York, p. 288

Berne E (1968) *Games People Play*, Penguin, Harmondsworth, pp. 158, 162

Berne E (1973a) *Sex in Human Loving*, Penguin, Harmondsworth

Berne E (1973b) *What Do You Say After You Say Hello?*, Bantam, New York, pp. 245, 376

Erskine R (1973) Six stages of treatment, *Transactional Analysis Journal 3(3)*: 149–150

James M (1977) *Techniques in Transactional Analysis: For Psychotherapists and Counsellors*, Addison-Wesley, Reading, Mass., p. 34

Steiner C (1974) *Scripts People Live*, Grove, New York

Suggested Further Reading

Abell R G (1977) *Own Your Own Life*, Bantam, New York

Berne E (1968) *Games People Play*, Penguin, Harmondsworth
Berne E (1973) *What Do You Say After You Say Hello?*, Bantam, New York
Goulding M M, Goulding R L (1979) *Changing Lives Through Redecision Therapy*, Brunner/Mazel, New York
Woollams S, Brown M (1978) *Transactional Analysis*, Huron Valley Institute, Dexter, Mich.

Chapter 10   Rational-Emotive Therapy

Windy Dryden

Historical Context and Developments in Britain

Historical context

Rational-emotive therapy was established in 1955 by Albert Ellis, a clinical psychologist in New York. Ellis received his original training in psychotherapy in the 1940s in the field of marriage, family and sex counselling. In the course of his practice he realized that this kind of counselling was limited because 'disturbed marriages (or premarital relationships) were a product of disturbed spouses; and that if people were truly to be helped to live happily with each other they would first have to be shown how they could live peacefully with themselves' (Ellis 1962). He thus embarked on a course of intensive psychoanalytic training and received his training analysis from a training analyst of the Karen Horney group whose technique was primarily Freudian. In 1949, Ellis began to practise orthodox psychoanalysis with his patients, but was disappointed with the results he obtained. His patients appeared to improve, claimed to feel better, but Ellis could see that their improvement was not necessarily sustained. He then began to experiment with various forms of face-to-face, psychoanalytically oriented psychotherapy. Although he claimed that these methods brought better results and within a shorter period of time than orthodox psychoanalysis, he was still dissatisfied with the outcome of the treatment. In 1953, he began to research a monograph and a long article on new techniques in psychotherapy (Ellis 1955a, 1955b) which influenced him to practise a unique brand of psychoanalytic-eclectic therapy; still, Ellis remained dissatisfied.

Throughout his career as a psychoanalytically inspired therapist from the late 1940s to 1955, Ellis had become increasingly disenchanted with psychoanalytic theory, claiming that it tended to be unscientific, devout and dogmatic. He had always maintained his interest in philosophy and enjoyed thinking about how this field could be applied to the realm of psychotherapy. He used his knowledge of philosophy to help him answer his most puzzling question: 'Why do highly intelligent human beings, including those with considerable psychological insight, desperately hold on to their irrational ideas about themselves and others?' (Ellis 1962). The writings of Greek and Roman Stoic philosophers (especially Epictetus and Marcus Aurelius) were particularly influential in this respect. These philosophers stressed that people are disturbed not by things but by their *view* of things. Ellis began to realize that he had made the error of stressing a psychodynamic causation of psychological problems (namely that we are disturbed as a result of what happens to us in our early childhood); instead, he started to emphasize the philosophic causation of psychological problems (namely that we remain disturbed because we actively and in the present re-indoctrinate ourselves with our disturbance-creating philosophies).

From this point he began to stress the importance that thoughts and philosophies (cognition) have in creating and maintaining psychological disturbance. In his early presentations and writings on what has become known as rational-emotive therapy, Ellis (1958) tended to overemphasize the role that cognitive factors play in human disturbance and consequently de-emphasized the place of emotive and behavioural factors. This was reflected in the original name that he gave to his approach: rational psychotherapy. In 1962, Ellis published his pioneering volume entitled: *Reason and Emotion in Psychotherapy*. In this volume he stressed two important points: first, that cognitions, emotions and behaviours are interactive and often overlapping processes, and second, that 'human thinking and emotions *are*, in some of their essences, the same thing, and that by changing the former one *does* change the latter' (Ellis 1962). He thus concluded that the label *rational-emotive therapy* more accurately described his therapeutic approach.

As noted above, the theory of rational-emotive therapy has from its inception stressed the importance of the interaction of cognitive, emotive and behavioural factors in both a) human functioning and dysfunctioning and b) the practice of psychotherapy. Ellis has acknowledged, in particular, his debts to theorists and practitioners who have advocated the role of action in helping clients to overcome their problems (Herzberg 1945; Salter 1949; Wolpe 1958). Indeed, Ellis employed a number of *in vivo* behavioural methods to overcome his own fears of speaking in public and approaching women (Ellis 1973).

Initially, rational-emotive therapy received unfavourable and even hostile responses from the field of American psychotherapy. Despite this, Ellis persisted in his efforts to make his ideas more widely known; and as a result RET is now flourishing. Its popularity in the United States increased markedly in the 1970s, when behaviour therapists became interested in cognitive factors, and the present impact of cognitive-behaviour therapy has helped RET to become more widely known there. Currently, RET is practised by literally thousands of mental health professionals in North America. It is taught and practised in Holland, Germany, Italy, India, Pakistan, Australia and other parts of the world, including, of course, Britain.

Developments in Britain

Although Ellis's writings have been widely available in Britain since 1962, and despite the fact that he visited these shores twice in the 1970s, RET is not widely practised here. I was the first Briton to receive formal training in RET when I visited the Institute for Rational-Emotive Therapy, New York, in 1978. In 1979 I arranged for Dr Richard Wessler, then the Institute's director of training, to visit Britain, and together we ran the first accredited RET training course here. Since then several accredited training courses have been run in various parts of Britain and also in Eire; in addition, numerous shorter and non-accredited training courses have been run throughout Britain, mainly with groups of clinical psychologists, counsellors, psychotherapists, nurses and social workers. Thus, although there are only two *fully* accredited rational-emotive therapists in Britain (myself and Dr Al Raitt, a psychologist from Bristol), an increasing number of mental health professionals are now using rational-emotive methods in their work. It is my impression that most people in Britain prefer to integrate such methods into their own eclectic brand of psychotherapy rather than undertake complete formal training in rational-emotive therapy; cost, however, may be a deterring factor in this respect. In my view, therapists need to be fully trained in rational-emotive methods before integrating their use into the practice of eclectic psychotherapy.

The signs are, however, that as cognitive-behaviour therapy becomes increasingly popular in Britain, more mental health professionals are beginning to interest themselves in RET, thus paralleling the development of RET in North America. With such developments in mind, Al Raitt, Jack Gordon (a lay advocate of RET since the mid-1960s) and myself founded the Institute for Rational-Emotive Therapy (UK) in 1982. This superseded the Centre for Rational-Emotive Therapy and Education (CRETE) which Jack Gordon and I established in 1979. Our parent New York Institute has granted us permission to run accredited training courses in RET, and in addition we run non-accredited training programmes for professionals and courses for the general public.

Theoretical Assumptions

The image of the person

Rational-emotive therapy holds that humans are essentially *hedonistic* (Ellis 1976): their major goals are to stay alive and to pursue happiness efficiently, that is, in a non-compulsive but self-interested manner enlightened by the fact that they live in a social world. It is stressed that people differ enormously in terms of *what* will bring them happiness, thus rational-emotive therapists show clients not what will lead to their happiness but *how* they prevent themselves from pursuing it and how they can overcome these obstacles. Other basic concepts implicit in RET's image of the person include those listed below.

Rationality   In RET, 'rational' means that which helps people to achieve their basic goals and purposes, whereas 'irrational' means that which prevents them from achieving these goals and purposes.

Human fallibility   Humans are deemed to be by nature fallible and not perfectible. They naturally make errors and defeat themselves in the pursuit of their basic goals and purposes.

Human complexity and fluidity   Humans are seen as being enormously complex organisms constantly in flux, and are encouraged to view themselves as such.

Biological emphasis   Ellis (1977a) argues that humans have two basic biological tendencies. First, they have a tendency towards irrationality; they naturally tend to make themselves disturbed. Ellis (1976) makes a number of points in support of his 'biological hypothesis'. These include:

(a)   virtually all humans show evidence of major human irrationalities;
(b)   many human irrationalities actually go counter to the teachings of parents, peers and the mass media (for example, people are rarely taught that it is good to procrastinate, yet countless do so);
(c)   humans often adopt other irrationalities after giving up former ones;
(d)   humans often go back to irrational activity even though they have often worked hard to overcome it (Ellis 1976).

Second, and more optimistically, humans are considered to have great potential to work to change their biologically-based irrationalities.

Human activity   Humans can best achieve their basic goals by pursuing them *actively*. They are less likely to be successful if they are passive or half-hearted in their endeavours.

Cognitive emphasis   Although emotions overlap with other psychological processes such as cognitions, sensations and behaviours, cognitions are given special emphasis in RET theory. The most efficient way of effecting lasting emotional and behavioural change is for humans to change their philosophies. Two types of cognition are distinguished in Ellis's (1962) ABC model of the emotional/behavioural episode. A cognitions refer to the person's *inferences* about events and include such cognitive activities as making forecasts, guessing the intentions of others and assessing the implications of one's behaviour for self and others; A cognitions may be descriptive or evaluative, but do not account for the person's emotions and/or behaviours at C. B cognitions – beliefs – are evaluative in nature and indicate the personal significance of the event for the person concerned; B cognitions *do* account for the person's emotions and/or behaviours at C.

Concepts of psychological health and disturbance

Rational and irrational beliefs   Ellis (1962) has distinguished between two types of evaluation of personal significance: rational and irrational beliefs. Rational beliefs are evaluations of personal significance which are non-absolute in nature. They indicate desires, preferences and wishes. Feelings of pleasure result when humans get what they desire, whereas feelings of displeasure (sadness, annoyance and concern) result when they fail to get what they want. Such negative emotions are deemed to be appropriate responses to negative events since they do not significantly interfere with the pursuit of established or new goals.

Irrational beliefs are evaluations of personal significance stated in absolute terms such as 'must', 'should', 'ought' and 'have to'. It is noted that people often escalate their desires into demands: negative emotions such as depression, anger, anxiety and guilt occur when people make demands on themselves, others and/or the world. Ellis regards these negative emotions as inappropriate responses to negative events since they generally impede the pursuit of established or new goals. Ellis (1982) claims that rational beliefs underlie functional behaviours, whereas irrational beliefs underpin dysfunctional behaviours such as withdrawal, procrastination, alcoholism, substance abuse and so on.

The process of making absolute demands on reality is called 'musturbation'. It is linked to a process called 'awfulising'. 'Awfulising' is the process of making grossly exaggerated negative conclusions when one does not get what one 'must' or when one gets what one 'must not'. Ellis considers awful to mean 'more than 100% bad' and to stem from the demand 'It should not be as bad as it is.'

Self-damnation vs. self-acceptance   Self-damnation occurs when I either fail to do what I must or do what I must not. It involves: a) the process of giving my 'self' a global negative rating and b) 'devil-ifying' myself as being bad or less worthy. This second process rests on a theological concept, and implies either that I am undeserving of pleasure on earth or that I should rot in hell as a subhuman (devil). The RET alternative to global negative self-rating and self-damnation is unconditional self-acceptance: unconditional acceptance of oneself as a fallible human being who is constantly in flux and too complex to be given a single legitimate rating. RET theory advocates that it is legitimate, and often helpful, to rate one's traits, behaviours, etc., but that it is not legitimate to rate one's self at all, even in a global positive manner, since positive self-rating tends to be conditional on doing good things, being loved and approved, etc.

Discomfort disturbance vs. discomfort tolerance According to RET there are two types of fundamental human disturbance. These are, firstly, *ego disturbance* (as outlined in the previous section) where demands are made on one's self and, secondly, *discomfort disturbance*, which stems from the irrational belief: 'I must feel comfortable and have comfortable life conditions.' Conclusions that stem from this premise are a) 'It's awful' and b) 'I can't stand it when these life conditions do not exist.' Discomfort disturbance occurs in different forms and is central to a full understanding of a number of emotional and behavioural disturbances such as anger, agoraphobia, depression, procrastination, alcoholism and so on. Demands made on other people either involve ego disturbance (for example, 'You must approve of me or I'd be less worthy') or discomfort disturbance ('You must approve of me and give me what I must have'), and thus do not represent a fundamental human disturbance.

Discomfort disturbance usually impedes people from working persist-ently hard to effect productive psychological change. The ability to tolerate discomfort and frustration, not for its own sake but in order to facilitate constructive psychological change is a primary criterion of psycho-logical health in RET theory. It forms the basis of a philosophy of long-range hedonism: the pursuit of meaningful long-term goals while tolerating the deprivation of attractive short-term goals which are self-defeating in the longer term.

Psychological health Ellis (1983a) shows how 'musturbation' is involved in dogmatism, devout belief (religious and secular) and religiosity, since these are all based on absolute demands on reality. He thus equates much emotional disturbance with these processes. He advocates a scep-ticism which is based on a non-absolute view of reality as the emotionally healthy alternative. Thus non-absolutism is at the core of the rational-emotive view of psychological health, as can be seen as Ellis's (1979b) criteria of positive mental health are outlined: (a) self-interest, (b) social interest, (c) self-direction, (d) tolerance, (e) acceptance of ambiguity and uncertainty, (f) flexibility and (g) scientific thinking (employing the rules of logic and scientific analysis in solving emotional and behavioural problems). Psychologically healthy people are not cold and detached, as those with a scientific approach to life are commonly but erroneously assumed to be; indeed, they experience the full range of appropriate emotions, positive and negative, namely h) commitment, i) calculated risk-taking, j) self-acceptance and k) acceptance of reality.

The acquisition of psychological disturbance

Rational-emotive therapy does not posit an elaborate theory concerning how psychological disturbance is acquired. This follows logically from Ellis's (1976, 1979b) hypothesis that humans have a strong *biological* tendency to think and act irrationally. While Ellis is clear that humans' tendency to make absolute commands and demands on themselves, others and the world is biologically rooted, he does acknowledge that environmental factors *contribute* to emotional disturbance and thus *encourage* humans to make their biologically based demands (Ellis 1979a). He argues that because humans are particularly influenceable as young children they tend to let themselves be over-influenced by societal teachings such as those offered by parents, peers, teachers and the mass media (Ellis 1979b). However, one major reason why environmental control continues to wield a powerful influence over most people most of the time is because they tend not to be critical of the socialization messages they receive. Individual differences play a part here also. Humans vary in their suggestibility; thus, while some humans emerge relatively unscathed emotionally from harsh and severe childhood regimes, others emerge emotionally damaged from more benign regimes (Werner and Smith 1982). Thus Ellis strongly believes that we, as humans, are not made disturbed simply by our experiences; rather, we bring our ability to disturb ourselves to our experiences.

While past experiences do contribute but do not cause humans to make absolute demands on reality, such experiences do tend to have a greater impact on the inferences that humans make about reality. Thus, if a woman is exposed to many harsh critical males early on in her life, she will tend to expect that *most* men will be harsh and critical. However, she will then, Ellis would argue, have the biological tendency to a) conclude that all men are like this, and b) needlessly upset herself about this 'reality', that is, to 'musturbate' and 'awfulise' about this 'fact'.

The perpetuation of psychological disturbance

While, as noted above, RET does not put forward elaborate theories to explain the acquisition of psychological disturbance, it does deal more extensively with how such disturbance is perpetuated. First, most people perpetuate their psychological disturbance precisely because of their own theories concerning the 'cause' of their problems. They do not have what Ellis (1979b) calls 'RET Insight 1': that psychological disturbance is 'caused' mainly by the beliefs that people hold about the negative events in their lives. They tend to attribute the 'cause' of their problems to situations, rather than to their beliefs about these situations. Lacking 'Insight 1', people are ignorant of the major determinants of their disturbance; consequently they do not know what to change in order to overcome their difficulties. Even when individuals see clearly that their beliefs determine their disturbance, they may lack 'RET Insight 2': that they remain upset by re-indoctrinating themselves *in the present* with these beliefs. People who do see that their beliefs determine their disturbance tend to perpetuate such disturbance by devoting their energy to attempting to find out *why* and *how* they adopted such beliefs instead of using such energy to change the presently held beliefs. Some people who have both insights still perpetuate their disturbance because they lack 'RET Insight 3': 'Only if we constantly *work* and *practice* in the present as well as in the future to think, feel and act *against* these irrational beliefs are we likely to surrender them and make ourselves significantly less disturbed' (Ellis 1979b). People who have all three insights see clearly that just acknowledging that a belief is irrational is insufficient for change to take place.

Ellis (1979b) stresses that the major reason why people fail to change is due to their philosophy of 'low frustration tolerance' (LFT). By believing that they must be comfortable, people will tend to avoid the discomfort that working to effect psychological change very often involves, even though facing and enduring such short-term discomfort will probably result in long-term benefit. As Wessler (1978) has noted, such people are operating hedonistically from within their own frames of reference. They evaluate the tasks associated with change as 'too uncomfortable to bear' – certainly more painful than the psychological disturbance to which they have achieved a fair measure of habituation. They prefer to opt for the comfortable but disturbance-perpetuating discomfort of their problems rather than face the 'change-related' discomfort which they rate as 'dire'. Clearly, therapists have to intervene in this closed system of beliefs if psychological change is to be effected. This philosophy of low frustration tolerance which impedes change can take many different forms. One prevalent form of LFT is 'anxiety about anxiety'. Here, individuals may not expose themselves to anxiety-provoking situations because they are afraid that they might become anxious if they did so: a prospect which they would rate as 'terrible' because they believe 'I must not be anxious.'

'Anxiety about anxiety' represents an example of a phenomenon that explains further why people perpetuate their psychological disturbances. Ellis (1979b) has noted that people often make themselves *disturbed about their disturbances*, thus they block themselves from working to overcome their original psychological disturbance because they upset themselves about having the original disturbance. Humans are often inventive in this respect, therefore they can make themselves anxious about their anxiety, depressed about being depressed, guilty concerning their anger, and so on. Consequently, people often have to overcome their secondary disturbances before embarking on effecting change in their original problems.

Ellis (1979b) has observed that people sometimes experience some kind of perceived *payoff* for their psychological disturbance other than the gaining of immediate obvious ease. Here such disturbance may be perpetuated until the perceived payoff is dealt with, in order to minimize its impact. For example, a woman who claims to want to lose weight may not take the necessary steps because she fears that losing weight would make her more attractive to men: a situation which she would view as 'dire'. Thus, remaining fat protects her (in her mind) from a 'terrible' state of affairs. It is to be emphasized that the rational-emotive theorists stress the phenomenological nature of these payoffs: in other words, it is the person's view of the payoff that is important in determining its impact, not the events delineated in the person's description.

A final major way that people tend to perpetuate their psychological disturbance is explained by the 'self-fulfilling prophecy' phenomenon (Jones 1977; Wachtel 1977): by acting according to their predictions, people often elicit from themselves or from others reactions which they then interpret in such a way as to confirm their initial self-defeating forecasts.

In conclusion, Ellis (1979c) believes that humans tend naturally to perpetuate their problems and have a strong innate tendency to cling to self-defeating, habitual patterns, thereby resisting basic change. Helping clients change, then, poses quite a challenge for RET practitioners.

Practice

Goals of therapy

In trying to help clients to overcome their emotional difficulties and achieve their self-enhancing goals, rational-emotive therapists have clear and well-defined aims.

In this discussion it is important to distinguish between outcome goals and process goals. Outcome goals are those benefits which clients hope to derive from the therapeutic process. Ideally, rational-emotive therapists try to assist clients to make profound philosophic changes. This would first involve clients refusing to rate themselves, a process which would help them to accept themselves unconditionally. Second, clients would refuse to rate anything as 'awful'. Moreover, they would persistently work to increase their tolerance of frustration while striving to achieve their basic goals and purposes. As a result, if therapists are successful in this basic objective, clients would be minimally prone to future ego disturbance or discomfort disturbance. They would still experience appropriate negative emotions such as sadness, annoyance, concern and disappointment, since they would clearly retain their desires, wishes and wants; however, they would rarely experience inappropriate negative emotions such as depression, anger, anxiety and guilt since they would have largely surrendered their absolutistic 'musts' 'shoulds' and 'oughts' which underly such dysfunctional emotional experiences. In achieving such profound philosophic changes, clients would clearly score highly on the eleven criteria of positive mental health mentioned earlier in this chapter. If such ideal client goals are not possible, rational-emotive therapists settle for less pervasive changes in their clients. Here clients may well achieve considerable symptomatic relief and overcome the psychological disturbance which brought them to therapy, but will not have achieved such profound philosophic change as to prevent the development of future psychological disturbance. In this case, clients benefit from therapy either a) by making productive behavioural changes which lead to improved environmental circumstances at A in Ellis's ABC model or b) by correcting distorted inferences at A.

Process goals involve therapists engaging clients effectively in the process of therapy so that they can be helped to achieve their outcome goals. Here Bordin's (1975, 1976) concept of the therapeutic alliance is helpful. There are three major components of the therapeutic alliance: bonds, goals and tasks.

Effective bonds   These refer to the quality of relationship between therapist and client that is necessary to help clients achieve their outcome goals. Rational-emotive therapists consider that there is no one way of developing effective bonds with clients: flexibility is the key concept here, as will become apparent when this topic is developed in the section on therapeutic style (see page 249).

Agreement on goals   Effective RET is usually characterized by therapists and clients working together towards clients' realistic and self-enhancing outcome goals. The role of therapists in this process is to help clients distinguish between a) realistic and unrealistic goals and b) self-enhancing and self-defeating goals. Moreover, rational-emotive therapists help clients see that they can usually only achieve their ultimate outcome goals by means of reaching a series of mediating goals. Some rational-emotive therapists like in addition to set goals for each therapy session. Thus, client goals can be negotiated at three levels: a) ultimate outcome goals, b) mediating goals and c) session goals. Effective rational-emotive therapists help their clients explicitly to see the links between these different goals and thus help to demystify the process of therapy for clients.

Agreement on tasks   RET is most effective when therapist and client clearly acknowledge that each has tasks to carry out in the process of therapy, clearly understand the nature of these tasks and agree to execute their own tasks. The major tasks of rational-emotive are: a) to help clients see that their emotional and behavioural problems have cognitive antecedents; b) to train clients to identify and change their distorted inferences and irrational beliefs; and c) to teach clients that such change is best effected by the persistent application of cognitive, imagery, emotive and behavioural methods. The major tasks of clients are: a) to observe their emotional and behavioural disturbances; b) to relate these to their cognitive determinants; and c) to work continually at changing their distorted inferences and irrational beliefs by employing cognitive, imagery, emotive and behavioural methods.

The person of the therapist

Unfortunately, no research studies have been carried out to determine the personal qualities of effective rational-emotive therapists. Rational-emotive theory does put forward a number of hypotheses concerning this topic (Ellis 1978), but it is important to regard these as both tentative and awaiting empirical study.

(a) Since RET is a fairly structured form of therapy, its effective practitioners are usually comfortable with structure but flexible enough to work in a less structured manner when the situation arises.

(b) RET practitioners tend to be intellectually, cognitively or philosophically inclined and become attracted to RET because the approach provides them with opportunities to fully express this tendency.

(c) As will be shown in the section on therapeutic style (p. 248), Ellis argues that RET should often be conducted in a strong active-directive manner; thus, effective RET practitioners are usually comfortable operating in this mode. Nevertheless, they have the flexibility to modify their interpersonal style with clients so that they provide the optimum conditions to facilitate client change.

d) As will be shown in the section on major therapeutic techniques (page 250), RET emphasizes that it is important for clients to put their therapy-derived insights into practice in their everyday lives. As a result, effective practitioners of RET are usually comfortable with behavioural instruction and teaching and with providing the active prompting that clients often require if they are to follow through on homework assignments.

(e) Effective rational-emotive therapists tend to have little fear of failure themselves. Their personal worth is not invested in their clients' improvement. They do not need their clients' love and/or approval and are thus not afraid of taking calculated risks if therapeutic impasses occur. They tend to accept both themselves and their clients as fallible human beings and are therefore tolerant of their own mistakes and the irresponsible acts of their clients. They tend to have, or persistently work towards acquiring, a philosophy of high frustration tolerance, and do not get discouraged when clients improve at a slower rate than they desire.

Thus effective practitioners tend to score highly on most of the criteria of positive mental health outlined earlier in this chapter (page 241), and serve as healthy role models for their clients.

(f) RET strives to be 'scientific, empirical, anti-absolutistic and undevout in its approach to people's selecting and achieving their own goals' (Ellis 1978). Thus effective practitioners of RET tend to show similar traits and are definitely not mystical, anti-intellectual and magical in their beliefs.

(g) RET advocates the use of techniques in a number of different modalities (cognitive, imagery, emotive, behavioural and interpersonal). Its effective practitioners are thus comfortable with a multi-modal approach to treatment and tend not to be people who like to stick rigidly to any one modality.

Finally, Ellis (1978) notes that some rational-emotive therapists often modify the preferred practice of RET according to their own natural personality characteristics. Thus, for example, some therapists practice RET in a slow-moving passive manner, do little disputing and focus therapy on the relationship between them and their clients. Whether such modification of the preferred practice of RET is effective is a question awaiting empirical enquiry.

Therapeutic style

Taking their lead from Ellis (1977d), most rational-emotive therapists tend to adopt an active-directive style in therapy. They are active in directing their clients' attention to the cognitive determinants of their emotional and behavioural problems. While they can often adopt a collaborative style of interaction with clients who are relatively non-disturbed and non-resistant to the therapeutic process, Ellis (personal communication) argues that they ought to be forceful and persuasive with more disturbed and highly resistant clients. Whichever style they adopt, they strive to a) show that they unconditionally accept their clients as fallible human beings and b) be empathic and genuine in the therapeutic encounter. They tend not to be unduly warm towards their clients, since they believe that showing clients undue warmth is counter-productive from a long-term perspective, in that clients' approval and dependency *needs* may be inappropriately reinforced.

While an active-directive style of interaction is often preferred, it is important to note that this is not *absolutely* favoured (Eschenroeder 1979). What is important is for therapists to convey to clients that they are trustworthy and knowledgeable individuals who are prepared to commit themselves totally to the task of helping clients reach their goals. It is important that therapists develop the kind of relationship with clients that the latter will, according to their idiosyncratic positions, find helpful. This might mean that, with some clients, therapists might emphasize their expertise and portray themselves as well-qualified individuals whose knowledge and expertise form the basis of what social psychologists call *communicator credibility*. Such credibility is important to the extent that certain clients will be more likely to listen to therapists if they stress these characteristics; other clients, however, will be more likely to listen to therapists if the latter portray themselves as likeable individuals. In such cases, therapists might de-emphasize their expertise but emphasize their humanity by being prepared to disclose certain aspects of their lives which are both relevant to clients' problems and which stress liking as a powerful source of communicator credibility.

For example, I recently saw two clients on the same day with whom I emphasized different aspects of communicator credibility. I decided to interact with Jim, a 30-year-old bricklayer, in a casual, 'laid-back' style. I encouraged him to use my first name and was prepared to disclose some personal details because I believed, from what he had told me in an assessment interview, that he strongly disliked 'stuffy mind doctors who treat me as another case rather than as a human being'. However, in the next hour with Jane, a 42-year-old unmarried fashion editor, I portrayed myself as 'Dr Dryden' and stressed my long training and qualifications because she had indicated, again in an assessment interview, that she would strongly dislike therapists who were too warm and friendly towards her; she wanted a therapist who 'knew what he was doing'. The point here is that therapists should be flexible with regard to changing their style of interaction with different clients. They should come to a therapeutic decision about what style of interaction is going to be helpful in both the short and long term with a particular client. Furthermore, therapists need to recognize that the style of interaction that they adopt may in fact be counter-productive (Beutler 1979); for instance, they should be wary of adopting a) an overly friendly style of interaction with 'hysterical' clients and b) an overly directive style with clients whose

sense of autonomy is easily threatened. No matter what style of interaction therapists may adopt with particular clients, it is important that
the former should be concerned, genuine and empathic in the
encounter.

Major therapeutic techniques

The primary purpose of the major therapeutic techniques of RET is to
help clients give up their absolute philosophies and adhere to more relative ones. However, before change procedures can be used, therapists
need to make an adequate assessment of clients' problems.

Assessment of client problems   Clients often begin to talk in therapy
about the troublesome events in their lives (A) or their dysfunctional
emotional and/or behavioural reactions (C) to these events. Rational-
emotive therapists use concrete examples of A and C to help clients identify their irrational beliefs at B in the ABC model. In the assessment stage,
therapists particularly look to assess whether clients are making themselves disturbed about their original disturbances as described earlier in
this chapter (page 244).

Cognitive change techniques   Here both verbal and imagery
methods are used to dispute clients' irrational beliefs. Verbal disputing
involves three sub-categories. First, therapists can help clients to *discriminate* clearly between their rational and irrational beliefs. Then,
second, while *debating*, therapists can ask clients a number of Socratic-
type questions about their irrational beliefs: for example, 'Where is the
evidence that you must ...?' Finally, *defining* helps clients to make
increasingly accurate definitions in their private and public language.
These verbal disputing methods can also be used to help correct their
faulty inferences (Beck et al. 1979).

To reinforce the rational philosophy clients can a) be given books to
read (bibliotherapy); self-help books often used in conjunction with RET
include *A New Guide to Rational Living* by Ellis and Harper (1975) and
A Guide to Personal Happiness by Ellis and Becker (1982). They can also
b) employ *written rational self-statements* which they can refer to at
various times; and c) *use RET with others* – a technique which gives

clients practice at thinking through arguments in favour of rational beliefs.

Written homework forms such as that presented in Figure 10.1 is another major cognitive technique used in RET as is *rational-emotive imagery (REI)*. REI is the major imagery technique used in RET. Here clients get practice at changing their dysfunctional emotions to functional ones (C) while keenly imagining the negative event at A; what they are in fact doing is getting practice at changing their underlying philosophy at B.

Emotive-evocative change techniques   Such techniques are quite vivid and evocative in nature, but are still designed to dispute clients' irrational beliefs. Rational-emotive therapists *unconditionally accept* their clients as fallible human beings even when they act poorly or obnoxiously: they thus act as a good *role model* for clients. In this respect they judiciously employ *self-disclosure*, openly admitting that they make errors, act badly, etc., but that they can nevertheless accept themselves. Therapists often employ *humour* at times in the therapeutic process, believing that clients can be helped by not taking themselves and their problems *too* seriously, such humour is directed at aspects of clients, never at clients themselves.

Clients are often encouraged to do *shame-attacking exercises* in which they go and practice their new philosophies of discomfort tolerance and self-acceptance while doing something 'shameful' but not harmful to themselves or others: examples might include asking for chocolate in a hardware shop and wearing odd shoes for a day. Repeating rational self-statements in a *passionate* manner is often employed in conjunction with shame-attacking exercises and also at other times.

Behaviour change techniques   Rational-emotive therapists can employ the whole range of currently used behavioural techniques (see Chapter 11); however, they prefer *in vivo* (in the situation) rather than imaginal desensitization. Ellis (1979d) favours the use of *in vivo desensitization* in its '*full exposure*' rather than its gradual form, because it offers clients greater opportunities profoundly to change their ego and discomfort disturbance-creating philosophies. This highlights the fact that behavioural methods are used primarily to effect cognitive changes. Careful negotiation

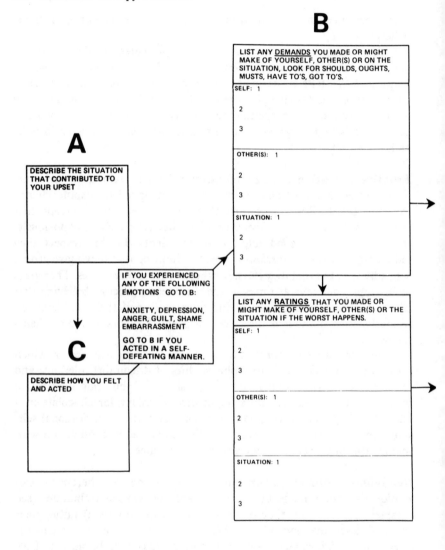

B

LIST ANY <u>DEMANDS</u> YOU MADE OR MIGHT MAKE OF YOURSELF, OTHER(S) OR ON THE SITUATION, LOOK FOR SHOULDS, OUGHTS, MUSTS, HAVE TO'S, GOT TO'S.

SELF: 1

2

3

OTHER(S): 1

2

3

SITUATION: 1

2

3

A

DESCRIBE THE SITUATION THAT CONTRIBUTED TO YOUR UPSET

IF YOU EXPERIENCED ANY OF THE FOLLOWING EMOTIONS GO TO B:

ANXIETY, DEPRESSION, ANGER, GUILT, SHAME EMBARRASSMENT

GO TO B IF YOU ACTED IN A SELF-DEFEATING MANNER.

C

DESCRIBE HOW YOU FELT AND ACTED

LIST ANY <u>RATINGS</u> THAT YOU MADE OR MIGHT MAKE OF YOURSELF, OTHER(S) OR THE SITUATION IF THE WORST HAPPENS.

SELF: 1

2

3

OTHER(S): 1

2

3

SITUATION: 1

2

3

Figure 10.1 A guide for solving your emotional and behavioural problems by re-examining your self-defeating thoughts and attitudes (Dryden 1982)

D

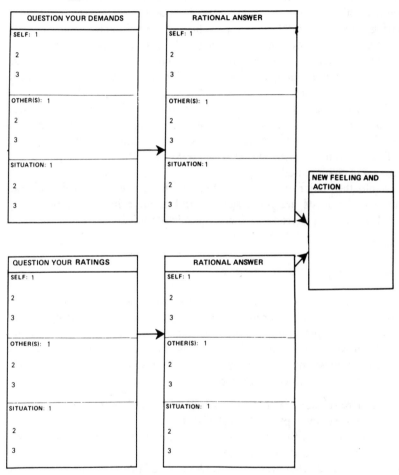

QUESTION YOUR DEMANDS

SELF: 1

2

3

OTHER(S): 1

2

3

SITUATION: 1

2

3

RATIONAL ANSWER

SELF: 1

2

3

OTHER(S): 1

2

3

SITUATION: 1

2

3

NEW FEELING AND ACTION

QUESTION YOUR RATINGS

SELF: 1

2

3

OTHER(S): 1

2

3

SITUATION: 1

2

3

RATIONAL ANSWER

SELF: 1

2

3

OTHER(S): 1

2

3

SITUATION: 1

2

3

concerning *homework assignments*, where clients aim to put into practice what they have learned in therapy, is advocated, and it is to be realized that clients will not always opt for 'full exposure, *in vivo* homework. Other behavioural methods often used in RET include: (a) *'stay-in-there' activities* (Grieger and Boyd 1980) which help clients to remain in an uncomfortable situation for a period while tolerating feelings of chronic discomfort; (b) *anti-procrastination exercises* which are designed to help clients start tasks earlier rather than later, thus behaviourally disputing their dire need for comfort; (c) *skill-training methods*, which equip clients with certain key skills in which they are lacking (for instance, social skills and assertiveness training are often employed, but usually after important cognitive changes have been effected); (d) *self-reward and self-penalization* (but not, of course, self-damnation!) which can also be used to encourage clients to use behaviour change methods.

While the major treatment techniques have been outlined, rational-emotive therapists are often flexible and creative in the methods they employ tailoring therapy to meet the client's idiosyncratic position.

The change process in therapy

As has been shown, rational-emotive therapists are quite ambitious in setting as their major therapeutic goal helping clients to effect what Ellis often calls a 'profound philosophic change'. This primarily involves clients surrendering their 'demanding' philosophy and replacing it with a 'desiring' philosophy. In striving to achieve these changes in philosophy, such clients are helped in therapy to:

(a) adhere to the idea that they manufacture and continue to manufacture their own psychological disturbance;

(b) acknowledge fully that they have the ability to change such disturbance to a significant degree;

(c) understand that their psychological disturbance is determined mainly by irrational beliefs;

(d) identify such irrational beliefs when they become disturbed and distinguish these from rational beliefs;

(e) dispute such beliefs using the logico-empirical methods of science and replace these with their rational alternatives (more specifically, such clients work towards unconditional self-acceptance and raising their frustration tolerance);

(f) reinforce such cognitive learning by persistently working hard in employing emotive and behavioural methods. Such clients choose to tolerate the discomfort that this may well involve because they recognize that without acting on newly acquired insights, change will probably not be maintained;

(g) acknowledge that as humans they will probably have difficulty in effecting a profound philosophic change and will consequently tend to backslide. Taking such factors into account, such clients re-employ and continually practise RET's multi-modal methods for the rest of their lives. In doing so, they learn to experiment and find the methods that work especially well for them. They specifically recognize that forceful and dramatic methods are powerful ways of facilitating philosophic change and readily implement these, particularly at times when they experience difficulty in changing (Ellis 1979e).

In helping clients achieve such profound change, effective rational-emotive therapists are unswerving in their unconditional acceptance of their clients. They realize that the achievement of profound philosophic change is an extraordinarily difficult task, and one which frequently involves many setbacks. Consequently, while tolerating their own feelings of discomfort they dedicate themselves to becoming a persistent and effective change agent. Thus they strive to (a) identify and work to overcome their clients' resistances (Ellis 1983b, 1983c); (b) interpret and challenge the many defences that their clients erect against such change; and (c) continually encourage, persuade and cajole their clients to keep persisting at the hard work of changing themselves; and (d) generally experiment with a wide variety of methods and styles to determine which work best for individual clients.

Rational-emotive therapists acknowledge that not all clients can achieve such far-reaching philosophic change. This knowledge is usually gained from clients' responses to the therapeutic process. When deciding to settle for less ambitious outcome goals, RET practitioners limit themselves to help clients: a) effect situationally-based philosophic change; b) correct distorted inferences (Beck et al. 1979); and c) effect behavioural changes so that they can improve negatively perceived life events. Profound philosophic change would, of course, incorporate these three modes of change.

· Case Example

The client

Teresa is a 38-year-old woman who is happily married to Fred, her second husband, and whose 17-year-old son by her previous marriage lives with them. She was referred to the clinic I run for a local general practice, complaining of depression and anxiety. Although it is not my practice to obtain detailed background information, I did learn the following. Teresa is one of seven children born to a Pakistani father and an English mother. She did not feel accepted by either of her parents, and described her mother as particularly rejecting of her since she was not 'pure Asian'. As a half-caste, she believed that she could not please anybody and thus concluded that she. was inferior, just not coming up to standard. One of the consequences of her 'inferiority' was that she spent lengthy periods of time beneath a sun-lamp so that she could gain a tan and thus become more acceptable to her mother!

Assessment of client problems in rational-emotive therapy is an on-going process throughout therapy which, in Teresa's case, revealed the following problems:

(a) Excessive worry and anxiety concerning her son.
(b) Difficulty in refusing requests, particularly those made by her mother and sisters.
(c) Extreme anxiety concerning disruption to her plans.
(d) Difficulty in 'making up' with her husband after a row.
(e) Anger towards her mother for her non-acceptance of Teresa. She reported hating going to see her mother, although she did so every week. She also felt that she needed her mother's approval.
(f) She reported that her husband's family made her feel like an outcast: 'Even if I am a half-caste, they don't have to show it.'
(g) Anxiety about meeting people. This centred around her feelings of shame concerning firstly, her failed marriage, secondly, the prospects of crying, revealing anxiety or acting foolishly in public, and thirdly, her poor spelling.

(h) Feelings of hurt that her mother and sisters did not understand her and put her in 'upsetting' situations.
(i) Anxiety concerning failure to live up to what she considered to be her husband's expectations of her.
(j) Feelings of loss of control and fears of going mad as a result of experiencing intense pre-menstrual tension.
(k) Excessive smoking.
(l) Feeling lost after completing her household chores.

The following irrational beliefs were revealed as underlying the above problems:

(i) 'My happiness is totally dependent on my son's happiness. If he is miserable, then I have to be miserable. There I *have to* do the right things to make him happy' (problem a).
(ii) 'If other people (particularly my family) think I'm inferior then *I am inferior*' (problems b, d, e, f, g).
(iii) 'Things *have* to be the way I want them to be. I *can't stand it* if my routine is disrupted' (problems c, k).
(iv) 'I *can't stand it* if others make a fuss of me if I'm upset. It means that I am at fault and I *must not* make such mistakes' (problem d).
(v) 'My sister *should* recognise that I am sensitive and not put me in upsetting situations' (problem h).

In addition, Teresa was prone to the following inferential distortions (Beck et al. 1979):

(vi) 'Other people are to blame for my problems': 'faulty attribution' (problems c, d, e, f).
(vii) Predicting that other people would consider her inferior and that this would occur frequently: 'negative prediction', 'magnification' (problems b, d, g, h).
(viii) 'I will lose control and go mad at certain times of the month': 'faulty attribution', 'emotional reasoning' (problem j).
(ix) 'I cannot be the source of my own enjoyment': 'negative prediction' (problem l).

The acquisition and perpetuation of psychological disturbance

Whilst there is no doubt that Teresa's upbringing contributed to her psychological problems, it did not 'cause' these problems. A number of people have had childhood and adolescent experiences similar to those of Teresa without becoming disturbed (Werner and Smith 1982). Moreover, other people experience problems similar to Teresa's even though they have had most favourable early experiences. As a rational-emotive therapist, I consider that Teresa brought her tendency to disturb herself to her early experiences. The following analysis of how she perpetuated her psychological disturbance should be regarded as tentative.

Once her belief that she was worthless was fully formed, she perpetuated it by redoubling her efforts to gain her parents' approval. The more she tried to win her parents' love the more she failed, since her parents, from her account, seemed to be prejudiced against her because of her 'half-caste' status and thus rebuffed her attempts. The more they conveyed to her that they did not accept her, the more she re-confirmed her belief in her own worthlessness. Believing herself worthless, she then tended to predict that others would also consider her so. She would thus get anxious, tending either to withdraw from others and thereby to deprive herself of disconfirming experiences (Wachtel 1977), or to misinterpret the responses of others as evidence that they, too, considered her inferior. These perceived experiences at A activated her by now deeply entrenched belief: 'I'm worthless.' Since she held other people, not her own beliefs, responsible for her feelings of inferiority and worthlessness, she was unable to address herself to the philosophic cause of her emotional problems (lack of RET Insight 1). It is also likely that her failed first marriage contributed to her feelings of failure. From her perspective, her one source of joy left was her son; it now became imperative to make him happy, particularly as she herself had had an unhappy childhood. Cut off by her own beliefs from other sources of enjoyment, she invested her remaining chance of happiness in her son's happiness. Since she believed she *must* make him happy, however, she remained anxious even when he was happy since he might at some future time become unhappy. Getting married for the second time did not provide the answer to her psychological problems, even though it was and still is a good marriage, since she believed that it would be only a matter of time before her husband 'found her out' as being inferior. Her behaviour with him confirmed this. She believed she had to make herself attractive to him at all times lest he should discover her to be unattractive and therefore in her eyes worthless. I have focused here mainly on Teresa's ego disturbance and will not, due to limited space, consider the development and perpetuation of her discomfort disturbance as manifested in problems (e), (h) and (i).

Therapy

From her favourable response to initial attempts at cognitive restructuring, I offered Teresa a ten-session brief therapy contract. These ten sessions were in fact spread out over a period of eight months. While Teresa wanted to experience depression less often, she was realistic enough to know that she would still have such experiences; however, she wanted to gain some tools to help her cope with these experiences so that she would not have to rely on drugs. Therapeutic outcome goals were then chosen by Teresa and myself in collaboration. I would help her to identify her irrational beliefs (demands) underlying her shame, anxiety and depression and show her the rational alternatives (desires). Together we explored what different emotional and behavioural consequences would stem from such a change in philosophy. I would often remind her that she did not *have to* choose the consequences based on rational thinking – but she invariably did. I was thus able to develop an effective, collaborative working alliance with Teresa from the outset. We agreed on outcome goals, and she saw that the achievement of such goals required work and effort which she invested from the start.

Major therapeutic techniques *Cognitively,* I verbally disputed Teresa's irrational beliefs. I helped her to discriminate between her desires and demands, and by asking her a number of Socratic questions helped her to see that:

(a) She did not have to do the right things to make her son happy and that her own happiness was not dependent on his.
(b) She could accept herself as a fallible human being even if others regarded her as inferior or worthless.
(c) She could tolerate disruption to her routine without liking it.
(d) She could stand being fussed over; even if she caused a row, she could accept herself for this.

(e)   Other people have a right to their value systems even though this may conflict with her own values.

In addition, I showed her that she (Big 'I') was comprised of many different aspects (little 'i's). Moreover, I helped her to distinguish between 'I' and 'iiii' and encouraged her to rate 'iiii' while accepting 'I' (Lazarus 1977).

Emotively, I accepted her as a fallible human being and showed her that I could be viewed as her equal, not her superior. To help her to distinguish between *doing* something stupid and *being* stupid, I on one occasion humorously and vividly flung myself to the floor barking like a dog (Dryden 1982). I thus did not take myself too seriously in the therapeutic situation.

Behaviourally, she took risks and started refusing unreasonable requests from her family. She began to speak up to her mother and acted more in her own interests. She forced herself to speak after rowing with her husband and generally began to reveal her imperfections to him. She began to socialize more, and deliberately showed herself in public when *not* tidily dressed and coiffured. All these behavioural tasks were backed up by *in vivo* cognitive disputing, and were designed to effect cognitive changes mainly in her self-downing philosophy.

The change process   Teresa began to change when she saw that her problems were determined by her own beliefs and not caused by other people. She was somewhat unique in taking full responsibility for her change at the outset of therapy, and saw that going from intellectual to emotional insight involved frequent re-examination of her beliefs and acting on new beliefs (Ellis 1963). In my opinion, she was successful in effecting a situationally based philosophic change at the end of the ten sessions. She appeared to be more self-accepting with her mother, sisters and husband, although she did not have the opportunity to test this out fully since her family did not react that unfavourably to her self-assertive efforts. She became somewhat less anxious with other people because she corrected inferential distortions rather than challenged irrational beliefs (i.e. she reminded herself that others were not *that* likely to regard her as inferior). However, she was still prone to problems in this regard at the end of therapy, since she had not exposed her weaknesses in public while accepting herself forcefully and had not had many opportunities to accept herself in the face of public rejection/disapproval.

During several sessions I exposed and disputed her dependency needs: 'I *need* Dr Dryden to look up to and seek help from.' Although potentially disrupting, this attitude was not strongly held and did not obstruct Teresa's independent improvement since she effectively challenged and counteracted it. No other forms of 'resistance' were present in treatment.

A recently conducted follow-up session, nine months after therapy had ended, revealed that Teresa had maintained the gains she had made during therapy; indeed, she had effected a more profound philosophic change than at the end of the ten sessions. She had in the interim period exposed some of her weaknesses in public and accepted herself in the face of some public rejection. She had adopted and maintained a responsible voluntary position in the probation service, meeting a variety of people without anxiety. She reported feeling on equal terms with others. The only area in which she had not maintained improvement concerned smoking. She had increased her daily consumption from six to fifteen cigarettes, and I spent some time in the follow-up session disputing her belief, 'I *have to* have the pleasure of the moment.' I plan to see Teresa again for a final follow-up session in a year's time.

References

Beck A T, Rush A J, Shaw B F, Emery G (1979) *Cognitive Therapy of Depression*, Guilford, New York

Beutler L E (1979) Toward specific psychological therapies for specific conditions, *Journal of Consulting and Clinical Psychology* 47: 882–897

Bordin E S (1975) 'The generalizability of the psychoanalytic concept of working alliance', paper presented at the meeting of the Society of Psychotherapy Research, Boston

Bordin E S (1976) 'The working alliance: basis for a general theory of psychotherapy', paper presented at the meeting of the American Psychological Association, Washington, D C

Dryden W (1982) *Vivid RET*, Institute for RET (UK), London

Ellis A (1955a) New approaches to psychotherapy techniques, *Journal of Clinical Psychology* (Brandon, Vermont)

Ellis A (1955b) Psychotherapy techniques for use with psychotics, *American Journal of Psychotherapy* 9: 425–476

Ellis A (1958) Rational psychotherapy, *Journal of General Psychology* 59: 35–49

Ellis A (1962) *Reason and Emotion in Psychotherapy*, Lyle Stuart, Seacausus, NJ, pp. 3, 14, 122

Ellis A (1963) Toward a more precise definition of 'emotional' and 'intellectual' insight, *Psychological Reports* 13: 125–126

Ellis A (1973) 'Psychotherapy without tears' in Burton A and associates *Twelve Therapists: How They Live and Actualize Themselves*, Jossey-Bass, San Francisco

Ellis A (1976) The biological basis of human irrationality, *Journal of Individual Psychology 32*: 145–168

Ellis A (1978) Personality characteristics of rational-emotive therapists and other kinds of therapists, *Psychotherapy: Theory, Research and Practice 15(4)*: 329–332

Ellis A (1979a) 'Toward a new theory of personality' in Ellis A and Whiteley J M (eds.), *Theoretical and Empirical Foundations of Rational-Emotive Therapy*, Brooks/Cole, Monterey, Cal.

Ellis A (1979b) 'The theory of rational-emotive therapy' in Ellis A and Whiteley J M *Theoretical and Empirical Foundations of Rational-Emotive Therapy*, p. 47

Ellis A (1979c) 'The rational-emotive approach to counseling' in Burks Jr H M and Stefflre B (eds.) *Theories of Counseling*, McGraw-Hill, New York

Ellis A (1979d) 'The practice of rational-emotive therapy' in Ellis A and Whiteley J M *Theoretical and Empirical Foundations of Rational-Emotive Therapy*

Ellis A (1979e) The issue of force and energy in behavioral change, *Journal of Contemporary Psychotherapy 10(2)*: 83–97

Ellis A (1982) The treatment of alcohol and drug abuse: a rational-emotive approach, *Rational Living 17(2)*: 15–24

Ellis A (1983a) *The Case Against Religiosity*, Institute for Rational-Emotive Therapy

Ellis A (1983b) Rational-emotive therapy (RET) approaches to overcoming resistance 1: common forms of resistance, *British Journal of Cognitive Psychotherapy 1(1)*: 28–38

Ellis A (1983c) Rational-emotive therapy (RET) approaches to overcoming resistance 2: how RET disputes clients' irrational, resistance-creating beliefs, *British Journal of Cognitive Psychotherapy 1(2)*: 1–16

Ellis A, Becker I (1982) *A Guide to Personal Happiness*, Wilshire, North Hollywood, Cal.

Ellis A, Harper R A (1975) *A New Guide to Rational Living*, Wilshire, North Hollywood, Cal.

Eschenroeder C (1979) Different therapeutic styles in rational-emotive therapy, *Rational Living 14(1)*: 3–7

Grieger R, Boyd J (1980) *Rational-Emotive Therapy: A Skills-Based Approach*, Van Nostrand Reinhold, New York

Herzberg A (1945) *Active Psychotherapy*, Grune and Stratton, New York

Jones R A (1977) *Self-Fulfilling Prophecies: Social, Psychological and Physiological Effects of Expectancies*, Lawrence Erlbaum, Hillsdale, New Jersey

Lazarus A (1977) 'Toward an egoless state of being' in Ellis A and Grieger R (eds.) *Handbook of Rational-Emotive Therapy*, Springer, New York

Salter A (1949) *Conditioned Reflex Therapy*, Creative Age, New York 1949

Wachtel P L (1977) *Psychoanalysis and Behavior Therapy: Toward an Integration*, Basic Books, New York

Werner E E, Smith R S (1982) *Vulnerable but Invincible: A Study of Resilient Children*, McGraw-Hill, New York

Wessler R A (1978) The neurotic paradox: A rational-emotive view, *Rational Living 13 (1)*: 9–12

Wolpe J (1958) *Psychotherapy by Reciprocal Inhibition*, Stanford University Press, Stanford

Suggested Further Reading

Dryden W (1984) *Rational-Emotive Therapy: Fundamentals and Innovations*, Croom Helm, Beckenham

Ellis A, Abrahms E (1978) *Brief Psychotherapy in Medical and Health Practice*, Springer, New York

Grieger R, Boyd J (1980) *Rational-Emotive Therapy: A Skills-Based Approach*, Van Nostrand Reinhold, New York

Walen S, DiGiuseppe R, Wessler R (1980) *A Practitioner's Guide to Rational-Emotive Therapy*, Oxford University Press, New York

Wessler R A, Wessler R L (1980) *The Principles and Practice of Rational-Emotive Therapy*, Jossey-Bass, San Francisco

Chapter 11   Behavioural Psychotherapy

Dougal Mackay

Historical Context and Developments in Britain

Historical context

Although the term 'behaviour therapy' was first used by the American psychologist B.F. Skinner in the 1950s to refer to operant conditioning work with psychotic patients, the establishment of the psychotherapy school of this name is usually associated with Joseph Wolpe (1958), a psychiatrist who worked at that time at the Maudsley Hospital in London. Other Maudsley psychiatrists and psychologists, such as Isaac Marks and Hans Eysenck, joined forces with him in an endeavour to promote a school of psychotherapy to rival psychoanalysis. Consequently, despite the influential writings of Skinner, Hull and other American psychologists, behaviour therapy has its roots in Britain.

In contrast to other forms of psychological treatment, which emerged largely from clinical practice, behaviour therapy was regarded by its founders as the applied branch of a basic science. Since it had proved possible to create phobias experimentally through classical conditioning (Watson and Rayner 1920), it was argued that all neurotic disorders could be seen as inappropriate learned responses which could be 'unlearned' through the application of procedures derived from the work of Pavlov and Skinner. Thus Wolpe (1958) defined this approach as 'the use of experimentally established principles of learning for the purpose of changing unadaptive behaviour'.

However, whether experimental work on conditioning is directly relevant to the genesis of neurotic disorders or, indeed, to the practice of behaviour therapy has long been questioned. Breger and McGaugh

(1965), in one of the earliest theoretical critiques of this treatment approach, argued that the relationship between laboratory studies and clinical practice is, at best, analogous. For example, the development of agoraphobia, where the concept 'outside the home' is the essential feature, is much more readily explained in terms of cognitive processes than by reference to stimulus generalization, which has been shown to operate strictly on the basis of physical similarity. Moreover, the speed with which phobics respond to behavioural techniques indicates that they are learning strategies rather than undergoing extinction training.

In America, the inadequacies of the simple conditioning model were quickly appreciated, and it was not long before more sophisticated theories of normal and abnormal behaviour were being offered. Of these, that proposed by Albert Bandura (1969) proved to be the most influential. While not dismissing altogether the importance of conditioning paradigms, he maintained that the effectiveness of behaviour therapy techniques was due in part to the generation of symbolic activities and the facilitation of attitude change. With the limitations of stimulus-response theory exposed, clinicians were quick to adapt their style of working. For instance, Kanfer and Phillips (1970) argued that behavioural assessment should involve the analysis of both covert and overt events. This led to the development of cognitive change methods to be used in conjunction with standard behavioural techniques.

Developments in Britain

On this side of the Atlantic, there was marked resistance to the idea that behaviour therapists should concern themselves with events which are not directly observable. It was felt by many that the whole scientific basis of this approach would be seriously undermined if such 'soft' variables as images, thinking processes and attitudes were to be included. Eysenck (1976) reformulated the learning theory model of neuroses in an attempt to demonstrate that conditioning paradigms could adequately account for all the phenomena and that speculations about cognitive functioning were quite unnecessary. On the therapeutic side, British behaviour therapists continued to develop and refine techniques, such as flooding and social skills training, the aim of which was to produce change at the overt behavioural level. Thus by remaining blindly loyal to the traditional learning theory approach British behaviour therapists gradually fell behind their American counterparts, not only with regard to theoretical formulations of human behaviour but also in so far as the development of innovative treatment methods was concerned.

There were two important developments in the mid-1970s which finally led therapists in this country to recognize that it is possible to work with cognitive processes without abandoning the behaviourist philosophy. The first of these was the publication of Meichenbaum's (1975) work on cognitive behaviour modification. He argued that it was possible to regard statements that we make to ourselves as discriminative stimuli which control behaviour in much the same way as observable events do. In other words, covert stimuli, responses and reinforcers can be understood and worked with in terms of the operant conditioning model. In addition, he demonstrated that it was possible to change maladaptive sequences of this kind by direct means. From this point onwards, cognitions became 'scientifically respectable' in British behaviour therapy circles.

The second important event was Seligman's (1975) proposal that depression can be regarded as a state of 'learned helplessness'. Drawing on his experimental work on Pavlovian conditioning with animals, Seligman had observed that when significant outcomes are made independent of responses, a generalized passivity response occurs which has many of the hallmarks of clinical depression. Given the academic credibility of the source, and the body of well-conducted laboratory research to support the message, it was inevitable that this work would be well received in this country: almost overnight, British behaviour therapists began to use such cognitive terms as 'expectations' and 'perceived controllability'. Moreover, as the shortcomings of Seligman's model gradually became appreciated, they began to devour the cognitive psychology and social learning theory literature in an attempt to better understand these newly adopted concepts.

As a result of these developments, behaviour therapy has moved a long way from Wolpe's original definition. Clinicians are more concerned to help their clients develop effective coping strategies than to directly eliminate maladaptive responses. Technology has been replaced, to a large extent, by 'talking treatments'. This change of emphasis is reflected in the titles given to the major interest groups in this country: the Behavioural Engineering Association disbanded in the mid-70s and its functions were taken over by the British Association for Behavioural

Psychotherapy. This contemporary term 'behavioural psychotherapy' indicates that British clinicians have finally come to accept the fact that the person in need of help is far removed from the bar-pressing pigeon and the salivating dog!

Theoretical Assumptions

The image of the person

According to the contemporary behavioural model (Bandura 1977), man is concerned to see himself as master of his own, unique environment. He is constantly attempting to sustain or increase the control he perceives himself to have over both his inner and outer world. He is happiest when he has evolved a clear plan for living, when his body behaves as he wants it to and when he has the skills and aptitudes necessary to achieve the goals he has set himself. His choice of goals is determined by past learning events such as parental modelling, selective reinforcers and punishments from teachers and friends, and self-evaluation of personal experiences. The achievement of a goal is rewarding to the degree that it enables him to perceive himself as master of his chosen environment.

Stimulus control and environmental contingencies The traditional behavioural model was unashamedly deterministic; it was assumed that, as a result of having been through a variety of classical and operant conditioning procedures, the individual learns to make specific responses in the presence of particular stimuli because they have been associated with certain consequences in the past. The early behaviourists dismissed such notions such as 'thoughts' and 'expectations', as hypothetical constructs which added nothing to our understanding of human behaviour. The 'man as a robot' model has been largely discredited (Mackay 1983), and there are few contemporary behavioural psychotherapists who would argue that this is an adequate explanation of human functioning. Nevertheless, a much more elaborate version of the stimulus-response-reinforcement sequence provides the theoretical basis for this approach.

The three-systems model According to Lang (1969), the term 'behaviour' should be broadened out to include cognitive functioning, physiological responses and overt actions. He argues that these three behavioural systems do not always operate in harmony with one another: for example, a specific stimulus may trigger off a particular chain of thoughts in an individual but have no effect on his autonomic nervous system or his observable behaviour. Bandura (1978) accepts this general principle, but rejects the notion that the systems operate as 'a disjointed triadic family'. He argues that cognitions can create physiological arousal just as autonomic functioning can influence thought. Consequently he finds it more useful to regard the three types of behaviour as 'partially independent response systems regulated by different determinants'.

Self-efficacy theory While acknowledging that the relationship between the three systems is a complex one, Bandura (1978) claims that cognitive processes are of primary importance when it comes to understanding human behaviour. According to self-efficacy theory, the degree to which the individual regards himself as competent in his dealings with the world has a far more significant effect on his emotional state and his actions than external contingencies as such. Although different modes of influence can strengthen or weaken expectations of personal efficacy, it is the person's self-conception which tends to govern his reactions in particular situations.

Concepts of psychological health and disturbance

Problem-solving vs. impulsive action As D'Zurilla and Goldfried (1971) point out, 'our daily lives are replete with situational problems which we must solve in order to maintain an adequate level of effective functioning'. Most of us muddle along without any coherent plan for living, and accept philosophically the fact that some days are rewarding whereas others are frustrating or disappointing in some way. It is only when we find that the failure experiences are increasing, and that we are seemingly unable to reverse this trend, that we are forced to admit that we have a problem. The poor problem-solver is slow to recognize that difficulties are mounting up and, when eventually he finds himself to be in a crisis situation, acts on impulse without properly considering alternative solutions or indeed the consequences of his chosen course of action. Impulsive action usually compounds the problem still further, leaving him confused, bewildered and anxious. He then either escapes from the situation altogether or seeks outside help to sort out the mess he has helped to create. The good problem-solver utilizes a combination of cognitive and behavioural strategies to avoid most obstacles and setbacks and to deal effectively with those he is unable to prevent.

Stress control vs. fear of fear From time to time each of us experiences episodes of high levels of physiological arousal combined with a sudden disintegration of our rational thinking patterns. If an individual is unable to bring this disruptive reaction under control, it will escalate and lead to a 'panic attack'. As a result of this traumatic experience, the person will feel significantly less confident in his ability to control his internal environment; consequently, he will approach similar situations in the future with a considerable degree of anticipatory anxiety. This, in turn, makes it more likely that the fear response will be re-instigated with another panic attack the inevitable outcome. In view of his perceived inability to overcome this 'fear of fear', the individual begins to avoid a wide range of situations which he feels might set the upward spiral into motion. This will necessarily involve shunning a variety of potentially enriching experiences. The well-adjusted person is able to monitor and control both his thinking processes and autonomic nervous system so as to ensure that his fear reactions are always contained. This involves utilizing coping strategies which comprise a variety of cognitive, physical relaxation and behavioural skills.

Self-regulation vs. uncontrolled behaviour According to Skinner's model of operant conditioning, the individual will engage in behaviours which are rewarding to him and refrain from those which have aversive consequences. Although this is a relatively straightforward proposal when applied to the laboratory rat, it has its limitations as an explanation of human behaviour. There are a variety of activities, such as cigarette smoking, eating cream cakes and consuming alcohol, which are reinforcing in the short term but lead eventually to a negative outcome. If the person recognizes this but still regards immediate gratification as more important than increasing the risk of lung cancer, obesity or alcoholism, then he can be said to have his life under his control. If, however, he wishes to stop smoking, overeating or heavy drinking but cannot, then he is clearly not master of his environment. Each failure experience results in self-criticism and guilt feelings. According to Kanfer (1980), the ability to monitor and regulate one's behaviour is an important feature of the well-adjusted person. This involves counteracting the self-generated cues which are potential triggers of maladaptive behaviour and rearranging the contingencies which would help to maintain it, should it occur.

Assertion vs. learned helplessness As stated earlier, helplessness is the belief that one cannot influence the outcome in a particular situation. Under these circumstances, the individual expends far less effort on goal achievement. If the situation is a significant one, such as his marriage or his career, this tendency towards passivity will carry over to other important areas of his life. At this stage, the individual is considered to be 'depressed' and in need of professional help. Bandura (1978) makes the important point that failure to reach particular targets does not in itself lead to a state of helplessness. It is only if the frustrating experience lowers the individual's perceived self-efficacy that significant performance deficits will occur; as a result, those who view themselves as having little control over their lives are much more likely to become anxious and depressed when faced with obstacles or other sources of frustration. By contrast, the well-adjusted person will not permit failure in one situation to affect his behaviour in other areas. He will continue to think and act assertively in his ongoing attempt to achieve maximal control over his total environment.

Social competence vs. social inadequacy It is generally acknowledged that the individual who is not actively involved in a social network – be it a marriage, a circle of friends, or a group of work colleagues – has made a poor adjustment to life. According to the behavioural model (Trower et al. 1978), the extent to which the person has formed satisfactory relationships depends not on a hypothetical concept such as 'personality' but on the quality and range of social skills he has acquired from childhood onwards. The well-adjusted person emits responses during his social interactions which others find rewarding.

Psychological health According to the behavioural model, the well-adjusted person is someone who has learned to see himself as master of his cognitive processes and physiological functioning, and who has acquired the necessary skills and aptitudes to influence events in his outer world. At the cognitive level, he can perceive choices open to him in all significant areas of his life and can decide which option to follow at a particular point in time. When faced with an obstacle, he is able to formulate the problem clearly to himself, generate alternative courses of action and put into effect the strategy he considers to be most appropriate. If he cannot overcome the obstacle, he is capable of engaging in internal dialogues which prevent him from becoming unduly anxious, frustrated or depressed. Once a goal has been achieved, he is able to recognize this and reinforce himself appropriately. With regard to physiological functioning, he can quickly detect the occurrence of any unwanted response pattern and deal with it without escaping from the situation or resorting to medication. So far as overt behaviour is concerned, he has the social skills to enable him to communicate effectively with others in order to achieve the particular interpersonal goals he considers to be important. Armed with this collection of learned attributes, he is constantly seeking ways of enriching his life and developing his potentialities still further.

The acquisition of psychological disturbance

Traumatic learning experiences The traditional behaviourist explanation of neuroses is that irrational fears are acquired through classical conditioning: in other words, a harmless object or situation comes to elicit anxiety as a result of having been associated with an aversive stimulus. Through the process of stimulus generalization, this powerful emotional response can subsequently be evoked by a wide range of apparently similar stimuli. An elaborate version of this model is provided by Eysenck (1976). Bandura (1978) is highly critical of attempts to explain the genesis of neurotic disorders in terms of acquired physiological response patterns, and cites evidence from both the clinic and the laboratory which demonstrates the inadequacies of this model. He accepts the principle that traumatic experiences are likely to lead to maladaptive ways of behaving but argues that 'conditioning operations serve principally as ways of conveying information rather than as mechanical conditioners of behaviour'. In other words, a traumatic experience produces behaviour change by modifying the individual's knowledge of himself and his environment.

Reinforcement contingencies for disapproved behaviour It is common in British psychiatry to view people who engage in antisocial acts as suffering from a personality disorder. Behaviourists take the view that many individuals who drink alcohol excessively, engage in unusual sexual practices, or commit aggressive acts for no apparent gain, have learned to do so through social reinforcement. Bandura (1969) argues that, in certain subcultures, disapproved behaviour can be highly instrumental in gaining the admiration of peer group members. Since the approval of the reference group is such a powerful incentive, particularly for school-age children and adolescents, it follows that the tendency to engage in disapproved behaviour can be acquired by individuals who are well adjusted in every other way.

Modelling of maladaptive behaviour   According to social learning theory, people often acquire neurotic or depressive patterns of behaviour through observing the ways in which significant others interact with their environment. The child who watches his phobic mother panic and try to escape from a stressful situation is likely to become anxious when he finds himself in similar circumstances in the future. Similarly, the father who becomes passive and helpless when difficulties arise is modelling depressogenic behaviours for his children. Bandura (1969) offers a cognitive-behaviourist explanation of the vicarious learning phenomenon. As he sees it, the stimuli which are elicited through perception of the model become associated with the images and thoughts to which these stimuli give rise. When these cognitions are subsequently revoked, they trigger off the maladaptive response sequence in much the same way as discriminative stimuli do in the operant conditioning paradigm. Even if the individual does not display overt signs of disturbance in childhood, inappropriate modelling will predispose him to develop a neurosis later in life. Whether this manifests itself or not depends on the particular set of circumstances he finds himself in.

The perpetuation of psychological disturbance

Avoidance and escape   In the traditional behaviourist model of neuroses, the classical conditioning model was used to explain the genesis but not the persistence of maladaptive response patterns. It was assumed that phobias do not become extinguished in the same way as laboratory-induced conditioned responses because the individual engages in instrumental acts which prevent this process from taking place. For example, the claustrophobic *avoids* lifts and aeroplanes and immediately attempts to *escape* should he inadvertently find himself in a confined place. In other words, it is the performance of acts that are negatively reinforced through the reduction of anxiety which helps to maintain the disturbed behaviour. Bandura (1978) has reformulated this explanation in cognitive terms. He states that by the very act of running away from difficult situations the individual is providing himself with information concerning his ability to master his environment. By lowering his perceived self-efficacy in this way, he is less likely to confront the problem on the next occasion.

Negative self-talk   Meichenbaum (1977) claims that anxious and depressed persons engage in self-defeating thinking patterns which act as cues for maladaptive behaviour. The individual who says to himself, 'I know I will fail' on entering a test situation will perform relatively poorly, and the outcome is likely to be a negative one. Following this experience of failure, it is likely that his forecast will be at least as gloomy on the next occasion and the vicious circle will be reactivated. Thus by allowing negative cognitions to govern his behaviour the person is, in effect, helping to perpetuate his problem. Meichenbaum's proposals are entirely consistent with self-efficacy theory and the social learning explanation of modelling.

Reinforcement of maladaptive behaviour   Psychological disturbance is particularly likely to persist if its occurrence is accompanied by sympathy or attention from significant others in the client's life. The well-meaning wife who only 'mollycoddles' her husband when he is distressed is making social reinforcement contingent upon non-coping behaviour; by adopting such a strategy, she is actively contributing to the chronicity of the problem. There are numerous studies which indicate that similar reinforcement schedules are operating in the chronic wards of psychiatric hospitals where nurses are inadvertently rewarding patients for undesired behaviour (Ayllon and Michael 1959). Negative reinforcement can also help to maintain 'illness behaviour'. If, by being psychologically incapacitated, the individual is able to evade unwanted responsibilities at work or in the home, his motivation to start coping again will be that much less. In this situation, he will be reluctant to develop more positive attitudes or behave in a more effective way.

Significant others as 'mastery' models   According to self-efficacy theory, the individual's perception of himself is not simply a function of the degree to which he is able to control his environment. If he fails to achieve particular goals but observes that those around him are no more successful, then he will resign himself to a dreary life. However, if the significant others are achieving these goals, he will lower his perceived self-efficacy still further, and depression will be the likely consequence. Thus the passive, ineffectual husband is more likely to remain in the helpless role if his wife is able to take over his responsibilities with apparent ease than if she is clearly having difficulty in coping with the additional burden. By modelling mastery behaviour in this crisis situation she is, in effect, lowering his self-esteem still further.

Practice

Goals of therapy

The achievement of specific targets   The behavioural model holds that the client's 'symptoms' can be regarded as discrete psychological entities which can be removed or altered by direct means. The therapist's main task is to define clearly the problem behaviour, analyse clearly the contingencies which are maintaining it and implement techniques which will interrupt the stimulus–response–reinforcement sequence. It is the identification and modification of very specific targets which most clearly differentiates this form of treatment from traditional psychotherapy approaches.

Greater self-awareness   Although the primary task is to eliminate the target behaviour, the behavioural psychotherapist sets out to achieve goals of a less tangible nature. By being actively involved in the analysis of his behaviour patterns (Kanfer and Phillips 1970), the client should achieve both an understanding of how the presenting problem links in with other aspects of his psychological functioning and an appreciation of the historical factors which have contributed to his current difficulties. It is assumed that this awareness should not only facilitate the change process but should lead the client to reappraise his life-style, either within the therapeutic context or without.

The development of problem-solving skills The behavioural analysis process involves close collaboration between therapist and client. As a result of this experience, the client learns the importance of defining the problem clearly, how to set up hypotheses to account for the data and ways of collecting evidence systematically to test out these hypotheses. These are problem-solving skills which may well enable him to deal with any difficulties which might arise in the future, without the need for professional help.

Increased self-efficacy By demonstrating to the client that he can achieve greater control over one aspect of his environment, the therapist uses this information to increase his overall perceived self-efficacy. Therapy ends with the clinician, saying, in effect: 'Largely through your own efforts, you have been able to overcome a problem which you previously thought to be insoluble. Just think of the other difficulties you can deal with if you approach them in the same way.' There is now considerable evidence (e.g. McPherson et al. 1980) to suggest that behavioural interventions aimed at specific targets lead to improved functioning in other areas of the client's life and that these positive generalized effects persist in the longer term.

The person of the therapist

The early behaviour therapists were reluctant to acknowledge the role played by the therapist as a facilitator of change, so convinced were they that the techniques themselves were the only active therapeutic ingredients. For example, in his much publicized paper on 'automated desensitization', Quirk (1973) argued that the therapist's services could be virtually dispensed with altogether:

> Moreover, by virtue of the relative absence of verbal interchange in the method, both at the initial investigation and during the procedure itself, even much of the feeling of a human 'presence', which might be construed as a 'relationship', may be essentially excluded from the treatment program.

By contrast, the contemporary behavioural psychotherapist would maintain that the effectiveness of the techniques depend to a large extent on the building up of a facilitative therapist-client relationship. The following therapist variables have been isolated as significant determinants of outcome:

a) The *confidence* of the therapist in his approach, and his ability to communicate this sense of conviction to the client (Ryan and Gizynski 1971).
b) His *flexibility* in terms of adapting his style to suit the needs of the client (Ford and Kendall 1979).
c) The degree to which he is perceived as *warm* and *empathic* by the client (Morris and Suckerman 1974).

However, there is some confusion in the literature as to whether the effective therapist is someone who is characterized by certain inherent traits or qualities or whether he is a skilled clinician who has learnt to apply relationship enhancement methods at appropriate times. In his plea for more research in this area, Ford (1978) implies that the person of the therapist is more than his collective responses and suggests that there is a complex relationship between these variables within a particular therapeutic context:

> We must attempt to determine what it is in the moment-to-moment behaviors of therapists that affects clients and how these specific behaviors interact with behavior change techniques – and differences in therapists, clients, settings, and target objectives – to produce more or less successful outcomes.

These issues will be explored further in the next section.

Therapeutic style

A caricature of the old-style behaviour therapist would be of a white-coated laboratory research worker who applied standardized techniques as objectively as possible, with little regard for the particular needs of his 'subjects'. His interventions were motivated more by academic curiosity than by a genuine desire to help the person. The contemporary behavioural psychotherapist is concerned to understand the individual's problems as fully as possible in order to be able to design and implement a treatment programme to meet the unique requirements of the particular case. The client is encouraged to participate both in the formulation of his own problem and in the selection of the most appropriate techniques to suit his needs. The roles of the client and therapist have been compared to those of the research student and his supervisor. The student knows the literature in his field of interest far better than his supervisor ever will, but he lacks the expertise to design a properly controlled experiment. The supervisor has a thorough knowledge of research methodology and is able to help the student to set up hypotheses, test them out and interpret the data. The project which emerges is the result of close collaboration between the two parties. The same holds true for behavioural psychotherapy.

Continuing with this analogy, it is apparent that the therapist, just like the supervisor, is ultimately responsible for the success of the 'experiment'. If the desired change does not take place, it is he who has to suggest a return to the 'drawing-board' stage with a view to producing a better treatment plan. This can involve anything from a completely new set of procedures to the inclusion of an additional component into the existing programme. He may also decide to modify his own behaviour in relation to the client with a view to producing a better outcome.

This latter point takes us on to the more subtle aspects of the therapeutic relationship. Behavioural psychotherapists do not adopt a fixed style of working in their various client relationships. This is a point which is made very forcibly by Turkat and Brantley (1981): 'Before anyone can claim that non-specific factors such as warmth and empathy should be utilized with all cases, these factors must be operationalized, evaluated in terms of their outcome and mechanisms, and demonstrated to be indicated by the formulation of each individual case.' This should not be interpreted as a plea for therapists to be as impersonal and detached as possible in their work with clients; rather, these authors are suggesting that when conducting the behavioural analysis the therapist should be seeking guide-lines as to which style of working will be best suited to the individual. For example, humour can enhance the relationship in certain cases and almost destroy it in others. The same is true of warmth:

> Some patients will feel frightened and vulnerable with a therapist towards whom they feel attracted, particularly if from past experience they perceive such relationships as dangerous (danger of being hurt emotionally). With such a patient, a somewhat more distant and impersonal relationship may in fact be more desirable in that it will facilitate the patient's involvement in the treatment, following the treatment regimen, etc. (Goldfried 1980)

Flexibility of style, based on systematic observations rather than 'hunches', is therefore an important characteristic of the effective behavioural psychotherapist.

Major therapeutic techniques

There are over fifty well-established formal treatment methods in behavioural psychotherapy, and it will only be possible here to look at the ones which are most commonly used. Before doing so, however, it will be necessary to examine the procedures for assessing the individual case and negotiating the treatment contract, both of which should be carried out thoroughly before implementing the more specific techniques.

Behavioural analysis The corner-stone of behavioural psychotherapy is the functional analysis of the interactions between the problem behaviour and the environment (Kanfer and Phillips 1970). This complex assessment procedure enables the therapist to formulate the disturbance in behavioural terms and design a treatment programme to meet the requirements of the particular case. Moreover, since its execution involves a close collaboration between therapist and client, it facilitates the building up of a good rapport before formal treatment commences. In addition, by helping the client to achieve greater understanding of his difficulties, the behavioural analysis is an important therapeutic technique in its own right.

It is customary to begin by obtaining a clear description of the presenting problem behaviour together with the antecedents and consequences which are currently maintaining it. Data from the client's past history are not collected until the therapist has produced at least one hypothesis concerning the nature of the disturbance at this point in time. Information about the genesis and development of the problem is used by the therapist to check out the validity of each of these preliminary conceptualizations. Only when he has evolved a formulation which is consistent with all relevant facts from both the present and the past is he in a position to design a treatment programme to suit the needs of the individual case. Failure to carry out this procedure properly can lead to the implementation of techniques which are ineffective or possibly even harmful to the client.

Mackay (1982) has proposed that the behavioural analysis comprises the following seven stages:

(a) *Obtain a precise description of the maladaptive behaviour:* Self-report inventories, psychophysiological measures, behavioural ratings, and *in vivo* observations are just some of the devices which assist the therapist in his initial task of defining the problem (Hersen and Bellack 1976). It must be emphasized that a comprehensive assessment involves the collection of information concerning the client's cognitions and physiological functioning, in addition to his overt behavioural responses.

(b) *Define the controlling stimuli:* The careful isolation of the environmental factors which influence the frequency and/or intensity of the response in question is the most critical stage in the behavioural analysis. Unless the therapist succeeds in uncovering all the relevant antecedents, his subsequent interventions are unlikely to be particularly effective. A variety of checklists and observational procedures are available to enable him to tease out the relevant cognitive, physiological, interpersonal and situational triggers in a systematic fashion (Hersen and Bellack 1976).

(c) *Determine the reinforcers:* It often emerges that a significant person in the client's life is deliberately or unwittingly helping to maintain the problem by making social reinforcement contingent upon maladaptive behaviour. It is important that the therapist should take account of this when designing the programme. In addition, care should be taken to uncover any 'gain' the client might be deriving from having the problem; failure to take account of such subtle reinforcers is the main reason why inexperienced therapists frequently encounter 'resistance' on the part of their clients.

(d) *Formulate the problem:* By this stage, the therapist should be in a position to offer one or more hypotheses to account for the data he has collected. These can often be presented to the client in the form of flow charts.

(e) *Elicit relevant historical information:* By collecting facts concerning the onset and development of the problem, the therapist is able to quickly discard false hypotheses, leaving himself with the formulation which has the greatest apparent validity. This usually has to be modified to some degree in the light of the data which emerges during this stage of the investigation.

(f) *Design and implement a treatment programme:* Provided that the problem has been properly conceptualized, the selection of procedures to suit the client's requirements is a relatively straightforward process. It must be emphasized that the contemporary behavioural psychotherapist creates 'tailor-made' treatment programmes, based on his formulations, unlike his predecessors who tended to administer 'off the shelf' techniques according to diagnostic category.

(g) *Re-evaluate the formulation periodically:* The behavioural analysis is an ongoing process which terminates only when the client has achieved his objectives. Should he appear to be resisting change by failing to attend regularly or carrying out agreed homework assignments, the likelihood is that the formulation is faulty or incomplete; the same is true if he responds well to the early interventions but fails to progress beyond a certain point.

A comprehensive behavioural assessment of this kind will occupy a minimum of three one-hour sessions and is rarely completed in so short a time. It is potentially a very powerful tool for developing good rapport, and care should be taken to ensure that it does not take the form of a lengthy interrogation. Throughout, the therapist should present the client with the rationale underlying each stage of questioning and should encourage him to participate in the setting up and testing out of hypotheses. If he is able to take some responsibility for the formulation of his own problem, he is much more likely to co-operate fully with the treatment programme which is derived from it.

Treatment contract   Following this structured assessment procedure, the behavioural psychotherapist is in a position to discuss therapeutic goals, techniques to be used, and duration of treatment with his client. It is not uncommon for the client to accept the formulation and understand the logic underlying the proposed therapeutic plan but feel unable to commit himself to it. For example, he may be unwilling to devote sufficient time to enable the goals to be achieved. Alternatively, because of excessive pressures at work or at home he may be reluctant to subject himself to a programme which will make heavy demands on his resources. Under these circumstances, it will be necessary to negotiate a contract which is acceptable to both parties. On the few occasions where it is not possible to reach an agreement, the therapist should withhold his offer of help and discuss with the client alternative forms of treatment which could be made available to him.

Having established a broad plan for therapy, the next stage is to specify the respective responsibilities of therapist and client. In most behavioural treatment contracts, the client is expected to commit himself to attend regularly, undergo the procedures which have been decided on, carry out homework assignments and not to terminate without prior discussion. The therapist agrees to take responsibility for implementing the programme while, at all times, taking account of the client's welfare. He expresses his willingness to re-negotiate the contract should techniques prove ineffective or too stressful for the client to continue with. Finally, he makes it clear that he is not prepared to play a general supportive role and will discourage discussions on issues which are not strictly relevant to the task in hand.

Behavioural psychotherapists differ in their opinions as to how rigidly the treatment contract should be enforced. In America, clients are often required to pay a deposit, a portion of which they forfeit should they fail to carry out a particular activity. Most British psychotherapists would regard such a practice as excessively rigid and punitive, if not unethical. In any event, non-compliance is an interesting piece of behaviour in its own right which should be incorporated into the ongoing behavioural analysis. It may indicate, for example, that the therapist has over-estimated the client's resources or has adopted a therapeutic style that is inappropriate for the particular case. Under these circumstances, it will be necessary to discuss the problems which have arisen and attempt to modify the programme accordingly.

Systematic desensitization   The phobic client is asked to rank in order clearly defined situations which cause him distress. He is then trained in relaxation and taken carefully through the hierarchy by the therapist. Although this can be carried out in fantasy, there is clear evidence (Matthews 1978) that *in vivo* desensitization is more effective. It is essential, at each stage in this procedure, that the therapist should wait until the client is completely at ease in a particular situation before presenting the next item. In view of the relaxation component, it is particularly useful with clients who typically experience considerable physical discomfort under conditions of stress.

Exposure   This is a more cost-effective procedure for eliminating phobias although it can prove more distressing for the client. Here the therapist encourages the client to face up to the feared situation, cither in imagination or in real life, for prolonged periods. As a rule, the more severe the problem, the longer the client should be exposed to the anxiety-eliciting cues. This technique is particularly effective with those phobic clients who engage in extreme avoidance and escape behaviour at the prospect of confronting their fear directly. However, since it is not always possible to engage their co-operation in such a venture, systematic desensitization may have to be offered as an alternative.

Anxiety management training   This is particularly useful with clients whose presenting complaint is, essentially, a 'fear of fear' (Suinn and Richardson 1971). Clients are trained to control their autonomic responses under increasingly stressful circumstances. Having coached the client in basic relaxation skills, the therapist presents an aversive stimulus or describes a traumatic scene until tension is evident. The source of stress is quickly removed, and the client is instructed to relax. Biofeedback devices can be helpful here.

Cognitive behaviour modification   This is a technique for enabling clients to overcome the 'doom-laden prophecies' which are helping to maintain the anxiety or depressive response (Meichenbaum 1977). The therapist teaches the client to devise coping statements which will enable him to better prepare for, and confront, situations which formerly caused him difficulty. Therapeutic aids, such as cue cards or specially recorded cassettes, are used to facilitate generalization to situations outside of the therapeutic context.

Training in problem-solving   With clients whose thought processes rapidly become disorganized under conditions of stress, it is necessary to provide special coaching in the cognitive skills which are required to deal with problematic situations (Goldfried and Davison 1976). Through modelling and guided training, the client learns to master each stage in the sequence: general orientation; problem formulation; generation of alternatives; decision-making; verification. Once he has become competent under low-stress conditions, he is encouraged to test out his skills by confronting a problem or situation which he could not cope with formerly.

Assertiveness training This is a useful technique with clients who experience anxiety in interpersonal situations, who find it difficult to express emotions directly or who are frustrated at their inability to influence the attitudes and behaviour of certain others. Treatment is normally carried out in small groups and a programme would normally include role-play, feedback, modelling, behaviour rehearsal, and homework assignments (Liberman et al. 1975).

Covert sensitization For clients who have difficulty in refraining from activities which they later regret, this form of cognitive aversion therapy (Cautela 1967) can be particularly useful. The client is asked to imagine a scene which normally evokes the temptation to execute the unwanted behaviour. When he has achieved a clear image, the therapist introduces strongly aversive stimuli into the fantasy. After a number of presentations of this kind, the negative features of the situation begin to predominate over the positive ones. As a result, he finds himself avoiding those places which provide the cues for carrying out the undesired response.

Training in self-control This is a less traumatic approach for helping those clients who wish to stop smoking, cut down on alcohol, eliminate unwanted sexual habits or give up bingeing. The stimulus-response-reinforcement sequence is analysed with great precision, and the client is encouraged to carry out adjustments to his environment and rehearse adaptive self-statements in order to interrupt the pattern. By reducing the cues which precipitate the 'bad habit', the probability of its recurrence decreases.

Thought-stopping Clients who are troubled by obsessional thought patterns which they cannot control may benefit from this simple but effective technique. The client is requested to ruminate deliberately and, when it is apparent that he is overwhelmed by these disturbing thoughts, the therapist shouts 'Stop!' or creates some other form of disturbance. This is repeated on several occasions until the client is convinced that the obsessions can be reliably interrupted in this way. He is then encouraged to use the distraction himself.

Finally, he is encouraged to develop a less obtrusive strategy which will enable him to control the unwanted thoughts in everyday situations.

The change process in therapy

According to Bandura (1978), the effectiveness of behavioural techniques is due mainly to the fact that they provide the client with information which leads to some degree of change in his perception of himself. Faced with indisputable evidence that he has become more competent at managing his anxiety, evolving problem-solving strategies, controlling unwanted behaviour or asserting himself, he is obliged to question the validity of his previous negatavistic self-image. The resulting increase in perceived self-efficacy will enable him to progress more quickly through the latter stages of the programme. Its successful completion will facilitate further cognitive change, not only in relation to the presenting problem but also with regard to his life as a whole. The knowledge that he has been able to overcome one long-standing difficulty will alter his perception of other sources of frustration and dissatisfaction. Consequently, at the termination stage the therapist should be able to make the following statements with regard to his client:

(a) the problem behaviour has been eliminated or contained;
(b) his cognitive, physiological and behavioural functioning is now much more under his control;
(c) he is performing more effectively in other areas of his life;
(d) he sees himself as having achieved greater mastery over his environment;
(e) he has a greater understanding of himself as a person, both in his current life situation and in the context of his past history;
(f) he has learned how to analyse and overcome personal problems without the need for professional help in the future;
(g) he recognizes that the interaction between his behaviour and his environment is a two-way process.

It is rare for all these goals to be achieved. Limiting factors are the motivation and competence of the therapist, the level at which the client wishes to work, domestic or occupational environments which cannot easily be modified, and time constraints for both parties. However, even if one focusses exclusively on the target behaviour, the achievement of this goal will inevitably be accompanied by some degree of change in these other aspects of psychological functioning.

Case Example

The client

Barbara is a 28-year-old-lady who was referred by a consultant psychiatrist for 'relaxation training for her anxiety symptoms, which occasionally border on panic'. At the time of assessment she had been married for two years and was employed as a temporary secretary. Three months before seeking help, she had been obliged to leave her post as personal assistant to the director of a large company, due to staff redundancies.

Although she describes her childhood as moderately happy, the family moved around a great deal, which meant that she never felt properly established anywhere nor established long-lasting friendships. She felt rather remote from her father, who seemed more involved with his career as a solicitor than with the family. She depended a great deal on her mother, whom she saw as a strong, coping figure who would provide her with comfort and sympathy whenever she was worried or upset. However, she cannot recall having been cuddled as a child, and felt that displays of affection between family members were taboo.

She was sent to boarding school at the age of eleven and adapted reasonably well to this change of environment. Two years later, however, her father died suddenly from a heart attack. Although she had never been close to him, she was extremely upset by his death and spent the next six months at home with her mother before resuming her studies. She can recall little of what took place during this period, but describes it as the most distressing episode in her life. Her mother became very depressed after the death, started drinking heavily and has been incapable of organizing her own life ever since.

On leaving school at eighteen, Barbara went off to live in France, where she obtained a secretarial post. After a year she moved on to Italy, where she also found employment. For the next six years she travelled extensively, never staying anywhere for any length of time. She describes this as the most enjoyable phase in her life. However, towards the end of her extended itinerary across Europe, her problems suddenly manifested themselves. At the time she was working as secretary to the purser on a cruise liner, and found the job very demanding. She was not allowed off the ship at its various ports of call because she was so behind with her work. She began to have panic attacks and was eventually referred to the ship's doctor who prescribed tranquillizers. When she was eventually allowed shore leave in Greece, she 'jumped ship' and made her own way back to Britain.

In the two years that followed, she was in a constant state of high anxiety, which she tried to cope with by using alcohol excessively. She then met Geoffrey, her husband-to-be, who helped her to gain more control over her life. She obtained a good job, felt much more stable emotionally and stopped drinking heavily. However, her problems returned when she was made redundant and had to seek temporary work.

Following a comprehensive behavioural analysis, it became clear that, although Barbara's difficulties involved all three response systems, her distorted thinking processes and perceptions were the primary problem:

First, at the *cognitive* level, she was almost totally preoccupied with thoughts of nuclear war. On probing, it became apparent that this was more like an irrational obsession than realistic concern about world events. She was terrified of death and, in particular, of what might lie ahead. The prospect of eternity, which for her conjured up images of unpredictability, helplessness, and endlessness, caused her considerable emotional distress. Consequently she tried to avoid thinking directly about life after death and instead focused her attention on events which could threaten her existence on earth.

Secondly, her *physiological* manifestations of anxiety involved physical tension, increased heart rate and shortness of breath. Two or three times a month she would suffer major panic attacks which would necessitate her husband being called home from work.

Thirdly, her abnormal *behavioural* pattern took the form of a 'compulsion' to perform as many tasks as she could each day, on the assumption that her death was imminent. She read three national newspapers and listened to every news broadcast in an endeavour to gain as much information as she could about world events. In addition, she wrote hundreds of letters each year to politicians, urging them to fight for nuclear disarmament. It must be emphasized that, although these activities are not in themselves abnormal, the motivation behind them is very different from that of the majority of anti-nuclear campaigners. For her, the threat of the holocaust was not the destruction of mankind but the prospect of her premature entry into eternity.

The acquisition and perpetuation of psychological disturbance

The next stage in the behavioural analysis was to identify the stimuli and reinforcers which were maintaining this irrational or exaggerated fear response. It quickly became clear that her attempts to understand, predict and control the threat of nuclear war, by means of the strategies outlined above, were contributing to the problem. For example, the reading of a newspaper item, which suggested mounting tension between the major powers, would immediately trigger off a panic attack. Moreover the awareness that events of such magnitude were far beyond her power of influence served to increase her sense of helplessness. This was exacerbated by the change in her job situation, which meant that she had far less control over her everyday life. This lowering of perceived self-efficacy was a major factor which led to her seeking help at that particular time.

Further investigations suggested that Geoffrey had been unwittingly reinforcing the problem behaviour by providing her with attention and reassurance each evening when she recounted to him her fears about the world situation. However, although his explanations served to reduce her level of anxiety, their effect never lasted more than a few hours. It should be noted that Geoffrey took her concern about nuclear war at face value and had no appreciation of the primary fear which lay behind it.

The preliminary formulation therefore was that the client had an irrational or exaggerated fear of life after death which she was unable to confront. Instead, she had become preoccupied with more tangible events which had some bearing on this fear. However, her goal of understanding, predicting and controlling these events was inevitably a futile one. Moreover her attempts to achieve it were directly feeding into her primary fear and consequently perpetuating the self-defeating sequence. In addition, the behavioural manifestations of the problem were being reinforced by her husband. She became unable to cope when a change in her life situation decreased her perceived self-efficacy still further.

There were a number of events from her past history which supported such a hypothesis:

(a) Between the ages of five and ten, she worried incessantly about dying before going to sleep, and had regular nightmares involving this theme.

Even in childhood, it was her inability to comprehend eternity, rather than the more common fear of death itself, which disturbed her particularly.

(b) During this period, her normally undemonstrative mother would spend time with her until she settled down for the night. By making social reinforcement contingent upon overt displays of distress, her mother was effectively training her to talk openly about her fears. This role has been taken over by her husband.

(c) Her mother's attempts to comfort her involved pointing out the activities she could look forward to on the following day. She did not offer explanations as to how other people cope with the unpredictable. This ploy of distraction, through planning the next twenty-four hours, was an ineffectual coping mechanism still used by the client. Its shortcomings are clearly revealed by the sudden increase in her anxiety symptoms following redundancy.

(d) Her 'catastrophic' reaction to her father's death was due in part to the fact that it renewed her fears concerning mortality and life after death. Her mother's inability to cope with the loss reinforced this maladaptive behaviour through modelling.

(e) Her subsequent travels seem to have been motivated by a constant need for distraction in order to escape from her disturbing thoughts.

(f) Her first panic attack occurred when she was confined in a small office, below the water-line, in an ocean-going vessel. She found it difficult to cope with a working environment from which there was no easy exit should an emergency arise. The strict disciplinary measures taken against her, which prevented her from escaping from the situation, served to exacerbate the anxiety symptoms.

(g) At the age of twenty-three she became preoccupied with thoughts about cancer and believed that her death was imminent. Two years later, she became concerned about environmental pollution and joined the ecology movement. This would suggest that the focus of the primary fear changes according to the particular issue which is topical at the time.

(h) She describes her 'alcoholic phase' in her mid-twenties as a period when she was overwhelmed by her fears about death. Following the traumatic incident abroad, she no longer had the confidence to use travel as both a distracting and escape strategy. Following the model set by her mother, she began to drink heavily in an endeavour to rid herself of the distressing thoughts.

(i) This phase ended when she met Geoffrey. He was an active member of CND, and it was not long before she had a new vehicle for her fears. His political stance made him an ideal candidate for the role of comforter.

Therapy

At our first meeting, Barbara presented her problem in somatic terms and requested treatment for her anxiety symptoms and panic attacks; however, she agreed to my suggestion that it would be useful to conduct a full assessment of her difficulties before proceeding with therapy. Due to her well-rehearsed cognitive avoidance strategy, it required three sessions before her primary fear emerged. Given the degree of distress this disclosure evoked in her, I was obliged to proceed cautiously, and consequently a further three sessions were required before I considered the behavioural analysis to be complete. Barbara was actively involved in this process and agreed with the eventual formulation of the problem, but with one reservation: she found it difficult to accept my suggestion that Geoffrey was helping to perpetuate the problem.

The contract we made was that I would help her to cope better with her fear of eternity, manage her anxiety more effectively and evolve a plan for leading a more rewarding life. She agreed to participate fully in treatment, carry out agreed homework tasks, provide open and honest feedback as to progress, and not to terminate without having discussed it first. We decided to meet for eight weekly sessions initially and review the situation at that stage. In view of our difference of opinion as to the part played by her husband in the perpetuation of the problem, it was agreed to let the matter rest until the review session.

Major therapeutic techniques In view of her concern about handling panic attacks, we decided to work initially with the manifestations of the problem before looking at the underlying factors. Consequently we embarked on a brief course of *anxiety management training*, the aim of which was to help her to gain more control over her thinking processes and physiological responses under conditions of stress. With the assistance of a biofeedback device and a specially prepared relaxation cassette, she learned a variety of skills for countering sudden increases in autonomic nervous system activity. At the same time, it was necessary to devise effective coping statements to replace the self-defeating cognitions which typically accompanied the experience of heightened physiological arousal. These messages, which were the result of close collaboration between therapist and client, were typed on to filing cards which Barbara could have in her possession at all times. One such self-statement was as follows:

> That twinge I just experienced is a signal to me to use my relaxation skills. Provided I keep my breathing steady and ease the tension from my body, I will be able to cope. I managed quite well on the last two occasions, and this has given me a lot of confidence. So there is every reason to suppose that I will fare even better this time.

Since much of anxiety management training involves home practice, this stage of treatment was completed after only three sessions. Now that Barbara's 'fear of fear' had lessened considerably, she felt able to work on the primary problem. Given that her strategy of cognitive avoidance had proved ineffective as a coping mechanism, it was decided that a procedure should be employed which would enable her to confront her distressing thoughts and restructure them in such a way as to reduce the anxiety they elicited; thus the chosen procedure was a combination of *exposure in fantasy* and *cognitive behaviour modification* (Meichenbaum 1977). However, before undergoing this part of the programme, Barbara expressed her curiosity as to how other people coped with thoughts of life after death. Consequently, I decided to include a *modelling* component which could be helpful to her as a basis for forming her own adaptive self-statements. The therapist's disclosures can be summarized as follows:

> I have learned not to plan too far ahead because situations rarely turn out the way I expect them to. If there is life after death, I have no idea what problems I will face or what resources I might have to deal with them. My philosophy therefore is to set myself obtainable goals and deal as effectively as possible with obstacles to them, as and when they arise. Since I feel that I am coping reasonably well in this world, I am reasonably confident that I will adapt well to any environment I find myself in.

Barbara and I worked together to produce a modified version of the above which felt right for her. She was then instructed to repeat these statements to herself during the exposure phase of treatment. This involved a guided fantasy procedure, during which I suggested images and concepts which had previously elicited considerable anxiety in her.

After three two-hour sessions she reported that she was no longer experiencing any discomfort and felt well able to cope with thoughts of 'endlessness' and 'eternity'. To ensure generalization to situations other than the consulting room, she was encouraged to listen to a recording of one of our sessions at home as often as possible.

At the review session which followed, Barbara reported that she was far less preoccupied with thoughts about nuclear war, felt generally more relaxed, and was no longer 'compelled' to carry out significant tasks each day. However, she reported that she was now very much aware of 'gaps' in her life which she did not know how to fill. Further exploration revealed that she had no goals to work towards in her marriage, social life or career. We discussed the fact that, since she had spent most of her life escaping from stress, she had had little experience in providing herself with positive incentives to work towards. Consequently we decided to extend our contract for a further six sessions with a view to helping her to set up targets, decide on strategies and tactics and acquire *problem-solving skills* to deal with the obstacles that would inevitably arise. Given the fact that she had been able to overcome the initial problem without her husband being involved, we decided to continue with individual therapy.

In this final phase of treatment, she was encouraged to set up a variety of specific homework assignments and behavioural 'experiments' to help her to collect information about the kinds of activities she found rewarding. This led to her applying for a business studies course, making contact with friends from the past, and undergoing marriage guidance counselling with Geoffrey! Given the extent of my therapeutic involvement with her, we both felt that her goal of enhancing the marital relationship would best be tackled in an entirely different therapeutic context.

The change process Given the speed with which the client responded to the techniques, and the degree to which generalization occurred, it is clear that the behavioural techniques were instrumental in facilitating a considerable degree of cognitive shift. The evidence that she could control her thinking processes and her physiological responses not only led to a reduction in escape behaviour but increased her perceived self-efficacy. However, given her lack of experience in working towards positive incentives, it proved necessary to administer additional techniques to help her to redirect her resources towards the achievement of goals which would be rewarding in themselves. As a result, she learned strategies which increased her perceived control over events in her external environment.

It is interesting to speculate why she refused to allow her husband to be involved in therapy from the outset. Three possible explanations are as follows:

(a) She valued the therapist's exclusive attention.
(b) She was concerned lest her marital difficulties manifested themselves before she felt ready to address herself to them.
(c) For therapy to be successful, it was necessary that she should feel that change occurred through her efforts alone.

When this issue was raised during our final session, Barbara claimed that, although there was a degree of truth in all three, the last explanation rang most true. Given that termination proceeded smoothly and that she subsequently went on to pursue her relationship difficulties, it would seem likely that increased perceived self-efficacy was the *sine qua non* in this particular case.

References

Ayllon T, Michael J (1959) The psychiatric nurse as a behavioral engineer, *Journal of the Experimental Analysis of Behavior 3*: 323–334

Bandura A (1969) *Principles of Behavior Modification*, Rinehart and Winston, New York

Bandura A (1977) Self-efficacy: Toward a unifying theory of behavioral change, *Psychological Review 84*: 191–215

Bandura A (1978) Reflections on self-efficacy. *Advances in Behaviour Research and Therapy 1*: 237–269

Breger L, McGaugh J (1965) Critique and reformulation of 'learning theory' approaches to psychotherapy and neurosis, *Psychological Bulletin 63*: 338–358

Cautela J R (1967) Covert sensitization, *Psychological Reports 20*: 459–468

D'Zurilla T J, Goldfried M R (1971) Problem solving and behavior modification, *Journal of Abnormal Psychology 78*: 107, 197–226

Eysenck H J (1976) The learning theory model of neurosis – a new approach, *Behaviour Research and Therapy 14*: 251–267

Ford J D (1978) Therapeutic relationship in behavior therapy. *Journal of Consulting and Clinical Psychology 46*: 1302–1314

Ford J D, Kendall P O (1979) Behavior therapists' professional behaviors: Converging evidence of a gap between theory and practice, *The Behavior Therapist 2*: 37–38

Goldfried M R (ed.) (1980) Special issue: Psychotherapy process, *Cognitive Therapy and Research* 4: 269–306

Goldfried M R, Davison G C (1976) *Clinical Behavior Therapy* Holt, Rinehart and Winston, New York

Hersen M, Bellack A S (eds.) (1976) *Behavioral Assessment: A Practical Handbook*, Pergamon, New York

Kanfer F H (1980) 'Self-management methods' in Kanfer F H and Goldstein A P (eds.) *Helping People Change*, Pergamon, New York

Kanfer F H, Phillips J S (1970) *Learning Foundations of Behavior Therapy*, Wiley, New York

Lang P J (1969) 'The mechanics of desensitization and the laboratory study of fear' in Franks C M (ed.) *Behavior Therapy: Appraisal and Status*, McGraw-Hill, New York

Liberman R P, King L W, De Risi W, McCann M (1975) *Personal Effectiveness*, Research Press, Champaign, Ill.

Mackay D (1982) 'Techniques of behaviour therapy' in Priest R G (ed.) *Psychiatry in Medical Practice*, MacDonald and Evans, Plymouth

Mackay D 'Principles of learning' (1983) in Weller M (ed.) *The Scientific Basis of Psychiatry*, Baillière Tindall, London

Matthews A (1978) Fear-reduction research and clinical phobias, *Psychological Bulletin* 85: 390–404

McPherson F M, Brougham L, McLaren L (1980) Maintenance of improvements in agoraphobic patients treated by behavioural methods in a four-year follow-up, *Behaviour Research and Therapy* 18: 150–152

Meichenbaum D (1975) 'Self-instructional methods' in Kanfer F H and Goldstein A P (eds.) *Helping People Change*, Pergamon, New York

Meichenbaum D (1977) *Cognitive Behavior Modification*, Plenum, New York

Morris R J, Suckerman K R (1974) The importance of the therapeutic relationship in systematic desensitization, *Journal of Consulting and Clinical Psychology* 42: 147

Quirk D A (1973) An automated desensitization. In Rubin R D, Brady J P and Henderson J D (eds.) *Advances in Behavior Therapy* 4, Academic Press, New York pp. 103–116

Ryan V L, Gizynski M N (1971) Behavior therapy in retrospect: patients' feelings about their behavior therapies, *Journal of Consulting and Clinical Psychology* 37: 1–9

Seligman M E P (1975) *Helplessness: On Depression, Development and Death*, Freeman, San Francisco

Suinn R M, Richardson F (1971) Anxiety management training: a non-specific behavior therapy program for anxiety control, *Behavior Therapy* 2: 498–510

Trower P, Bryant B, Argyle M (1978) *Social Skills and Mental Health*, Methuen, London

Turkat I D, Brantley P J (1981) On the therapeutic relationship in behavior therapy, *The Behavior Therapist* 4: 16

Watson J B, Rayner R (1920) Conditioned emotional reactions, *Journal of Experimental Psychology* 3: 1–14

Wolpe J (1958) *Psychotherapy by Reciprocal Inhibition*, Stanford University Press, Stanford, p. 9

Suggested Further Reading

Bandura A (1977) *Social Learning Theory*, Prentice-Hall, Englewood Cliffs, NJ

Fensterheim H, Glazer H I (eds.) (1983) *Behavioral Psychotherapy: Basic Principles and Case Studies in an Integrative Clinical Model*, Brunner/Mazel, New York

Franks C M, Wilson G T, Kendall P C, Brownell K D (1982) *Annual Review of Behavior Therapy 8*, Guilford, New York

Goldfried M R, Davison G C (1976) *Clinical Behavior Therapy*, Holt, Rinehart and Winston, New York

Kanfer F H, Goldstein A P (eds.) (1980) *Helping People Change: A Textbook of Methods*, 2nd edition, Pergamon, New York

Chapter 12 Individual Therapies: A Comparative Analysis

Windy Dryden and Associates

Up to now, ten discrete approaches to individual therapy have been presented. To attempt a comprehensive comparative analysis of the similarities and dissimilarities among all ten approaches would require another book, yet to forgo any attempt to compare and contrast the different therapies presented in this book would be shirking editorial responsibility. A compromise thus needed to be reached, so I decided to ask each contributor to rate the therapeutic approach about which they had written on: (a) a set of personality dimensions and (b) a set of dimensions focused on therapist behaviour.

This strategy, of course, has its pitfalls. First, each contributor has his or her own idiosyncratic opinions on their own school of therapy which may not correspond to the views of other practitioners of that particular school. Second, each contributor probably has some reservations about being asked to rate his or her approach on the dimensions presented; most therapists do not relish being asked to make generalizations about therapy, being mindful of exceptions to the general rule. Third, the correlation between stated therapeutic practice and actual therapeutic practice is known not to be very high, thus the validity of the ratings on the therapist behaviour dimensions may be questionable. Fourth, contributors are likely to use different standards in making judgements. Yet if the reader bears these pitfalls in mind, some value may be gained from inspecting the contributors' views and making comparisons among them. While the reader will probably wish to make his or her own comparisons from the data presented, I will focus here on the major similarities and dissimilarities that have emerged from the information provided by the contributors.

Personality Dimensions: A Comparative Analysis

Each contributor was asked to consider the theoretical underpinnings of their approach to therapy with special reference to where the approach stood on ten personality dimensions. These dimensions were put forward by Corsini (1977), who himself relied heavily on Coan's (1968) work. Contributors were given the information outlined in Table 1 to guide them in their ratings. Figure 12.1 presents the views of the contributors which were obtained by this method. A unidirectional arrow → or ← indicates the pole which is stressed in the theoretical underpinnings of

1. *Objective-subjective.* Objective theories feature explicit, observable, unequivocal behaviour that can be counted and numbered. Subjective theories are concerned with the inner personal life of an individual - his ineffable self - and are of the introspective type.

2. *Elementaristic-holistic.* Elementaristic theory sees the person as composed of parts: organs, units, elements put together to make the whole. Holistic theories see the person as having a central unity, and the parts as aspects of the total entity. The individual is seen as indivisible.

3. *Apersonal-personal.* Apersonal theories are impersonal, statistically based, and consider generalities rather than individualities. They are based on group norms. Personal theories deal with the single individual, or are idiographic.

4. *Quantitative-qualitative.* A quantitative theory makes it possible to measure units of behaviour. A qualitative theory does not see behaviour as able to be measured exactly, holding that behaviour is too complex for such dealings.

5. *Static-dynamic.* Static theory sees the individual as a unit reactor, not a learner; filled with instincts, and based on generalizations preestablished by heredity. Dynamic theory is concerned with the individual as a learner, with interactions between behaviour and consciousness and between consciousness and unconsciousness.

6. *Endogenistic-exogenistic.* Endogenous theories view the person as biologically based. They are constitutional theories. Exogenistic theories are social learning theories.

7. *Deterministic-indeterministic.* Deterministic theories in effect see the individual as not responsible for his behaviour, as being the pawn of society, heredity, or both. Indeterministic theories put emphasis on self-direction of the individual. Control is within the person, and prediction is never completely possible.

8. *Past-future.* Some theories see the individual in terms of what he has inherited or learned in the past, and others see the individual as explained by his anticipation of future goals.

9. *Cognitive-affective.* Cognitive theories are the so-called ego theories which see man as essentially rational, with the emotions subserving the intellect. Conversely, affective theories see man as operating on an emotional basis, and with the intellect at the service of the emotions.

10. *Unconsciousness-consciousness.* Theories that stress the unconscious see the person as having considerable investment below the level of awareness. Consciousness refers to awareness, and such theories see the individual as rational.

Table 12.1 Descriptions of 'personality' dimensions (Corsini 1977)

	SUBJECTIVE / OBJECTIVE	HOLISTIC / ELEMENTARISTIC	PERSONAL / APERSONAL	QUALITATIVE / QUANTITATIVE	DYNAMIC / STATIC	EXOGENISTIC / ENDOGENISTIC	INDETERMINISTIC / DETERMINISTIC	FUTURE / PAST	COGNITIVE / AFFECTIVE	UNCONSCIOUS / CONSCIOUS
BEHAVIOURAL	↕	↓	↑	↕	↑	↑	↓	PRESENT FUTURE	—	↓
RATIONAL-EMOTIVE	↕	↑	↑	↑	↑	↓	↑	PRESENT FUTURE	↕	↕
T.A.	↕	→	↑	↑	↑	↑	↑	PAST PRESENT FUTURE	↕	↓
GESTALT	↓	↑	↑	↑	↑	→	↑	PRESENT	↕	↕
EXISTENTIAL	↑	↑	↑	↑	↑	→	↑	PAST PRESENT FUTURE	↕	↓
PERSONAL CONSTRUCT	↑	↑	↑	↕	↑	↑	↑	PAST PRESENT FUTURE	↕	↓
PERSON-CENTRED	↑	↑	↑	↑	↑	↑	↑	PAST PRESENT FUTURE	↕	↓
JUNGIAN	↑	↑	↑	↕	↑	↓	↑	PAST PRESENT FUTURE	↓	↑
KLEINIAN	↑	↑	↑	↑	→	→	↑	↓	↓	↑
FREUDIAN	↑	↑	↑	↑	↑	↑	→	↓	↕	↑

Figure 12.1 'Personality' dimensions

Source: Corsini 1977

each approach. The sign ↔ indicates that the theory encompasses both poles of the dimension while the sign ⊥ indicates that the theory occupies a central position between both poles.

Before the comparative analysis is presented, it is interesting to note that if a majority view is taken on each dimension then the following 'normative' personality theory emerges from the ten approaches presented: personal, dynamic, indeterministic, holistic, qualitative, affective ↔ cognitive, subjective, past–present–future, exogenistic and conscious. The position of person-centred therapy on these dimensions corresponds exactly to the 'normative' view, while that occupied by behavioural psychotherapy is most discrepant from it.

In Figure 2, the major similarities and dissimilarities are presented among the approaches on the ten personality dimensions combined. The numbers in parentheses denote the number of differences between two approaches. A score of 1 is given to a primary difference where the arrows on a single compass point in opposite directions, i.e. → vs. ←, whereas a score of ½ is given to every other (secondary) difference. Figure 2 clearly indicates that from this analysis behavioural psychotherapy is most dissimilar to eight of the other therapeutic approaches on the personality dimensions combined.

Therapist Behaviour: A Comparative Analysis

Each contributor was then asked to consider therapist behaviour as advocated by their particular therapeutic approach on four major aspects of therapist behaviour suggested by Beutler (1983). These are:-

(a) 'Relationship style': three dimensions are presented which centre on the type of therapist–client relationship considered desirable by each therapeutic approach;

(b) 'Focus/structuring': five dimensions are presented which represent how much therapist structuring of the therapeutic process is advocated and what type of focus the therapist is recommended to adopt;

(c) 'Directed activity': seven dimensions are presented concerning how much and the nature of therapist directed activity recommended by each approach;

(d) 'Expressive/evocative' therapist behaviour: eight dimensions are

	MOST SIMILAR		MOST DISSIMILAR	
FREUDIAN	KLEINIAN; PERSON-CENTRED; PERSONAL CONSTRUCT	(2)	BEHAVIOURAL	(4½)
KLEINIAN	JUNGIAN	(1½)	BEHAVIOURAL	(6)
JUNGIAN	KLEINIAN	(1½)	BEHAVIOURAL	(6½)
PERSON-CENTRED	EXISTENTIAL	(½)	BEHAVIOURAL	(4)
PERSONAL CONSTRUCT	PERSON-CENTRED	(1)	BEHAVIOURAL	(4)
EXISTENTIAL	PERSON-CENTRED	(½)	BEHAVIOURAL	(4½)
GESTALT	RATIONAL EMOTIVE	(1½)	BEHAVIOURAL	(5)
T.A.	PERSON-CENTRED	(1)	KLEINIAN	(4)
RET	GESTALT	(1½)	BEHAVIOURAL	(4½)
BEHAVIOURAL	T.A.	(3)	JUNGIAN	(6½)

Figure 12.2 'Personality' dimensions – major similarities and dissimilarities

presented to show how therapists differ in eliciting and dealing with client material.

Contributors were asked to rate each dimensin on a 1–5 scale and the dimensions converted to show where the major emphasis lay on each one: →, ← or __|__ (to denote a middle-of-the-dimension position). Figures 12.3, 12.5, 12.7 and 12.9 present the emphases on all dimensions across therapeutic approaches; in figures 12.4, 12.6, 12.8 and 12.10, the major similarities and dissimilarities are presented among the approaches on all dimensions in the four respective areas. Again, the numbers in parentheses indicate that a score of 1 is given to a primary difference (→ vs. ←) and a score of ½ given to a secondary difference (→ vs. ← and and a score of ½ given to a secondary difference (→ vs. ↓ and ↓ vs. ←).

When the data on major similarities and dissimilarities across all four aspects of therapist behaviour are considered, the picture which emerges is presented in Figure 12.11. The data in this figure have been collated from Figures 12.4, 12.6, 12.8 and 12.10. Only major similarities and dissimilarities that occur in two or more of the comparisons made in these figures are included in Figure 11. Thus, with regard to therapist behaviour, Freudian psychotherapy is overall most similar to the Kleinian and Jungian therapies since it is revealed as being most similar to each on three of the four specific aspects of therapist behaviour presented here. Overall it is most dissimilar to behavioural psychotherapy on therapist behaviour, having been revealed as such on two of the four specific aspects.

This analysis reveals, for example, expected major similarities among the psychodynamic therapies – although they are by no means identical – and expected major dissimilarities between the psychodynamic therapies and behavioural psychotherapy. Kleinian psychotherapy is found in the major dissimilarity group on seven occasions, indicating that Kleinian therapists behave quite differently from all but the other psychodynamic therapists. Person-centred therapists, on the other hand, while being similar to a number of other therapists on one of the four specific aspects of therapist behaviour, share no greater similarity to any of them beyond that.

Summary

Contributors of chapters on specific approaches to individual therapy were asked to rate the position which their particular therapeutic approach occupied on a number of personality dimensions and aspects of therapist behaviour. Major similarities and dissimilarities from the resultant data were presented. Readers are further invited to make their own comparisons, as it is recognized that different readers have different reasons and therefore different purposes for making comparisons. Care should nevertheless be exercised when generalizing from this data, since only a representative sample of possible dimensions have been used here.

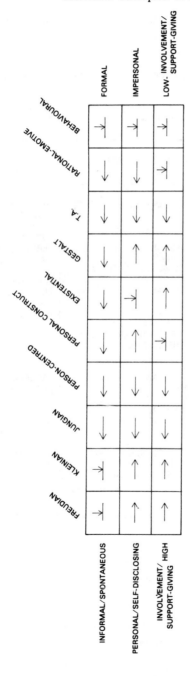

Figure 12.3 Therapist behaviour 'relationship style' dimensions

	MOST SIMILAR		MOST DISSIMILAR	
FREUDIAN	KLEINIAN	(0)	JUNGIAN; PERSON-CENTRED; T.A.	(2½)
KLEINIAN	FREUDIAN	(0)	JUNGIAN; PERSON-CENTRED; T.A.	(2½)
JUNGIAN	PERSON-CENTRED; T.A.	(0)	FREUDIAN; KLEINIAN	(2½)
PERSON-CENTRED	JUNGIAN; T.A.	(0)	FREUDIAN; KLEINIAN	(2½)
PERSONAL CONSTRUCT	GESTALT	(½)	JUNGIAN: PERSON-CENTRED: T.A.; RET	(1½)
EXISTENTIAL	GESTALT	(½)	JUNGIAN: PERSON-CENTRED; T.A.	(1½)
GESTALT	FREUDIAN; KLEINIAN PERSONAL CONSTRUCT; EXISTENTIAL	(½)	T.A.	(2)
T.A.	JUNGIAN; PERSON-CENTRED	(0)	FREUDIAN; KLEINIAN	(2½)
RET	JUNGIAN; PERSON-CENTRED; T.A.	(½)	KLEINIAN	(2)
BEHAVIOURAL	FREUDIAN; KLEINIAN; PERSON-CENTRED; EXISTENTIAL; RET	(1)	JUNGIAN; PERSON-CENTRED; GESTALT; T.A.	(1½)

Figure 12.4 'Relationship style' dimension: major similarities and dissimilarities

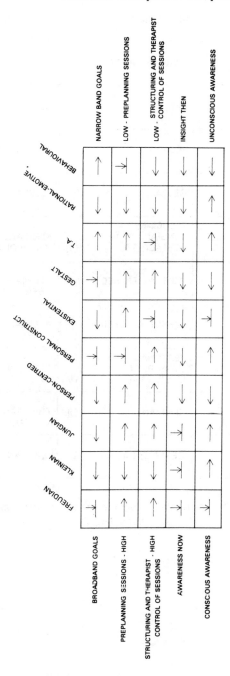

Figure 12.5 Therapist behaviour: 'focus/structuring' dimensions

	MOST SIMILAR		MOST DISSIMILAR	
FREUDIAN	JUNGIAN; GESTALT	(1)	RET	(3½)
KLEINIAN	RET	(½)	GESTALT	(4)
JUNGIAN	FREUDIAN	(1)	BEHAVIOURAL	(4)
PERSON-CENTRED	GESTALT	(½)	KLEINIAN	(3½)
PERSONAL CONSTRUCT	FREUDIAN; JUNGIAN; GESTALT; T.A.	(1½)	KLEINIAN; BEHAVIOURAL	(2½)
EXISTENTIAL	PERSON-CENTRED	(1)	KLEINIAN; BEHAVIOURAL	(2½)
GESTALT	PERSON-CENTRED	(½)	KLEINIAN	(4)
T.A.	PERSONAL CONSTRUCT; EXISTENTIAL	(1½)	KLEINIAN	(3)
RET	KLEINIAN	(½)	FREUDIAN; GESTALT	(3½)
BEHAVIOURAL	GESTALT; T.A.	(2)	JUNGIAN	(4)

Figure 12.6 'Focus/structuring' dimensions: major similarities
and dissimilarities

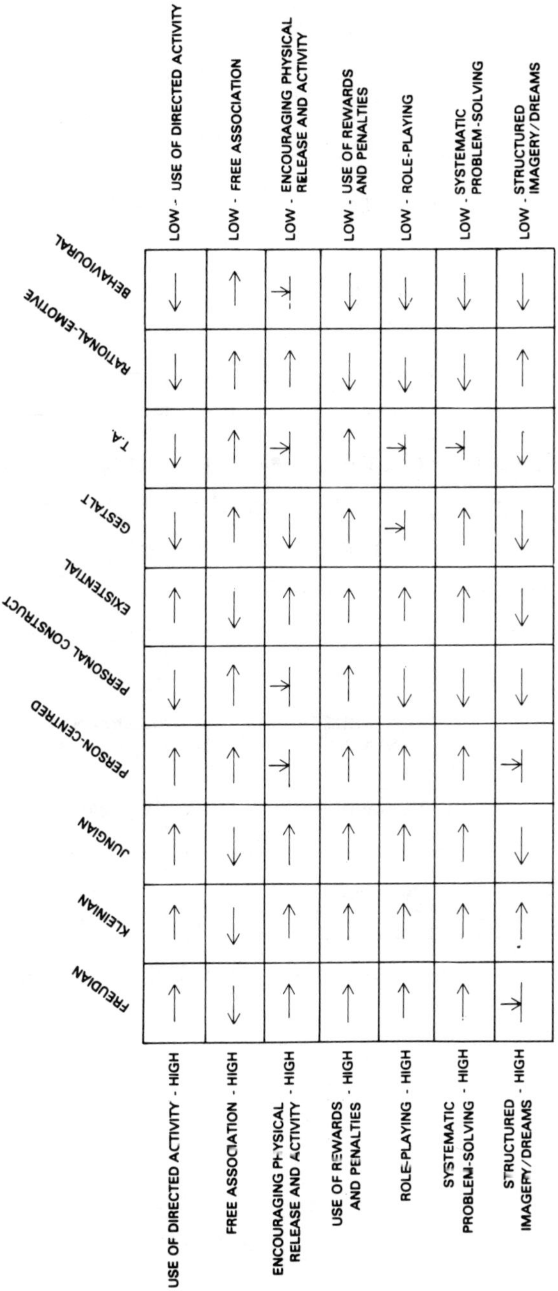

Dimension (HIGH ↑ / LOW ↓)	BEHAVIOURAL	RATIONAL-EMOTIVE	T.A.	GESTALT	EXISTENTIAL	PERSONAL CONSTRUCT	PERSON-CENTRED	JUNGIAN	KLEINIAN	FREUDIAN
USE OF DIRECTED ACTIVITY	↓	↓	↓	↓	↑	↓	↑	↑	↑	↑
FREE ASSOCIATION	↑	↑	↑	↑	↓	↑	↑	↓	↓	↓
ENCOURAGING PHYSICAL RELEASE AND ACTIVITY	→	↑	→	↓	↑	→	→	↓	↑	↑
USE OF REWARDS AND PENALTIES	↓	↓	↑	↑	↑	↓	↑	↑	↑	↑
ROLE-PLAYING	↓	↓	→	→	↑	↓	↑	↑	↑	↑
SYSTEMATIC PROBLEM-SOLVING	↓	↓	→	↑	↑	↓	↑	↑	↑	↑
STRUCTURED IMAGERY/DREAMS	↓	↑	↓	↓	↓	↓	→	↓	↑	→

Figure 12.7 Therapist behaviour: 'directed activity' dimensions

	MOST SIMILAR		MOST DISSIMILAR	
FREUDIAN	KLEINIAN; JUNGIAN; EXISTENTIAL	(½)	BEHAVIOURAL	(6)
KLEINIAN	FREUDIAN	(½)	BEHAVIOURAL	(6½)
JUNGIAN	EXISTENTIAL	(0)	RET	(6)
PERSON-CENTRED	FREUDIAN	(1½)	RET	(5)
PERSONAL CONSTRUCT	T.A.; BEHAVIOURAL	(1)	KLEINIAN	(5½)
EXISTENTIAL	JUNGIAN	(0)	RET	(6)
GESTALT	T.A.	(1)	KLEINIAN; RET	(4½)
T.A.	PERSONAL CONSTRUCT; GESTALT	(1)	KLEINIAN	(4½)
RET	BEHAVIOURAL	(1½)	JUNGIAN	(6)
BEHAVIOURAL	PERSONAL CONSTRUCT	(1)	KLEINIAN	(6½)

Figure 12.8 'Directed activity' dimensions: major similarities and dissimilarities

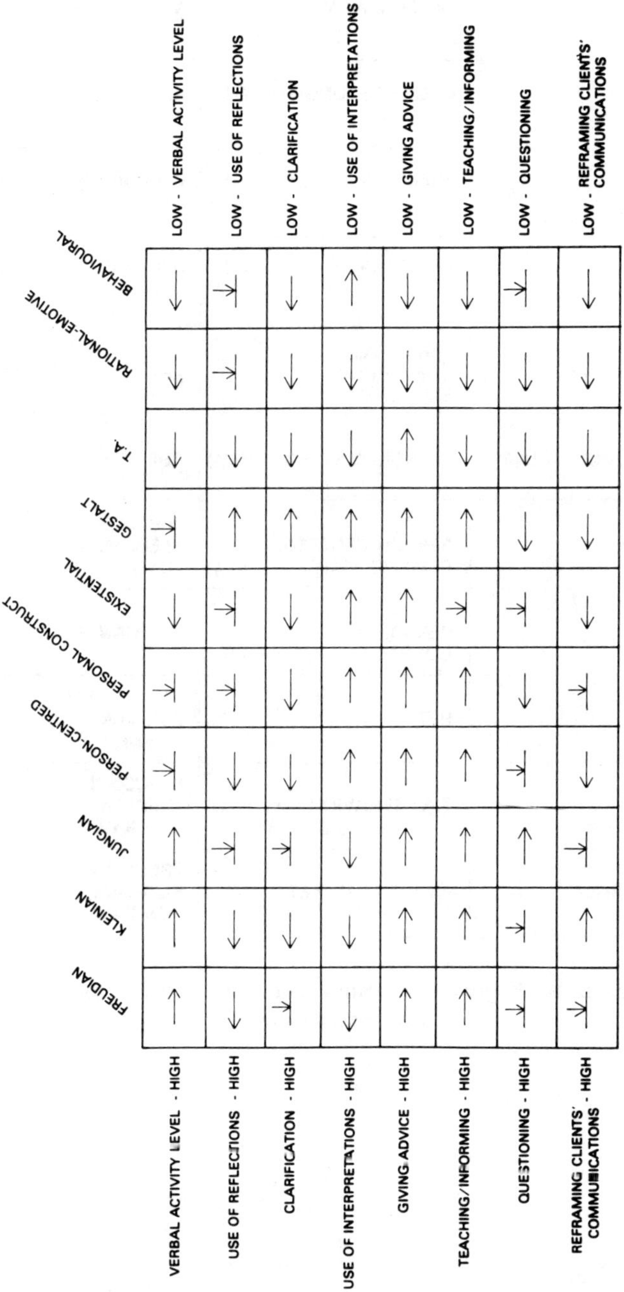

Figure 12.9 Therapist behaviour 'expressive/evocative' dimensions

	MOST SIMILAR	MOST DISSIMILAR
FREUDIAN	KLEINIAN; JUNGIAN (1)	BEHAVIOURAL (5½)
KLEINIAN	FREUDIAN (1)	BEHAVIOURAL (5½)
JUNGIAN	FREUDIAN (1)	BEHAVIOURAL (5½)
PERSON-CENTRED	PERSONAL CONSTRUCT; EXISTENTIAL (1½)	RET (4½)
PERSONAL CONSTRUCT	PERSON-CENTRED (1½)	RET (4½)
EXISTENTIAL	PERSON-CENTRED; BEHAVIOURAL (1½)	FREUDIAN; KLEINIAN; JUNGIAN (4)
GESTALT	PERSONAL CONSTRUCT (2)	KLEINIAN; RET (5)
T.A.	RET (1½)	JUNGIAN; GESTALT (4½)
RET	T.A.; BEHAVIOURAL (1½)	FREUDIAN; KLEINIAN; JUNGIAN (5)
BEHAVIOURAL	EXISTENTIAL; RET (1½)	FREUDIAN; KLEINIAN; JUNGIAN (5½)

Figure 12.10 'Expressive/evocative' dimensions: major similarities and dissimilarities

	MOST SIMILAR		MOST DISSIMILAR	
FREUDIAN	KLEINIAN; JUNGIAN	(3)	BEHAVIOURAL	(2)
KLEINIAN	FREUDIAN	(3)	BEHAVIOURAL	(2)
JUNGIAN	FREUDIAN	(2)	BEHAVIOURAL	(2)
PERSON-CENTRED	—		KLEINIAN; RET	(2)
PERSONAL CONSTRUCT	GESTALT; T.A.	(2)	KLEINIAN; RET	(2)
EXISTENTIAL	PERSON-CENTRED	(2)	KLEINIAN; JUNGIAN	(2)
GESTALT	PERSONAL CONSTRUCT	(2)	RET (2) KLEINIAN (3)	
T.A.	PERSONAL CONSTRUCT	(2)	KLEINIAN	(3)
RET	T.A.; BEHAVIOURAL	(2)	JUNGIAN (2) KLEINIAN (2) FREUDIAN (3)	
BEHAVIOURAL	EXISTENTIAL; RET	(2)	KLEINIAN (2) JUNGIAN (3)	

Figure 12.11 Therapist behaviour: major similarities and dissimilarities (four aspects combined)

References

Beutler L E (1983) *Eclectic Psychotherapy: A Systematic Approach*, Pergamon New York

Coan R W (1968) Dimensions of psychological theory, *American Psychologist 23*: 715–722

Corsini R J (ed.) (1977) *Current Personality Theories*, Peacock, Itasca, Ill.

Chapter 13 Individual Therapies: Limitations

Windy Dryden and Associates

Each approach to therapy has its limitations, and yet these are often glossed over in the published literature. To ensure that this does not happen in this book, I decided to include a separate chapter on 'limitations' and invited the contributors to address themselves to this particular theme, giving them each a thousand words for the purpose. Their replies are printed as received.

Psychodynamic Therapy: The Freudian Approach (Michael Jacobs)

Since Freudian psychotherapy requires not only considerable time, but also experienced therapists whose training is long and costly, there is an obvious limitation upon the number of people who can avail themselves of this type of therapy. This is one of the reasons for the development of techniques for better assessment and treatment in brief psychotherapy, as outlined in Chapter 2. The briefer and less frequent the therapy, the more limitations there are upon those who can best use this form of Freudian therapy. The requirements of clients for brief psychotherapy are also outlined in my chapter, and the absence of these are obvious contra-indications for taking such people on.

In the varied experience of Freudian psychotherapy and psychoanalysis, it is not easy to delineate those people for whom the therapy is limited in its effectiveness. Individual instances are cited of very disturbed clients achieving profound change, but in general the greater the degree of disturbance, dependency and demands of the client, the more need there is for a therapeutic environment which can contain and work with such features; since such an environment is not readily available, there are obvious limitations on who can be helped. There is a need for therapists with an even higher degree of training and experience who are able to provide time and accessibility such as is unusual in the briefer forms of therapy; there will probably also need to be a supportive environment, such as a therapeutic community, where others can share the daily care, support and therapy of the individual. Thus, while lack of sufficient ego strength to continue living tolerably between sessions is normally a contra-indication for psychotherapy on a once- or twice-weekly basis, it is possible to work with such clients given the right conditions; but such decisions cannot be taken lightly. The therapeutic environment needs to be capable of dealing with the possibility of severe regression to infantile states of mind and behaviour. Here the individual Freudian psychotherapist, working in isolation, is at a disadvantage.

The limitations outlined above are those of resources and expertise. Other limitations present themselves on the part of the client, even in the briefer and less intensive types of psychotherapy likely to be of interest to the reader. Certain characteristics of the client suggest the likelihood of a poor outcome for this particular approach to 'talking' things through.

The first limiting factor is the client who shows more concern with getting rid of symptoms than with understanding their significance; of course clients wish to be free of those aspects of their behaviour or experience which cause discomfort, but what matters is the approach to their difficulties. A symptom can be tackled head on (e.g. through medication) or from behind and within, so that through an understanding of its function it can be given up. For example, a headache can be tackled with analgesics and to all intents and purposes removed. Exploring the source of the tension, on the other hand, will probably take longer; but by bringing the tension into the open, much more than the headache can be relieved. The client who will find the Freudian approach limiting is the person who wants symptoms to be taken away by the therapist through 'magical words', advice or managing situations which cause stress. This is especially so where the client presents just one symptom and yet feels that there is nothing else wrong in life worth talking about. It can also apply to some clients who present a series of difficulties but with the expectation that these can be 'dumped' upon the therapist and that he will prescribe them away (by drugs, advice or by some superior knowledge of human beings). Unless the client has sufficient psychological mindedness to acknowledge that it is probably personal and emotional factors that lie at the root of his or her problems (even in psychosomatic or apparently somatic symptoms), Freudian therapy will either fail to get off the ground or will proceed on such different underlying assumptions that the working alliance between therapist and client will not occur.

The second major limiting factor in the client is the inability to relate to the therapist, both in the sense of finding difficulty in relating his thoughts and feelings and also in the sense of making a relationship. Although the difficulty in speaking may arise from the passivity referred to above, or from shame and guilt, all these difficulties might, during the session, be amenable to change through being worked on by the therapist. But some clients find it impossible to relate, even though they are reasonably intelligent. This limitation is nothing to do with lack of education, although a reasonable capacity to think objectively, empathically and subjectively is necessary. It is fairly obvious with some people that all the remarks or questions offered by the therapist are met only with mono-syllabic answers and that free-floating conversation, let alone free association, is unlikely to occur.

The third limitation is when the client is reluctant to engage in therapy either because he has come under some sort of duress or pressure from others or because his symptoms are too comfortable to be given up – they are what is called 'ego-syntonic'. There certainly needs to be some degree of discomfort for anyone to engage in a therapy which is likely to arouse even more discomfort before things get better. Even if changing is felt to be difficult, the desire and motivation of the client is an important factor.

There is, finally, an ongoing limitation to therapy, which lies in the client's unconscious resistance: either to change or to uncovering repressed aspects which are feared. That this is so much part of Freudian psychotherapy, the analysis of resistance, indicates that this is not in itself a barrier to therapy; but the degree of resistance, and the skill of the therapist in meeting it, impose limitations on the depth of change that is likely to occur. Given the important limitations on time (and money) for therapy, it is likely to be resistance which marks the premature end of therapy. When the client has gone as far as he or she is prepared to go,

and the therapist as far as he is capable of going, termination marks sufficient change but also avoidance of deeper aspects of the self with which
the experienced therapist is ready to engage.

Psychodynamic Therapy: the Kleinian Approach (Cassie Cooper)

In present-day society, there is a proliferation of differing methods of psychotherapy, many of which do not emphasize self-awareness and which open
wide the question of the causation of therapeutic change. They postulate
that change is not engendered by the growth of self-awareness but
actually stems from the process by which that self-awareness is
brought about.

Any scientific examination of the causes of therapeutic change must
involve an examination and description of the variables which, in context,
facilitate the changes. Experimental methods can then be evolved which
will test the hypotheses that are formed. Kleinian therapy, as judged by
these contemporary standards, is still unable to provide the scientific
evidence which is necessary to meet the basic criteria of discon-
firmability. Moreover, it becomes increasingly evident that it is an over-
simplification to look at psychopathology as if it could be isolated from
the changing attitudes of the nuclear age.

My patients and their problems are not entirely separable from the
outside environment they have created and in which they function. With
a good conscience, I, as the psychotherapist, cannot divorce my patients
from their social and cultural background; they are, after all, a specific
group of people who have reacted in a specific way to their problems and
who come to me seeking psychotherapy. A human being does not live in a
sterilized plastic bubble: he is conceived at the coming together of his
parents who contribute to this act of creation the essence of their own
personalities at this given moment in time. He is born at a predicted
season of the year, in a special place and in a particular way. He depends
throughout life on the availability and proximity of other human beings.
In the wheatfields of America, a man will sow the wheat that gives him
bread; and in the sweatshops of Hong Kong a child will labour to cut the
clothes that cover him.

Few, if any, of the methods of psychotherapy described in this book
can encompass the broad sweep of these extraneous human factors. Only

certain parts of the interaction between therapist and patient can be focused upon. In Kleinian therapy, as in others, there is no rigorous way of describing the interchange between the person who wishes to change and the person who sets out to change him.

The broader social context and the subjective processes which brought these two human beings together is left out of the counselling room; the focus is on manoeuvrability and tactics. Kleinian therapy holds the view that external events are not of primary importance, but that these events can exacerbate or alleviate certain aspects of the personality. It is the undeclared intention of the therapist to relieve anxiety, intending that this relief will later help the patient to succeed in life, to become happy, to remember his past life and past experiences so that he can learn to discriminate between those he wishes to repeat and those he wishes to avoid.

Inevitably, the point of view on what process to use with a patient in effecting these changes is shaped by one's theoretical approach. However, if the therapist practises his therapy all day and every day from only one viewpoint, then there is a real danger of the therapist becoming subsumed and consumed by his own stance. This contrasts sharply with other strategies of intervention where the emphasis has shifted from the processes within an individual to those in the context of his relationships with others.

Kleinian therapists tend to forget that because they see their patients in such a strictly controlled analytic setting they can be insulated from a view of their patient in the external world. True, the patient reports on his daily life, but these reports are highly selective and often only pertinent to the failures rather than to the successes of life outside the consulting room.

Anxious behaviour on the part of a patient can be interpreted as a repression of unconscious ideas which are threatening to become conscious. The same anxious behaviour could be viewed externally as a way of appealing for a sympathetic approach from another person. These two interpretations of behaviour represent astonishingly different theoretical systems. In this way the view of the therapist can be distorted.

The reader of this book will have noted that various theorists have differed on the postulation of central motives or goals for *all* human beings. Why do they differ so much? Is it not that the task of ferreting out the central motives of all human beings is an impossible task? Is it not an unattainable goal to poll every patient on their expectations of life and their private responses to 'the slings and arrows of outrageous fortune'?

The crucial question for any therapist remains: what effect does the assumption of a particular theoretical stance have on the behaviour of that therapist? Does this assumption always dictate the therapist's goals for patients? Does the therapist only find out what he expects to find? Does the therapist, in order to fit his own expectations, distort what information the patient provides?

Would Kleinian therapy suffer if each patient's motives were seen as unique? Psychoanalytical psychotherapy has been defined as a perspective which is essentially pre-theoretical in nature, but perspectives are often constricted by ideological underpinnings, whether we are aware of them or not.

Psychodynamic Therapy: the Jungian Approach (Kenneth Lambert)

Analytical psychology arose out of the attempt to respond to the neurotic and psychotic suffering of patients. Its special focus came to be upon problems of meaning as met with at the different phases of an individual's developing life-span. Despite that focus, however, Jung's interest was in a general psychology: open-ended and accommodating to extensions in psychological studies as a whole. In practice, however, analytical psychology has focused upon new technical developments in analytic practice both from within and without its ranks, and upon interacting with medicine, ethology, philosophy, literature, history, socio-political, religious and mythological studies, and not least the academic study of alchemy.

My own chapter has, however, dealt mainly with clinical matters, and so it is with the limitations of the clinical foci and practice of analytical psychology that we shall now be concerned – limitations that demand of diagnostic interviewers a good sense of the practicalities of the patient's situation and a good clinical judgement of his suitability for treatment.

Limitations may be understood as *accidental* or *inherent* – or both. Under *accidental limitations* we may subsume the problem of financing long and detailed treatments; the problem of location and of that of the relatively small number of analysts available – especially outside London; and those of the relative curtailment of freedom during the working week that regular sessions impose and of the patient's lack of freedom to change his home location drastically owing to the fact that he needs to live within striking distance of his analyst's rooms. Indeed, there are patients who have to make quite complicated arrangements to obtain analytical treatment, and the number of those who have the means to achieve this remains limited indeed.

Inherent limitations, on the other hand, are sometimes imposed by the extent and intensity of damage and distortion suffered by the patient at the beginning of his life and sometimes cumulatively throughout its course so far.

In describing this state of affairs, I shall draw, with gratitude, upon Alan Edwards's seminal paper on the subject, namely 'Research studies in the problems of assessment' (1983). In it Edwards describes five areas of damage. In the first place, for instance, we find *psychosis*: florid, latent or borderline. Here, the analytic method, as described in Chapter 4, is likely to fail or to result in serious, if not hardly manageable, difficulties. Its application may release hitherto quite unconscious and really primitive aggression as well as transferences to the therapist of a violently persecutory and psychotic nature and of a sort that cannot be decently resolved.

The same could be said of individuals whose *early dependency* needs have been almost entirely unmet by their early environment and who yet, at a later time in their lives, may form unresolvable dependent transferences to their analysts. For these people, the threat of any separation can lead to a sense of almost total disintegration into rage and terror; thus some analyst or other may have to be responsible for such a patient for many years, if not the remainder of the patient's life. Such demands can cause stress to the therapist to a degree of intensity that goes far beyond any relief the patient may experience.

Again, there are personalities whose damage is so intense and whose rage and terror is so unbearable that *totally rigid defences of an obsessional paranoid or schizoid* type come into operation in such a way that both the presence and the interpretative functions of the analyst are totally resisted.

Then there are *histrionic* personalities whose inner emptiness, deadness and horror at the thought of abandonment propel them towards an intense and dramatic acting-out for the purpose of seeking attention or, alternatively, into manipulative behaviour or desperately self-destructive manoeuvres. Such individuals can hardly attend to their therapist's analytic or other interpretations, for any fuller consciousness of their manipulative behaviour towards their therapists and others might lead to suffering that is perhaps even more unbearable than that which they seek to deny through their histrionic style of behaviour.

Finally, there are the people who, no doubt out of a wide variety of reasons or, more likely, causes, have become severely addicted to alcohol, cannabis, heroin, etc. The addiction diminishes the patient's attention to any interpretations offered by the therapist that could in any way be suspected of the aim of undermining the addictive compulsion.

It should be stated that Edwards is describing, in each of these areas, somewhat extreme disturbance, and that there are less severe cases where greater therapeutic gains are possible. A fine clinical judgement needs to be made as to whether the patients' ego consciousness is sufficiently developed for him to be able both to observe and to relate to the pressure of archetypes, internalized objects and internalized archetypal objects. A further judgement concerns whether these archetypal forces are in an untouched primitive condition so that the patient is, so to speak, at their mercy, or whether the patient can identify with the therapist sufficiently to be able to develop ego strength and flexibility. Edwards quotes Greenson's (1967) concept of 'antithetical ego functionings', and considers its relevance in this context. Such functionings include the capacity to be flexible enough to work within a wide spectrum that includes the capacity to regress or to progress, the capacity to control or to give up control by standing aside, and the capacity to renounce reality testing or to return to it.

When the clinical judgement is that the damage has been too great and that the patient's ego is insufficiently developed, then other methods of treatment may need to be prescribed. These include supportive psychotherapy, preferably carried out by an analytically sophisticated therapist who uses his analytic insights for the purpose of understanding the kind of support the patient needs but not necessarily in order to convey them to his patient. Other methods of handling may include symptom alleviation or shifting – through drug therapy, behavioural therapy, occupational therapy, institutionalism or varying mixtures of some or all of such – or possibly, under certain aspects, group therapy.

It should nevertheless be remembered that in making his penetrating assessment of the limitations of analytic therapy, Edwards quotes Jung's hint that there is no knowing what enthusiasm on the part of the therapist may not achieve. Evidence exists to suggest that the enthusiasm of young therapists may sometimes work wonders; sometimes, too, the imagination of experienced therapists may be touched by something in the kind of patient we are considering that calls out in a special way his capabilities for enthusiasm, care, devotion and hope. However this may be, there are many differing kinds of human condition, and not all are treatable by analytic methods. We are, however, these days witnessing the rise of a plethora of psychotherapeutic methods. Most of them can, in some way, be effective in meeting different and special kinds of therapeutic need – or at least in alleviating urgent pain. It can, however, only be desirable that some mutual understanding and sense of the significance of each such contribution within a general context should be fostered. Analytical psychology certainly supports this as a general desideratum. To achieve this, rigorous observation is needed, and it is to be hoped that the present book will make a contribution to increased consciousness in this field.

Person-Centred Therapy (Brian Thorne)

After nearly sixteen years as a person-centred therapist, I am drawn to what seems to me the wholly logical conclusion that the limitations of the approach are a reflection of my own limitations as a human being. As these limitations have not been constant over time, and as, presumably, they differ from those of other person-centred practitioners, I am sceptical about the usefulness of debating the limitations of the approach in any generalized fashion. I am however, intrigued by the issue because it throws considerable light on my own personality and its shortcomings.

Rogers himself reflected on the matter some years ago when he gave a recorded interview to Susan Bearn of the magazine *Psychology Today* (1975). He referred then to the largest research project he had ever supervised, which was an elaborate investigation of the effect of psychotherapy on schizophrenics. The results of that research, said Rogers, were mildly positive in so far as the person-centred therapists were of help in reducing the measures of schizophrenic quality in those patients involved in the project despite the fact that most of these had been hospitalized for a lengthy period of time. It was clear, however, that although the patients had profited, the degree of benefit was not nearly as great as that which

Rogers and his colleagues were accustomed to expect in clients presenting for therapy at clinics or counselling offices. During the interview Rogers offered the opinion that psychotherapy of any kind, including person-centred therapy, is probably of the greatest help to the people who are closest to a reasonable adjustment to life. As I see it, however, it would have been equally reasonable to conclude that person-centred therapists were only mildly effective with long-term schizophrenics because such people are immensely difficult to accept and to understand and because they place enormous demands on the therapist's own ability to conduct himself authentically. In other words, the fault – if fault it is – might well lie not with the approach but with the practitioner's ability to embody and apply the approach consistently and effectively.

I recall from my first year as a therapist a young female client who within twenty minutes evoked in me such rage that I was deprived of all ability to accept her or empathize with her. I was certainly genuine enough in so far as I experienced almost uncontrollable anger and yelled at her to get out of my room and never return. Although she subsequently did come back, to consult a colleague, I can scarcely boast that she constituted a therapeutic triumph for me as a fledgling person-centred therapist. I am aware now, however, that her attitude towards me in those brief twenty minutes was one of contempt, both for me as a person and for the therapy which I professed to practise. She demanded to be told what to do and rapidly concluded that I was totally incapable of being the expert she felt I ought to be. At that stage of my life I was utterly incapable of tolerating such scorn and immediately felt threatened and undermined; today, I feel reasonably confident that I could understand and accept her desperate need for direction and gently offer her the acceptance which might then have made it possible for us to work constructively together. The unfavourable outcome of the actual interview I had with her in 1968 was the direct result of the combination of her attitude and the shakiness of my own self-esteem.

Some years ago, to take another example, I often felt unnerved and anxious in the presence of a client who was expressing a veiled or direct intention to commit suicide. Filled with fear about my own responsibility, I would quickly start thinking of psychiatric help, hospitalization or some other dramatic intervention. Such anxiety on my part made it almost impossible to listen to the client and certainly rendered empathic understanding at any depth quite impossible. Nowadays I am not anxious to the same degree, and discover that suicidal clients often find it incredibly supportive to be understood and not condemned, to be with a therapist who is prepared to go with them into the despair and to stay there until they no longer feel alone; in short, I often now find it possible to enter into communion with a suicidal person, and believe that this is the most effective way of drawing the sting from self-destructive thoughts. After all, interventive ways of preventing suicide do not really prevent it, as is clear from the large number of people who actually commit suicide in hospital.

The thesis that the limitations of the approach lie in the extreme demands it places on the practitioner rather than in the approach *per se* finds confirmation in the extensive research work performed by Reinhard Tausch and his colleagues at Hamburg University (Tausch 1975). They found that there was no relationship between therapeutic success and the symptoms or problem behaviour that clients presented; success seemed rather to be related to the attitudinal climate established between client and therapist. Clearly in most instances the creation of this climate will depend upon the ability of the therapist to offer the core conditions of acceptance, empathy and genuineness (this, in turn, depending on the level of his self-acceptance and ability to be other-directed). There will, however, be occasions when the attitudinal stance of the client is such that the establishing of the necessary climate will be unlikely or seemingly impossible. Such a stance is most likely to occur when the client is highly authoritarian in outlook and seeks direction from external experts (my female client of 1968 fell into this category, although she was was young enough to find rapid liberation from it if I had not been so callow), or when the client is accustomed to find answers to problems by the rigidly disciplined exercise of the intellect through logical reasoning. This is not to suggest that the person-centred approach is anti-intellectual, but it does assume in the client a willingness to offer parity of esteem to the worlds of feeling and intuition. It has seemed to me, in passing, that traditional psychoanalysis often commends itself initially to high-flying academics or intellectuals because of the beauty of its conceptual framework and the ease with which it lends itself to a rational, historical approach. This is not of course, to pass unfavourable judgement on the efficacy of analysis, nor on what happens to such clients once they are launched upon analytical therapy.

One final thought is prompted by the findings of the recent psychotherapy meta-analysis of Smith, Glass and Miller (1980). This immense research undertaking (which concluded that psychotherapy, whether it be verbal or behavioural, psychodynamic, person-centred or systematic, is beneficial, consistently so and in many different ways) revealed that person-centred therapy is, as one might hope to expect, particularly successful in improving a client's self-esteem. It is, however, according to this research, less powerful in promoting behavioural change. For my own part, I like to feel that even this is perhaps not a limitation; it could, after all, be a response to that ancient prayer which asks for the serenity to accept the things we cannot change, the courage to change the things we can and the wisdom to know the difference.

Personal Construct Therapy (Fay Fransella)

It is interesting to ask oneself why there should be limitations to things. The answer seems to go along the lines that nothing is perfect, that everything has faults and that this is human. It is part of the Protestant ethic that to err is human and the only thing without flaws is the Almighty. So when one says that, to date, the limitations of personal construct psychotherapy are not apparent, one is seen to be doing the unforgivable: claiming it has divine qualities (not in so many words of course, but the implication seems to be there). From this same line of thought comes the dictum 'Something that explains everything explains nothing'. It is a dictum that is somewhat difficult to understand – at least, to me.

To say that personal construct psychotherapy has no obvious limitations does not mean that it explains everything and therefore nothing. It may well have an explanation for everything *within the context of helping the human being*, but it makes no claim to explain earthquakes, the movements of the stars or the flow of electric current along a neurone –at least, I do not think it does, yet. But there are now amazing ideas coming from physics which suggest, for instance, that electrons construe! However, these can be regarded as outside the range of convenience of personal construct psychotherapy (and its whole psychology, for that matter) for the time being at least.

One of the reasons for the absence of limitations is the very abstract level at which the theory is pitched. It is far more a metatheory than any other in psychology, and it is certainly a more abstract theory about psychotherapy than any other. Because of its abstract nature it can subsume most other approaches: these are different ways of looking at human distress and ways of alleviating that distress. There is one great advantage to having a metatheoretical system: it provides a framework for designing research which gets away from the 'brand A versus brand B' variety: you look instead at the 'process' of change and why a particular technique is useful for that particular person at that particular time.

For limitations we must therefore look at the practitioners rather than at the practice. There are three main limitations here, I believe. One is that, because of the very nature of this type of therapy, the personal construct therapist has to be a person who is not threatened by *giving over total control to the client* at some stage, by which I mean being willing to allow his own construing to be put completely on one side while they try to 'get inside' the client's world. This is *not* just a cognitive exercise, but an experiential one: it is an exercise in which, for a few moments, the distance between the client and therapist is reduced to approaching nil.

The second is also to do with control, but of a different sort. *The therapist does not have a cookbook*; he does not have the answers. His ability to subsume the client's ways of construing the world may give him guide-lines, but the client has all the answers in the long run. It was no idle comment when Kelly called his approach 'the psychology of the unknown'. With construing being about anticipations and behaviour being the testing out of these anticipations, the therapist has to be able to tolerate a considerable amount of uncertainty.

The third limitation of therapists is related to control and uncertainty, and is to do with creativity and aggressiveness. The personal construct therapist *has to be creative*, for, having no cookbook, he has to create the therapy and the techniques. There are, of course, some techniques which Kelly suggested and some that have been described since then, but even in the case of the self characterization the therapist needs a creative streak to be able to get the most out of it. Aggression, defined by Kelly as the active elaboration of the construing system, is as much a necessary characteristic of the therapist and goes with being creative.

Where the limitations of practitioners are most obvious is in areas where language cannot be used as the prime mode of interaction and communication. Finding ways of getting into the personal worlds of those who are dysphasic, mentally handicapped or autistic stretches most therapists to their limits – but some are trying. The theory, of course, has no problem here.

Existential Therapy (Emmy van Deurzen-Smith)

The philosophical nature of the existential approach is at the core of its strengths and at the same time determines its limitations.

Commitment

This way of working can only be effective with clients who are motivated to address life issues seriously. Those clients who want to tackle a specific symptom without considering the inner attitudes related to the creation of that symptom will probably not be helped by this method. No specific techniques are proposed to overcome symptoms in this exclusive way, and no technique is proposed to overcome the initial resistance to uncovering personal attitudes and values. Clients are expected to come to existential therapy with the firm intention of examining assumptions and prejudices, conflicts and ideals as honestly as possible. Without that sustained intention, existential therapy is likely to be ineffective.

As the client is expected to be a co-worker with full commitment to the therapeutic process as described above, the therapist is never prepared to force-feed the client back to life. The saying 'You can lead a horse to water, but you cannot make him drink' illustrates the boundaries of the existential way of working particularly well. It is with existential therapy as with existence: you have to commit yourself to it to make it work.

The implications of this are that people cannot be referred by prescription; the method can only be made available to those who wish to explore their problems in living in this way.

Change

It follows from this that the approach is unsuitable for use as a method for readjustment. It is unlikely that the result of existential therapy will be that of fitting the person back into the *status quo*. More likely, a person who begins to examine and face his life in this way will tend to want to make changes in accordance with the priorities that are discovered under the dust of previous self-deception. This may have ideological or political implications.

Paradoxically, the approach is sometimes considered as being limited by its potential to make people accept or come to terms with certain situations or facts that they might otherwise have evaded or rejected. For example, the concept of internal freedom allows people to come to terms with pressures that would have seemed unacceptable if external freedom had been the main goal. The concept of autonomy might make the client willing to establish or maintain a relationship, where a former desire for independence made this a threat. The concept of commitment might make the client willing to die or live for a cause that seemed insignificant as long as life was considered less carefully. Bringing one's life in line with one's inner values may mean going against the mainstream and the established situation; it may also mean adapting to what some would consider external pressures or limitations.

Evaluation

This brings us to considering the limitations of the approach in terms of evaluation. As the goal of existential therapy is always internally determined by the client, the assessment of the outcome of therapy can only be done by the client herself. No one, other than the client, can decide whether the fact that she has stopped smoking, got married, visited Wales on holiday or remained unemployed is an expression of health or unhealth, whether it shows that the therapy has been successful or not. Ultimately all that matters is the client's ability to evaluate for herself how consistent she is being with her inner self, how authentically she is living. There is no possibility of quantifying this search for quality. This makes the approach less accessible for objective evaluation, which may be considered a limitation by some.

In the same way, the therapist's consistency with her own inner values and professional criteria which rests on this same continuous, evaluative inner process would be contradicted by any external evaluation procedures that aimed at standardization. This makes it undesirable to videotape therapy sessions regularly for instance, as this could easily shift the focus of evaluation from an internal to an external point of reference. It is considered that meaning can never be completely caught by images, gestures or words, but only by reference to an inner source of understanding and comprehension – meaning can certainly not be reached by conformity to certain ways of behaving, speaking or relating.

Communication

The verbal nature of this method is another limitation worth considering. As with most forms of psychotherapy, the emphasis is on insight through talking about problems, which limits its application to work with people who are capable of such verbal expression and reflection. However, because the existential approach favours the use of a vocabulary that is as close to the client's inner frame of reference as possible, this makes it feasible to communicate symbolically.

Gestures, neologisms, pieces of music, drawings and dream symbols may all be used as long as the client initiates this process and providing their underlying meaning is explored and comprehended. It is therefore possible to work existentially wherever meaning is expressed in some way.

The real limitation lies where talk about meaning replaces meaning itself and empty philosophical discussions replace true contact. To guard against this danger the existential method needs to re-invent its own process at each session rather than become ossified in jargon or technique. Ultimately, the limitations of this approach will therefore be those of each existential therapist and her client at each session, rather than exclusively those that the method as such brings with it.

Gestalt Therapy (Faye Page)

Gestalt therapy, developed by Fritz Perls, is one of the most vigorous and exciting therapies practised today. It offers a theory and techniques that focus on the unity and wholeness within an individual and in her ongoing interaction with her environment.

Perls' interest was more in process than in content, practice rather than theory. He did not present his theory in a conventional, organized form and his writings are sometimes abstruse:

> Clearly, Perls addresses aspects of highly complex human experience. His writing, when followed closely, leads the reader on a valuable journey of insights about the commonplace and the sublime. But his thinking is often

difficult to follow, and virtually impossible to validate in an experimental setting. This does not diminish its value; it simply makes it difficult to attract the attention of scientists who must eventually pass judgement on it (Corsini and Marsella 1983).

Clinebell (1981) observes that there are a number of weaknesses in Gestalt therapy which he attributes to the 'reductionistic elements in Perls' thought'. Perls dismissed all moral values as 'shouldisms' without considering that some values are essential for living with ourselves and other people. He reduced intellectual activity to intellectualizing and rationalizing 'mind games', whereas understanding is necessary for insight, decision-making, etc. and can assist in initiating change. Perls' emphasis on the extreme side of self-responsibility promotes a position of ultra-individualism and denies the concept of social responsibility. Dependency and interdependency are necessary in order to change ourselves or our society.

Perhaps it is not so much in the theory, but in those who use it that the limitations are seen. Enwright, who studied with Perls and knew him for many years, when interviewed by Kogan (1976), offers some observations concerning the practice of Gestalt therapy. He notes that Perls had difficulty in maintaining close relationships and always needed to be the centre of attention. Enwright says these 'are the two flaws in the way that Fritz manifested Gestalt, and both are in the process of being redeemed now. But a lot of people picked up both of those. Picked up the showmanship. Dependence is a fact of life, and the massive putdown of that by gestaltists is a perversion.'

For the effective practice of Gestalt therapy as for any therapy, it is necessary for the therapist not only to have skill and experience in its use but also knowledge and understanding of both its applications and limitations. There is much written today on the theory and practice of psychotherapies, but little on their limitations. This is also the case with Gestalt therapy. An exception is Shepherd's (1972) article in which she says: 'Probably the most effective application of Gestalt techniques (or any other therapeutic techniques) comes with personal therapeutic experiences gained in professional training workshops and work with competent therapists and supervisors.' With inadequately trained or untrained practitioners, there is the possibility that Gestalt therapy could become extremely authoritarian and used as a vehicle for 'power trips'.

Gestalt, like most psychotherapies, is generally appropriate for people who can function in society, if only in a limited or inconsistent way. Gestalt therapy is not advised, without certain provisions, for psychotic people who have little contact with reality or with those whose difficulties are in 'acting out' or sociopathic behaviours. One provision is that of a long-term therapy commitment. Another is that work in this area requires thorough knowledge, training and experience of severely disturbed individuals, and some degree of back-up is usually desirable.

The use of Gestalt therapy can sometimes be limited by the person's attitude toward therapy. She may not be willing or able to participate. The different systems, such as family, work and philosophical or religious beliefs, that could be affected by full involvement in Gestalt therapy need careful consideration, as does the amount and degree of change that these systems will tolerate.

Gestalt therapy is not widely known in Britain's psychiatric establishments, which tend to rely on the traditional concepts of therapy. There are limitations when a Gestalt therapist functions as part of an interdisciplinary team, which might include a psychiatrist, nurse, social worker and occupational therapist. The degree of limitation depends on the models, goals, etc. each member has and the co-operation among team members: for example, if a medical model is predominant, then the administration of drugs and or electroconvulsive therapy limits the extent and effectiveness of Gestalt therapy.

Paradoxical though it may be, the result of effective Gestalt therapy could itself hold limitations for certain individuals. Shepherd (1972) states:

> The consequences of successful Gestalt therapy may be that by teaching the patient to be more genuinely in touch with himself, he will experience more dissatisfaction with conventional goals and relationships, with the hypocrisy and pretence of much social interaction, and may experience the pain of seeing the deficiencies and destructiveness of many social and cultural forces and institutions. Simply stated, extensive experience with Gestalt therapy will likely make patients more unfit for or unadjusted to contemporary society. However, at the same time, they may hopefully be more motivated to work toward changing the world into a more compassionate and productive milieu in which human beings can develop, work, and enjoy their full humanness.

Transactional Analysis (Laurence Collinson)

In my view, there is only one base to which a counsellor or therapist working as a transactional analyst can return for renewal, refreshment, information, or 'enlightenment', and that is the canon of Eric Berne's books and the books and ideas of his direct followers. However simple or however profound his subject-matter, Berne wrote of it with wisdom, humanity, and a dry, irreverent wit. His approach to language was much the same as his approach to psychotherapy: intelligent, creative and illuminating.

I am not suggesting that Berne was beyond criticism; he was a man of his time, albeit a brilliant one, and inevitably subject to the influences of his time. In a period significant for its changing attitudes toward the gender roles of women and men and its recognition that homosexuality was simply a variation on statistical norms (as well as a scapegoat target for those insecure in their own heterosexuality), Berne, despite his radical turnabout in regard to psychoanalysis, was still taking much Freudian – and particularly post-Freudian – doctrine as axiomatic. It might be said that just as many psychoanalysts since Freud have hardened his theories into 'fact' and thus treat their patients according to a rigid set of 'how to' rules, so many transactional analysts adhere to 'rules' derived from Berne by TA enthusiasts and made into a dogma that has already split TA into 'schools', some of which add to the usefulness of TA and some of which detract from it. Berne, for instance, conceived the idea of the Parent, Adult and Child ego states and, after a time, contributed to the development of this theory by positing the existence of the three ego states within each main ego state: as for example, the Parent in the Child, the Adult in the Child, and the Child in the Child. The 'larger' ego states are generally expressed as P2, A2, and C2, while the ego states within each ego state are known as P1, A1, and C1. Difficulties in distinguishing between ego-state structure and ego-state function have been inherent in TA since its beginning; but now there are theorists who go further and attempt to identify ego states within ego states within ego states, etc., which I personally find confusing.

However engrossing or even useful this may be to a therapist with a strong 'Try hard' driver, it serves little if any practical purpose; all it does in the long run is to add mystification to a psychotherapy that Berne intended to be without mystification. And it goes against Berne's adherence to efficient models based on the principle of scientific economy, best known in English as 'Occam's razor'.

In my work I experience a dilemma that I never expected would arise for me, and that is TA's de-emphasis – in practice, if not always in theory – on the unconscious. Berne (1973) writes in *What Do You Say After You*

Say Hello? 'there is no proscription against the script analyst dealing with unconscious material . . . if he is equipped to do so. And he will do so, because, of course, it is these very experiences which form the basic protocol for the script.' He also says, prior to the above, that 'Script analysts believe in the unconscious, but they emphasise the conscious when dealing with patients for whom orthodox psychoanalysis is more or less unsuitable . . .' When I first began using TA, I tended – as indeed did most of the therapists and trainers with whom I worked as well as a large body of TA literature – to dismiss the unconscious aspects of treatment; I spoke of certain matters as simply being 'out of awareness' at the present moment. It now seems to me important to stress – to myself, at least – that the client's unconscious, irrespective of whether I call it Freud's 'unconscious' (without the additional infrastructure of id, ego, and super-ego), an altered state of conscious, a trance induction or right-brain function, is, except for a few less salient problems in everyday living that can be resolved by means of logic or brainstorming, an essential element in change; and that while TA analyses, whether script, game, transactional or structural, give comparatively swift and easy access to awareness and understanding, the therapist's ability to 'cure' (that is, to help the client to greater autonomy or develop positive attitudes toward his or her script or belief system) is the more difficult aspect of treatment and requires the co-operation of the unconscious – which is not such a contradiction in terms as it might at first appear. There are few individual TA practitioners who offer guide-lines about treatment processes – the Gouldings, the Lanktons, Muriel James, Graham Barnes, and Richard Erskine, for example, do so – but TA *per se* does not. And treatment seems usually to involve the use of other kinds of therapy or resources; indeed, one of TA's greatest advantages is its flexibility to incorporate other methods while it itself provides the necessary basis of understanding, awareness and enlightenment.

The limitations described above are the more important ones for me personally. There are others, however. One of them – the matter-of-fact language – is usually regarded as a virtue. This very simplicity, unfortunately, has led many people to believe that their knowledge and comprehension of the basic concepts is sufficient to allow them to act as TA trainers or therapists without undertaking to obtain the skills involved in the practice of *any* method, and which require time-consuming and committed study.

Another criticism levelled at TA is that it can be used manipulatively, particularly in personal relationships where one of the persons knows TA and uses it to obtain an unfair advantage over the other(s) in the relationship. Since I believe that in relationships it is impossible, without either a contract (as in an employer-employee situation) or unconscious collusion (as with lovers or partners), *not* to manipulate, actively or passively, I do not feel any great concern about this aspect of TA. All communication is an attempt to manipulate; as, indeed, is all therapy, including the so-called 'non-directive' methods of psychoanalysis and person-centred therapy. What I do see as being of consequence here are the ethics of those using TA: that is, the intended result of their attempted manipulation. It does not seem to me to be ethical, for example, to train managerial staff in industry to use TA if the explicit or implicit aim is to try to keep the workers happy; the workers need also to learn TA. On the other hand, I believe it valuable to instruct airline staff in the use of TA when the function of doing so is to help allay the passengers' fears about flying and any traumatic event that happens en route.

I object also to the notion of TA as a universal panacea; it then becomes something of a religion with evangelists and proselytes. The missionary zeal with which someone newly enthusiastic about TA tries to convert others often has the opposite effect. One of the reasons, I think, that Thomas Harris's *I'm OK – You're OK* became a continual best seller is its attempt to present TA as a solution to the world's ills; and that is one of the reasons I do not recommend it to beginners.

The last, but not least, limitation that I have space to deal with is the language of TA concepts, which may be categorized by those who like it as 'colloquial' and by those who dislike it as 'jargon'. The language, which Berne created in order to help the layman understand his own therapy, is frequently used to avoid accepting responsibility. Although in my work I ask clients to learn the TA concepts and the terminology, I customarily ask clients to use the words only as a last resort if they have difficulty in expressing themselves more personally. I use the words myself primarily as a form of shorthand in explaining and/or diagramming the problems that the client brings to the session.

Rational-Emotive Therapy (Windy Dryden)

I have been practising rational-emotive therapy now for over seven years in a variety of settings. I have worked in a) a university counselling service, b) a general practice, c) a local marriage guidance council and d) a private practice. I have seen, in these settings, a wide range of moderately to severely disturbed individuals who were deemed to be able to benefit from weekly counselling or psychotherapy. While I do not have any hard data to substantiate the point, I have found rational-emotive therapy to be a highly effective method of individual psychotherapy with a wide range of client problems.

However, I have of course had my therapeutic failures, and I would like to outline some of the factors that in my opinion have accounted for these failures. I will use Bordin's (1979) useful concept of the therapeutic working alliance as a framework in this respect (see Chapter 10 for a fuller account of this concept).

Goals

I have generally been unsuccessful with clients who have devoutly clung to goals where changes in other people were desired. (In this regard, I have also failed to involve these others in therapy.) I have not been able to show or to persuade these clients that they make themselves emotionally disturbed and that they ought to work to change themselves before attempting to negotiate changes in their relationships with others. It is the devoutness of their beliefs which seems to me to be the problem here.

Bonds

Unlike the majority of therapists of my acquaintance, I do not regard the relationship between therapist and client to be the *sine qua non* of effective therapy. I strive to accept my clients as fallible human beings and am prepared to work concertedly to help them overcome their problems, but do not endeavour to form very close, warm relationships with them. In the main, my clients do not appear to want such a relationship with me (preferring to become close and intimate with their significant others). However, occasionally I get clients who do wish to become (non-sexually) intimate with me. Some of these clients (who devoutly believe they need my love) leave therapy disappointed after I have failed either to get them to give up their dire need for love or to give them what they think they need.

Tasks

As Bordin (1979) has noted, every therapeutic method requires clients to fulfil various tasks if therapy is to be successful. (I have outlined what these tasks are with respect to RET in Chapter 10.) In my experience, clients who are diligent in performing these tasks generally have a positive therapeutic outcome with RET, while those who steadfastly refuse to *work* towards helping themselves outside therapy generally do less well or are therapeutic failures.

It may of course be that I am practising RET ineptly and that these failures are due to my poor skills rather than any other factor. Ellis (1983), however, has recently published some interesting data which tend to corroborate my own therapeutic experiences in this respect. He chose fifty of his clients who were seen in individual and/or group RET and were rated by him, and where appropriate by his associate group therapist, as 'failures'. In some ways, this group consisted of fairly ideal RET clients in that they were individuals of

> above average or of superior intelligence (in my judgement and that of their other group therapist); (2) who seemed really to understand RET and who were often effective (especially in group therapy) in helping others to learn and use it; (3) who in some ways made therapeutic progress and felt that they benefited by having RET but who still retained one or more serious presenting symptoms, such as severe depression, acute anxiety, overwhelming hostility, or extreme lack of self-discipline; and (4) who had at least one year of individual and/or group RET sessions, and sometimes considerably more.

This group was compared to clients who were selected on the same four criteria but who seemed to benefit greatly from RET. While a complete account of this study – which, of course, has its methodological flaws – can be found in Ellis (1983), the following results are most pertinent:

> 1. In its cognitive aspects, RET ... emphasizes the persistent use of reason, logic, and the scientific method to uproot clients' irrational beliefs. Consequently, it ideally requires intelligence, concentration, and high-level, consistent cognitive self-disputation and self-persuasion. These therapeutic behaviours would tend to be disrupted or blocked by extreme disturbance, by lack of organization, by grandiosity, by organic disruption, and by refusal to do RET-type disputing or irrational ideas.

All these characteristics proved to be present in significantly more failures than in those clients who responded favorably to RET.

2. RET also, to be quite successful, involves clients' forcefully and emotively changing their beliefs and actions, and their being stubbornly determined to accept responsibility for their own inappropriate feelings and to vigorously work at changing these feelings (Ellis & Abrahms 1978; Ellis & Whiteley 1979). But the failure clients in this study were significantly more angry than those who responded well to RET; more of them were severely depressed and inactive, they were more often grandiose, and they were more frequently stubbornly resistant and rebellious. All these characteristics would presumably tend to interfere with the kind of emotive processes and changes that RET espouses.

3. RET strongly advocates that clients, in order to improve, do in vivo activity homework assignments, deliberately force themselves to engage in many painful activities until they become familiar and unpainful, and notably work and practice its multimodal techniques. But the group of clients who signally failed in this study showed abysmally low frustration tolerance, had serious behavioral addictions, led disorganized lives, refrained from doing their activity homework assignments, were more frequently psychotic and generally refused to work at therapy. All these characteristics, which were found significantly more frequently than were found in the clients who responded quite well to RET, would tend to interfere with the behavioral methods of RET.

Thus it appears from the above analysis that the old adage of psychotherapy applies to RET: namely that clients who could most use therapy are precisely those individuals whose disturbance interferes with their benefiting from it.

It is worth noting that RET can be successful with clients with lower intelligence as long as the therapist is flexible enough to modify his or her strategies and interventions with such clients. In addition, RET can be practised ineffectively, and factors opposite to those others in Chapter 10 (pages 247–248) are likely to be operative in this respect.

At present, it is not known whether clients who 'fail' with RET are likely to benefit more from other therapies. Hopefully, we will have some data on this issue before too long to ensure that such clients get appropriate help on grounds other than 'trial and error'.

Behavioural Psychotherapy (Dougal Mackay)

Behavioural psychotherapy has traditionally emphasized the importance of adopting a 'scientific' stance in relation to the study and amelioration of psychological disturbance. Its theoretical models are clearly presented in postulate form so that they may be easily subjected to experimental investigation. The major techniques have been carefully evaluated through properly controlled outcome studies in order that clinicians should employ the most cost-effective procedures. The behavioural analysis, which involves the systematic testing out of empirically derived hypotheses, allows little room for clinical speculation or therapist intuition. In these respects, the behavioural model differs significantly from those approaches to psychotherapy which have emanated from the consulting room as opposed to the laboratory.

Although such a close adherence to scientific methodology is undoubtedly a major strength of this model, it can also be seen as a limiting factor. Human experiences and behaviour cannot always be broken down easily into stimulus–response–reinforcement terms, even if cognitions are included in these categories. Consequently, on those occasions when the behavioural analysis fails to demonstrate a readily identifiable pattern of events, the therapist has little to offer but techniques on a trial-and-error basis. This is rarely successful and is often demoralizing for the client. A second limitation of this avowedly reductionist approach is that it fails to provide the clinician with a clear set of guide-lines as to the particular problems he should focus on and the order in which they should be tackled; in contrast to the psychoanalytic models, behavioural psychotherapy lacks a schema for making sense of the balance and interplay of the various aspects of the individual's functioning. Another deficiency of the model is that thoughts and feelings are generally worked with only in so far as they are related to the target behaviours. To explore these covert experiences at a deeper level would be to deviate too far from the fundamental principle of objectivity wherever possible. Finally, by attempting to make the client's internal and external environments more orderly and controllable, the therapist may well be depriving him of the opportunity for growth; a structure which helps one individual to contain strong feelings may well block the personal development of another. These deficiencies can be seen in the following characteristics of the behavioural model.

The cross-sectional approach to the analysis of behaviour

A fundamental assumption of this model is that behaviour is always orderly: in other words, given a thorough knowledge of an individual's past learning history, it should be possible to predict the circumstances under which he will perform a particular response. The initial task facing the clinician is therefore to isolate the stimuli which act as triggers for the target behaviour and to identify the reinforcers which are maintaining it. Hypotheses which emerge from this can then be tested out by analysing critical episodes from the past in a similar fashion. In this way, the relevant antecedents and consequences can be teased out. Failure to detect a recognisable pattern is regarded as evidence that the assessment procedure is incomplete and that more data should be collected.

In the case of maladaptive emotional reactions, it is now generally accepted that cognitions play a significant triggering function and that information concerning the individual's self-statements must be collected. It follows that the clinician must succeed in unearthing the thoughts or images which precipitate the affective response if he is to design an appropriate treatment programme. However, according to Zajonc (1980), there is considerable clinical evidence that emotional responses are often more fundamental, rapid and, indeed, quite independent of cold cognitive appraisals. One implication of this proposal is that the clinician who is concerned to isolate the external events and inappropriate thoughts which trigger off intense feelings will often search in vain.

This issue has also been taken up by Rachman (1980) in his contro-versial paper on 'emotional processing'. He argues that if an emotional disturbance is not absorbed satisfactorily, it will manifest itself periodically through such channels as nightmares, pressure of talk, irritability and impulsive behaviour. An interesting aspect of Rachman's thesis is that, although he uses cognitive and behavioural terms throughout, he con-stantly refers to Freud's treatment of the celebrated case, Anna O., to illustrate his points! Of particular importance here is the implicit notion that the conventional behavioural analysis would be unable to account for data of this kind: in other words, the assumption that all behaviour can be broken down into stimulus–response–reinforcement sequences must be seen to be questionable in the light of this argument.

Problem behaviours as discrete psychological entities

Traditional behaviour therapists took the view that each response in the individual's repertoire has its own particular antecedents and consequences and can therefore be worked with in isolation. This assumption has two implications: first, the removal of an unwanted 'symptom' should have little effect on other aspects of the individual's psychological functioning;

and second, the order in which the various problem behaviours are tackled should be immaterial. Contemporary behavioural psychotherapists are more aware of the interplay between different response patterns and use the behavioural analysis to design programmes which will minimize the risk of 'resistance' or 'symptom substitution'. However, according to Fensterheim and Glazer (1983), even the more sophisticated behavioural model pays insufficient attention to the biological and intrapsychic context within which the problem behaviour developed. They argue that the experienced behavioural psychotherapist, who has little understanding of psychodynamic concepts, will often make the mistake of choosing an inappropriate target or working on problems in the wrong order: 'While it is true that there are rules for behavioural analysis, there are no rules for determining which behaviors to analyze.'

Cognitions as discriminative stimuli

Cognitive behaviour modification is based on the assumption that emotions and behaviour are controlled, to a significant degree, by the client's self-statements. It follows from this that if he can be trained to provide himself with more appropriate messages, he will cope more effectively with stress, obstacles, and setbacks. Behavioural psychotherapists, however, do not concern themselves with the reasons why such self-defeating strategies evolved in the first place. By contrast, cognitive therapists such as Beck et al. (1979) regard these 'automatic thoughts' as indicators of the irrational primary assumptions which lie at the core of the distressed individual's personality. It follows from this model that unless these assumptions can be modified the client will continue to generate unhelpful self-statements in the future. By his reluctance to work with the individual's conceptual system in a holistic fashion the behavioural psychotherapist is unlikely to bring about a fundamental change in the way in which the client perceives his world.

The reason for this is clear. Behaviourist philosophy has always emphasized the importance of objectivity and has eschewed such hypothetical constructs as attitudes, beliefs and assumptions. To concede that covert events have a significant influence on behaviour was a major break with tradition. To go further and postulate how cognitions might be organized would be to abandon the principles of objectivity which lie at the core of this approach.

Controllability through the provision of structure

Behavioural techniques can be seen as structured learning experiences which enable the client to gain more control over events in both his internal and external environments. They are employed by the therapist as the most cost-effective methods available for eliminating or reducing psychological distress. In other words, it is tacitly assumed in behavioural psychotherapy that such emotional states as anxiety, anger and depression are aversive experiences which must be brought under control as quickly as possible. However, this assumption is open to question: in certain cases it could be argued that the individual is experiencing distress because he is undergoing a change process which might ultimately be in his best interests to continue with. Under these circumstances, to help him to contain these feelings by devising a coping strategy would be to interfere with his growth as a person.

The therapist as a research supervisor

Although contemporary behavioural psychotherapists no longer administer standard techniques in a mechanistic fashion, they are still influenced to a significant degree by the experimental model which underlies their approach. As Fensterheim and Glazer (1983) point out: 'Emphasis on procedure may also lead to the demand that the patient conform to our style of doing things, distracting us from the need to tailor the treatment situation so that the patient can best function.' For example, the client who makes it clear during a particular session that he is not motivated that day to work within the terms of the agreed contract tends to be regarded as 'difficult' or 'manipulative'. However, his apparent non-compliance may be a deliberate or unconscious desire to attempt to re-define his problem or to explore different avenues towards change; the therapist who insists on following the treatment programme, at least until the review session, may be depriving his client of the opportunity to explore such important issues. With an approach which emphasizes targets, contracts and procedures, this is always a risk, regardless of the experience and personal qualities of the clinician.

From what has been said it is clear that the laboratory model of human behaviour has its deficiencies as well as its strengths. Moreover, behavioural psychotherapy, no matter how skilfully or humanely it is applied, can tighten when it should loosen and block when it should free. It is the responsibility of the individual clinician to recognize these dangers and be prepared to offer the client a different kind of help when his problems lie outside the range of this approach.

References

Beck A T, Rush A J, Shaw B F, Emery G (1979) *Cognitive Therapy of Depression*, Wiley, New York

Berne E (1973) *What Do You Say After You Say Hello?*, Bantam, New York, pp. 400, 404

Bordin E S (1979) The generalizability of the psychoanalytic concept of the working alliance, *Psychotherapy: Theory, Research and Practice 16(3)*: 252–260

Clinebell H (1981) *Contemporary Growth Therapies: Resources for Actualizing Human Wholeness*, Abingdon, Nashville, Tenn., p.179

Corsini R J, Marsella A J (1983) *Personality Theories, Research, Assessment*, Peacock, Itasca, Ill., p. 376

Edwards A (1983) Research studies in the problems of assessment, *Journal of Analytical Psychology 28*: 299–311

Ellis A (1983) 'Failures in rational-emotive therapy' in Foa E B and Emmelkamp P M G (eds.) *Failures in Behaviour Therapy*, Wiley, New York, pp. 160, 165

Ellis A, Abrahms E (1978) *Brief Psychotherapy in Medical and Health Practice*, Springer, New York

Ellis A, Whiteley J M (eds.) (1979) *Theoretical and Empirical Foundations of Rational-Emotive Therapy*, Brooks/Cole, Monterey, Cal.

Fensterheim H, Glazer H I (eds.) (1983) *Behavioral Psychotherapy: Basic Principles and Case Studies in an Integrative Clinical Model*, Brunner/Mazel, New York pp. 12, 18

Greenson R R (1967) *The Technique and Practice of Psychoanalysis*, Hogarth, London

Kogan J (1976) 'Perspectives: Interviews with James Simkin and John Enwright' in Hatcher C and Himelstein P (eds.) *The Handbook of Gestalt Therapy*, Jason Aronson, New York, p. 750

Rachman S (1980) Emotional processing, *Behaviour Research and Therapy 18*: 51–60

Rogers C R (1975) 'Client-centered Therapy,, cassette recording of interview with Susan Bearn, *Psychology Today* series

Shepherd I L (1972) 'Limitations and cautions in the gestalt approach' in Fagan J and Shepherd I L (eds.) *Gestalt Therapy Now*, Penguin, Harmondsworth, pp. 264, 269

Smith M L, Glass G V and Miller T I (1980) *The Benefits of Psychotherapy*, Johns Hopkins University Press, Baltimore.

Tausch R (1975) Ergebnisse und Prozesse der klientenzentrierten Gesprächspsychotherapie bei 550 Klienten und 115 Psychotherapeuten. Eine Zusammenfassung des Hamburger Forschungsprojektes, *Zeitschrift für Praktische Psychologie 13*: 293–307

Zajonc R (1980) Feeling and thinking, *American Psychologist 35*: 151–175

Chapter 14 Issues in the Eclectic Practice of Individual Therapy

Windy Dryden

Introduction

So far in this book, specific schools of therapy have been presented and discussed. However, an increasing number of therapists describe themselves as 'eclectic' (Garfield and Kurtz 1977), that is to say they claim to choose what appears to be best from diverse therapeutic sources, systems and styles. As Garfield (1982) has noted, if eclectic therapists indeed choose what appears to be best, it is difficult to criticize them. However, is this what they actually do? In their study of 154 eclectic psychologists, Garfield and Kurtz (1977) found that 145 of them used thirty-two different combinations drawn from a wide range of therapeutic schools. Most combinations seemed to be blended and employed in idiosyncratic fashion; therefore when therapists describe themselves as eclectic they do not adequately communicate to others what they actually do in therapy sessions.

The aim of this chapter is to discuss the pertinent issues involved in the eclectic practice of individual therapy. This will serve to set the scene for the in-depth presentation of two types of eclecticism in the following two chapters.

Eclectic Therapy: Its Prevalence and Practitioners

Since there is a dearth of research carried out into the practices and self-descriptions of British therapists, a consideration of American research on this issue is again in order. Whereas an earlier study of 855 American clinical psychologists found that 55% of the sample identified themselves as eclectic, later surveys have indicated that electicism seems to have slightly declined in popularity. Smith (1982), in a survey of 800 members of the American Psychological Association (Divisions 12, clinical psychology and 17, counselling psychology), found that 42.1% of the sample described themselves as eclectic. Prochaska and Norcross (1983) found that 30.2% of a sample of 410 psychologists belonging to Division 29 (psychotherapy) of the APA chose 'eclectic' as their predominant therapeutic orientation. In a similar survey of a representative sample of clinical psychologists from Division 12 of the APA, Norcross and Prochaska (1982) found that 30.1% of the sample chose to describe themselves as eclectic. There is some evidence (Prochaska and Norcross 1983) that this slight decline in the popularity of eclecticism seems to coincide with a resurgence in popularity of psychoanalytic/psychodynamic approaches to therapy among APA members.

As mentioned above, Garfield and Kurtz (1977) found that thirty-two different combinations of therapeutic orientations were used by their sample of eclectic therapists who were asked to choose two orientations that were most characteristic of their eclectic approach. The top five of the combinations in order of frequency were: (a) psychoanalytic and learning theory; (b) neo-Freudian and learning theory; (c) neo-Freudian and Rogerian; (d) learning theory and humanistic; (e) Rogerian and learning theory. In their research into Division 29 (psychotherapy) members of the APA, Prochaska and Norcross (1983) asked subjects who selected eclecticism as their primary or secondary orientation (211 of a sample of 410) to select one of four theoretical perspectives underlying their eclectic approach. Their results showed that 45% chose psychodynamic, 24.6% humanistic and existential, 17.5% behavioural and 12.8% other. Thus it seems that psychoanalytic and psychodynamic orientations comprise a significant and sustained element in the eclectic approaches adopted by psychotherapists and psychologist members of the APA.

In addition, there has been some research carried out into the views of eclectic therapists. Garfield and Kurtz (1977) asked their sample of 154 eclectic therapists to 'try to define or explain your eclectic theoretical view' (Garfield and Kurtz 1977). Seventy-two responded that they used 'whatever theory or method seemed best for the client'. These therapists select procedures according to the requirements of individual clients and thus consider themselves 'pragmatic'. Nineteen responded that they basically employ and combine two or three theories in therapy. Twenty-two claimed to attempt an amalgamation of theories or aspects of theories, while ten responded rather vaguely that 'no theory is adequate and some are better for some purposes than others'. Prochaska and Norcross (1983) asked their sub-sample of 211 psychotherapists who selected eclecticism as their primary or secondary orientation to select from three types of eclecticism the one that best approximated to their own views. Sixty-five per cent of eclectic therapists said that they integrated a diversity of contemporary approaches and 31% that they used a variety of techniques within a preferred theory, while only 4% claimed to have no preferred theoretical orientation. This finding must be considered with caution since, as the next section shows, there are more than three types of eclecticism on the therapeutic scene.

While the foregoing information is of interest, and comparative British research much needed, this survey research does not reveal what eclectic therapists actually do in therapy, how they make therapeutic decisions, the nature of such decisions and what factors influence such decisions. As Garfield (1982) has observed, this type of research is lacking and needed if we are to unravel the mysteries of eclecticism. The lack of relevant research into eclecticism in action having been noted, a consideration of the different types of eclecticism will now be made.

Types of Eclecticism

As Dryden (1980) has noted, to refer to *the* eclectic approach to therapy falls prey to a therapeutic 'uniformity myth' (Kiesler 1966). There appear to be well over a dozen different types of eclecticism referred to in the psychotherapy literature. My intention here is to describe ten such types to show the range of eclectic endeavours currently being practised.

1. Theoretical eclecticism

Theoretical eclectics adhere to a specific therapeutic school but are prepared to use particular techniques developed by other schools; in doing so they do not subscribe to the theoretical postulates of the other schools but use their techniques for therapeutic purposes consistent with their own orientation. An example of theoretical eclecticism has been provided by Dryden (1982), who outlined the use of a variety of methods and techniques (e.g. Gestalt, psychodrama) within a rational-emotive approach to psychotherapy. Theoretical eclectics acknowledge the technical limitations of their own orientation and believe that the effectiveness of their approach to psychotherapy can be enhanced by the use of techniques spawned by other therapeutic orientations. Because they basically show allegiance to a particular orientation, theoretical eclectics, like their non-eclectic colleagues, have been criticized for having a restricted perspective on the complexity of human psychological problems.

2. Structural eclecticism

Structural eclecticism is outlined by Murgatroyd and Apter in Chapter 16. In this approach to eclecticism, a framework known as reversal theory is used to guide therapists in their selection of diverse therapeutic techniques. A number of dimensions are put forward to account for clients' variability, and therapeutic techniques are selected according to the individual client's position at any specific time on one or more of these salient dimensions. A fuller account of structural eclecticism can be found in the said chapter.

3. Combination eclecticism

Combination eclectics attempt to integrate two or more approaches to psychotherapy. In doing so they generally try to effect theoretical integration at a high order level, although other combination eclectics may not attempt this integrative task. Much has been written on integrating psychoanalytic and behavioural approaches to therapy. Some, like Yates (1983), consider this task impossible since the two approaches have such a different perspective on psychological disturbance; while others, such as Wachtel (1977), believe that such theoretical integration is not only possible but also valuable in that it provides therapists with the use of a broader range of therapeutic techniques.

Drawing upon Sullivan's (1953) interpersonal theory, Wachtel (1977) argues that disturbed behaviour is perpetuated not by a constellation of forces established in childhood and 'frozen in the unconscious' – as outlined in the traditional psychoanalytic view – but by the way the person presently lives his life. The client's behaviour in the present is deemed to elicit reactions in others which in turn help to maintain pathological structures of perception, thought and feeling. The client can be helped to break such vicious circles by *both* the therapist's analytic *and* behavioural interventions. The analytic interventions are designed to help the client gain insight into the determinants of his present behaviour, while behavioural interventions are used to effect actual changes in present behaviour, so that the client, by behaving differently, can elicit more favourable reactions from others. Wachtel hypothesizes that changes in perception, thought and feeling can be effected by both types of intervention and more powerfully when they are used in concert.

4. Existential eclecticism

This type of eclecticism has been identified by Robertson (1979), who states that such therapists adhere to a 'loosely knit set of existential propositions related to the process of encountering and coping with the exigencies of life. The therapist moves quickly to expose the client's existential dilemma, confronts him/her with the choices and options, and then proceeds to utilise whatever methods may assist the client to live out the new, albeit tentative life decisions'. To my knowledge no extensive writings on existential eclecticism appear in the literature, although the position is similar to that outlined by Greenwald (1973) in his book *Direct Decision Therapy*.

5. Technical eclecticism

Lazarus (1981) has argued that technical eclecticism 'implies using many techniques drawn from different sources without also adhering to the theories or disciplines that spawned them'. Such eclectics are much more concerned with pragmatic clinical issues than theoretical ones. They are concerned with the question: What technique works for whom, and under which particular conditions?

The best example of technical eclecticism is perhaps Lazarus's (1981) 'Multi Modal Therapy'. He regards his approach as systematic in that he methodically covers seven basic modalities of human functioning and dysfunctioning in therapy: behaviour, affect, sensation, imagery, cognition, interpersonal relationships and drug-taking/physiological – hence the acronym BASIC ID. Lazarus argues that, in the first instance, therapists should use the most obvious methods and techniques at their disposal for a particular client problem (i.e. those which research has deemed to be most effective). However, should failure result more careful analysis across the client's BASIC ID, including second-order BASIC ID analyses for the problems concerned, should be undertaken. Lazarus's approach rests on a set of basic theoretical concepts which are none the less not very closely related to his pragmatic clinical approach. He argues that the following concepts can explain most of the psychological processes across the BASIC ID: classical and operant conditioning, modelling and vicarious processes, private events, non-conscious processes and defensive reactions, and meta-communications (our ability to communicate about our communications).

6. Systematic – persuasive eclecticism

This type of eclecticism has recently been introduced by Beutler (1983), and represents an admirable attempt to integrate research and clinical considerations within an approach which views psychotherapy as a process of social influence. Beutler's approach is systematic in that a *wide* range of therapeutic variables are reviewed to help therapists plan a comprehensive treatment programme.

Therapeutic techniques are selected according to the following criteria: The first is which intermediate treatment objective they are designed to meet. Six such objectives are covered by Beutler, namely (a) insight enhancement, (b) emotional awareness, (c) emotional escalation, (d) emotional reduction, (e) behavioural control and (f) perceptual change. The second is whether they are designed to emphasize cognitive, affective and/or behavioural experience. The third is whether and to what extent they are designed to have a broad-band or narrow-band therapeutic impact; and finally there is the question of whether and to what extent they are designed to be confrontative or non-confrontative.

Client variables are conceptualized in a number of ways. First a client's problems are classified according to which core-conflictual theme underlies these problems. Beutler, identifies four 'pure' themes but recognizes that they may often occur in combination. The four themes are: attachment, detachment, separation and ambivalence. Second, a client's coping style is assessed according to whether the client uses an internalizing or externalizing style of coping. Third, a client's locus of control is assessed according to his level of reactance potential. Reactance refers to 'an individual's investment in maintaining personal control and freedom, and is described by one's unwillingness to comply with external restraints' (Beutler 1983); it is hypothesized that clients with a high level of reactance will respond differently to a number of therapeutic procedures from clients with low reactance. Finally, a client's level of symptom complexity is assessed according to whether his problems are mono-symptomatic at one extreme or show complex adjustment patterns at the other.

Beutler's achievement is that he specifies different therapeutic programmes and plans for different types of client based on an integration of the above factors. While a detailed discussion of these plans is outside the scope of this chapter (see Beutler 1983, especially Chapter 9), Beutler does outline different plans for the following: high reactant/externalizing clients, low reactant/externalizing clients, high reactant/internalizing clients and low reactant/internalizing clients. Different treatment plans are put forward for each of these groups according to whether they are mono-symptomatic or have complex adjustment patterns. While Beutler's schema is impressive, it awaits further empirical enquiry before its utility can be properly assessed.

7. Integrationism

Therapeutic integrationists (who, incidentally, dislike the term 'eclecticism') strive 'to delineate and operationalise clearly some of the common variables which seem to pay a role in most psychotherapies and . . . to regard them as a basis for a clearer delineation of psychotherapeutic principles and procedures' (Garfield 1982). Integrationists point out that, apart from the fact that behavioural procedures are shown by some studies to be more effective than non-behavioural procedures for selected disorders, there is no clear-cut superiority of any therapeutic orientation over others. Thus the search for therapeutic variables needs to be shifted to another level: to the existence of therapeutic factors which are common to most psychotherapies. Garfield (1980, 1982) is perhaps the leading exponent of this view. He has specified the following therapeutic variables as being common to different therapeutic approaches: the therapist/client relationship; interpretation, insight and understanding; catharsis, emotional expression and release; reinforcement in psychotherapy; desensitization, relaxation; information in psychotherapy; reassurance and support; modelling; confronting one's problems; clarifying and modifying client expectancies and providing both a credible therapeutic framework for the client's problems and a credible rationale for treatment. The effectiveness of therapeutic procedures and techniques is seen as being derived from the potency of one or more of these common factors.

This approach gives therapists a broader perspective for viewing the therapeutic value of widely different techniques and thus provides them with the possibility of using alternative techniques for similar therapeutic ends. Goldfried (1982) has similarly argued that the delineation of common therapeutic principles provides therapists with a common therapeutic language which, hopefully, may facilitate mutually beneficial dialogue. Goldfried (personal communication) hopes that such dialogue may lead to the development of a superordinate theoretical framework, acceptable to a wide variety of clinicians, which may help to unify the field.[1] This unification would then lead to new developments in both research in psychotherapy and clinical practice. The strengths of integrationism are that it rests on a fairly sound empirical base and offers a framework which is capable of incorporating new developments in psychotherapy.

8. Developmental eclecticism

Developmental eclectics see the practice of therapy as a set of developmental sequences or stages. Theory, when considered, is regarded as secondary and as helping to explain the changing nature of therapists' tasks over time. An example of this type of eclecticism is Robertson's (1979) 'radical eclecticism'. Here 'requirement of a theoretical framework is bypassed and the therapist selects an intervention on the basis of whether the thought, feeling or action component of a unit of behavior is primarily involved' (Robertson 1979). In his paper, Robertson describes his approach of using person-centred, Gestalt and behavioural methods in sequence. His rationale is as follows: person-centred methods help to establish a relationship between therapist and client so as to allow the client to respond positively to the quick-acting Gestalt methods. These Gestalt methods are used to help both parties become aware of how the client's 'problems of living are particularised in the client's lifestyle'; moreover, they help prepare therapist and client to individualize the application of behavioural interventions in later sessions.

A similar but better-developed example of developmental eclecticism is Egan's (1982) skills-based approach to therapy (as outlined in Chapter 15). Therapy is again seen as a set of developmental stages which generally, but not in every case, occur in sequence. These stages may be repeated for different problems that a particular client might discuss. Therapists have different tasks at different stages. In Stage 1, the therapist's major task is to help the client explore his concerns and clarify the problems; in Stage 2, the client is helped to set goals based on dynamic self-understanding, and in Stage 3, he is helped to take appropriate goal-oriented action. Egan (1982) notes that different therapist skills are required at different stages and that therapists are free to select from a wide range of techniques with a view to the successful execution of their stage-appropriate tasks.

9. Transtheoretical eclecticism

This type of eclecticism has emerged from the work of Prochaska and his colleagues at the University of Rhode Island in America (Prochaska 1979; Prochaska and DiClemente 1982; McConnaughty, Prochaska and Velicer 1983). Transtheoretical eclectics are guided in their therapeutic work by integrating five processes of change with four stages of change in psychotherapy (See Table 14.1). They are thus striving to bring together the work of integrationists and development eclectics.

STAGES:	PRE-CONTEMPLATION	CONTEMPLATION	ACTION	MAINTENANCE
PROCESSES:	CONSCIOUSNESS-RAISING	CHOOSING	CONTINGENCY CONTROL	
		CATHARSIS	CONDITIONAL STIMULI	

Table 14.1 Integrating change stages and processes (adapted from Prochaska and DiClemente 1982)

The five processes of change were identified from an overview of major schools of psychotherapy and behaviour therapy (Prochaska 1979). Each process of change is sub-divided into two levels, an experiential (inner-directed) level and an environmental level, since it is recognized that psychological change can be affected by modifying both intrapersonal and interpersonal/environmental factors. Table 14.2 shows how Prochaska (1979) has conceptualized the resulting ten change processes. (See Prochaska 1979 for a fuller description).

The four stages of change were identified from research carried out with people who had effected or tried to effect change either as a result of

Verbal Therapies	Action or Behaviour Therapies
CONSCIOUSNESS-RAISING:	CONDITIONAL STIMULI:
Experiential level - feedback	Experiential level - counter conditioning
Environmental level - education	Environmental level - stimulus control
CATHARSIS:	CONTINGENCY CONTROL:
Experiential level - current emotional experiences	Experiential level - re-evaluation
Environmental level - dramatic relief	Environmental level - contingency management
CHOOSING:	
Experiential level - self-liberation	
Environmental level - social-liberation	

Table 14.2 Therapeutic change processes at experiential and environmental levels (Prochaska 1979)

their own efforts (self-changers) or as a result of seeking therapy (therapy-changers). In the pre-contemplation stage of therapy, the person either does not think he has a problem or does not want to change. At the contemplation stage, the person is beginning to recognize that he has a problem, has committed himself to change and at the end of this stage is beginning to make efforts to effect change. At the action stage, the person has actively begun to change his behaviour or the environment, either successfully or unsuccessfully. At the maintenance stage of therapy, the person has already effected changes and is involved in maintaining those changes, either successfully or unsuccessfully.

This promising work is still at an early stage of development, and various client profiles based on a 'stage of change' instrument have recently been identified (McConnaughty et al. 1983). However, Prochaska's work provides a means of testing the following predictions: (a) 'that particular processes of change are most effective with clients working in particular stages of change' – see Table 1; (b) 'that resistance to therapy increases if the therapist is working on a different stage of change than what the client is in'; and (c) that 'by matching the client's stage profile with the appropriate processes of change, progress in therapy can be optimised' (McConnaughty et al. 1983).

10. Haphazard eclecticism

This rather uncharitable label describes those eclectics who are haphazard in their therapeutic approach. Not surprisingly, since journal editors tend not to recommend such papers for publication, such examples of this type of eclecticism rarely appear in the professional literature. None the less, it is very likely that at least some self-professed eclectics deserve this label. Such eclectics are likely to choose their theories, methods and techniques on the basis of subjective appeal; 'I use whatever makes sense to me and whatever I feel comfortable with' (Lazarus 1981)[2] is a frequent refrain. Such eclectics attend many weekend workshops and then try out techniques on the next few 'unfortunate' clients whether or not their clients' problems warrant such methods. These therapists wander around in a daze of professional nihilism, experimenting with new 'fad' methods indiscriminately. A sub-type of haphazard eclecticism is what I call 'hat-rack' eclecticism. These therapists have a range of hats and will wear, for example, a Gestalt hat with one client, a psychoanalytic hat with another, and so on.

Haphazard eclectics have a very restricted view of psychotherapy, tend to overvalue the therapeutic potency of techniques, underplay the value of developing and maintaining a therapeutic alliance and do not have a thorough understanding of common therapeutic variables and their importance. If rigid adherents to one therapeutic school are tight construers, then haphazard eclectics tend to be extremely loose construers (see Chapter 6).

I have included haphazard eclecticism as a separate type to indicate that adopting an eclectic stance, although currently popular, is no guarantee of increased therapeutic effectiveness. Although there is very little outcome data on eclectic approaches to therapy, it is conceivable that eclectic therapists will show the same range of therapeutic effectiveness as do adherents to a specific therapeutic school. Indeed, it is possible that some therapists, particularly those who are likely to practice haphazard eclecticism, would be more successful by operating from a well-defined therapeutic orientation.

It is noteworthy that, with the exception of Murgatroyd and Apter's work on structural eclecticism (see Chapter 16), all the above-mentioned

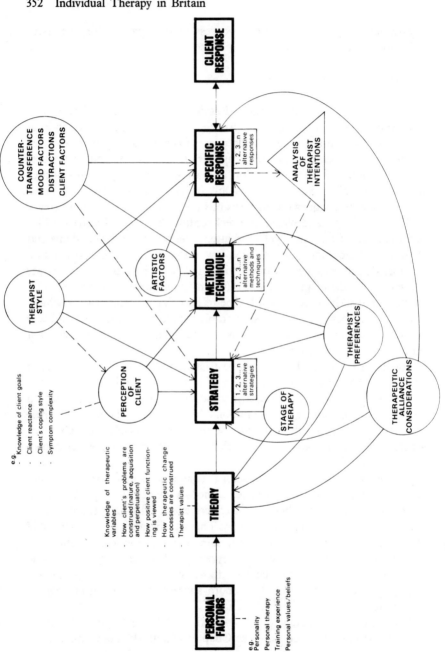

Figure 11.1 A model of therapist decision making in eclectic individual

writers on eclecticism are .American; British therapists have, in general, not written on the subject of eclecticism, and it is not known how many consider themselves eclectics. It is my hope that the following model of therapist decision-making in eclectic individual therapy and subsequent discussion of its elements might provoke greater discussion and research on eclecticism in Britain.

Therapist Decision-Making

Eclecticism has been defined as selecting what appears to be best from diverse therapeutic sources, systems and styles. In order to explain this process of selection, a model of therapist decision-making will be put forward (see Figure 14.1). This model can be used as an aid to understanding the decisions that therapists make in the process of psychotherapy whether or not they adopt an eclectic stance. It is my contention that studying therapist decision-making in eclectic therapy is probably the best way of understanding what eclectic therapists actually do in practice.

In summary, the model shows that, despite some arguments to the contrary, eclectic therapists are more or less guided by theoretical concepts which are in turn determined in part by a set of personal factors. The theoretical notions which underpin the work of eclectic therapists determine in the first instance a set of therapeutic strategies which in turn determine what range of techniques or methods is selected for possible use with a particular client. Therapeutic techniques are made up of a number of therapist-client response exchanges.

The major elements in the model and the factors that influence them will be specified in greater detail below. However, it is worth while noting at this juncture that eclectic therapists, like other therapists, are influenced by a set of imprecise personal factors which guide their behaviour. A number of writers have written on the topic of therapist intuition. Although it is my contention that studies which focus on therapist decision-making in psychotherapy are probably the best route to understand this intuitive process, it must be recognised, however, that we may never be able to *fully* understand what guides therapists in their selection of strategies, techniques and specific responses. A good example of this appears in the work of Standal and Corsini (1959). In this edited book a number of therapists outlined how they handled 'critical' incidents in psychotherapy. The conclusion which can be gained from this material is that therapists often handle such critical incidents in a 'spontaneous' fashion which they do not fully understand either at the time or even after some reflection. Indeed, their attempts to make sense of these experiences after the event are open to the accusation of post-hoc rationalisation. With this in mind the model of therapist decision-making will now be presented.

The role of theory in therapeutic decision-making

Cornsweet (1983) has argued that a theory in psychotherapy is 'primarily a model, a way of structuring and understanding a complex set of phenomena. It provides the clinician, in particular, with a framework from which to view the patient and with a rationale for intervention'. In this sense, therapists cannot help but be theoretical in that (a) they structure what they observe, and (b) this structuring is based on explicit or implicit assumptions which influence their actions to some degree. Thus therapists who claim to be atheoretical and conduct therapy in a highly individualistic, eclectic fashion are in fact probably operating from an implicit, informal system of beliefs; while therapists who choose not to understand why client problems develop or why therapeutic techniques work and merely use those techniques that are deemed to be effective are, as Cornsweet (1983) has shown, operating from a 'radical empirical theory which operates on observational data alone'.

A current view of psychotherapeutic effectiveness is that outcome is dependent on a process of persuasion or social influence. 'Successful' clients, according to this view, emerge from therapy more closely identified with the beliefs of their therapists (Beutler 1983). It is therefore important for therapists to be reasonably consistent in their beliefs or values if they are not to 'persuade' clients to adopt a set of incoherent, contradictory beliefs. This suggests that eclectic therapists should pay close attention to their implicit assumptions and think through important theoretical issues. Important issues, in the author's opinion, include those that are dealt with in the 'theoretical assumptions' section of the approaches to therapy covered thus far, namely: (a) the image of the person; (b) how psychological disturbance and health are construed; (c) how psychological problems develop and are perpetuated; and (d) how therapeutic change processes are construed. It is, however, debatable whether all these factors have equal influence in determining which strategies eclectic therapists develop in treatment. Davis (1983), for example, has argued that the way therapists understand the *origin* of a problem may have little influence in determining which therapeutic procedures are selected for dealing with the problem. In addition, a knowledge of therapeutic variables (common factors) will enhance eclectic therapists' theory of psychotherapy (Garfield 1980).

It is understandable that some eclectic therapists shy away from an examination of their theoretical assumptions, since at first sight it seems as if to attempt a theoretical integration of several established perspectives is an insurmountable task. However, as Davis (1983) has shown, monolithic theories do not need to be swallowed whole and theories constantly evolve. Eclectics do not need to integrate all parts of all available theories, but only those parts which have validity and are helpful clinically. Wachtel (1977) has shown that such meaningful integration is possible and points out that valid perspectives from different approaches can be combined into a new structure (Wachtel 1983). One point needs reiteration: verbal dismissal of theory does not mean that theory is actually dismissed. An explicit examination of theoretical issues is, if Beutler's (1983) thesis is valid, a therapeutic factor. Unexamined theory is, as Cornsweet (1983) has shown, potentially damaging to clients.

There are other reasons for the explicit examination of theoretical issues. As the model shows, a therapist's theory is partly determined by a number of personal factors and personal preferences. Unless the impact of these determinants is examined explicitly, eclectic therapists are open to the criticism that they adopt a theoretical perspective that suits them personally rather than one which has any clinical utility and validity.

A final argument for eclectic therapists making their theoretical perspectives explicit to themselves is that these perspectives are likely to have a 'for better or worse' impact on their clients. According to Bordin's (1979) concept of the therapeutic alliance, the probability of effective therapy is enhanced if therapist and client have a shared understanding of the nature of the latter's problems. If eclectic therapists are to communicate such understanding to their clients, a prior and explicit examination of the foundations of such understanding is necessary if inconsistent, incoherent and thus unhelpful conceptions are to be avoided. Whether, in fact, eclectic therapists conceptualize their clients' problems from a base broader than that of other therapists is as yet unknown.

Developing effective therapeutic strategies

Goldfried (1978, 1980) has argued that the most likely arena where therapists of different persuasions may find meaningful consensus lies at a level of abstraction between theory and technique. This is the level of 'clinical strategies'. Such strategies imply principles of therapeutic change. Goldfried (1982) argues that to increase the likelihood of productive dialogue between therapists of different persuasions, therapists need to use a neutral language in explaining their clinical strategies, i.e. one which is free from the jargon of specific therapeutic schools. Whether this enterprise will facilitate therapeutic *rapprochement* remains to be seen, but the idea is particularly appealing to those eclectic therapists known as integrationists. Goldfried (1980) quotes two examples of such clinical strategies, the first being that of providing the client with new corrective emotional experiences and the second that of offering the client direct feedback. Having conceptualized clinical strategies in this way, therapists are then faced with a number of different ways of implementing such strategies. They can best do this by using a variety of therapeutic methods and techniques.

A number of important points need to be made at this juncture. First, the selection of strategies is to some degree based on a therapist's theoretical formulations, as described in the previous section. Thus, if the therapist's strategy is to help a client modify a faulty cognition, the therapist is operating on the assumption that faulty cognitions are involved in the client's problem and that changing it will help to overcome his problem. Thus, once again, eclectic therapists cannot avoid operating on theoretical assumptions.

Second, eclectic therapists are likely to pay close attention to client variability in the selection of clinical strategies. Here, Beutler's (1983) work is important, since eclectic therapists will use different strategies dependent upon (a) the client's coping style, (b) the complexity of the client's symptoms and (c) the client's reactance level.

Third, eclectic therapists are likely to pay close attention to the stage of therapy in selecting clinical strategies (for example, Egan 1982; McConnaughty et al. 1983). Richert (1983) has shown that different clients require different strategies and techniques at the initial stage of therapy. Using two dimensions – an authority continuum covering issues of therapist power and status and a therapist orientation towards problems – he has identified four types of client on the basis of their role expectations for therapist behaviour. *Medical modellers* are clients who prefer therapists to be high on the authority dimension and to focus directly on problems. *Revelationists* prefer therapists to be high in power but to scrutinize their personal feelings and experiences closely. *Problem-solvers* prefer therapists to occupy a position of lesser authority and focus upon their problems. Finally, *explorers* want their therapist to be companions (low authority) on a trip into their psychological space. Clearly, if therapists are to engage all such clients productively in therapy, care has to be taken in selecting appropriate clinical strategies at the outset either to meet a particular client's role expectations or to modify them.

Fourth, eclectic therapists are likely to give careful consideration to the most appropriate style to adopt in implementing strategies with particular clients in accordance with their perceptions of these clients on salient dimensions (Anchin and Kiesler 1982). Such therapists are aware that particular therapeutic styles may reinforce a client's psychological problems by re-confirming negative and disturbance-perpetuating schemata, while other styles may provide disconfirming evidence for the client and thereby promote change: for example, adopting a very active-directive style with a very passive client may reinforce that client's passivity, while adopting a moderately expressive style with a client who uses intellectualization as a defence may promote change.

Fifth, therapeutic alliance considerations are salient here (as they are throughout the model). If therapist and client share a common understanding as to the purpose of the therapist's clinical strategies, and if the client can see that the implementation of such strategies will help him reach his therapeutic goals, then the chances of productive therapy will be enhanced.

It is possible that eclectic therapists use a broader range of clinical strategies than do those belonging to a particular school, although this is a matter for empirical enquiry. It is likely, however, that eclectic therapists' personal preferences will also play a role in strategy selection; but again this question awaits research. In this regard, Clara Hill (in preparation) is currently engaged in important research which may prove valuable in promoting greater understanding of the range of clinical strategies that eclectic therapists employ. She is studying the intentions that therapists have which determine their responses in therapy. She is asking therapists to listen to tape recordings of therapy sessions and to check which intention(s) guided every therapist response in the session.

1.   **To set limits or make arrangements:** to structure, establish goals and objectives of treatment, outline methods to attain goals, correct expectations about treatment, or establish rules or parameters of relationship (e.g., time, length, fees, cancellation policies, homework, content, etc.).

2.   **To gather information:** To find out specific facts about history, client functioning, future plans, etc.

3.   **To give information:** To educate, give facts, correct misperceptions or misinformation, give reasons for therapist's behaviour or procedures.

4.   **To support and build rapport:** To provide a warm, supportive, empathic environment; to increase trust and rapport and build relationship, to help client feel accepted, understood, supported, comfortable, reassured, and less anxious: to help establish a person-to-person relationship.

5.   **To focus:** To help client focus, get back on track, change subject, channel or structure the discussion if he/she is unable to begin or if he/she has been diffuse, rambling, or shifting topics.

6.   **To clarify:** To provide or solicit more elaboration, emphasis, or specification when client or therapist has been vague, incomplete, confusing, contradictory, or inaudible.

7.   **To instill hope:** To convey the expectation that change is possible and likely to occur; that the therapist will be able to help the client; to restore morale; to build up the client's confidence to make changes.

8.   **To promote relief from tension or unhappy feelings:** To allow the client a chance to cathart, let go, or talk through feelings and problems.

9.   **To identify maladaptive cognitions:** To point out illogical or irrational thoughts or attitudes (e.g., 'I must be perfect' etc.).

10.   **To identify maladaptive behaviours:** To give feedback about the client's inappropriate behaviour and/or its consequences; to do a behavioural analysis; to point out games.

11.   **To encourage a sense of self-control:** To help the client own or gain a sense of mastery or control over his/her own thoughts, feelings, behaviours, or impulses; to help become more appropriately internal rather than in-appropriately external in taking responsibility for one's role.

12.   **To identify, intensify, and/or enable acceptance of feelings:** To encourage or provoke the client to become aware of or deepen underlying or hidden feelings or affect or to experience feelings at a deeper level.

13.   **To stimulate insight:** To encourage understanding of the underlying reasons, dynamics, assumptions, or unconscious motivations for cognitions, behaviours, attitudes or feelings. May include an understanding of client's reactions to other's behaviours.

14.   **To build more appropriate behaviours or cognitions:** To help develop new and more adaptive skills, behaviours, or cognitions to inculcate new ways of dealing with self and others. May be to instill new, more adaptive assumptive models, frameworks, explanations or conceptualisations. May be to give an assessment, or opinion about client functioning that will help client see self in a new way.

15.   **To reinforce change attempts:** To give positive reinforcement of feedback about behavioural, cognitive, or affective attempts at change in order to enhance the probability that the change will be continued or maintained; to encourage risk-taking and new ways of behaving.

16.   **To overcome obstacles to change:** To analyze lack of progress, resistance, or failure to adhere to therapeutic procedures, either past or possibilities of relapse in future.

17.   **To challenge:** To jolt the client out of a present state; to shake up current beliefs or feelings; to test validity; adequacy, reality, or appropriateness of beliefs, thoughts, feelings, or behaviours; to help client question the necessity of maintaining old patterns.

18.   **To resolve problems in the therapeutic relationship:** To deal with issues as they arise in the relationship in order to build or maintain a smooth working alliance; to heal ruptures in the alliance; to deal with dependency issues appropriate to stage in treatment; to uncover and resolve distortions in client's thinking about the relationship which are based on past experiences rather than current reality.

19.   **To relieve therapist:** To protect or defend the therapist, to take care of the therapist's needs; to alleviate anxiety; to try unduly to persuade, argue, or feel good or superior at the expension of the client.

Table 14.3 Therapist intentions (Clara Hill)

While this method is open to the criticism of *post hoc* rationalization, it is an important step forward in furthering understanding of therapist decision-making. Table 14.3 lists nineteen such therapist intentions. It is noteworthy that Hill includes the item: 'to relieve therapist' as an intention; this serves as another reminder that some clinical strategies may be implicitly employed to protect the therapist rather than help the client.

Hill (personal communication) has observed that while these therapist intentions can be conceptualized as referring to strategies, these strategies tend to be more immediate in focus. Therapeutic strategies, then, vary along a time-focus continuum. A strategy may be adopted for a short period of time within a session, for an entire session or even over a number of sessions. In addition, strategies may be organized hierarchically. A therapist may implement a particular strategy to enable him at a later date to implement another.

Employing different therapeutic methods and techniques

Having developed a set of clinical strategies to use with a particular client, the eclectic therapist can now select from a wide range of therapeutic methods and techniques to implement these strategies. A technique is a well-defined, circumscribed therapeutic manoeuvre, such as behavioural rehearsal, the two-chair technique or rational-emotive imagery; whereas a therapeutic method can be seen as a more general therapeutic manoeuvre, for example responding from within a client's frame of reference or the use of therapist immediacy. It is at this point in the model that the therapist's eclectic stance is likely to become most apparent in that he selects from a diverse range of therapeutic methods and techniques culled from different schools of therapy. Once a particular clinical strategy has been selected and agreed with the client, the therapist can use a variety of different techniques to achieve the same therapeutic end. Another advantage of eclecticism at this stage is that the eclectic therapist can use a variety of alternative methods and techniques if a given therapeutic technique or method fails. Indeed, therapeutic alliance considerations would suggest that it would be productive for therapists to discuss with their clients the different methods and techniques that could possibly be employed to implement clinical strategies and thereby achieve therapeutic goals. Letting the client choose the most appropriate method or technique for his own particular situation would be particularly beneficial. There is, in fact, evidence that clients who receive a form of treatment for which they have expressed a preference achieve better results than do clients who receive randomly assigned or non-preferred treatment (Devine and Fernald 1973).

It is important to observe at this stage that eclectic therapists should distinguish between the possible short- and long-term effects of particular therapeutic methods and techniques. Some methods and techniques may promote short-term benefits but lead to problems later in therapy. For example, some cathartic techniques may be helpful for clients in the short term but reinforce disturbance-creating philosophies in the long term (Dryden 1982). Judging the short- and long-term consequences of employing given methods and techniques is dependent upon: (a) a knowledge of the client's personality structure and patterns, (b) one's theory of healthy functioning and disturbance and (c) outcome research.

With regard to the use of techniques and methods in eclectic therapy the following points are pertinent. First, in the same way that certain eclectic therapists have preferences for particular clinical strategies, it is probably true that therapists will use certain methods and techniques more frequently than others. Second, being sensitive to the needs of individual clients, eclectic therapists are likely to use different ways of employing a given method or technique with different clients; the point about therapeutic style has already been made. However, the artistic nature of therapeutic work is also relevant here. Lazarus (1978) makes an important point in this respect:

> when I select systematic desensitization as one of the techniques to be used with a given client, I do so because scientific studies have suggested that this method has a high success rate in certain instances. But the different way in which I explain its rationale to specific clients, the individual pace, manner and structure I employ with different people and the variety of ways in which I introduce scenes embroider images, and embellish tailor-made themes, rest heavily on ... artistic skill.

The selection of specific methods and techniques and the way these are executed are determined not only by the above 'rational factors'; it is well known that occasionally therapists respond to their clients in non-therapeutic ways. Counter-transference factors (see Chapter 2), mood factors, the impact of certain client factors on certain therapists and general distractions are all potential determinants that may interfere with therapist decision-making. This is why having their therapeutic work supervised is highly desirable for all therapists.

Specific therapist responses

Methods and techniques have been defined as general and specific therapeutic manoeuvres respectively, used in the service of broad clinical strategies. As such they are composed of a number of discrete therapist responses known as therapist 'turns'. A therapist turn is defined as everything a therapist says between two client statements and, as can be seen from Figure 1, is influenced by similar factors that impinge on the use of methods and techniques as well as by preceding client responses. When therapist behaviour is analysed at this level, it may be difficult to detect differences between therapists of different orientations and eclectic therapists; yet it is at this level that therapists have direct impact on their clients. This perhaps accounts for the therapeutic equivalence of widely different theoretical approaches to therapy.

As noted above, this level of therapist behaviour is being studied by Hill (in preparation) with the aim of identifying therapist intentions to implement clinical strategies. Thus although the direct study of specific therapist responses may not help us to understand the work of eclectic therapists, it is important to examine this level of behaviour so as to help illuminate the decision-making processes of eclectic therapists.

In conclusion, it should be noted that the model outlined in Figure 1 assumes that therapists will offer clients a minimum level of appropriate therapeutic conditions (such as empathy, genuineness and respect), and these factors should be given due consideration along with the other elements in the model when reasons for therapeutic failure are sought.

Having outlined some general issues involved in the practice of eclectic individual therapy, we are now in a position to consider in detail two types of eclecticism currently practised in Britain.

Notes

1 A number of integrationists have recently, formed the Society for the Exploration of Psychotherapy Integration. The society exists to further constructive dialogue among therapists interested in therapeutic *rapprochement*. Further details can be obtained from:

Dr M R Goldfried
Department of Psychology
State of University of New York at Stony Brook
Stony Brook
New York, NY 11794
USA

2　This quote should not be attributed to Lazarus's view of his own approach. His statement implies criticism of haphazard eclectics.

Readers may be interested in the International Academy of Eclectic Psychotherapists. The major objective of the IAEP is 'to bring psychotherapy into a new era, through closer collaboration of eminent professionals of diverse expertises'.

Further details can be obtained from:

Dr J Hariman
84 Hunter Avenue
St Ives
NSW 2075
Australia

References

Anchin J C, Kiesler D J (eds.) (1982) *Handbook of Interpersonal Psychotherapy*, Pergamon, New York

Beutler L E (1983) *Eclectic Psychotherapy: A Systematic Approach*, Pergamon, New York, p. 39

Bordin E S (1979) The generalizability of the psychoanalytic concept of the working alliance, *Psychotherapy: Theory, Research and Practice 16(3)*: 252–260

Cornsweet C (1983) Nonspecific factors and theoretical choice, *Psychotherapy: Theory, Research and Practice 20(3)*:307–313

Davis J D (1983) Slaying the psychoanalytic dragon: An integrationist's commentary on Yates, *British Journal of Clinical Psychology 22*: 133–134

Devine D A, Fernald P S (1973) Outcome effects of receiving a preferred, randomly assigned or nonpreferred therapy, *Journal of Consulting and Clinical Psychology 41(1)*: 104–107

Dryden W (1980) Eclectic approaches in individual counselling, *The Counsellor 3(2)*: 24–30

Dryden W (1982) Rational-emotive therapy and eclecticism, *The Counsellor 3(5)*: 15–22

Egan G (1982) *The Skilled Helper: Model, Skills and Methods for Effective Helping*, 2nd edition, Brooks/Cole, Monterey, Cal.

Garfield S L (1980) *Psychotherapy: An Eclectic Approach*, Wiley, New York

Garfield S L (1982) Eclecticism and integrationism in psychotherapy, *Behavior Therapy 13*: 610–623

Garfield S L, Kurtz R (1977) A study of eclectic views, *Journal of Consulting and Clinical Psychology 45*: 75, 78–83

Goldfried M R (1978) On the search for effective intervention strategies, *The Counseling Psychologist 7(3)*: 28–30

Goldfried M R (1980) Toward the delineation of therapeutic change principles, *American Psychologist 35*: 991–999

Goldfried M R (1982) On the history of therapeutic integration, *Behavior Therapy 13*: 572–593

Greenwald H (1973) *Direct Decision Therapy*, Edits, San Diego, Cal.

Kiesler D J (1966) Some myths of psychotherapy research and the search for a paradigm, *Psychological Bulletin 65*: 110–136

Lazarus A A (1978) Science and beyond, *The Counseling Psychologist 7(3)*: 24–25

Lazarus A A (1981) *The Practice of Multimodal Therapy*, McGraw-Hill, New York pp. 4–5

McConnaughty F A, Prochaska J O , Velicer W F (1983) Stages of change in psychotherapy: Measurement and sample profiles, *Psychotherapy: Theory, Research and Practice 20(3)*: 368–375

Norcross J C, Prochaska J O (1982) A national survey of clinical psychologists: Affiliations and orientations, *The Clinical Psychologist 35(3)*:1–6

Prochaska J O (1979) *Systems of Psychotherapy: A Transtheoretical Analysis*, Dorsey, Homewood, Ill.

Prochaska J O, DiClemente C C (1982) Transtheoretical therapy: Toward a more integrative model of change, *Psychotherapy: Theory, Research and Practice 19*: 276–288

Prochaska J O, Norcross J C (1983) Contemporary psychotherapists: A national survey of characteristics, practices, orientations and attitudes, *Psychotherapy: Theory, Research and Practice 20(2)*: 161–173

Richert A (1983) Differential prescription for psychotherapy on the basis of client role preferences, *Psychotherapy: Theory, Research and Practice 20(3)*: 321–329

Robertson M (1979) Some observations from an eclectic therapist, *Psychotherapy: Theory, Research and Practice 16(1)*: 18–21

Smith D (1982) Trends in counseling and psychotherapy, *American Psychologist 37(7)*: 802–809

Standal S W, Corsini R J (eds.) (1959) *Critical Incidents in Psychotherapy*, Prentice-Hall, Englewood Cliffs, NJ

Sullivan H S (1953) *The Interpersonal Theory of Psychiatry*, Norton, New York

Wachtel P L (1977) *Psychoanalysis and Behavior Therapy: Toward an Integration*, Basic Books, New York

Wachtel P L (1983) Integration misunderstood, *British Journal of Clinical Psychology 22*: 129–130

Yates A J (1983) Behaviour therapy and psychodynamic psychotherapy: Basic conflict or reconciliation and integration? *British Journal of Clinical Psychology 22*: 107–125

Chapter 15   Developmental Eclecticism: Egan's Skills Model of Helping

Francesca Inskipp with Hazel Johns

Historical Context and Developments in Britain

Historical context

In 1975, Gerard Egan's *The Skilled Helper: A Model for Systematic Helping and Interpersonal Relating* was published. He stated that it was not a presentation of any one theory but an endeavour to integrate some of the existing psychological theories and to try to provide a way of training that could be relied upon to produce effective helpers. The emphasis was on setting up a *reliable* method of training people in the skills of helping.

Gerard Egan is Professor of Psychology at Loyola University, Chicago, and currently co-ordinator for the programme in Community and Organizational Development; his doctorate is in clinical psychology. His earlier publications were three books on human relations training in groups. In these books, he castigates the goallessness and ambiguity of much human relationships training and suggests that waiting for people to learn interpersonal skills experientially in groups by pointing out negative behaviours is not as useful as defining the skills people need to relate well and then helping them learn and practise those skills systematically. He cites the research of Carkhuff (1969a, 1969b) which states that skills in relating to others do not just happen but have to be learned and that training in this most important area is the most neglected in education.

In *The Skilled Helper*, Egan (1975) developed these ideas and suggested that most training courses for professional helpers have high cognitive content on psychological theories but do not teach students how to implement these theories in their work with clients. The book sets out to do this by producing a three-stage skills model of helping which analyses and suggests ways of learning and practising the skills. (There is also a book of exercises which develops training methods further. Egan 1981). Egan calls his eclectic model 'developmental' – not to be confused with the Developmental Counselling of Blocher (Blocher 1966) or Tyler (Tyler 1969) – because, first, it have developed out of several theories and, secondly, it goes on developing and changing as research continues to suggest new clinical ideas. The three stages build on one another: if the skills of the first stage are not learned and used, the other stages cannot follow.

Egan cites three main influences on the development of this model:

The work of Robert Carkhuff and his associates Their research concerned the differences between high-level functioning helpers, whose clients improve, and low-level functioning helpers, whose clients get worse. The seven qualities or skills identified as essential for high-level functioning – empathy, respect, concreteness, genuineness, self-disclosure, confrontation and immediacy – are the basis of the skills developed in the three stages of Egan's model (Carkhuff 1969a). Egan acknowledges that Carkhuff's work is built on the work of Carl Rogers, and Stage 1 of the Egan model relates very closely to Rogers's theories (Rogers 1957).

Social/Influence theory process Egan says that this theory, which views helping as a social influence process, may be a radical departure from some traditional ways of helping; but he cites research in support of it, saying that it is better to study the principles of social influence and learn to use them creatively rather than be 'victims' of them. He gives extensive references, among them Strong (1968) Frank (1973) and Corrigan, Dell, Lewis and Schmidt (1980).

Learning theory and the principles underlying the maintenance and change of behaviour Again, Egan acknowledges that this is a controversial area, but says that it would be a step backwards in the science and art of helping if helpers were to ignore the principles of behaviour modification. In a helping model dependent on skill-learning, 'the helper must have a thorough grasp of the basic principles underlying learning, unlearning and relearning ... if the helper and/or the helpee ignores these principles, they will be ground up by them' (Egan 1975).

Important influences here include the works of Skinner (1953), Sherman (1973) and Watson and Tharp (1973, 1981).

Other influences apparent in the model are: Brammer's work on analysing skills to promote 'understanding of self and others' (Brammer 1973); Ivey and associates' work on training in skills using 'micro-counselling' (Ivey 1971); and Kagan and associates' use of video for training in skills and sensitivity, particularly the techniques associated with 'interpersonal process recall' (Kagan 1975).

In 1979 Egan published, with Michael Cowan, *People in Systems*, and in this he outlines a developmental model of personality which focuses on life stages, tasks and skills and emphasizes the influence of 'systems' on the human developmental process. He suggested that this is a way of looking at healthy development in human beings rather than focusing on 'abnormal psychology'. These ideas were further developed in his second book with Michael Cowan, *Moving into Adulthood: Knowledge and Skills for Effective Living* (Egan and Cowan 1980). The books need to be read in conjunction with *The Skilled Helper* in order to identify Egan's 'image of the person'.

In 1982 Egan produced a second edition of *The Skilled Helper*, expanding, clarifying and updating the three-stage model. He renamed it 'a problem-management' model, and added a further influence to those outlined above: 'the rich body of theory and research associated with problem solving'. He urged readers to use his model as a map for integrating theories and as a springboard for developing ideas and finding ever better ways of increasing skilled helping. He demonstrated in his second edition that he has done this. The model mirrors his image of the person – in the process of development.

Developments in Britain

Since the first appearance in Britain of *The Skilled Helper* in the summer of 1976, Egan's model has spread rapidly, particularly in the field of counselling. The book appeared at a time when counselling and counsellor training were undergoing a period of expansion. Most counselling in this country is carried out not by professional counsellors but by teachers, social workers, nurses, doctors, ministers of religion, youth workers, etc. in the course of their work, or by a host of people working in voluntary organizations or peer groups such as Womens' Aid. Egan's model has much value for this large group of people, and courses offering 'skills training in counselling' are widespread.

The Centre for Studies in Counselling at the North-East London Polytechnic taught Egan's model from 1976 onwards, running courses mainly for teachers, careers officers, nurses, health visitors and other workers in the health professions.

In 1978 the Catholic Marriage Advisory Council invited Egan to Britain to discuss and demonstrate his methods, and since then he has run annual workshops for their tutors and counsellors. Their head of training and other CMAC tutors have spent time working with Egan at Loyola University and have subsequently shared knowledge and skills with trainers from other organizations.

Also in 1978, the tutor responsible for counselling training at the Royal College of Nursing visited Egan in Chicago, and since that date RCN courses have been influenced substantially by Egan's skills model. Both the CMAC and the RCN train a considerable number of helpers in counselling skills each year.

The South-West London College's Diploma in Counselling course, which now trains about seventy counsellors annually, uses the Egan model to draw together the wide range of counselling theories presented programmes on their training courses.

Probably the greatest influence in spreading Egan's three-stage model has been the two series of BBC programmes 'Principles of Counselling', which were written and presented by us. The first series of eight programmes was broadcast in 1978 and repeated five times between then and 1982; the second was broadcast three times in 1983. We used the Egan three-stage model to explain and demonstrate counselling, and several thousand people wrote requesting repeats and further information. These requests came from a very wide variety of professions and organizations, and there is evidence that many trainers use tapes of the programmes on their training courses.

As a result of the first series of broadcasts, the British Association for Counselling ran workshops on 'skills training', and in 1980 invited Egan to run workshops at their Northern Trainers' Conference in York. This was followed by two workshops run by Egan in London, both of which could have been filled twice over.

This evidence shows the widespread dissemination of Egan's ideas, but research is needed to show if using this model does in fact produce more effective skilled helpers.

Theoretical Assumptions

The image of the person

In *The Skilled Helper* (Egan 1975), the helping model is based on humanistic and eclectic personality theories, with roots in self theories, social influence and social learning theories. Such a general statement – the only direct reference made to personality theory – suggests that in this and other early books Egan does not present a specific 'image of the person'.

However, the second edition (Egan 1982) emphasizes that when professional helpers listen to clients they need a model of man which presents a healthy rather than a pathological view. It suggests that because professional helpers in training learn about psychopathology and abnormal behaviour they may have a tendency to 'read' psychopathology into what clients do or say. To enable helpers to listen to their clients in focused ways with a minimum of bias, Egan offers what he calls a 'broad-band, people-in-systems' model. This is an integration of many psychological theories and is spelt out in detail in *People in Systems* (Egan and Cowan 1979). The elements of this broad-band model include the following.

Uniqueness   Man is a builder of models that enable him to transform experience and create psychological meaning from the events of his life. Meaning, and the action it leads to, is generated in a four-phase cycle: perception–attention–transformation–action. An understanding of man's capacity to transform events is crucial. His response to a stimulus is never direct but mediated by an active construction of the meaning of the event. This transformation is always internal and therefore non-observable, though the resulting action can be seen. Transformation is affected by (a) cognitive or rational thinking, (b) emotion and (c) values and attitudes (which Egan describes as 'thinking with a feeling charge'). The balance of influence of those three elements varies from person to person. People may have a preferred or habitual style, filtering experiences cognitively, emotionally or through particularly strong values. These variations may be genetically or culturally derived.

So each individual has a unique transformational style which influences his perception, attention and behaviour, and these three are also responsive to his immediate social environment. This perception–attention–transformation–action cycle offers a model of a human being *at a particular moment.* This understanding is crucial for the helper who is dealing with unique human beings at particular points in their lives. Since each individual creates his own unique world, he can only be understood if others are willing to enter *his* frame of reference.

The developmental framework   Although each individual is unique, there is a developmental framework within particular cultures so that any individual life cycle fits into a common pattern. Human beings, as they develop, move through relatively predictable stages. Skills and knowledge have to be acquired at each stage in order to accomplish increasingly complex tasks and fulfil new roles. (A comprehensive developmental map of the life cycle in American culture is given in Egan and Cowan 1979). The transition from one stage to another may be a time of crisis, which can provide opportunities for growth. These crises are part of normal healthy human development.

Human systems   Egan stresses the importance of the environment, both social and physical, in which human development takes place; in particular, the social 'systems' in which a person exists have major effects on development. He suggests that psychology has been too much focused on the individual: 'a theoretical view giving primacy to the individual's thoughts, feelings and behaviour, while disregarding the socio-cultural settings in which these emerge has led to highly individual-centred approaches to helping' (Egan and Cowan 1979). In *People in Systems* (Egan and Cowan 1979) he sets out four levels of system which can help clarify the interaction between the individual and his environment: (a) the immediate personal settings: family, school, work-place; (b) the network of personal settings: the interaction of family, school and work-place; (c) larger institutions: government, organized religion, etc.; and (d) culture: language, mores. Egan suggests that at each developmental stage there are 'key systems' which are needed to provide support, challenge, knowledge and skills, thus bringing about healthy development. People are important resources at all stages of life. 'Mutuality' – the willingness of people to invest themselves in one another's lives in order to contribute to their mutual growth and development – is a human value Egan promotes strongly.

The Integration of 'Models'   Egan defines a model as a cognitive map with practical potential, complex enough to make sense of reality and simple enough to use. He integrates two models to form a 'working model' for helpers. The four-phase perception–attention–transformation–action cycle provides a model of how people learn and change which the counsellor can use to facilitate learning. The developmental model suggests what stage clients might be at and which tasks, knowledge and skills are relevant. The helper can use this to predict the client's particular learning needs.

Skill learning, self-direction and human potential   Egan sees the learning of skills, particularly interpersonal skills, as the foundation for human living. The models of man he outlines help define what skills are needed at each stage of life and how they can be learned or taught. Helpers are skill learners and skill trainers, and Egan is confident that skills can be taught and learned – and that people can enjoy learning. Man is capable of self-direction, or of setting his own goals and meeting the challenges of his complex development in a complex world, provided he has support and challenge. Unused human potential is a serious social problem. Egan relates this to Maslow's view of 'the psychopathology of the average' (Maslow 1968) and William James's remark that few people bring to bear more than about 10% of their human potential on the problems and challenges of being human. Helpers should be supporting and challenging their clients not just to cope with problems but to move towards optimum growth.

Concepts of psychological health and disturbance

Egan presents a clear picture of the healthy personality based on individual development within social systems. The 'healthy person' completes developmental tasks effectively and copes with crises which may occur in the transition periods between one stage and the next: for example, the move from full-time work to retirement. Anxiety and emotional upset may be normal in these crises, and the individual needs adequate skills, knowledge and resources, both internal and external, to cope with these. Healthy growth depends not only on the interaction between the person and the system he lives in, but also on the interaction between the different systems: for example, between family, school and government. This may enhance or stultify growth. 'Under ideal conditions, enlightened and skilled individuals and systems work synergistically, each contributing to the development of the other' (Egan and Cowan 1979). People are an important resource for healthy development: they provide support and challenge, serve as models for effective behaviour, and may be teachers of skills and providers of knowledge. People bring both resources and deficits to their interactions, and influences may be positive or negative, so healthy development depends on the *quality* of the interaction. The quality of interaction between people depends on the skills they have, and Egan describes six areas of skill in which the healthy person needs to be competent. (Egan and Cowan 1979)

(a) Skills related to physical development – health, fitness;
(b) Skills related to intellectual development – learning how to learn;
(c) Self-management skills – the ability to use a working theory of personality, to apply the basic principles of behaviour change and problem-solving
(d) Value clarification skills;
(e) Skills of interpersonal involvement – self-presentation, responding and challenging skills;
(f) Skills of small-group involvement – initiating, goal-setting, using group resources, and the skills necessary for effective participation in communities and organizations.

Abnormal behaviour or 'emotional disturbance' may be described as ineffective behaviour and its consequences, arising from a lack of knowledge or skills: a 'deficiency' view rather than a pathological view of human behaviour.

Those who appear psychologically disturbed may include:
(a) Individuals not able to move to a new developmental stage or to undertake new tasks and roles and cope with the crises of transition;
(b) Individuals who are unable to relate to others;
(c) Individuals who are alienated, feel helpless and powerless to influence the systems of their lives;
(d) Individuals who are unable to change behaviour which is destructive to themselves or others;
(e) Individuals who are 'victims of society', suffering from poverty, bad housing, etc.

The healthy person strives to develop his potential and use the crises and transitions of his life as opportunities for growth – but the social systems in which he lives may need changing in order to provide the appropriate conditions for that growth.

The acquisition and perpetuation of psychological disturbance

In essence, Egan's view of how people acquire and perpetuate psychological disturbance depends as much on factors from the environment as on factors within the individuals themselves. He spends little time on 'why' a client is 'disturbed', and while admitting that the past affects present behaviour, is more concerned with helping the client explore his present perceptions and behaviour. In this respect he agrees with the following statement by Carl Rogers: 'Present tensions and present needs are the only ones which the organism endeavours to reduce and satisfy. While it is true that the past experience has served to modify the meaning which will be perceived in present experiences, yet there is no behaviour except to meet a present need' (Rogers 1951).

Egan suggests that one way of looking at 'crazy behaviour' might be that when people face stressful life situations they do not have the skills needed to deal with the crisis and stress and so 'fall apart', try bizarre, ineffective solutions or give up. He does not advocate that a simplistic 'lack of skills' model should take the place of a medical model of psychopathology, but suggests that erratic and immature behaviour can often be traced to a lack of skills, and skill deficit may be an important part of any behaviour problem. Emotional disturbance may be a normal reaction to a difficult developmental crisis: for example, excessive anxiety may be due to a lack of knowledge and skills.

Psychological disturbance may be caused or perpetuated by the following *factors within the person.*

(a)   Passivity or learned helplessness, blaming others for problems, not able to take control.

(b)   Low self-concept, self-defeating attitudes, perhaps learned from experiences in the environment or from the person's perception of their experiences.

(c)   The individual has been reinforced for dysfunctional behaviour and may still be repeating old patterns. He does not have the knowledge or skills he needs in order to work at changing behaviour.

(d) Confusion or conflict over values may lead to passivity, depression and an inability to make decisions.

(e) 'The psychopathology of the average': the individual is not using the strengths and resources he has.

(f) The individual has not learned to manage his emotions, and these are distorting his perception: fear, fixed habits, perfectionism or dependence on authority keep him from living effectively.

(g) The individual has neither the knowledge nor the skills to tackle his problems systematically: he continues to apply inappropriate solutions or cannot risk new ways of behaving.

(h) He has insight into his problems but not the support and challenge he needs to act on them.

(i) He has too many crises in his life at once and is immobilized.

(j) He is stuck in a transition period between developmental stages and has no ability to make new commitments or risk new roles: he cannot ask for help.

In addition to all these internal factors, the following *environmental factors* may be influential:

(a) People are victims of social systems which limit their options for action: for example poverty and bad housing may be prime causes of psychological disturbance.

(b) Individuals may be helped by therapists to cope with problems and then returned to a destructive 'system' which raises more problems. The locus of the problem is in the system but the individual lacks knowledge and skills to attempt to change the system.

(c) 'Key systems', for example, family, education, peers, may not provide support, challenge or the opportunities to acquire knowledge and learn skills for healthy development. Education does not normally teach 'human skills' and prepare people for developmental tasks and transitions; it is falsely assumed that people grow into human skills without having to learn them. Human support is vital at every stage of development, and its lack retards growth.

(d) The environment and developmental stages make demands which the person has not the skills and support to meet, particularly if earlier developmental tasks have not been completed at the appropriate stage: for example, if group play is not experienced in mid-childhood the person may not have developed skills in relating to peers.

(e) The present state of the world and the individual's inability to affect what happens (for instance, nuclear disarmament) may produce alienation, despair and a loss of hope for the future.

Practice

Goals of helping

The principal aim of the Egan model of helping is to assist clients to 'manage the problem situations of their lives a bit (or even a great deal) more effectively' (Egan 1982). Egan argues that clients can be helped to deal with even the most serious problems a *little* more effectively; even in the face of chaos, therapists should be able to help the client do *something*. Within that aim there are, then, two kinds of goals.

Goals central to the helping process itself

(a) to establish a warm, accepting relationship that helps the client explore freely; to help him understand more objectively so that he sees the need for action; to help him establish specific concrete goals and to help him plan and take action. Egan emphasizes that establishing a relationship is not a goal in itself, but a means to an end, helping the client manage his problems so that he lives more effectively;

(b) to help the client participate in and 'own' the helping process, thereby maintaining the client's self-responsibility;

(c) to make the counselling process as explicit as possible so that the client can understand and share in the process as a partner;

(d) to teach the client 'problem management' so that he can transfer his newly learned skills and knowledge to other situations.

Goals leading to specific outcomes for the client

In this model, goal-setting is the central point of the helping process; the importance of helping the client set clear workable goals cannot be overstressed. Some of these goals leading to positive outcomes might include:

(a) to help the client set his own goals which are appropriate to his developmental stage and realistic in terms of both his inner resources and the resources and constraints of the social systems of his life;

(b) to help the client develop realistic self-direction and self-determination;

(c) to help the client change behaviours that are self- and other-destructive and acquire the knowledge and skills of behaviour change;

(d) to help the client acquire skills, especially interpersonal skills that help him live more effectively;

(e) to develop the client's responsibility for himself so that he handles problems and refashions his life according to his own values;

(f) to give the client knowledge of developmental stages, tasks and crises and to help him acquire life skills to pursue the tasks in his particular setting;

(g) to help the client discover what kind and degree of problem management is possible (some situations are less manageable than others);

(h) to help the client recognize and develop his internal and external resources and strengths so that he leaves the helping process better equipped to live more effectively;

(i) to stimulate the client to live more fully, develop his potential, rise above 'the psychopathology of the average'.

These goals are both therapeutic and educational.

Because goal-setting is central to this model it is important that the client is helped to move from stating a general aim or intent towards deciding what he would like to do in concrete terms. He is helped to set goals which are:

(a) clear and very specific;

(b) measurable or verifiable;

(c) realistic in terms of the client's resources – within his control, finances, etc.

(d) adequate – contributing to managing the problem;

(e)   in keeping with the client's values;
(f)   set in a reasonable time frame.

Egan suggests that setting concrete and specific goals may not be a natural part of a client's style; many people prefer to jump to action or hope goals will just 'emerge'. However, he sees it as the helper's responsibility to reach goal-setting as part of problem management.

The person of the helper: helping style

In Egan's model, the person and style of the helper, what she is, what skills and knowledge she has and how she uses them, and particularly her level of interpersonal skills, are the most important factors in determining whether or not the client is helped. Egan's view of the skilled helper is based on the core qualities and skills which Carkhuff identified as essential for the 'high-level functioning helper', that is to say *empathy, respect, concreteness, genuineness, self-disclosure, confrontation and immediacy* (Carkhuff 1969a, 1969b); indeed, helpers who are deficient in these qualities may actually make their clients worse. Effective helpers have to be able to communicate those qualities so that they can both support and challenge their clients. Support without appropriate challenge may be ineffective; challenge without adequate support may be damaging.

Egan links the core qualities with the idea that helping is a social influence process (Strong 1968) and that the skills which communicate respect, genuineness and accurate empathy are behavioural ways of establishing the expertness, trustworthiness and attractiveness of the helper.

Respect is expressed by attitudes towards the client, regarding him as unique, valuing him and seeing him as having his own resources (even if these are currently blocked) and capable of self-determination. Respect is also demonstrated by attending, by suspending critical judgement and by communicating warmth. The degree of warmth may vary with different clients' needs: some are helped by a more intimate relationship and some by a more matter-of-fact one. The helper has to judge the needs and respond appropriately.

Genuineness is expressed by being a person, not just 'in role' as helper, by being spontaneous (though not necessarily verbalizing every thought to the client); by being assertive without being aggressive, by not being defensive, and by being capable of deep self-disclosure when appropriate.

Accurate empathy is the communication of the helper's understanding of the client's thoughts, feelings and experiences. It reflects the helper's ability to perceive the world 'as if' through the client's eyes and to use his frame of reference.

The expression of these qualities – respect, genuineness and accurate empathy – gives the helper power and influence over the client. How she uses or misuses this power is determined by her own values. Egan suggests that the social influence process at its best does not rob clients of self-responsibility but rather promotes it; helpers can be seen as 'consultants in effective living' who influence their clients to take responsibility for both the helping process and their own lives.

Egan gives a 'portrait of a helper' which seems an ideal at which to aim. It begins: 'Ideally (helpers) are first of all committed to their own growth – physical, intellectual, social-emotional and spiritual – for they realize that helping often involves modeling the behavior they hope others will achieve. They know they can help only if, in the root sense of the term, they are 'potent' human beings – that is people with both the resources and the will to act' (Egan 1982). The portrait also emphasizes that helpers

> have respect for their bodies and need a high level of energy; read actively and hungrily and make what they read work for them; turn good theory and research into practical programmes; have common sense and social intelligence; are not afraid of deep human emotions and are able to respond spontaneously and effectively; can see the world through their clients' eyes and genuinely care for those who come for help; are not afraid to challenge clients with care and to help clients place demands on themselves; are pragmatists and will draw on all possible helping resources that will enable the clients to achieve their goals; may use a variety of techniques, follow a helping model but are not rigid in its application; are not afraid to enter someone's world, no matter how distressing; can handle crises, mobilize their energies and help others to do so; have their own human problems and do not retreat from them, knowing what it means to be a client.

If they are to assist others, helpers must be seen to be living effectively; yet they know they, too, are 'in process' and that each stage of their own lives has its own developmental tasks, crises and challenges which they must meet. In essence, helpers are 'consultants', 'trainers in skills' and 'educators' modelling 'man in process of becoming'.

Major therapeutic techniques

The hallmark of the Egan helping model is the sensitive use of a range of skills in response to clients' needs, mediated through a caring relationship in which the helper can both support and challenge her client. The skills needed by both helper and client are defined in detail and with clarity in *The Skilled Helper* (Egan 1982), which outlines a three-stage helping model. This is offered as a flexible, humanistic, broadly based problem-management approach: Stage 1, *explore*; Stage 2, *understand*; Stage 3, *act*. It is practical and presents clearly defined helping skills. It aids the helper to make sense of the clutter – or richness – of the techniques available from a variety of theories. Egan describes it as a 'map for integrating eclectic approaches', a clear conceptual framework to enable systematic borrowing, useful both for training helpers and working with clients. The model is developmental, that is, systematic and cumulative: the work in Stage 2 is dependent on the quality of the helping in Stage 1, while Stage 3 is directly affected by the quality of the work in Stages 1 and 2.

The three-stage helping model

Stage 1: exploration and focusing; clarifying the problem
The helper aims to establish a rapport and relationship with the client by giving close attention, listening actively, responding genuinely and demonstrating that she is 'being with' him by empathic, accepting responses. Because of the way the helper responds the client is encouraged to explore specifically and concretely his feelings, thoughts, behaviour and experiences which relate to the problem situation, and to clarify his specific concerns. Salient helping skills at this stage are: attending; observing; good unbiased listening; communicating empathy and respect by responding accurately; picking up core messages, reflecting feelings, summarizing, using appropriate open questions to help the client be concrete and focus on specific concerns.

Stage 2: promoting new perspectives and deeper understanding leading to goal-setting
The helper assists the client in piecing together the picture that has emerged in Stage 2, helps him to see themes, broader issues and patterns where relevant and so develop new perspectives on himself and his situ-

ation and then decide what he might do about it. The skills of Stage 2 help the client deepen his self-understanding, increase his awareness of the need for action and help him set specific goals. Salient helping skills at this stage are all the skills of Stage 1, plus: summarizing; integrating themes; offering new perspectives or alternative frameworks; offering information when appropriate; communicating advanced accurate empathy; self-sharing; challenging and helping the client challenge himself; immediacy (expressing what is happening in the interaction); timing and pacing, goal-setting. Any of these skills can be used to provide the right balance of challenge or support for the client.

Stage 3: designing and implementing action
The helper aims to help the client to act, making use of his new understanding of himself and his situation. She explores with the client a variety of ways of achieving the goals that have been set, and helps him identify what resources and strengths he has and can use. She helps the client choose and work out a specific plan of action, taking into account costs and gains for himself and others. She supports him in implementing the plan, and afterwards helps him to evaluate it. Salient helping skills at this stage are all the skills of Stages 1 and 2 plus: an ability to be creative, use divergent thinking and encourage the client in these skills; the knowledge and ability to use (and teach) theories of how behaviour is changed and maintained; decision- and problem-solving skills; the ability to teach the skills of 'effective living'; a knowledge of resources.

The *Skilled Helper* (Egan 1982) presents, in detail, methods of learning and using the skills and applying them to a wide range of clients, including resistant and reluctant ones. The model is supported by and developed from extensive research with detailed references.

The three-stage model can be seen as having eight steps:

Stage 1   Exploration (1)
            Focus on specific concerns (2)
Stage 2   Developing new perspectives (3)
            Setting specific goals (4)
Stage 3   Exploring possible ways to act (5)
            Choosing and working out a plan of action (6)
            Implementing the plan (7)
            Evaluation (8)

The eight steps are helpful 'milestones' for assessing what is happening in the helping process and planning subsequent progress. Although the model is developmental, it is not a blueprint for all helping relationships but needs to be used flexibly; the helper should move backwards and forwards among the stages as seems helpful to the client.

Thus the three-stage model itself is the major therapeutic tool in this approach to helping. It subsumes and is supported by other particular techniques, of which the two most notable therapeutic features are as follows. The first is making available to the client the skills and 'working knowledge' (i.e. that which has immediate practical application) he needs in order to help himself live more effectively and change the 'passivity of learned helplessness' into positive action. Secondly, helpers working with the Egan model legitimately and pragmatically use any techniques from other approaches to counselling and therapy which enable clients to reach their goals.

Within those two overall approaches, the main therapeutic techniques are chosen to provide the client with adequate support, offer appropriate challenge and enable him to move to take effective action. In order to provide *support*, essential techniques are: establishing a caring relationship, chiefly through the communication of empathy, acceptance and genuineness; facilitating the exploration of problems and issues – especially those causing pain and dissonance – in a safe, warm climate; and helping a client to focus on and take responsibility for his own concerns in concrete and specific language. Therapeutic techniques which offer *challenge* include: the communication of advanced empathy (bringing into focus and making sense of feelings or thoughts that have been 'unavailable', out of reach of the client, but which involve significant themes); helping a client gain new perspectives by offering alternative frameworks, facing him with inconsistencies or identifying patterns and 'connecting islands'; applying specific techniques from Gestalt, transactional analysis or rational-emotive approaches; and enabling a client to set clear, workable goals which feel within reach.

If the balance of support and challenge is appropriate, clients will be able to move to *action*. Relevant therapeutic techniques may then involve behaviour change methods: applying the principles of changing and maintaining behaviour, such as reinforcement, extinction, punishment, avoidance and shaping. The client can be helped to understand the operation of such forces (either for or against him); and if he shares with and learns from the helper the relevant knowledge and skills involved in changing behaviour, he is able to avoid possible manipulation and retain self-responsibility and self-direction. Other techniques include: generating teaching and learning methods, such as brainstorming and creative imagining; assertiveness training; self-management skills; problem-solving methods, notably the 'force-field analysis' approach with the clear weighing of costs and consequences; and the use of homework to extend work done in helping sessions. This can encourage a client to take responsibility for his own progress; it might cover trying out practical skills, doing written exercises, reading to extend 'working knowledge', writing a journal, keeping records or planning the use of time.

The use of *contracts*, whether for support, challenge or action, is a powerful therapeutic technique. Since helping, like any interpersonal relationship, is affected by implicit contracts and unspoken agreements, the negotiation of explicit contracts may clarify and simplify some of the processes and enable the client to feel a participant in, and responsible for, the helping process.

Finally, a major and consistent therapeutic feature of the Egan model is its emphasis on helping clients to identify and use their *strengths*, whatever the context of problems, so that self-esteem can grow and enable them to face their difficulties and take action to live (if only a little) more effectively.

The change process in helping

Clients seek help because they are experiencing difficulties or are in pain; because they want to make choices or changes or reduce confusion; or because they are not living as fully as they wish. In Egan's model, clients are influenced by the helper to undertake ways of learning how to cope with their problems and how to act so that they live more effectively. Such change is mediated by the following.

The social influence process Through this process the helper encourages the client to involve himself in, and work at, the learning process. Egan quotes (among others) Strong's, (1968) view of helping as an 'interpersonal influence process': briefly, when a helper attempts to aid a client bring about change in his life, dissonance is produced in the client; he will attempt to get rid of the dissonance by discrediting the counsellor or by discrediting the issue. Strong postulates that the extent to which a counsellor is seen as 'expert, attractive, and trustworthy' will reduce a client's attempts to discredit the helper. In Stage 1 of Egan's model the helper, by communicating empathy, acceptance and genuineness, is seen as competent, attractive and trustworthy; this gives her power to influence the client to move on through the stages of the learning process which may be painful and difficult. Such power can be misused, but in this model the helper uses her power to encourage the client to learn and take responsibility for himself, so making him a partner in the learning process.

Techniques which help the client learn and act The helper has an image of the client as learner. One way of seeing human development is that as the individual develops and meets new challenges in his life, his cycle of perceiving–attending–transforming–acting needs to increase in complexity so that he can respond flexibly in the way he perceives. transforms and acts. The three-stage model outlined above is a systematic way of promoting this learning process, but it should be used as a map, not as a strait-jacket. The salient points of change can be summarized as follows.

In Stage 1, exploration and clarification are sufficient to help some clients perceive differently, attend perhaps to neglected areas and transform their perception so they can go away and take action (which may be just thinking differently) without further help. The change process stems from the 'climate' which frees them to explore and change their perceptions – and sometimes self-defeating emotions subside when listened to. Other clients need further help and, indeed, Egan warns against using exploration and insight as the only way to bring about change in all clients. He castigates the 'eternal search for deeper insights divorced from action' and suggests that the client who believes everything will be all right if he can only understand himself fully, is indulging in 'magical thinking'.

Clients who need Stage 2 help are encouraged: to view themselves, others and the world from different perspectives; to attend to new information to enlarge their view; to see the world differently by loosening old constructs, releasing emotions and clarifying values. Exploration and self-disclosure can release 'healing forces' or resources in the client, or may produce disequilibrium, disorganization, shame and crisis. The counsellor needs to support the client through this and help him use the crisis to initiate change. The change in a client's perception may alter his view of himself as a 'victim' blaming others for his problems, and may enable him to begin to see how he can set goals to bring about change and so move from passivity towards being an agent in his own life. Such a client may need no further help, or may need to go on to Stage 3, in which he will learn to act.

Clients get stuck and cannot act because their perceptual field is too narrow. The helper may challenge the client's perception: there may be many ways he could 'act' in order to achieve his goal. The helper further encourages the client to change his perception of himself as 'helpless' to 'potent' human being by: attending to his strengths and to the possible resources that he is not using; helping him break action down into small enough steps to get some success and so increase his confidence; helping him learn to use behaviour modification techniques so as to increase his power to change his behaviour; helping him learn the skills he needs; giving the appropriate balance of support and challenge throughout the helping process so that change can take place at the right pace for the client; and finally, because the helper has a working knowledge of human development processes, she can help the client use transition and crisis periods as opportunities to learn and grow.

Case Example
The client

Linda, aged 35, was referred by a friend because of being depressed and unhappy in her job. Working with Stages 1 and 2 of the helping model (exploration leading to understanding) gave the following picture of the client for her and for me.

She was an accountant who had worked for a firm of accountants since she qualified and now felt she was stuck and would like to move. She lived and kept house for her widowed father, and any other job she took would have to be fairly local. This fact did not yield many prospects.

Home and job both seemed dull, and she seemed to lack the initiative to change but felt that unless she did so she would be stuck for the rest of her life. She was generally fed up with work, but recently another of the accountants had begun to make sexual remarks to her which she found very distressing and she dreaded any contact with him. This had spurred her into thinking about leaving, but her father said she should not give up a safe job in these times of job shortage. She had looked after her father for the last ten years, since her mother died. Although he was perfectly fit, she felt she could not leave him to look after himself – and of course there were few or no local opportunities for jobs. She was very frustrated with the restrictions this imposed. In addition, her father did not like having anybody to stay, so she could not invite friends for extended visits; also, he liked her to take him out in the car at weekends. She was fond of him and did not want to hurt him; but as she explored these issues she became very angry and tearful about her feelings of being trapped, with life 'passing her by'. She had had boyfriends in the past but had not wanted to make any commitment to them, and they had disappeared. She rarely met any 'free men' now. She had one or two close women friends but now did not make enough time and effort to see them frequently. She had no links with her community, belonged to no church, clubs or classes, and seemed to spend her leisure time at home watching TV, reading and knitting. Weekends were spent on housework and taking her father out. As she explored herself and her life, she became increasingly angry, and from feeling helplessly trapped began to think about how life could be different. She had the following strengths: physical fitness, an attractive appearance, intelligence, good qualifications, sensitivity, a willingness to work on herself and liveliness when released from anxiety.

The acquisition and perpetuation of psychological disturbance from a developmental perspective

Linda was in the early adulthood stage (22–40) but had not completed many of the tasks of moving into adulthood from adolescence, such as achieving autonomy, loving and making a commitment to another person, becoming an active community member and citizen and learning how to use leisure time. Using this framework assisted me in helping Linda to assess what was wrong and what was right in her life and what she might begin to do about it.

She was a woman who 'let things happen to her', and seemed to have developed a passive attitude to life which meant she was not developing much of her own potential. It took some sort of crisis at work to bring her to ask for help. Underlying this was the mid-thirties stage in development. She began to recognize that marriage and children were becoming increasingly unlikely, and yet she was not clear what other purpose her life could have – with the exception of looking after her father. Egan suggests that the transitions between one developmental stage and the next, which may be at times of crisis, uncertainty and emotional disturbance, are opportunities for personal growth provided the right balance of support and challenge are there.

The helping process

In the first two sessions, in terms of the model, we moved backwards and forwards between Stages 2 and 3, creating a warm relationship so that she was able to explore (Step 1) in more depth and, as insight developed, focus on some of the feelings about herself, about her father and about her anger and fear at work, her depression about her life and its pointlessness (Step 2). She had held on to her emotions for most of her life, and it was difficult for her to let go. However as she began to trust me she was able to express her misery, by crying, and her anger towards both her co-worker and her father. By putting themes together I helped her look at her passivity, her feelings of being a 'victim', and at what resources she had which might help her to act (Step 3).

In the third session, we looked at areas she could work on: (a) the difficulties at work and how to cope with them; (b) exploring what sort of life she wanted; (c) looking for and preparing for a new job; and (d) getting more freedom to do what she wanted to do. She chose the situation at work, and I reinforced this as it seemed immediate: if she coped with that, it would give her some sense of control over her life and some confidence (Step 2). She defined a specific goal: 'to cope with the sexual remarks without getting upset'. This brought us to Step 4 and the end of Stage 2 (deeper understanding, leading to planning possible action). We made a contract at this stage to work on this goal in forthcoming sessions. This brought us to Stage 3.

Step 5 was to look at all the possible methods she could use to reach her goal. Egan suggests that many people are trapped in their problems because they only see one solution and the counsellor needs to be creative in helping clients to generate many possibilities and then assess the costs and consequences of each. We used a felt-tip pen and a large sheet of paper to write down possibilities: ignore him, change her job, become desensitized to sexual remarks, report him to superiors, ask him to stop, tell him how it makes you feel. We looked at the costs and consequences of each of those, and she chose 'to tell him how she feels and ask him to stop' (Step 6). We discussed the skills she would need to carry this out, and I explained to her 'assertive' skills and 'body management' skills which would enable her to talk to him and cope with her feelings while she did it. She agreed to spend the next session learning and practising these skills, and I gave her some homework to do in preparation: a tape on relaxation and breathing (Step 7).

We spent the next two sessions working on these skills, and role-playing situations in which she could practise being assertive. As she worked, we needed to continue to help her explore her feelings (Stage 1). Between sessions she practised her skills by taking some goods back to a shop and getting money refunded – this gave her some confidence. We finally planned the way she would approach the man at work and what she would say, and role-played possible responses. She needed support and a challenge to start behaving in new ways, and I was conscious of trying to keep the balance right. She found role-playing very difficult at first, and I used Stage 1 skills to help her express and explore her feelings. As we persevered and made some of the role-play fun, she began to enjoy it and produce creative ideas which I reinforced. She fixed a time to see the man and asked if she could telephone me when she had done it.

The next session was spent going over what had happened (Step 8). She was pleased that she had been able to confront him without being aggressive or withdrawing, but had found it very difficult to cope with first his angry feelings and then his hurt feelings. She recognized, too, that this was a major problem with her father. This led on to further exploration of her relationship with him (back to Stages 1 and 2). She wanted life to be different, but was not sure how. In preparation, I gave her some reading on developmental stages and tasks, and a 'life planning' exercise to work through and bring to the next session. This exercise formed the basis of the next sessions in which she began to plan and experiment with new ways of spending her time and new ways of relating to her father.

Major therapeutic techniques: the change process

The developing rapport between us enabled her to begin exploring thoughts and feelings she had not talked about before. Helping her to be specific in exploring enabled her to bring up deeper feelings and understand what was going on in her life and interactions – and what was missing. Deeper empathy, summarizing themes and gentle challenging helped her to take a different perspective on herself and her life and begin to see that she had some power to change things. This led her to formulate goals. Learning through role-play, practising and trying out skills of assertiveness with support helped her begin to behave in different ways. Success in working on one problem gave her confidence to go on working on others. This learning to work in a systematic way on problems may be extended to other areas of her life. A contract, formulated after two sessions, to work on the specific goal of 'coping at work', provided a structure and clarity on how we would work together, and helped her to begin to 'own' the helping process. This seemed to generate some energy and gave her a feeling that she could begin to make things happen instead of being a passive victim. Giving her homework assignments gave her a feeling of participation: she was not dependent on me and could work on her own. The material helped her to have a deeper understanding of herself and some working knowledge which she could use to clarify her values and so begin to define what she wanted.

The change process began with building a relationship. This enabled me to influence her to move forward through the three stages of the model and act to change her immediate problem. Taking action increased her trust in me and her confidence in herself; she could then begin to tackle the more difficult problems in her life. She is still working on them.

References

Blocher D H (1966) *Developmental Counseling*, Ronald, New York

Brammer L (1973) *The Helping Relationship: Process and Skills*, Prentice-Hall, Englewood Cliffs, N J

Carkhuff R R (1969a) *Helping and Human Relations 1: Selection and Training*, Holt Rinehart and Winston, New York

Carkhuff R R (1969b) *Helping and Human Relations 2: Practice and Research*, Holt, Rinehart and Winston, New York

Corrigan J D, Dell D M, Lewis K N, Schmidt L D (1980) Counseling as a social influence process: a review, *Journal of Counseling Psychology* 27:395–431

Egan G (1975, 1982) *The Skilled Helper: A Model for Systematic Helping and Interpersonal Relating*, Brooks/Cole, Monterey, Cal.; 1st edition, p. 7; 2nd edition, pp. 26, 33

Egan G (1981) *Exercises in Helping Skills*, revised edition, Brooks/Cole, Monterey, Cal.

Egan G, Cowan M A (1979) *People in Systems: A Model for Development in the Human-Service Professions and Education*, Brooks/Cole, Monterey, Cal., pp. 5, 8, 34–6

Egan G, Cowan M A (1980) *Moving into Adulthood: Themes and Variations in Self-Directed Development for Effective Living*, Brooks/Cole, Monterey, Cal.

Frank J D (1973) *Persuasion and Healing*, 2nd edition, John Hopkins University Press, Baltimore

Ivey A E (1971) *Microcounseling: Innovations in Interviewing Training*, Charles C Thomas, Springfield, Ill.

Kagan N (1975) *Influencing Human Interaction*, American Personnel and Guidance Association, Washington

Maslow A H (1968) *Toward a Psychology of Being*, 2nd edition, Van Nostrand Reinhold, New York

Rogers C R (1951) *Client-Centered Therapy*, Houghton Mifflin, Boston, p. 492

Rogers C R (1957) The necessary and sufficient conditions of therapeutic change, *Journal of Counseling Psychology* 21: 95–103

Sherman A R (1973) *Behaviour Modification: Theory and Practice*, Brooks/Cole, Monterey, Cal.

Skinner B F (1953) *Science and Human Behavior*, Macmillan, New York

Strong S R (1968) Counseling An interpersonal influence process, *Journal of Counseling Psychology* 15: 215–224

Tyler L E (1969) *The Work of the Counselor*, 3rd edition, Appleton-Century Crofts, New York

Watson D, Tharp R (1981) *Self-Directed Behavior*, 3rd edition, Brooks/Cole, Monterey, Cal.

Suggestions for Further Reading

Egan G (1975, 1982) *The Skilled Helper: A Model for Systematic Helping and Interpersonal Relating*, Brooks/Cole, Monterey, Cal

Egan G (1981) *Exercises in Helping Skills*, revised edition, Brooks/Cole, Monterey, Cal.

Egan G (1977) *You and Me: The Skills of Communicating and Relating to Others*, Brooks/Cole, Monterey, Cal.

Egan G, Cowan M (1979) *People in Systems: A Model for Development in the Human-Service Professions and Education*, Brooks/Cole, Monterey, Cal.

Egan G, Cowan M (1980) *Moving into Adulthood: Themes and Variations in Self-Directed Development for Effective Living*, Brooks/Cole, Monterey, Cal.

Chapter 16 Eclectic Psychotherapy: A Structural-Phenomenological Approach

Stephen Murgatroyd and Michael J Apter

Introduction

In this chapter we shall describe a theoretical system – reversal theory – which can act as a systematic basis for the choice of therapeutic plans by eclectic therapists. It requires the therapist to develop an understanding of the client's personality and motivation as well as an understanding of the relationship between different types of therapeutic intervention and the basic 'structural features' of the client's problem. We present this material since, first, it provides a systematic approach to the practice of eclectic psychotherapy; second, it provides a basis for evaluating both the process of psychotherapy and outcomes in terms that are neutral to particular therapeutic orientations; and third, it reflects our own practice as therapists working in a variety of settings.

It will be noted that we have not called this form of systematic eclecticism 'reversal therapy', since there is not a particular set of therapeutic practices which derive exclusively from the application of reversal theory to client problems. Rather, we see reversal theory as providing a thoroughgoing, empirically grounded basis for encouraging and enabling therapists to choose appropriate techniques for their clients and even to combine techniques from different forms of therapy. This chapter is unlike other contributions to this volume in that it describes an approach to counselling and therapy which both requires a redefinition of clients' presenting problems and presents a general framework within which different well-established therapeutic approaches have a place.

Historical Context and Developments in Britain

Unlike many therapeutic procedures, the idea and practice of systematic eclecticism using reversal theory originated in Britain and is being used in a number of countries at the present time. Developed in the period 1974–1980 by Dr K. C. P. Smith, a consultant psychiatrist, and Dr Michael J. Apter, a psychologist, the theory of psychological reversals began as a general description of the psychology of motivation and human action, and arose initially in the context of the child guidance clinic.

In essence, reversal theory sought to offer an explanation for various paradoxes in human behaviour: such as the fact that while an individual may be a sensation-seeker at a particular time, at others he may be a sensation-avoider, or that while he likes to plan ahead on certain occasions, he otherwise tends to lead his life as a series of instant responses to seemingly unexpected events. A particular concern of the theory was to understand three features of human action: (a) the inconsistency of the actions performed by a particular person, even over relatively short periods of time; (b) the bewildering complexity of motives which people use to account for their actions; and finally, (c) the fact that the same action performed by the same person on different occasions can be attributed such different meanings.

The theory has been described fully in Apter (1982), and Apter and Murgatroyd (forthcoming), the latter offering a detailed exposition of the value of the theory as a systematic basis for eclectic psychotherapy. In addition, material valuable to an understanding of the therapeutic implications of the theory can be found in Apter (1983), Apter and Smith (1979a, 1979b), Blackmore and Murgatroyd (1980), Murgatroyd (1981), Murgatroyd and Woolfe (1984) and Seldon (1980). Readers wishing to explore the experimental psychological basis of the theory, and not simply its therapeutic implications, should consult the work of Svebak and his co-workers, for instance: Svebak, Storfjell and Dalen (1982); Walters, Apter and Svebak (1982); Murgatroyd et al. (1978); and Svebak and Murgatroyd (1984). A critique of reversal theory is offered by Rowan (1981).

Theoretical Assumptions

The image of the person

The first assumption of the approach is that people can only be understood fully if the structure of their phenomenological field is taken into account. For this reason, the general approach which is adopted has come to be known as 'structural phenomenology' – a term which makes clear that it involves an attempt to understand the structure of individual experience (Apter 1981).

Since the terms 'structural' and 'phenomenological field' are used at various points in this chapter, it is necessary to be clear about their meaning from the outset. By 'phenomenological field' is meant (following Snygg 1941) the totality of an individual's experience at a given time: in other words, everything he is thinking about and aware of at that time. By the 'structural' features of some phenomenon are meant the way it is organized and the patterns it displays. Thus the concern of 'structural phenomenology' is with the way in which the phenomenological field is organized and how the particular contents of the field are assimilated to this organization. There are two respects in which the phenomenological field may be said to be structured. The first is the way in which it is organized at a particular time: for example, how focused or diffuse is it, and how far does it contain an awareness of the future? The second is the way it is organized over time: are there recognizable patterns of change from one type of structure to another, and if so, do these tend to recur? Both of these are of concern to structural phenomenology, as is the relationship of the said structure(s) to the individual's action. It is the second, temporal aspect which will be of particular concern to us here.

While these brief definitions may not seem particularly satisfactory, there are many entire texts devoted to structuralism (e.g. Levi-Strauss 1963) and to phenomenology (e.g. Thinès 1977) which explore these kinds of ideas fully. What is important to note here is, first, the idea that experience is essentially orderly and that this orderliness can be described in structural terms; and secondly, that a distinction can be made between the structure and the content of experience (although, of course, the two are intimately related). This distinction affects the way in which case histories are taken and cases documented since it emphasizes the need to explore structural features of the client's experience (and the relationship of these to his actions). It also crucially affects decisions about therapeutic programmes, as will be made clear in what follows.

In reversal theory, three pairs of phenomenological modes are identified. The characteristics of these so-called 'meta-motivational' modes are summarized in Figure 16.1. Each mode is a unique way of structuring the phenomenological field, especially in relation to motivational aspects of experience. (The way in which these modes can be characterized in structural terms is described more fully in Apter 1982.) The assumption is that one or other of each pair will be operative at a given time, so that at any one time the phenomenological field will be characterized by a subset of three of these six modes or states (the words 'mode' and 'state' being used interchangeably).

By way of illustration, let us examine two specific actions. First, consider someone who is driving his car faster than the official speed limit in a built-up area. He may be driving fast so as to ensure that he arrives in time for an important meeting (a telic reason), or because he enjoys the sensation of fast driving (a paratelic reason) or because he finds it exciting to defy the law in this way (paratelic negativism). A second example is persistent absenteeism from work. The person may be absent because of some anxiety about work (telic), because of some refusal to co-operate with others (negativistic) or because something has been found by the person concerned which gives instant rewards and sensations and which precludes attendance at work (paratelic).

These two examples make clear that identification of these different modes helps us understand a person's own motive for action – but they do more than this. The six modes outlined here involve meta-motives, and this is why they are called 'meta-motivational modes': that is, they are in a sense descriptions of the motives people have for having motives; they are the general motivational basis for the particular motives people have for specific actions. A glue sniffer might say that his motive for sniffing glue at a particular time was 'to get a buzz'; reversal theorists would ask what his motive was for having this motive, and see it as one way of satisfying his paratelic needs. Equally, a young adult who copies the behaviour of others in a particular gang to the detriment of his or her own individuality could be said to be motivated by a strong need for conformity which was being expressed in this particular form. All these examples should help to clarify the meaning of the term 'meta-motivational'; and they bring out the way in which different particular motives can be associated with the same meta-motivational modes, and the same motive can be associated with different meta-motivational modes. It is for this reason that simply identifying people's motives is not enough to understand the full significance of their actions.

Figure 16.1 presents the six meta-motivational modes so far identified within reversal theory as three pairs of opposite modes. Specific motives

TELIC

The person is seriousminded, planning-oriented and seeks to avoid arousal.

PARATELIC

The person is arousal-seeking, 'here and now' oriented, and pursues goals only insofar as they add to the immediate pleasure of a situation.

NEGATIVISTIC

The person does not wish to conform to a salient pressure that is felt to be imposed from outside.

CONFORMIST

The person wishes to conform to a salient pressure that is felt to be imposed from outside.

SYMPATHY

The individual feels a need to be sympathised with by the other with whom he is interacting, and transactions are experienced as involving 'giving' or 'receiving'.

MASTERY

The individual feels a need to dominate or control the other with whom he is interacting, and transactions are experienced as involving 'taking' or 'yielding up'.

Figure 16.1 Six meta-motivational states
Murgatroyd and Apter, 1984

for action at a given time can be related to one or other of the modes within each pair. What is important to note about these modes is that they are descriptions of *states* and not traits; more specifically, they are descriptions of the states from within which individuals 'view' their own specific motives for specific actions.

It may be thought that the reversal theory view of the person is rather 'static' – but this is not the case. Another part of the theory suggests that individuals will switch between pairs of meta-motivational states with some regularity; thus at any one time a person is either telic or paratelic, either negativistic or conforming, displaying either sympathy or mastery. But from time to time the person is seen to switch or *reverse* from one of the meta-motivational modes outlined in Figure 1 to the opposite member of the pair: hence the name of the theory.

This reversal process can occur as a result of many different factors. So far, three general categories have been identified.

(a)   *satiation*: after a prolonged period in one state (e.g. telic) there will be an increased likelihood of a reversal to the opposite (e.g. paratelic) state occurring;

(b) *frustration*: when the psychological needs of one state (e.g. the need to feel that one is behaving negativistically) are not being met, there will be a tendency for reversal to occur;

(c) *contingency*: the intrusion into the individual's psychological world of some social or other factor which leads to reversal: for example, imagine a sexual encounter that involves two persons mutually agreeing to mild aggression as a feature of their sexual repertoire. If one partner became unduly violent, the other would be likely to reverse from the paratelic state, in which the aggression had hitherto been enjoyed, to the telic state, in which the aggression would now be experienced as upsetting and avoidance of the aggression would be sought.

Whilst the basic description of the theory as outlined here provides an image of a person frequently changing operative states, this description can also be used to understand something of a person's enduring personality; for while individuals can be seen to be switching between states with some regularity, it is also clear from research (see Murgatroyd et al. 1978; Svebak and Murgatroyd 1984) that individuals have a tendency to spend more time in one state (e.g. telic) than another (e.g. paratelic). Although some might regard this as a trait, our view is that it is better to consider this as a form of 'dominance' or bias. Thus a person can be said to be telic or paratelic dominant, negativistic or conformist dominant, or sympathy or mastery dominant. This dominance does not preclude reversals from taking place; rather, it suggests that a person can be regarded as likely to spend more time in his or her dominant state than in its opposite, for each pair of states, during the course of reversals over time.

Reversal theory thus provides a vocabulary and grammar for understanding the inconsistency of individual actions. In addition, it helps us appreciate the importance of looking not only at the motives for a given piece of behaviour but also at the 'motives of the motives'. For, as we have seen, the theory makes clear that a person can perform a grossly similar piece of behaviour on different occasions not only for different motives but also for different 'meta-motives': hence the enigmatic quality of a person's experiences and actions.

As Hetherington (1983) has observed, reversal theory is concerned with the individual both as a biological *organism* and also as a *person* who is a part of a social milieu. The potential of the theory is that it offers a general, structural model for human action of all kinds.

Concepts of psychological health and disturbance

The previous section outlined the concepts of meta-motivation, reversal and dominance. It also provided brief descriptions of the six meta-motivational modes or states within which a great many specific motives for specific actions can be viewed. How, then, does reversal theory see the psychologically healthy person? According to current descriptions (Apter and Murgatroyd, forthcoming), healthy people have the following characteristics:

(a) They reverse between different meta-motivational modes with some frequency, given that they may also display dominance. (Paradoxically, the psychologically healthy person is one who is, in this respect, inherently inconsistent.)

(b) They usually find themselves in combinations of states which are appropriate to both their social environment and their own needs, and are generally able to achieve the satisfactions of the states in which they find themselves at each point in time.

(c) They are able to achieve the satisfactions of the state they are in without creating undue stress or disturbance in other people with whom they are interacting.

(d) They are able to achieve the satisfactions of the state which they are in without creating difficulties for the achievement of satisfactions in this or other states on subsequent occasions, or without restricting the possibility of reversing under appropriate conditions at later times.

Psychological ill-health or disturbance arises from the absence of one or more of these four qualities. Thus disturbance can be regarded as a consequence of:

(a) the relative inability to reverse, with the consequence of being 'stuck' in one mode for most of the time;

(b) reversals occurring at times or places when such reversal is inappropriate;

(c) behaviour which satisfies the person's own needs but in socially inappropriate ways;

(d) the achievement of satisfactions in one state in a way which makes reversal more difficult or makes the achievement of satisfaction in the same or the alternate state less likely in future.

These four kinds of what we shall term 'structural disturbance' constitute a new way of classifying clients' presenting problems. When taken together with an identification of the particular meta-motivational mode(s) involved in these structural disturbances, they provide the therapist with a major tool for problem classification which adds new dimensions to existing classifications.

To explore such structural features further, let us examine chronic anxiety and psychopathy within reversal theory terms. The structural disturbance in both of these presenting problems is the same: clients are unable to reverse and are entrenched in a particular meta-motivational mode. What differentiates them is the mode they are 'locked' into. The chronically anxious person is unable to reverse from the telic state into the paratelic state; furthermore, he shifts to an extreme form of telic motivation in the sense that he is unable to reduce his level of arousal, which he experiences as increasingly unpleasant. In contrast, the psychopath is 'locked' in the paratelic state and can only achieve the excitement he seeks by extreme behaviour, often at the expense of others, such as vandalism or crime. (In this case there is both reversal failure and inappropriate behaviour within the operative mode.) Dominance of the negativistic state may also be implicated here.

As will be clear from these two examples, the analysis of the nature of psychological disturbance involves an understanding of both the structural features of the person's phenomenological field and an identification of the particular meta-motivational modes concerned. To illustrate this point further, let us look at depression. Reversal theory identifies four types of depression, derived from an understanding both of structural features of depression and the way in which depression relates to the telic and paratelic states (Apter 1982). Two of these types are described below.

Anxiety depression This is a term that is used widely in the available literature on depression. In reversal theory terms, it arises from a failure to reverse out of the telic mode and involves the inability of such clients to reduce their arousal levels; as a result, they become concerned not only about the goals which they pursue and which give rise to the arousal but also about the fact of the arousal itself. This is combined with a feeling of helplessness about ever being able to change the situation.

Boredom depression Such clients are unable to reverse from the paratelic state and yet are unable to achieve the satisfactions of this state, so that they experience extreme boredom in a great many areas of life, especially sex, sleep and eating. Again, this is combined with a feeling that nothing can be done to change the situation.

It is interesting that these two kinds of depression are the opposite of each other: they involve contrasting interpretations of the nature of arousal and contrasting depressive behaviours. This paradoxical nature of depression has hitherto been poorly understood (Beck 1976). An examination of the structural properties of the person's experience and the way he or she is interpreting arousal helps us establish a different aetiology of depression. All this highlights the value of reversal theory as a basis for understanding the phenomenological world of the depressed person whilst at the same time advancing our understanding of the structure of depression as a personal experience. In general, all these examples illuminate the value of a structural approach to the aetiology of clients' presenting symptoms and the need for therapists to be attuned to the phenomenological world of their clients.

The acquisition of psychological disturbance

The theory of reversals makes no assumptions about the acquisition of disturbance. Whilst there is some evidence linking telic or paratelic dominance to psychophysiological characteristics (Svebak and Murgatroyd 1984) there is as yet no evidence linking structural disturbance to genetic or biological predispositions or to maturational processes.

Rather than seeking to locate psychological disturbance in terms of a trait psychology, as many other theories have done, reversal theory seeks to locate disturbance either in the descriptions provided by clients (in the case of reversal failure, inappropriate reversal and reversal-potential inhibition) or in those provided by others with a detailed knowledge of clients' behaviour (most especially in the case of inappropriate behaviour). It is important to recognize that some of these structural disturbances occur because clients' needs are being satisfied but satisfied in ways which are felt by others to be socially inappropriate or unhelpful. In the latter case, disturbance is socially defined.

These brief comments suggest that considerably more work is needed if our understanding of the aetiology of different types of structural disturbance is to be improved. In particular, there needs to be a much more developed understanding of the relationship between 'self' concepts and actions – something which Apter and Smith are currently working on (Apter and Smith 1984).

The perpetuation of psychological disturbance

Once disturbance has been acquired it may be sustained, exacerbated or decreased as a result of the way the disturbed individual is treated by others: for example, the reactions of others to a particular action may serve to increase the frequency of that action. In the case of a paratelic dominant boy truanting from school, for instance, an extreme emotional over-reaction from parents, teachers, social workers or counsellors may have the effect of reinforcing the truanting behaviour since the boy finds their reactions exciting. Such pleasantly high arousal levels can then be achieved at will by the boy through the effects of the truanting itself. Similar counter-productive reactions have been observed in cases of agoraphobia in telic dominant children, where threats only increase the anxiety associated with leaving 'safe' locations and reduce such children's ability to leave the home setting. In both these examples, the actions taken by others are unhelpful because they do not take into account the meta-motivational mode of the individual concerned.

For this kind of reason whole sequences and cycles of maladaptive interactions may occur. This is illustrated by the following family situation:

(a) Jake (aged twelve) presents a problem: he expresses fears about school and develops a variety of physical illnesses (a telic action).

(b) Mother moves in to try to protect Jake – especially from Father, who threatens him (thus helping to consolidate Jake's telic mode).

(c) Mother is laughed at by Sue and Father (who are both paratelic dominant and who use this situation to promote high arousal confrontations which they find pleasurable whilst in the paratelic state). These two accuse Mother of treating Jake like a baby (and the threat to Jake implied by this accusation increases his anxiety in the telic mode).

(d) Mother reacts to these taunts physically, becomes ill and is hospitalized (a telic response, like Jake's). She also becomes depressed.

(e) Father runs the family home in a far more paratelic style than Mother did. Jake returns to school showing no signs of the previous telic anxiety reaction to school; Father, Sue and Jake all engage in a variety of forms of mutual pleasure such as watching TV, playing Scrabble or Monopoly, taking walks, having occasional meals out, visiting friends, etc., most of these being things which were rarely done when Mother was at home.

(f) Mother recovers, returns home and takes over the management of the household.

(g) Father begins to withdraw and shows signs of boredom and restlessness, followed by depression; he drinks more and smokes roughly twice as much as when he was in charge at home. (He finds himself in a 'telic environment' when in a paratelic state and so finds it difficult to satisfy his meta-motivational needs.)

(h) Arguments burst out between Father and the other members of the family. (Father seeks to increase arousal so as to satisfy his needs whilst in the paratelic state; in so doing he unwittingly helps to consolidate the telic state of Mother, and this appears to facilitate a reversal for Jake from a paratelic state to a telic state.)

(i) Jake presents a problem, not going to school and showing signs of a great many physical ailments and illnesses (a result of a shift within the telic state to what might be thought of as in some sense a more extreme telic position).

(j) Mother moves in to protect Jake ... (go to b) above).

This case of Jake and his family shows clearly how disturbance is related to meta-motivational mode (as, for example, in the way Jake is locked into the telic state when Mother manages the household), and shows the ways in which psychological disturbance in members of a family can be perpetuated by means of a complex interaction between their operative modes at different times, mode dominance, cognitive appraisal and social reinforcements and punishments.

Practice

Before describing the particular approach to eclectic therapy we are pursuing, it may be helpful to repeat again that it is not our intention to advocate new forms of therapy, but rather to suggest that reversal theory provides a rationale for the therapist to make appropriate selections of therapeutic techniques from a broad repertoire. It should also be recognized that reversal theory, in addition to providing a means of reconceptualizing clients' presenting problems, also provides a means by which it is possible to examine the effect which a given therapeutic technique is likely to have in relation to the structural aspects of the disturbance: does it help to alleviate reversal failure, for example, or inappropriate reversal, or inappropriate behaviour within a particular meta-motivational mode?

Goals of therapy

The goals of eclectic therapy are to restore the person to effective coping and to assist the person to develop psychological health as described above. These goals need to be agreed between the client and therapist and, in our experience, need to be explicitly contracted for. In order to achieve these aims it is necessary for the client and therapist to engage in establishing a climate which is both emotionally safe and trusting and enabling of 'diagnostic' activity. In addition, both client and therapist need to be clear about the criteria by which effective coping is to be assessed and the achievement of psychological health to be measured. These tasks will be achieved in different ways for different clients, but it is important to develop some systematic way of assessing needs and contracting if eclectic therapy is to be both thorough and effective.

It will be appreciated that different goals may be equally therapeutic, and reversal theory helps to make clear that these are choices to be made not only about which techniques to use to achieve a given goal but also about the goals themselves. For example, the therapeutic goal in treating a phobia may be to help the client to relax, which is the most usual goal; but in principle there is an alternative: namely to help the client to experience high arousal as excitement rather than anxiety, that is, to switch modes.

Some forms of therapy seem to be more concerned with mode switching (it could be argued that much of Gestalt therapy is about this – cf. Perls 1969), while other forms of therapy seem to operate within a mode. For example, biofeedback seems to be based on the assumption that the client is in the telic state and that therefore the technique should be used only to lower arousal. Svebak and Stoyva (1980) have in fact argued that this is an unnecessarily limiting assumption and that biofeedback could also be used with clients in the paratelic state to help them to increase their felt arousal to pleasantly high levels.

The person of the therapist

Eclectic psychotherapists, in addition to displaying and effectively communicating the qualitative conditions of empathy, warmth and genuineness, need to display a confidence in the specific method employed at a given time. Moreover, they need to have a knowledge of the assumptions and working practices of a number of types of therapeutic intervention and to be aware of the limitations of specific therapeutic tools. These observations suggest that eclectic therapists need to be technically competent in the use of a variety of therapeutic methods whilst at the same time behaving scientifically to select and evaluate the effects of their intervention. If eclectic therapy is to develop beyond *post hoc* rationalization, it needs to be founded upon some systematic principles of therapy selection as well as upon a thorough understanding of clients' presenting problems.

Therapeutic style

The therapeutic style of therapists working within the framework of a structural phenomenological approach involves them giving careful consideration to: first, the structural features of therapeutic interventions (how does an intervention tactic relate to the structural features of the client's presenting problem?); and, second, the degree of involvement they wish to have with the client (how intense will the therapeutic relationship be?).

A great many types of therapeutic intervention are possible, especially for the eclectic therapist willing to utilize interventions from a variety of therapeutic schools. But the eclectic therapist may have to make further decisions about the precise way in which he is going to use the method he has chosen. For example, Minuchin (1974) describes a number of therapeutic techniques which the systems-oriented family therapist may choose to utilize. These include: (a) *blocking transactional patterns* – interrupting the normal patterns of behaviour or thinking which the client displays; (b) *emphasizing differences*, especially in relation to thinking and behaviour or thinking and emotional content; and (c) *developing inner conflict* – turning differences into conflict. Each of these three types of intervention has the effect of increasing the arousal a person experiences during therapy; but the therapist has at the same time to help the client interpret that arousal. In terms of reversal theory, increasing arousal through these processes could be used by the therapist to create an intensely telic experience (the arousal is interpreted as unpleasant) or an intensely paratelic experience (the arousal is interpreted as pleasant). In addition, the therapist may in certain cases be seeking to create conditions in which the meta-motivational mode involved in the client's presenting problem is satiated or frustrated so as to enable a reversal to take place during therapy and/or on later occasions. In these examples, the therapist seeks to identify the effect which a particular type of intervention may have on the structural features of the disturbance so that he may utilize them in an effective way.

In examining the structural basis of a particular intervention, the therapist needs also to consider the impact which his or her own personal qualities will have upon the client when using that intervention. For example, the effective use of paradoxical intention in certain cases requires the therapist to make a skilled and careful use of humour (Frankl 1969). The kind of humour which therapists use will be a function of their own preferences and their own ability to work with clients within a paratelic mode. To 'carry off' an effective paradoxical strategy, the therapist often has to push the client hard to reverse from a telic state to a paratelic state (this is the most common structural quality of this tactic), and humour is a valuable tool in this respect. Not all therapists, however, are or can be effective in this task; indeed, some feel themselves unable to utilize humour in their work at all and could therefore not use this form of paradox effectively (Kubie 1971).

These comments suggest that eclectic therapists need to be mindful of the potential structural effects of the interventions they intend to utilize. In addition, they need to show high levels of communicated empathy with their clients since they need to relate the process of therapy to the world as experienced by the client. This in turn raises issues of the degree of involvement with the client. Intervention programmes will vary in duration depending both on the structural problem presented and the intervention selected. Typically, therapy lasts no longer than twenty-five sessions. Since a variety of interventions may be involved, it is difficult to be specific about the level of involvement between client and therapist. Some interventions, such as those involving massage or dynamic meditation, involve close physical contact; whilst others require some distancing between client and therapist in order to be effective. The degree of involvement is, however, a significant determinant of therapeutic style.

Major therapeutic techniques

In considering possible therapeutic interventions, eclectic therapists need to:

(a) establish clearly the impact which a particular intervention is likely to have upon the structural feature of their clients' presenting problems;

(b) understand the mode within which a particular intervention is likely to be viewed and experienced by the client;

(c) locate firmly the impact such an intervention is likely to have upon various specific features of the client's phenomenological field.

Therapeutic techniques can be taken from any of the approaches to therapy described so far in this text and from many other therapies described and elaborated elsewhere. In choosing a type of treatment, eclectic therapists have to ask such questions as the following.

Concerning the structural impact

(a) Is this type of intervention especially useful in relation to reversal failure? If not, is it likely to exacerbate the problem, e.g. in the case of reversal failure, to entrench yet further the mode from within which the client is currently reporting distress?

(b)   The therapist needs to repeat these questions in relation to inappropriate reversal, inappropriate behaviour and the other types of structural disturbance.

(c)   To what extent does the impact of this type of intervention depend upon the client being in a particular state (e.g. telic/paratelic, conformist/negativistic) during therapeutic sessions? If it does, what climate-setting activities need to be engaged in so as to help to induce this state?

(d)   To what extent does the utility of this type of intervention depend upon social support outside the therapeutic sessions? If it does, how can such support best be obtained? (For instance: Should the help of other members of his family be sought? Does he need referral to a therapy group?)

Concerning the mode sought

(a)   In which mode (i.e. telic/paratelic, negativistic/conformist, sympathy/mastery) is most progress likely to be made in relation to the client's presenting problem?

(b)   How can this mode be achieved and sustained?

(c)   Who else (especially within the family) needs to be involved so as to help the client to achieve this mode fairly regularly?

(d)   What structural dangers are associated with the achievement of this mode?

The precise nature of the importance of such questions will become clearer in the case study to be presented below.

One point worth emphasizing is that eclectic therapists need to recognize that some types of intervention are likely to be structurally inappropriate for particular clients: for example, the use of Valium in the treatment of boredom depression or apathy-related stress conditions actually contributes to these conditions rather than alleviating them, because individuals in these conditions need higher, not lower, levels of arousal. Equally, relaxation training can actually be stressful for some clients who are paratelic dominant (Heide and Borkovec 1983).

In order to be able to answer the questions listed above about the type of treatment which they propose, eclectic therapists need to develop an adequate and detailed knowledge of their clients' phenomenal worlds. We have found Arnold Lazarus's (1976) set of headings for case-history taking to be especially helpful in our initial work with clients in order to examine their phenomenal worlds as fully as possible. Specifically, we explore with them their *behaviour, affective states, sensations, imagery, cognitions, interpersonal relationships* and *drug-taking behaviour,* such exploration being not an end in itself but a means of understanding the structural patterns of their action. In particular, these areas of their phenomenal world are explored so that we can understand: (a) the reversal processes that characterize their daily lives; (b) the way in which they cognitively appraise their own psychological processes; (c) the dominance of one meta-motivational mode or cluster of modes over another; (d) the interrelationship between modes; (e) the precise 'fabric' or content of the modes, to see if each of the modes commonly utilized by the person has an associated image or action-example which the therapist can make use of; and (f) the experience of previous helper behaviour in terms of modes and structures.

The change process in therapy

In order to complete a thorough examination of these areas of the person's life, therapist and client need to develop a great deal of mutual trust. This is why climate-setting activities – sharing of contract frameworks, brief biographies, some art drawing of the way in which the client perceives himself to have needs, some exploration of the expectations of the client for change – are vital ingredients in any assessment of the structural amd phenomenal features of the client's world. Climate-setting can also be done through small group work (we have often involved clients in small groups so as to help both set the climate for a therapeutic relationship and to assess the ability of the client to reverse) and through homework tasks which help to establish appropriate roles for the therapist in the client's mind.

This climate-setting period, which can last for between four and seven sessions, needs also to be used by the therapist to establish the likely structural impact of any intervention deemed to be appropriate. In addition, it will establish the mode(s) from within which the client is likely to work in therapy itself: it will help to decide the appropriateness or otherwise of humour, role-play, monodrama and many other standard intervention processes.

Following climate-setting, contracting for change and the therapist's decision concerning the intervention most suitable for the achievement of structural change, the therapy itself can begin in earnest. This period requires the therapist to assess continually the impact of the treatment on the structural features of the person: is it a) enhancing the person's ability to reverse, is it unblocking blocked reversal; b) making reversals more appropriate in terms of their timing; c) improving the nature of the behaviour the person uses to achieve the satisfactions associated with a particular mode; d) reducing the extent to which certain activities engaged in by the client inhibit or restrict subsequent reversal? These kinds of evaluation are central to the practice of eclectic therapy within the structural-phenomenological framework. Having first identified the person's problem in terms of structural disturbance, there is a need to ensure that the type of intervention chosen is in fact enabling appropriate structural change to occur rather than further consolidating and accentuating the disturbance itself.

In addition to examining the structural impact of therapy, there is also a need to monitor closely the modes within which the person operates during therapy and between therapeutic sessions. If the task is to establish a greater frequency of telic to paratelic reversals, then there is a need to enable this to happen during therapy and to monitor its occurrence outside therapeutic sessions (through diaries, specific assignments, witness accounts and other forms of self-report). This applies equally to concerns with the other meta-motivational modes – negativism/conformity, mastery/sympathy – and to relevant combinations of these modes (i.e. telic-conformity, negativistic-mastery, etc.). The therapist needs to understand and monitor the structural and phenomenological features of the way the client responds to treatment.

Case Example

This case study illustrates the application of many of these principles and procedures to a particular client and his problems. The case of David is one of obsessional washing and checking, which was interpreted as involving the structural disturbance of inhibited reversal.

David, aged thirty-seven, is unemployed and not well educated. He has been unemployed for three years. He lives alone, though occasionally in the past he has been able to form relationships with women who have shared his flat for short periods. None of the relationships he has had with women have lasted for more than three months; he says, 'They just can't cope with me.' When he did work it was as a clerk in an accountancy company, a job he had had for 21 years.

He has two particular obsessions. First, he needs constantly to ensure that he has protected himself against potential harm. He fears harm from other people (burglars, assailants, fire-raisers) or from illness. This behaviour takes the form of repeatedly checking the locks on doors and windows, checking the wiring of electricity plugs, dampening down the log fires in his flat to prevent sparks from inadvertently getting onto carpets, carrying lighted torches at night, avoiding contact with strangers, washing hands up to twenty-five times each day, always taking two showers a day, cleaning his teeth ten to twelve times a day and flushing the toilet two or three times after use. His second compulsion is to record all of his feelings of ill-health – headaches, cramps, pins and needles, toothache, tiredness, tenderness, pain – and to report these regularly to his doctor.

The doctor regarded David as anxiety-laden and treated him with small, regular doses of Librium, with little success. He referred the patient after two years.

During the climate-setting and contracting period of therapy, the therapist noted the following.

Behaviour David is obsessional about checking, washing and recording his illnesses. His obsession occupies a large part of his life – so much so that it excludes other people. Others 'can't cope with David the obsessional'.

Affect David is anxious to achieve goals and feels great anxiety when something prevents him from achieving the goal of maintaining his ritualistic behaviour. Yet David has lost sight of the goal that triggered this behaviour originally and has created a new superordinate goal: to be well at all times and to minimize danger. Anxiety arises if he is able to brush his teeth only three or four times a day, since this threatens his superordinate goal.

Sensation David seems apathetic when he is not anxious. His dominant mode is telic, but he finds it difficult to achieve relaxation. His vocabulary of subjective feelings is extremely limited and related almost exclusively to words expressing anxiety.

Imagery   David has four images in particular which he says appear spontaneously in his conscious thoughts. These are: (a) an image of himself as a leper having to warn others about his illness; (b) an image of himself as the victim of a vicious attack in his own home; (c) an image of himself as a smelly person to whom others do not want to talk; and (d) an image of himself as the only live person in a sea of people who have died because of their own negligence. According to David, these images are present something like 40% of his waking life, though their impact upon him varies in intensity at different times.

Cognitions   The above images are accompanied by several irrational thoughts. Two in particular are prominent: (a) a person needs to be constantly aware of the dangers that exist in the environment since these dangers can affect physical health and general well-being – a momentary lapse can result in terminal illness, severe pain or immediate death; (b) others are not as vigilant as he is; therefore it is dangerous to get too close to them. Also, he sometimes believes he is 'crazy', and at these times he cuts down on his obsessional behaviour; it is also at these times that he strengthens his relationships with others.

Interpersonal   David makes few contacts with others, except for professional advice and support. He has had occasional sexual relationships with women, but these he has found exceptionally difficult to 'organise' (his word) and 'sustain'.

Drugs   David takes Librium on prescription and aspirin very occasionally. He does not drink (danger of alcoholic poisoning, sclerosis of the liver), smoke (danger of lung cancer), take snuff (danger of throat cancer and nasal infection), use hair conditioner (danger of scalp diseases, according to a piece he read in a Sunday newspaper). He takes aspirin only after badgering the chemist into assuring him that the drug is appropriate for the specific pain he is experiencing and that there have been no developments in the research into its side-effects (especially in relation to stomach cancer and stomach bleeding).

The therapist working with David hypothesized that David was telic-mode inhibited: that is, David was 'locked' in the telic state and unable to reverse into the paratelic state. His anxiety resulted from the failure he experienced in achieving his goals of total safety and security. His images reflected the supra-importance of his telic goals and possibly helped to make them more difficult to achieve. The therapist made the following observations about the therapeutic strategy for David, organizing these in terms of a scheme outlined briefly in Apter (1982) and developed fully in Apter and Murgatroyd (forthcoming).

Means-Ends David needs to be shown that his choice of goals is arbitrary and more likely to damage his health than to safeguard it. This will involve reducing the significance of current goals and substituting for them other goals which of themselves can be realistically achieved.

Time David is preoccupied with the very long-term time perspective and with trying to prevent his inevitable death; moreover, he is anxious to reduce to zero occasional feelings of ill-health or the onset of some organic illness. He rarely pursues short-term goals or behaves spontaneously. He does not seem to engage in any paratelic activity (for instance, sensation-seeking, game-playing, spontaneous actions). He spends approximately four and a half hours a day washing and teeth-cleaning.

Intensity David is behaviourally intense but says that he experiences few emotions apart from anxiety. He needs to be encouraged to experience a greater variety of emotions and to experience the telic mode in a greater range of ways than he is doing at present.

Using both the analysis of the client's structural disturbance (inhibited reversal) and the phenomenological analysis of the way in which this problem is experienced, the therapist is then able to move towards decisions about therapy. Here are the therapist's notes:

Means-Ends
(a) To escape from current rituals, David needs to be confronted with their consequences. Flooding will be used – we shall encourage him to increase his washing, showering, teeth-cleaning behaviour and checking routines by 100% (from four and a half to nine hours). This will need to be done with a little humour so that he can soon experience the futility of

these rituals. Therapist comments throughout the day will need to make intense use of paradoxical statements. The therapist will speak to David during this period about the behaviour others might engage in during these times, to give David a stronger feeling of his unusualness and the unreality of the goals he is pursuing. If David seems to respond well, then some systematic desensitization coupled with the affirmation of short-term goals not related to these rituals will be tried (Goldstein and Foa 1980). This will be an intense period of work, requiring out-patient or in-patient status. (In fact, he became an in-patient for four and a half weeks and then an out-patient for one and a half weeks).

(b) In order to replace David's ritualized goals with other goals, he will be encouraged to use guided fantasy to imagine shorter-term goals that can lead to more immediate gratifications (such as eating).

(c) RET will be used to change some of his irrational beliefs, but care will be taken that the specific techniques used will not be ones which increase the likelihood of the client being in the telic state at the time, as appears to be the case with some RET techniques. Rather, those more playful and humorous RET methods will be used which tend to induce the paratelic state.

Time

(a) A key task is to increase the frequency and intensity of spontaneous activity. Whilst associated with the therapy, David will participate in some of the therapy-game groups which encourage spontaneity. In individual therapy use will be made of drawings, conundrums and other devices which are intended to encourage and enable spontaneity.

(b) David also needs to be rewarded for acting and thinking spontaneously: some fantasy work will be used here as also will some agreed schedule of reinforcement for spontaneous activity.

Intensity

(a) We need to increase the extent to which David understands and creates combinations of ideas and images, especially those which can help to induce the paratelic state. Use will be made of tarot cards for David to tell stories with, and he will be reinforced for humour, spontaneous ideas and imaginative (unreal) versions.

(b) He also needs to be encouraged to engage in more social situations;

some modelling and shaping of his behaviour may also be needed here.

This case of David has been described at some length, since it illustrates that the therapist consciously chose strategies – RET, behavioural shaping and reinforcement, some counter strategies, some relaxation training with fantasy, some Gestalt, some humour therapy – to operationalize understanding of David's structural phenomenological problem. Considerable success was achieved with David in reducing the incidence of his obsessional behaviour, but the process designed to encourage and enable him to experience the paratelic state (sensation-seeking, here-and-now focused, spontaneous) took considerably longer than anticipated. At the time of writing, David's therapy is continuing (on a fortnightly basis) a year and a half after it commenced. The therapist writes:

> It has been especially difficult to achieve any progress with David at the level of changing his way of always interpreting arousal as unpleasant. I think the best we can generally hope for is a shift in the intensity of David's telic mode (making it less 'extreme') with occasional (though important) reversals into the paratelic mode. The good news (!) is that he now has a job and no longer avoids social contact like the plague ... But he does spend some time in the paratelic mode and is nowhere near as obsessional as he was on referral; he is able to engage in social interaction, he is able to be spontaneous more often than not and he is becoming (but that's it, becoming) more human.

The therapeutic strategy adopted with David is not one that is appropriate for all obsessionals; indeed, David's therapy has proved extremely demanding of therapeutic resources. The point to note is that the strategy – eclectic as it is – was derived from an assessment of the structural and phenomenological qualities of David as a person. The strategies developed reflected the therapist's understanding both of what it meant to be 'locked' into the telic mode, and the needs of the client in terms of the restoration of coping and the promotion of psychological well-being.

What has not been said in this case study (because of lack of space) concerns the way in which this structural-phenomenological understanding of the client excluded certain therapeutic options from the framework. Suffice it to say here that other strategies were considered and excluded because it was thought that they might further inhibit rather than facilitate the possibility of reversal into the paratelic state. A risk was taken in using paradox and flooding devices, since these could have exacerbated David's obsessionality; but it was judged (correctly) that the effects of this flooding procedure with paradox would facilitate a shift in the manner in which David experienced things in the telic mode. In the early stages of working with David this shift was regarded as a primary target for therapy, whereas later on there was an increasing focus on attempts to facilitate reversal into the paratelic mode.

Conclusion

This chapter has presented some complex ideas in a short space. Normally opposing positions (structuralism and phenomenology) have been brought together without explanation; complex and new psychological ideas have been briefly introduced and with no discussion of the empirical evidence which bears on them; the applications to therapy of a new taxonomy of client-presenting problems has been no more than sketched in; and a new model of eclectic therapy has been briefly illustrated. Our hope, nevertheless, is that you will find some of these ideas and resources to be relevant and interesting, and that you will want to find out more.

These are early days for eclecticism based on the structural-phenomenological approach. Reversal theory is itself a relatively new development in psychology: the first major text appeared only recently (Apter 1982), and the first international symposium devoted to reversal theory took place in 1983. What is particularly interesting from the point of view of the present book is that these theoretical constructs, developed primarily in Britain, are already finding a place in therapeutic practice.

References

Apter M J (1981) The possibility of a structural phenomenology: the case of reversal theory, *Journal of Phenomenological Psychology* 12(2): 173–187

Apter M J (1982) *The Experience of Motivation: A Theory of Psychological Reversals*, Academic Press, London

Apter M J (1983) 'Negativism and the sense of identity' in G. Breckwell (ed.) *Threatened identities*, Wiley, Chichester

Apter M J, Murgatroyd S *Reversal Theory and Psychotherapy*, Academic Press, London (Forthcoming)

Apter M J, Smith K C P (1979a) Psychological reversals: some new perspectives on the family and family communication, *Family Therapy 8(2)*: 89–100

Apter M J, Smith K C P (1979b) 'Sexual behaviour and the theory of psychological reversals' in Cook M and Wilson G (eds.) *Love and Attraction: An International Conference*, Pergamon, Oxford

Apter M J, Smith K C P (1984) 'Experiencing personal relationships' in Apter M J, Fontana D and Murgatroyd S (eds.) *Reversal Theory: Applications and Developments*, University College Cardiff Press, Cardiff

Beck A T (1976) *Cognitive Therapy and the Emotional Disorders*, Meridian, New York

Blackmore A, Murgatroyd S (1980) 'Anne: the disruptive infant' in Murgatroyd S (ed.) *Helping the Troubled Child: Interprofessional Case Studies*, Harper and Row, London

Frankl V (1969) *The Will to Meaning: Foundations and Applications of Logotherapy*, Plume, New York

Goldstein A, Foa E (1980) *Handbook of Behavioural Interventions: A Clinical Guide*, Wiley, New York

Heide F J, Borkovec T D (1983) Relaxation-induced anxiety: paradoxical anxiety enhancement to relaxation training, *Journal of Consulting and Clinical Psychology 51(2)*: 171–182

Hetherington R (1983) Sacred cows and white elephants, *Bulletin of the British Psychological Society 36*: 273–280

Kubie L (1971) The destructive potential of humor in psychotherapy, *American Journal of Psychiatry 127*: 861–6

Lazarus A (1976) *Multi-Modal Behavior Therapy*, Springer, New York

Lévi-Strauss C (1963) *Structural Anthropology*, Basic Books, New York

Minuchin S (1974) *Families and Family Therapy*, Tavistock, London

Murgatroyd S (1981) Reversal theory: a new perspective on crisis counselling, *British Journal of Guidance and Counselling 9(2)*: 180–193

Murgatroyd S, Rushton C, Apter M J, Ray C (1978) The development of the Telic Dominance Scale, *Journal of Personality Assessment 42*: 519–528

Murgatroyd S, Woolfe R (1984) *Helping Families in Distress*, Harper and Row, London

Perls F (1969) *Gestalt Therapy Verbatim*, Bantam, New York

Rowan J (1981) Reversal theory: critique, *European Journal of Humanistic Psychology: Self and Society 9(5)*: 244–246

Seldon H (1980) 'Patricia: a problem of adjustment' in Murgatroyd *Helping the Troubled Child: Interprofessional Case Studies*

Snygg D (1941) The need for a phenomenological system of psychology, *Psychological Review 48*: 404–424

Svebak S, Murgatroyd S (1984) Meta-motivational dominance: a multimethod validation of reversal theory, *Journal of Personality and social psychology* (in Press)

Svebak S, Storfjell O, Dalen K (1982) The effect of threatening context upon motivation and task-induced physiological changes, *British Journal of Psychology 73(4)*: 505–512

Svebak S, Stoyva J (1980) High arousal can be pleasant and exciting: the theory of psychological reversals, *Biofeedback and Self-Regulation* 5: 439–444

Thinès G (1977) *Phenomenology and the Science of Behaviour*, Allen and Unwin, London

Walters J, Apter M J, Svebak S (1982) Color preference, arousal and the theory of psychological reversals, *Motivation and Emotion 6(3)*: 193–215

Suggested Further Reading

Apter M J (1982) *The Experience of Motivation: A Theory of Psychological Reversals*, Academic Press, London

Murgatroyd S J (1981) Reversal theory: a new perspective in crisis counselling, *British Journal of Guidance and Counselling 9(2)*: 180–193

Apter M J, Svebak S (1984) 'Stress from the reversal theory perspective' in Spielberger C D and Strelau J (eds.) *Stress and Anxiety*, Hemisphere/McGraw-Hill, New York

Murgatroyd S J (ed.) (1980) *Helping the Troubled Child: Interprofessional Case Studies*, Harper & Row, London

Apter M J, Fontana D, Murgatroyd S (eds.) (1984) *Reversal Theory: Applications and Developments*, University College Cardiff Press, Cardiff

Appendices

1 Notes on Contributors

The editor:

Windy Dryden is one of Britain's leading counselling psychologists and counsellor educators. He was lecturer in counselling psychology at the University of Aston in Birmingham from 1975 to 1984. He has published over fifty articles and book chapters primarily on rational-emotive therapy and cognitive behaviour therapy and is the author of *Rational-Emotive Therapy: Fundamentals and Innovations*. He is the editor of four forthcoming books, all published by Harper & Row: *Marital Therapy in Britain: Volumes 1 and 2, Therapists' Dilemmas,* and *Cognitive-Behavioural Approaches to Psychotherapy* (with William L. Golden). His current professional interests are in the areas of rational-emotive therapy, cognitive psychotherapy, marital therapy, therapist decision-making and eclecticism in psychotherapy. He is an Associate Fellow of the British Psychological Society, Fellow of the International Academy of Eclectic Psychotherapists, Associate Fellow and Training Faculty Member of the Institute for Rational-Emotive Therapy in New York and Director of the Institute for Rational-Emotive Therapy (UK). He has practised as a counselling psychologist in university counselling, general practice, marriage guidance and private practice settings.

Biographical details of the other contributors follow in alphabetical order:

Michael J. Apter is senior lecturer in psychology at University College,

Cardiff. He has also lectured or carried out research in a number of other universities including Princeton (USA), University of British Columbia (Canada), Bristol and King's College, London. He is the author of five books (and co-editor of a sixth) which have, between them, been translated into eight languages. During his research career his interests have evolved from cybernetics and computer simulation through educational technology to the field of motivation and personality. In the last-named area, he has been involved in the development of reversal theory and its use in counselling and therapy.

Laurence Collinson was born in Leeds, Yorkshire, in 1925. He lived in Australia from infancy until 1964, and has lived in London ever since, except for a period of eight months, during which he lived in Vence, France, with the aid of a two-year fellowship from the Commonwealth Literary Fund. He held various jobs before training as a teacher at the age of twenty-eight. He worked for ten years with the Victorian Education Department, but had a nervous breakdown after a brief period of supply teaching in London. He went into a National Health therapy group for five years, where he experienced the first stirrings of interest in becoming a psychotherapist himself. In 1970 he co-founded the London TA Study Group, which remains successfully extant as the North London TA Study Group. In 1975 he became a special fields member of the International Transactional Analysis Association, his special fields being general counselling, gay counselling, and education. In 1978 he began his training as a provisional teaching member and has so far sponsored two candidates successfully. He is presently in clinical training. He works in private practice, leading three ongoing weekly groups in the evening, and individuals during the day.

He uses TA with a variety of other therapeutic or growth modes, including NLP, transpersonal psychology, Gestalt, guided fantasy, some bodywork, Zen, *est* and Jungian psychology. His major interests in TA include intuition, reading the 'Martian' and communication.

Cassie Cooper holds a first-class honours degree in psychology and has practised as a psychotherapist since 1969. She is now head of the student counselling service at Harrow College of Higher Education and continues to teach and to supervise other psychotherapists and counsellors in training. In addition, she retains a small private practice.

Emmy van Deurzen-Smith was born and raised in Holland. She undertook her academic studies and training in France. She obtained a master's degree in philosophy with a thesis on an existential analysis of schizophrenia. She has worked in psychiatric hospitals, where she trained in various therapeutic approaches, including Lacanian psychoanalytic therapy. During this time she also obtained her Master's degree in clinical psychology with a thesis on attempted suicide. She then moved to England where she became involved with the Arbours Association for a year and taught existential psychology in their training programme. For the last six years she has taught for Antioch University International, where she now directs the Master of Arts degree programme in the psychology of therapy and counselling. She also teaches existential counselling on South-West London College's counselling courses. She is married to an American psychotherapist and they live together with their young son, dog and cat in South London.

Fay Fransella received a BA degree in psychology at the University of London in 1961, a diploma in clinical psychology in 1962 and a Ph. D. in 1965. Since then she has held various research and university teaching posts, the last one being reader in clinical psychology until 1982 at the Royal Free Hospital School of Medicine, University of London. On leaving the University of London she was given the title of Emeritus Reader in Clinical Psychology. In 1982 she founded the Centre for Personal Construct Psychology in London and is now its full-time director.

Francesca Inskipp trained in counselling at Keele University in 1970. From 1973–81 she was senior lecturer in counselling at the Centre for Studies in Counselling, North-East London Polytechnic, running diploma and short courses in counselling for a wide range of professional and voluntary workers. In 1973, with Hazel Johns, she wrote and presented a series of eight programmes for the BBC entitled 'Principles of Counselling'. These were repeated five times and followed in 1983 by a second series. Both series were based on Egan's skills model of counselling. She has been an active member of the British Association for Counselling since its inception. At present she is working as a freelance trainer and consultant and is also producing cassette tapes and a manual as aids for trainers in counselling skills.

Michael Jacobs has been counsellor and psychotherapist at the University of Leicester since 1972. He also writes and teaches in the counselling field, and is director of the Certificate in Counselling Studies for the university's adult education department. Previously he worked as a chaplain at the University of Sussex, where his study of Freudian theory was translated into the practice of counselling students. He was educated at Dulwich College and Exeter College, Oxford, where he read theology. He is married with a family of three teenagers, and when he has time relaxes by growing vegetables and cruising the waterways.

Hazel Johns trained in counselling at Swansea University in 1972. She was a senior lecturer in counselling at the Centre for Studies in Counselling, North-East London Polytechnic from 1975 to 79 and is now advisor in social and pastoral education for the County of Avon. She wrote and presented the BBC programmes 'Principles of Counselling' Series I and II with Francesca Inskipp.

Kenneth Lambert MA, Litt.D, FBPsS was educated at Highgate School and St Peter's College, Oxford. He has been a professional member and a training analyst of the Society of Analytical Psychology for many years. He is a past chairman of the section of medical psychology and psychotherapy of the British Psychological Society and a Fellow of that society. He is the author of numerous articles, critical notices, comments and reviews in scientific journals, a co-author and contributor to several books, and the author of *Analysis Repair and Individuation* for which he was awarded a Litt. D. by Trinity College, Dublin. He is an assistant editor and sometime review editor of the *Journal of Analytical Psychology*, and also co-editor of *The Library of Analytical Psychology*. He is in private practice in Cambridge and London, and devotes a considerable amount of time to the teaching and training of potential psychotherapists and analytical psychologists.

Dougal Mackay is district top grade psychologist to Bristol and Weston Health Authority and has the honorary post of lecturer in mental health at the University of Bristol. His book *Clinical Psychology: Theory and Therapy* was published in the Methuen Essential Psychology series in 1975, and he is the co-author of *Marriage and How To Survive It*, which was published in 1983 by Piatkus. He was formerly Principal Clinical

Psychologist at St. Mary's Hospital, Paddington, and Honorary Lecturer in Psychology at St. Mary's Hospital Medical School, London. He is programme organizer for Psychotherapy Workshops and runs workshops regularly on depression, grief therapy, sexual dysfunction, interpersonal difficulties and behavioural marital therapy for the Institute of Behaviour Therapy, British Association for Behavioural Psychotherapy and Psychotherapy Workshops. His publications include papers on depression, social skills training, psychosexual counselling and cognitive/behavioural techniques for anxiety states.

Stephen Murgatroyd is one of Britain's leading counselling psychologists. Formerly a counsellor in schools and colleges, Stephen is now senior counsellor with the Open University and a private practitioner. He is associate editor of the *British Journal of Guidance and Counselling* and a frequent contributor to the counselling literature, both here and abroad. He is the author of *Helping the Troubled Child* and *Coping with Crisis* (with Ray Woolfe), both published by Harper & Row.

Faye Page is a senior clinical psychologist working part-time in an NHS psychiatric hospital. She does some private individual psychotherapy and facilitates an ongoing weekend residential Gestalt workshop once a month. She became interested in Gestalt therapy about ten years ago on a visit to the United States, where she attended some introductory workshops. She then continued her training in Britain. Her interests include her family, her friends, developing the use of Gestalt therapy within the NHS and reading science fiction. Her major concern at present is the individual lack of awareness of and personal responsibility for the nuclear arms race.

Brian Thorne, a Cambridge graduate in modern languages, began his professional career as a schoolteacher. From 1962 to 1967 he was an assistant master at Eastbourne College, and it was during this period he first met George Lyward, the remarkable founder and director of Finchden Manor, a therapeutic community for adolescent boys. Lyward had a deep influence on his thinking, and in 1967 he left Eastbourne to embark on a diploma in educational guidance and counselling at Reading University. It was at Reading that, as a student of Bruce Shertzer, a visiting Fulbright Professor from Purdue, he was first introduced to the work of Carl Rogers and trained as a client-centred counsellor. After training he took up his first counselling appointment as a member of Audrey Newsome's pioneering team at Keele University. With this apprenticeship behind him, he became the first director of student counselling at the University of East Anglia, Norwich, in 1974. From 1976 to 1980 he was Chairman of the Association for Student Counselling and in recent years he has worked extensively in several European countries (sometimes with Rogers himself) as a person-centred facilitator and group leader. In 1980, together with five other colleagues, he became co-founder of the Norwich Centre for Personal and Professional Development, the first independent counselling and training unit in Britain committed to the person-centred approach.

Some Useful Addresses for Those Wishing Information Concerning Therapy Services in Britain

1   *Psychodynamic Therapy: The Freudian Approach* Therapy and training:

British Association of Psychotherapists
121 Hendon Lane
London N3 3PR

2   *Psychodynamic Therapy: The Kleinian Approach* Therapy and training:

Institute of Psycho-Analysis
63 New Cavendish Street
London W1M 7RD

3   *Psychodynamic Therapy: The Jungian Approach* Therapy and training:

The Society of Analytical Psychology
1 Daleham Gardens
Hampstead
London NW3 5BY

The Association of Jungian Analysts (Alternative Training)
18 East Heath Road
Hampstead
London NW3 1AJ

4 *Person-Centred Therapy* Therapy and training:

The Norwich Centre for Personal and Professional Development
7 Earlham Road
Norwich NR2 3RA

5 *Personal Construct Therapy* Therapy and training:

Centre for Personal Construct Psychology
132 Warwick Way
London SW1V 4JD

6 *Existential Therapy* Therapy:

Philadelphia Association
14 Peto Place
London NW1

Training:

Course Director, M.A. (Psychology of Therapy and Counselling)
Antioch University
115–117 Shepherdess Walk
London N1 7QA

7 *Gestalt Therapy* Therapy and training:

The Gestalt Centre
7 Parliament Hill
London NW3

8 *Transactional Analysis* Therapy and training:

Institute Of Transactional Analysis
BM Box 4104
London WC1 3XX

9 *Rational-Emotive Therapy* Therapy and Training:

Institute for RET (UK)
13 Wellington Crescent
Horfield
Bristol BS7 8SZ

10 *Behavioural Psychotherapy* Therapy and training:

Rod Holland
Psychology Department
Basingstoke District Hospital
Park Prewett
Basingstoke
Hampshire

11 *Developmental Eclecticism: Egan's Skills Model of Helping* Training:

Peter Cook
Department of Psychology
North East London Polytechnic
Romford Road
London E15 4LZ

12 *Eclectic Therapy: A Structural Phenomenological Approach* Therapy and training:

Stephen Murgatroyd
Open University
24 Cathedral Road
Cardiff CF1 9SA

In addition, useful referral and training directories are available from:
British Association For Counselling
37A Sheep Street
Rugby
Warwickshire CV21 3BX

The author welcomes feedback on the present volume. Correspondence should be addressed to:
Windy Dryden
14 Winchester Avenue
Brondesbury Park
London NW6 7TU

AUTHOR INDEX

SUBJECT INDEX

ABC model: personal construct, 143;
rational-emotive, 239, 245
abreaction, 39
acceptance, 117–9
acquisition and perpetuation of
disturbance: behavioural, 271–4, 297–9;
developmental eclectic, 372–4, 385;
eclectic, 398–401; existential, 159–62;
Freudian, 30–2; Gestalt, 186–9, 198–
200; Jungian, 85–8; Kleinian, 53–7;
personal construct, 134-6; person-
centred, 109–11; rational-emotive, 242–
5, 250–9; transactional, 213–8
actualising tendency, 106, 108, 183
addiction, 318
affective theories, 296 *table*
agape, 89
aggression, 27, 323
analytical psychology, 76, 78, 81, 92, 316;
Society of, 78–9
analytic repair process, 95
anger, 222–3, 338
antithetical ego functioning, 318
anxiety, 56, 58, 73, 145, 338; about
anxiety, 244; management of, 282, 289–
90; *see also* fear of fear
anxiety depression, 197–8
apersonal-personal theories, 296 *table*
archetypal psychology, 97
archetypes, 80, 87, 318
arena, therapeutic comparison of involve-
ments in, 2–3, 2 *table*, defined, 1;
selection of, 3–21
'as if' view, 130, 132

aspects of being human, 164–5
assertiveness, 270, 283
assessment of problems, 250, 278–80
attitudes, 120–1, 162; facilitative, 116–20;
to therapy, 328; of wonder, 165
authenticity/inauthenticity, 158–60, 162,
170, 171, 222, 325
autonomy, 29–30, 209–11, 228, 232
aversion therapy, 283
aversive experience, 338
awareness, 184–5, 188, 189, 192, 196
table, 197, 274

'awfulising', 240, 242

bad faith, 159, 162
BASIC ID, 345–6
behavioural analysis, 278–80: cross-
sectional approach to, 335–6; treatment
programmes, 278–80
behavioural therapy, 264–94: anxiety-
management, 282; assertion/asstertive-
ness, 270, 283; avoidance and escape,
272–3; cognitive behaviour modification, 282; covert sensitization, 283;
exposure, 281–2; modelling of maladaptive behaviour, 272; negative self-
talk, 273; problem-solving, 268, 275,
282; psychological health, 270–1; reinforcement, 271–2, 273; self-awareness,
274; self-control, 283; self-efficacy,268,
275; self-regulation, 269, significant
others as 'mastery' models, 274; social
competence, 270; stimulus control, 267;

from sight, missed. But dear to
memory

From sight missed
But to memory dear